# Passive Income Ideas 2021

5 Books in 1

*The Beginner's Guide on How to Make Money Online*

*-*

*Blogging, Affiliate Marketing, Tik Tok Marketing, Amazon FBA, Dropshipping with Shopify*

*by*

Robert Kasey

# Table of Contents

## BOOK 1: MAKING MONEY ON BLOGGING

# BOOK 2: AFFILIATE MARKETING 2021

# BOOK 3: TIK TOK MARKETING FOR ENTREPRENUERS

# BOOK 4: AMAZON FBA

# BOOK 5: DROPSHIPPING & SHOPIFY

# MAKING MONEY ON BLOGGING

## *2021 EDITION*

*How to Start Your Blogging Blueprint and Make Profit Online With Your Blog*

\-

*How do People Make Money by Blogging?*
*How can I Make Money Blogging?*

\-

*A step-by-step guide for beginners*

# INTRODUCTION

The world has recorded tremendous growth in the last couple of years – especially within this century and the previous. We have seen widespread technological advancements and many paradigm shifts that have happened as a result of the many advances in technology. Technology has undoubtedly affected the way we do most things. It has transformed the way we communicate, eat, travel, etc. One area where technology has changed our mode of operation how we interact with one another.

Before the advent of the internet, many people were used to keeping diaries – such diaries were written on notepads or notebooks and held securely to prevent loss or damage. However, with the invention of online storage mediums and the internet, people can now keep digital diaries in the form of blogs on the internet. Such digital journals saved on the internet can be accessed repeatedly.

There is no single area of our lives that technology has not affected. It was wrong for a proper gentleman to walk up to a lady in a gathering and open a conversation with her in the past. The duo (man and lady) would need to be introduced to each other by a third party. Today, the reverse has become the case – with apps like Tinder, people can arrange a "meet n greet" or other forms of dates by just tapping some buttons on their mobile device while sitting in the comfort of their bedrooms.

Technology has also changed the way we make money. In the past centuries, to make money, one would have to either get a job or start a business. None of these options was as simple as we just made it seem. To get a job, you would need to get a college degree, which costs a lot of money. After graduating from college, you would need to start competing for the few available jobs. On the other hand, to start a business, you would need a lot of money as well.

However, money-making has become increasingly more accessible today – thanks to the internet, people, both young and old, could now sit in the comfort of their living room, wearing nothing more than briefs, and earn as much money as they desire. Several online earning models are available, which the average person can leverage and create a consistent stream of income for him/herself. One of these online business models is blogging. Yes, you heard that right, BLOGGING.

People often think that blogging is an outdated way of making money on the internet, however, nothing can be farther from the truth. Blogging has been a viable way of making money online and will continue to be a significant online money spinner for those who know how to do it right. The problem with blogging being an income stream is that when it comes to blogging, people are not willing to treat their blog like a business. Remember, anything you do not handle as a business will not pay you like a business.

To put things in the right perspective, people have always rumored that real estate is no longer a viable business that can make you money. However, many people are making millions every day by directly investing in real estate. There will always be naysayers and those who are willing to do the work – while the former group will be there giving reasons why it is not possible, the latter group will be smiling to the bank every day.

The term "blog" was initially derived from the word "weblog," a combination of web and log. It is essentially a log that is hosted on the web for more accessible and secure access. The word log means a record of day-to-day events. Gradually, weblog was shortened to blog. Initially, people used blogs as online diaries, where they update things that mattered to them. You can see people post about their life, things that happened in their home, and travel experiences on their blogs.

Gradually, blogs shifted from just what people used to keep online diaries to what can be used to write about general issues. Today, we have blogs that talk about politics, business, relationships, religion, etc. After blogs shifted from just being online diaries, a lot has happened – people have found a way of monetizing their blogs. Since the early 2000s, people have been making tons of money from different types of blogs. That will only continue as humans will keep seeking knowledge, information, and even entertainment till the end of time.

While blog posts used to be centered on the owners, today, you could start a blog and write about business, politics, wildlife, travel, or a whole lot of other issues that appeal to you. This means that anyone can start a blog today, grow it, and start making money from it. Starting a blog is no longer exclusively reserved for people who live super exciting lives, like celebrities. Even if your life is not as exciting, there are tons of other things you can share on your blog, monetize the blog and make money.

As mentioned earlier, blogging started as a hobby for some people; however, you can now build a blog and turn it into your own full-time business. We have seen a lot of young and older people do so. These people did not do anything spectacular; they only treated their blog as a business, and it started paying them like a business.

If you want to be among those currently earning money from blogging, you are at the right place as this definitive guide is for you. You might think that blogging is saturated, but is there really any business in the world that is not saturated? Let's face it; every business you could think of is already saturated, and what differentiates those who make it in one business from those who make excuses is the effort they put in.

One good thing with blogging is that if you put in the necessary effort and treat it like a business, it will pay you like a business. On the other hand, if you treat it like a hobby, it will cost you like a hobby. That being said, how do you create a blog and turn it into your personal cash cow? What type of blog do you need to create? What are the various blogging niches available to you? Ultimately, how do you run your blog like an actual business so that it can pay you like a business?

All these and more are what we will be discussing in this all-encompassing guide. If you have been dreaming of earning money online through blogging, then this is a read for you. Even if you have been blogging for some time but have not recorded success, you are most likely doing something wrong. Our goal will be to expose you to the correct strategies that, if applied, you will see your much-desired breakthrough.

Without further ado, let's get started.

# CHAPTER ONE

# <u>Is Blogging Really For Me?</u>

Anyone who runs a blog is called a blogger – people often have this common misconception that all bloggers are good writers, politically aware, or savvy young chaps who are extremely good at working with computers. This is nothing more than a misconception. The truth is that anybody who can operate a smartphone can venture into blogging and become quite successful at it.

Within the past few years, people from all walks of life, nationality, race, and age have turned into bloggers, which changed their lives for good. One good thing about blogging is that it is vast – there is always something to blog about. If you are not good at analyzing politics, you could be good at writing about dogs, cats, and other pets. If you are not good at explaining sports, you might be excellent at giving fashion tips. If you are not good at creating and posting food recipes, you might be good at writing travel blog posts. So, this simply means that there is something you can do as a blogger – blogging is not reserved for some select few.

The only thing that could make it hard for you to succeed as a blogger is a lack of motivation, determination, perseverance, and focus. We must mention that while blogging is not a get-rich-quick scheme, if you do it right, however, it has the potential to make you rich, but you must be willing to put in the needed effort.

One mistake that most people who stumble into blogging make is that they think they could create a blog today, monetize it tomorrow, and start making money next week. Unfortunately, it does not work that way. Your blog is like your typical business. You must give it time, nurture it until it grows into a money-making machine.

Another mistake that people make is that they want to treat their blog as a hobby and expect it to pay them like a business. As mentioned earlier, if you treat what you do like a business, it will pay you like a business, but if you treat it as a hobby, it will pay you like a hobby. While there are people who blog as a hobby, our focus in this book is to raise people who see blogging as a business. Now, if you really want to run a blog as a business, you'll need a certain level of commitment.

First, you have to see it as if you are running a typical brick and mortar store. Someone that has a brick and mortar store wakes up early in the morning to open their store. After opening the store, they take inventory of available stock. Then, they open their books for the day. As the day goes by, the store owner discusses with customers, closes sales, and at the end of the day, takes another inventory, closes their book for the day and go home.

Now, if a typical store owner does all that hard work, it means that a blogger has some tasks to do as well. However, the work aspect is what some bloggers do not want to do. This is connected to the fact that some acclaimed gurus had sold them some fake dreams in the past. They have been told that you don't need to work to make money online.

So, the answer to the question, "Is blogging really for me?" YES. Blogging can be for you as long you are ready to work. Even if you are not a writer, you can hire writers to do the writing aspect of the blogging business for you. It is also essential to state that writing is just a small fraction of what bloggers do. The more significant part of the blogging business involves driving traffic to your blog posts, social media marketing, and attracting brands to advertise their products on your blog so you could earn money. So, even if you are not a writer, you can still be a blogger. You only need to hire a writer to create the posts for you.

To succeed as a blogger, you need to create a clear roadmap and focus on your goals. With the right motivation, dedication, perseverance, and a learning spirit, you can turn your blog into a money-making machine in a short time.

# CHAPTER TWO

# <u>Why Start a Blog?</u>

There are a million make-money-online schemes that abound out there, so why should anyone ditch many of those and pitch their tent with blogging? This is a question that any logical person would want to ask. While the other numerous make money online schemes have great potential to make money for you, blogging is unique for so many reasons, and we are going to talk about these exclusive benefits of blogging shortly.

### 1. Blogging can make you rich

While blogging is not a get rich quick scheme, it does have the potential to make you rich. One good thing about the income you earn from blogging is its passive nature. This means that you only have to do the work once and watch your income flow in, even on the days you decide not to work. With such a passive income model, you can have all the time in the world to bond with your family, take vacations, and do other things that matter to you.

Another thing that makes blogging an excellent money-making business is that there are thousands of ways through which you can make money with your blog. You can sell ad space to advertisers – this is one of the most popular methods of making money with your blog. When it comes to selling ad space – you have many choices. You can let ad networks like Google and Bing place ads on your blog and pay you on a commission basis, or you can develop your own unique pricing model, negotiate with companies directly, and have them pay you money to place their advertisements on your blog.

Additionally, you can accept sponsored posts where businesses pay you money to place marketing content on your blog. This is how it works – a company writes a marketing post which they could use to drive traffic to their own website. Then, they pay you money to publish the post on your blog and link it to their website. You can accept as many guest posts as possible in a month, and you earn according to the number of such posts you publish on your blog. Also, how much you can earn through this income model solely lies in your hands. So, the better your negotiation skills, the more money you earn.

You can also promote affiliate offers on your blog and earn a commission when a sale happens through the link you promoted. Affiliate marketing is a highly profitable way of making money on the internet. With affiliate marketing, you do not need to develop a product. You simply promote the products already developed by other companies to your blog visitors. If a sale happens through your promotions, then the company that has the product pays you an affiliate commission.

Affiliate marketing is always a win-win for you, the company you're promoting, and the customer. It is a win for you because you get to earn money for promoting other's products. It is a win for the company that developed the affiliate product because its product has now been promoted to a broader audience. Lastly, it is a win for the customer because you help them gain access to products that can help solve their problems.

There are thousands of affiliate marketing networks you can partner with and earn money when you promote their products on your blog. Clickbank.com is a popular affiliate marketing network where you can find millions of products to promote to your audience and earn money. You can also consider joining the Amazon affiliate program where you promote Amazon products on your blog so that when people buy those products or even other products through your efforts, Amazon pays you money.

Most of the internet service providers you will be using their service as a blogger have affiliate programs which you can join and earn money by promoting some tools to your audience. For instance, you need a hosting service to host your blog; you also need a domain name provider. The chances are that these providers will have affiliate programs. When you promote their affiliate offers; and people get to buy hosting service through your affiliate links, you earn money.

There are also hundreds of other tools you need as a blogger, and most of them have affiliate programs as well. For instance, you need an autoresponder for email marketing purposes, and most autoresponders have affiliate offers you can promote to earn more money. Apart from the tools you make use of, you can promote a ton of affiliate software tools or products that you think your audience needs.

Another great way to earn money with your blog is by selling digital and physical products. In fact, digital products are best because you don't need to keep inventory – you simply develop a single copy of the product and sell it to millions of customers. The difference between a physical and digital product is that you can touch a physical product while you cannot do the same for a digital product. Digital products are held intangibly on offline and online storage mediums. Typical examples of digital products include eBooks, software programs, and digital games. Examples of physical products include wristwatches, shirts, hoverboards, etc.

Now, you don't need to be the developer of either the physical or digital products before you can sell them on your blog. If you want to start selling eBooks on your blog, for instance, you could hire a writer, provide them with an outline and have them create an excellent eBook that you can host and sell on your blog. As for physical products, you can enter into a partnership with major brands so you can drop ship their products on your blog. Once you have grown your blog's audience, selling products to them will not be a problem, and the return can be quite impressive.

Your blog can make you money through gated content. How this works is, you create unique, high quality, and high in demand content on your blog, then make it available on a subscription basis to only those readers who pay. You can create a members-only section and hide away the more valuable content there. Then, when a member pays a stipulated subscription fee, you give them access to the gated member's only section.

While what I mentioned above is not so popular, some bloggers still earn money through it. However, before you try incorporating such a model into your blog, you need to have grown the blog to a certain level. Obviously, you cannot adopt this model when you are just starting out, and you must have shown that you know your onions as well. If you want to make the model work for you, your free content must be compelling enough and packed with value to make the reader want to pay for more. If your available content is not good enough, no reader would want to pay you money to read more of your content.

The methods described above are some of the most popular means of earning through your blog. There are more ways through which you can make money with your blog; we have just discussed the popular ones. Depending on your audience, you can research and creatively come up with more ways of monetizing your content. In a subsequent section of this book, we shall do an in-depth analysis of each of these blog income models. For now, let's continue to look at the other benefits of running a blog.

## 2. Blogging will help you improve your writing and technical skills

Blogging gives you a chance to learn and perfect some critical skills, such as writing and other technical skills. Even if you aren't writing your blog posts yourself, you will still be working with some technological tools, and the more you work with these tools, the more you learn and improve. If you are the one writing your posts, blogging will definitely help you to improve your writing skills.

As a blogger, you will be using a lot of plug-ins and templates. You may also need to learn basic web design so you can always modify your blog without seeking the help of a professional that might be costly. The more you work with these online tools, the more you develop your technical skills.

Additionally, as a blogger, you will consistently need to do a lot of search engine optimization, email marketing, and content marketing. Learning and perfecting all these skills will not only help you to become a successful blogger, but you can also apply the skills in running your other online businesses.

**3. Blogging will help you develop healthier habits**

In addition to helping you develop valuable technical skills, blogging also helps you to learn the art of commitment and discipline. Healthy habits, like time management, dedication, etc., which you can learn while blogging, can come in handy when you are dealing with other aspects of your personal and professional life. So, blogging does not just put money in your pocket alone; it helps you to develop some critical skills and learn healthy habits.

**4. Blogging enables you to build a network**

When people face a challenge, the first thing they do is turn to the internet to seek a solution. By owning a blog and posting useful content, you can attract people who will see you as their hero – these people will consume your content, post their thoughts in the form of comments, and some will even send you personal messages.

Some of your readers can go all out to arrange a physical meeting with you. All these will increase your network beyond your imagination. Aside from your readers, specific brands can get in touch with you through the useful content you create and propose a deal to you. In all, running a blog will help you grow a network of friends and acquaintances that will be helpful to you in the long run.

## 5. Blogging enables you to increase your knowledge of things in your niche and beyond

There is a hidden researcher in you, and blogging helps to bring it out. As a blogger, you have to research, collate, sort information, and present it authoritatively to your audience. Remember, your readers are visiting your blog because they see you as an authority in your niche. So, you must do the proper research to ensure that you post only quality content. In your bid to put up new well-researched content regularly, your effort will lead you to the discovery of new things in your field and beyond.

## 6. Blogging gives you the perfect outlet to express yourself

Your blog, no matter the type of content you share with it, it is still your personal space. So, even if your blog is a niche, you can still intersperse your opinions in your posts and get your voice heard. You can use your blog to air your views on trending issues while still maintaining a defined niche. A blog is a perfect outlet for self-expression.

## 7. Blogging exposes you to new opportunities and ideas

As a blogger, you will practically live on the internet. This means you will always get exposed to numerous opportunities and ideas that abound on the internet. It could be ideas on ways of making money or improved ways of living a healthier life. Blogging exposes you more to different topics than the average Joe on the streets. The more information you get exposed to, the better your approach to life will. The people you will get to meet will also positively influence your life, and the fact that you have people who see you as a hero will make you want to be of good behavior.

## 8. You can make a difference in people's lives

Millions of people around the world are facing one issue or the other, and they usually turn to the internet to seek a solution. These people are just looking for a little glimmer of hope or something to assist them amid their despair and gloom. Even knowing it, your blog could be the tonic that someone needs to get their life back.

Stated above are just some of the few benefits of blogging. In the next sections of this guide, we will talk about different blogging niches and how to choose the one that is best for you.

# CHAPTER THREE

## Getting Started

If you have decided that blogging is something you would want to do, then welcome to this chapter, where we will introduce you to the first things you need to do as a blogger. For instance, if you want to go to college, there are some things you must do first before the others. For example, you need to decide first on the course you want to study, check with the admissions office, fill some forms, and write a statement of purpose. After you have been offered admission, you can proceed to accept the offer. Perform the necessary registrations, pay the required fees, and then start your studies.

The same way no one wakes up one day and starts attending college, that's the same way you should not just wake up one morning and start blogging. Blogging is a serious business, at least for now, and it requires a lot of planning on your part. You need to plan on what to blog about, how to attract traffic to your blog posts, how to monetize your blog, and how to scale up your blogging business.

## First things first – choose a niche

When people go to college, they study only one course out of the millions available in the school. The reason is simple. You cannot conveniently study all the courses that the university offers. You must choose one, stick with it, and excel at it. Even as you continue with your studies, you are further mandated to specialize in your field's specific area of interest.

Now, the same way you cannot study all the courses in the university, it is not advisable for you to create a blog and write about all the random topics that come to your mind. No, there has to be an order. People should know your blog for something; when they need that particular thing, your blog becomes their go-to place.

If you have an ear infection, for instance, and you visit the hospital to get help, which of the following doctors would you instead allow to attend to you?

Doctor A: a general practitioner who diagnoses and treats all kinds of common ailments.

Doctor B: An ear, nose, and throat (ENT) specialist who is an expert at treating those infections.

Typically, you would go for doctor B because he is a specialist and is more likely to understand what is wrong with you.

If you really want to make money blogging, you must find a niche and stick with it. Finding a blog niche might sound easy, but it is not as easy as it sounds. It is the essential first step you need to take before everything else. Although you can always switch to another niche later in the future, it is better to get it right once.

Your blog niche will be determined by the type of audience you want to serve. Once you know your audience, it will be easier for you to create blog posts and other types of products that satisfy their needs. More importantly, having a defined niche will help you to maintain focus, so you don't write on sports today and write on entertainment tomorrow. It will also help you determine the best marketing strategies for you – this is because the type of blog you have will significantly impact the blog income opportunities available to you. That being said, what is a niche?

## What is a niche?

A niche has to do with interests, services, or products that only appeal to a small, specialized segment or section of a larger audience or population. It can also be said to be the smaller part of a larger whole.

In the above definition, you will notice some keywords which include "specialized" and "larger audience" or "population." When you look at those keywords' everyday uses, it will be easier for you to understand what a niche means. For instance, the word "sport" is extensive and consists of different types of sporting events.

Now, when you talk about sports, you will begin to see that there are different types, which can include, for instance, soccer, basketball, baseball. These different types of sports are niches within the broad category. Even within the niches, you can still narrow down each niche. For instance, within baseball, you can find "major league baseball" and "national baseball." All these are sub-niches within the baseball niche. Your niche is the overarching topic that you focus your blog contents on when it comes to blogging. It is more like the umbrella category that houses and defines the types of content you will be publishing on your blog. For instance, soccer is quite a broad niche; you can narrow down and blog about European football leagues. You can narrow down further and blog about European league predictions.

**Why does your blog need a niche?**

This is an important question we must answer before proceeding. Why does your blog need a niche? Why can't you blog on something as broad as soccer, for instance? Why can't you blog on how to make money online? Why can't you blog on how to prepare delicious meals?

Your blog needs to focus on a specific niche for several reasons, and these reasons are not hard to guess. We have already named some of them earlier. Picture yourself in a large hall filled with people saying different things. Everybody in the hall wants to be heard. Now, picture yourself in another small room where there are only five people; everybody in this small room wants to be heard too. Which of these places do you think that your voice stands a higher chance of being listened to?

Obviously, in the large hall, everybody will be shouting, trying to get their voice heard, and this will make it extremely hard for your voice to make an impact because it will get buried amid other voices. However, since there are only about five people in the small room, you stand a higher chance of getting your voice heard. This is just the perfect explanation of why you need a niche for your blog.

If your blog targets a broad audience, it will be tough for you to draw traffic to it. It will also be hard for you to make money through affiliate sales – this is not to mention that your search engine ranking will suffer. Early starters have already monopolized such broad niches in the game or the big fishes in the ocean of blogging. As a starter, you will find it extremely hard to compete with all the established blogs that are already targeting those broad niches.

Targeting a general niche is also bad for engagement. When you blog about a broad topic, you will most likely attract people who are not quite interested in what you are saying, and this will negatively affect user engagement on your blog. So, from the very beginning, you need to define your niche and stick with it. For instance, instead of blogging on ways of making money online, narrow down and blog on one of the options or suggestions being created. There are many ways of making money online, and if you focus on one, your blog will record higher traffic and engagement.

With a niche blog, you will have a defined audience; you will understand what they truly need and feed them accordingly. For instance, if you create a blog that focuses on back pain, people who have back pain will easily relate to what you say and follow all your posts. Since you already know the kind of people you are dealing with, you won't waste time creating other posts that won't appeal to them.

Also, if you blog about a small audience, it is easy for you to truly understand all the problems they are facing so you can speak to them directly. When your readers notice that you are talking about the specific issues they are facing, it will be easier for them to trust you as an authority in the field.

With that said, let's look at some of the ways of finding a perfect niche for your blog.

# How to find a blog niche

When it comes to finding a blog niche, you have two options – to go with the most popular niches that everyone talks about or find your own niche that appeals to you. Some of the most popular blog niches arranged in no particular order include:

- Technology
- DIY/Home Décor
- Beauty & Fashion
- Finance
- Self-Help
- Dating & Relationships
- Making Money Online
- Weight Loss
- Fitness
- Health

One problem with all the popular niches above is that they are quite broad, and their competitive score is high as well. When most people want to start a blog, they typically blog about these mentioned competitive niches, which is why they are very saturated. If you start blogging about any of the niches, you would hardly record success. Your blog will find it challenging to rank on search engines. Hence, you will have to spend a lot of money on pay per click advertising.

Instead of blogging in any of the competitive niches, you can take one of the niches, break it down further, and continue to narrow your search until you get to a sub-niche within the niche that is yet to be saturated. For instance, "car" is a broad name, and under it, you can get a range of cars like Mercedes Benz, Volkswagen, BMW. If you take a Mercedes Benz, for instance, which is a type of car, you will find out that even within that sub-niche, you will find Mercedes Benz S-Class Coupe, GLE Coupe, etc. When you focus on GLE Coupe, you may still differentiate them by the model year. This is a prime example of how to breakdown a broad niche until it becomes very narrow and less competitive.

When choosing a blog niche, you have to take any of the competitive niches, then break it down until you get a very narrow sub-niche. In online business terms, this is called niching down because it is like climbing from the bottom of a tree and finding one of the numerous branches on the tree to sit on.

Here are the steps you need to take to find the perfect blog niche:

**Step 1: Consider your interests**

This sounds cliché, but for you to succeed in something like blogging, you cannot underestimate the importance of blogging in a niche that interests you. Remember, you will be positioning yourself as an authority, and if what you are blogging about is of interest to you, you will often go the extra mile to research and give your readers valuable content.

In life, we all have various interests. Some of us are interested in things like music or sports. If you know how to make money online or how to fish, you can turn that into your blog niche. Look inwards; there must be one thing you can talk about very well, even without consulting a source. The next thing you need to do is to convert your interest into your blog niche.

Next, open a text editor on your computer or open a new page on your notepad, then write down the phrase, "blog niche ideas." Move to the next two lines and list your passions or topics you are interested in blogging about.

These topics could include your general interests, hobbies, or passions. Make sure you list as many as you want.

Now, under each interest, start listing more child branches by thinking of specific topics or subtopics based on what you know best. This is one of the reasons you are advised to go for a niche that is of interest to you instead of one that you perceive is profitable. If you choose a niche that is of importance to you, you will be able to produce a lot of useful content, which will increase your chances of succeeding as a new blogger.

Additionally, when blogging in a niche that interests you, posting content will not be a problem. You will easily create new content that your visitors will love to read. Even if you don't post every day, your readers will always be confident that the content will be top quality anytime you post.

Furthermore, your readers want you to solve their problem, and how are you going to do that if you don't understand the kind of issues they have or if their problem doesn't interest you? If you blog about your passion and what you know, you will easily connect with your readers and speak personally to them.

So, once you have listed a passion, interest, or blog idea, and you have also listed many branches under each of the topics, proceed to add more child branches to the existing ones. You don't need to be a perfect expert on any of the child branches. You only need to have at least some adequate knowledge of them. For instance, if one of the broad topics you have chosen is "baseball" and you only know some rules of the game, then that's okay as there are people who don't even know these rules, and they can find your blog useful.

For Example:

Let's assume that your broad topic is fishing; you can get ice fishing and fly fishing under that. Now, both fly fishing and ice fishing are both branches of the central niche. For each of these branches, continue to narrow your search and find more child branches. For instance, if you focus on ice fishing, you could have trout fishing, walleye fishing, and bass fishing. Under fly fishing, you could have bass fishing and trout fishing as well. You might consider taking each of the child branches and niche down the more until you have arrived at a narrower topic.

In the above example, the broad topic "fishing" was narrowed down until we got more specific branches like "trout fishing." If you want to consider any of the branches or child branches, you need to examine it and see if you could turn it into a whole blog. For instance, if you have chosen "bass fishing," can you possibly create a year's worth of content around that topic or niche? That's a critical question you should ask yourself before settling for any sub-niche.

**Step 2: Use a keyword planner to get more ideas**

If you find it hard to break down your chosen niche or topic into sub-topics or child branches, you can use Google Keyword Planner to get ideas. Google Keyword Planner is owned by Google and incorporated into its advertisement platform. To use the tool, you will need to log in with your Google account or Gmail details. If you don't have a Google account, you can create one by visiting mail.google.com.

When you type some broad keywords into the Keyword Planner, the tool will return a list of possible child branches of the topic. This way, you can get a clear idea of sub-niches available within the niche.

To use the Keyword Planner, you need to visit ads.google.com, use your google account to log in. On the homepage that greets you upon login, click on "Tools," then "Keyword Planner." To conduct new keyword research, click on "Find new keywords," then enter a seed niche idea you want to get information about. See the image below.

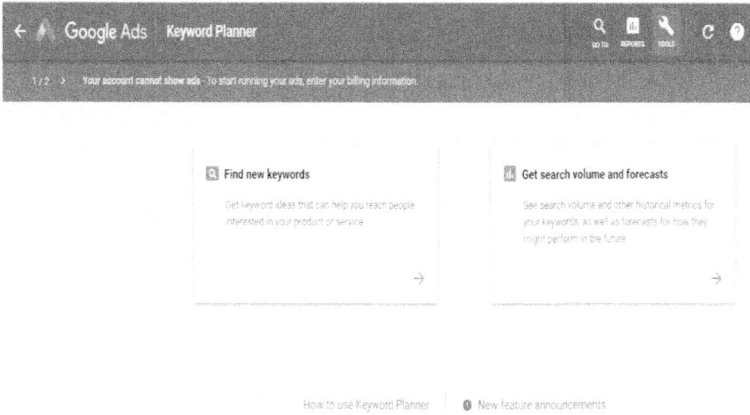

← Google Ads   Keyword Planner

1 / 2   >   Your account cannot show ads - To start running your ads, enter your billing information.

Find new keywords

Get keyword ideas that can help you reach people interested in your product or service

→

Get search volume and forecasts

See search volume and other historical metrics for your keywords, as well as forecasts for how they might perform in the future

→

How to use Keyword Planner      New feature announcements

The results you will get from the keyword research will look like the image below. "Ice fishing" was used as the seed keyword for this example.

| Keyword (by relevance) | Vol (US) | CPC (US) | Comp (US) | Avg. monthly searches | Competition |
|---|---|---|---|---|---|
| ice fishing ☆ 🖫 | 22,200 | $0.58 | 0.27 | 10K – 100K | Low |
| ice fishing gear ☆ 🖫 | 12,100 | $0.75 | 1 | 10K – 100K | High |
| ice shanty ☆ 🖫 | 18,100 | $0.54 | 0.68 | 10K – 100K | Medium |
| ice fishing house 🖫 | 3,600 | $0.68 | 1 | 1K – 10K | High |
| ice fishing shanty 🖫 | 4,400 | $0.40 | 1 | 1K – 10K | High |
| ice fishing shelter 🖫 | 2,900 | $0.49 | 1 | 1K – 10K | High |
| ice fishing equipme... | 1,000 | $0.71 | 1 | 1K – 10K | High |
| ice fishing clothing 🖫 | 1,000 | $0.76 | 1 | 1K – 10K | High |
| ice fishing jigs ☆ 🖫 | 2,400 | $0.23 | 1 | 1K – 10K | High |
| ice fishing tent ☆ 🖫 | 3,600 | $0.38 | 1 | 1K – 10K | High |
| ice fishing tackle 🖫 | 720 | $0.37 | 1 | 100 – 1K | High |

You can take any of the sub-niches shown in the image and turn it into your blog niche. Again, you will need to be sure that the topic can be developed into a whole blog. You can do this by ensuring that you can create a year's worth of blog posts around the subject.

You can enter each niche idea you have into the tool and generate as many sub-niches as possible. Once you are done, proceed to select one or two ideas from the many ones you have gotten.

**Step 3: Determine which niche is most profitable**

You may decide to choose a niche from the research and brainstorming you have done so far. However, you can still do further research to find the profitability of any niche you want to choose before settling for it.

One tool that helps you to research the profitability of a niche, topic, or keyword is Keyword Everywhere. It is a browser extension that you install on your Chrome or Firefox browser. What the extension does is that anytime you do a Google search, it will show you the number of people searching for that keyword or term in a month. The tool will also show you how much advertisers are willing to pay for the keyword or phrase.

For instance, let's search for "walleye fishing" on Google using a browser that has the Keyword Everywhere extension installed. See the screenshot below for the result of the search.

Google    walleye fishing

Volume: 22,200/mo | CPC: $0.37 | Competition: 0.3

Q All    Images    Videos    News    Maps    More         Settings    Tools

About 27,100,000 results (0.57 seconds)

**Walleye fishing - Wikipedia**
https://en.wikipedia.org/wiki/Walleye_fishing
Fishing for **walleye** is a popular sport with anglers. The current IGFA all tackle record is 11.34 kilograms (25 lb 0 oz), caught on August 2, 1960 in Old Hickory ...

People also ask

What is the best bait for walleye?                                    ∨

Are walleye fun to catch?                                             ∨

How deep do you fish for walleye?                                     ∨

Is Walleye good to eat?                                               ∨

Feedback

In the screenshot, you can see that 22,200 people search for Walleye fishing in a month, and CPC, which is the amount that advertisers are willing to pay for the keyword is $0.37. The keyword also has a competitive score of 0.3.

Now, what you need to do is install Keyword Everywhere extension on your browser and type all your selected blog niche ideas into Google. Click on the search button and record the figures returned by the extension in a spreadsheet or Word document.

See the screenshot below.

**Walleye Fishing**
- **Search Volume:** 18,100 searches/month
- **CPC:** $0.39

**Trout Fishing**
- **Search Volume:** 14,800 searches/month
- **CPC:** $1.66

**Bass Fishing**
- **Search Volume:** 49,500 searches/month
- **CPC:** $0.52

**Ice Fishing**
- **Search Volume:** 22,200 searches/month
- **CPC:** $0.58

**Fly Fishing**
- **Search Volume:** 90,500 searches/month
- **CPC:** $1.38

In the above document, we recorded the search volume and CPC for each niche idea we are using for this example.

Next, after you have determined the number of people searching for each blog niche idea and the keyword's CPC, you need to review the popularity of the niche idea over time. If a topic has just gained popularity over the past few months, you don't want to create a blog about that topic because it will soon fade away the same way it suddenly gained popularity. You also don't want to create a blog about a topic that is already dying. Your best bet is to choose a niche that has maintained its popularity consistently for many years.

The best tool for testing the popularity of a blog niche topic or idea is Google Trends. It's a tool by Google. To use the tool, visit trends.google.com, enter a keyword of interest, and you will see how the keyword has fared in terms of popularity over the months.

The screenshot below shows the popularity of "walleye fishing."

In the above screenshot, you can see that the popularity of the keyword dropped around November 2018. Ideally, you wouldn't want to choose a niche that doesn't attract consistent traffic throughout the year. Instead, you should continue your research and find other keywords or niche topics that are relatively popular throughout the seasons of a typical year.

So, enter the other topic ideas you have into Google Trends and observe how they maintained popularity throughout the year. Since we are using different types of fishing for this example, we may need to search for "ice fishing." Typically, ice fishing will be more popular around the winter months, so you may need to search for other topic ideas. You need to keep searching until you find a niche topic or idea that trends all through the year or for most of the year.

After you have sieved out some topic ideas, you should be left with just a handful. You still need to test the remaining ones for popularity on social media, and you can do that using Buzzsumo. Buzzsumo is a tool that shows you the amount of engagement (likes, shares, etc.) that a particular topic or keyword records on different social media platforms.

To check a keyword on Buzzsumo, visit the website, then in the search bar, type the keyword or niche topic, and hit "Go." The site will list current conversations on social media that contain the topic or keyword you just entered. Additionally, the tool will show you how many likes, shares, comments the keyword has received on each social media platform. The result the website will return will look like the screenshot below.

Now, go back to your spreadsheet where you recorded each niche topic as well as the information you have gathered about them. Next, include the popularity (on Google Trends and Buzzsumo) of each of the niche ideas.

**Check the sale potential of the niche idea**

At this point, you should be getting close to having one particular niche topic or idea that is most viable among the various options you have. The next thing you need to do is to check the niche topic's sale potential on platforms like Amazon and Udemy. The reason for checking on Amazon is that eBooks are among the most popular products developed by bloggers. So, if there are already eBooks in your preferred niche that are selling well on Amazon, it means that the niche topic has a high sales potential.

So, head on to Amazon, go to the eBook category, and type your preferred niche topic or idea in the search box. Sort your search by indicating that the books with the most reviews should appear first. Note the number of reviews that the first two books that show up in the results have. Repeat this process for all your niche ideas, then sieve out the niche ideas that have books with a few reviews.

**Check for competition**

The last thing you need to check before settling for a particular niche is the page authority and domain authority of the blogs that are already existing in the niche. A free method to do that involves creating a free account on moz.com and installing the MozBar browser extension. The MozBar extension works like Keyword Everywhere.

Search for each of your niche topics on Google; the MozBar extension will return the page authority and domain authority of each site that shows up in your Google search results. We are not interested in the page authority. We only want to consider the domain authority of each of the websites that show up in the search results. If the domain authority of a website is high, you will find it hard to compete with such a site.

For each niche topic that you search on Google, record the domain authority of the first website or blog that shows up in the search result. You need to round up the figures to the nearest whole number. If the first search result for any niche idea is a YouTube video, then skip that for the next result or website.

By this time, the spreadsheet you are using to record your figures or results should look like the screenshot below:

**Walleye Fishing**
- **Search Volume:** 18,100 searches/month
- **CPC:** $0.39
- **Interest Over Time:** popularity decreases in the fall and early winter
- **Most Shares:** 6,300
- **Amazon Reviews:** 34
- **Udemy:** no courses
- **Average DA:** 62

**Trout Fishing**
- **Search Volume:** 14,800 searches/month
- **CPC:** $1.66
- **Interest Over Time:** popularity decreases in the fall and winter
- **Most Shares:** 26,800 (Youtube); 3,200
- **Amazon Reviews:** 146
- **Udemy:** 1 course; 3 reviews
- **Average DA:** 56

**Bass Fishing**
- **Search Volume:** 49,500 searches/month
- **CPC:** $0.52
- **Interest Over Time:** popularity decreases in the fall and winter
- **Most Shares:** 10,000
- **Amazon Reviews:** 126
- **Udemy:** no courses
- **Average DA:** 69

Looking at the above screenshot, you will find out that "fly fishing" and "bass fishing" have the highest search volume. However, the domain authority for the websites that are already available in the different niches is relatively high. If you create a blog in such niches, you will find it hard to outcompete the already available blogs or websites.

"Trout fishing," as shown in the screenshot, has low search volume, but the average domain authority of the sites already available in the niche is 56, which is okay. Also, the CPC for the niche topic is even higher than that of "Bass fishing" and "Walleye fishing." So, if you want to choose one niche from the three shown in the screenshot above, you are better off settling with "trout fishing" as your blog will have higher chances of ranking on Google if you blog about that niche.

Notice how we have dedicated a lot of time and attention to talk about niches and how to choose one? The reason is simple. Once you have gotten this aspect of blogging right, then you can be rest assured that you are already halfway into becoming a successful blogger. If, on the other hand, you fail to get this stage right, then it means that your blog had already started failing before it even started.

Now that you have chosen your blog niche, the next thing you need to do is to choose the best blogging platform.

# CHAPTER FOUR

# <u>Building Your Blog</u>

Once you have chosen your preferred niche, the next step is to choose your preferred blogging platform. The two most popular blogging platforms are WordPress and Blogger (owned by Google). A blogging platform is simply a software that allows you to create, edit, update, delete, or generally manage your blog and posts.

Which of the blogging platforms is better? This is a question that people ask all the time. At the moment, bloggers, web designers seem to have reached a consensus that WordPress is better than Blogger for so many reasons. Be sure that this is not saying that Blogger is not equally good.

As mentioned earlier, Blogger is owned by Google, and it is an excellent platform for people who want to host a simple blog that they can update and edit easily. Once you have a Gmail account or Google account, then you can create a Blogger account, one of Google's integrated services. One good thing about using the Blogger platform is that you don't need to spend money on website hosting anymore. Google automatically hosts the created blog for free!

Furthermore, if you don't want to pay for a custom domain (which is highly recommended), then you can use a free subdomain provided by Google. Let's assume that your blog's name is Car Racing; if there is no other blog bearing the same on the Blogger platform, then you could choose carracing.blogspot.com as your domain name. The extension ".blogspot.com" is automatically attached to your blog name selected by Google.

If you want to remove the ".blogspot.com" attachment from your URL, you will need to buy a domain name. Then, redirect your blog on the Blogger platform to your new domain name. If you do that successfully, your new domain name will become "carracing.com." Note: the blog will still be hosted on Google. So, you are only paying for a domain name.

Once you have sorted out your domain name or blog name, you can choose any of Blogger blog themes, customize it as you please and then proceed to upload your first blog post. A theme shows how the different sections of your blog will look when viewed on desktop and mobile. If you don't like any of the default Blogger themes, you can pay for a premium Blogger theme or download one of the many available free Blogger themes on the internet.

One thing that makes many bloggers shy away from Blogger is that it has only limited themes and plug-ins. Many bloggers don't use the platform, and as a result, theme developers don't find it necessary to develop as many themes for the platform.

Plug-ins allow you to add several exciting features to the existing features of a software. Most software plug-ins are usually developed by a third party to improve the performance or add more functionalities to existing software. There are some plug-ins that, when you install them on your WordPress blog, will help you share your posts to your different social media pages. Some plug-ins help you maintain the security of your blog. Some plug-ins help you improve the search engine ranking of your blog.

When it comes to plug-ins, Blogger has a minimal number of plug-ins. The reason for that is – since most people are not using the Blogger platform, software developers who develop plug-ins concentrate their efforts on developing plug-ins for WordPress rather than Blogger.

With just a few available and boring themes, many bloggers ditch the Blogger platform for WordPress. Apart from the availability of a wide range of plug-ins and themes to choose from, several other reasons make people prefer WordPress to Blogger. Let's take an in-depth look at WordPress and some of the features that make it great.

# WordPress

WordPress is a content management system built using PHP (a programming language) and MySQL (a database management system). One thing that makes WordPress great is that you can install plug-ins for added functionalities. Also, you can make use of thousands of available templates or themes. All this makes it very simple to create or set up a blog using WordPress.

The simplicity of the use of WordPress is such that anybody who can send a text message on their mobile phone can use it. All you need is to download and install the content management system on your website host. Proceed to download and install any of the available WordPress themes. Download and install some essential plug-ins, then customize the theme according to your taste and start uploading your blog posts.

Many bloggers and website designers also prefer WordPress because of its improved security architecture. If you need added security, you can download and install plug-ins that will help you secure your site from hackers and cyber-attacks.

Also, there are available plug-ins that can help you improve the search engine ranking of your blog. This is another crucial reason why so many bloggers prefer WordPress. As a blogger, search engine optimization is vital to you because if you write the best blog posts in the world and people do not get to discover and read them, then you have just wasted your efforts. SEO plug-ins that can be installed on WordPress help increase the search engine ranking of your website such that when people are searching for content related to the one you have on your blog, your posts will show up in their search results.

With WordPress, you will always get support whenever you need it. For instance, if you are doing anything on your site and run into a problem or technical difficulty, you could easily search online and find your answers on any of the many available WordPress forums littering cyberspace. You may also get direct support from the WordPress support team.

Now that you have made up your mind to go with WordPress. Next, you need to purchase a domain name and hosting plan.

## **Domain name**

Your domain name is like the physical address of your blog on the internet. It is what visitors will use to locate your blog on the web. An example of a domain name is www.yourblogname.com.

Many people think choosing a domain is such an easy task; however, you will find out when you want to embark on the adventure that it is not as easy as it seems. You may discover that all the names you have been considering have all been taken.

Remember, your domain name is as important as the posts you put up on your blog. It is one of the first things that a visitor notices when they visit your blog. It also helps to improve the search engine ranking of your blog. Additionally, it helps visitors have a clear view of what your blog is all about. If you choose a domain name that does not convey your blog's message, you may be chasing away visitors.

Here are some tips on finding the right domain name:

**Use your niche topic**

Since you are starting a niche blog, there is no better domain name than one that contains the keywords in your niche. For instance, if you are blogging about guitars, make sure that "guitars" appear somewhere in your domain name. This way, if visitors come across your domain name, they do not have to think twice before knowing that the blog is about guitars and related stuff.

Unless it is highly necessary, try as much as possible to stay away from hyphenated domain names. Putting a hyphen in your domain name will reduce its smoothness and can be a significant turn off for visitors. Additionally, make sure the name is not unnecessarily prolonged. Once it starts exceeding two words, then it is already getting long. A domain name that consists of three words is already long, and if you try to go more than that, then what you have is a full sentence.

You must also avoid using your name as your domain name unless you are a lifestyle blogger. Even if you are a lifestyle blogger, it might still be necessary for you to separate your name from your business. In the past, some successful bloggers, both lifestyle bloggers and those in other niches who used their names as their domain names, have come out to regret the action.

Neil Patel, a famous blogger and internet marketer, once mentioned that he wouldn't use his name as his domain name if he were to start all over. So, think twice before using your name as your domain name, even if you are a lifestyle blogger.

**A ".com" domain is better**

The average blog reader already assumes that every website on the internet has a ".com" domain extension. So, when they want to type the URL of a website, they include ".com" at the end. If your blog uses a different extension, you may be losing visitors because if your potential visitor attaches the wrong domain extension to your domain name, they will be redirected to a different website, and in some cases, the domain name they typed may not even open.

Usually, when bloggers are searching for a domain name, they find out that all the names they have been nursing have all been taken. So, they often decide to choose a different extension as a way of preserving the name they love. You should still try some other variations of your domain name with the .com extension instead of going for a different extension. While some blogs are doing well with a .net extension, for instance, a ".com" extension is still your best bet.

Popular websites where you can buy a domain name include Namecheap.com, godaddy.com, and namesilo.com.

After choosing a domain name, the next step is to buy a hosting package, install WordPress, download a theme, install some required plug-ins, and start customizing your blog.

# CHAPTER FIVE

## <u>Populating **Your Blog with Content**</u>

After setting up your blog and doing all the necessary customizations, the next thing you want to do is to populate your blog with incisive posts. Earlier, we mentioned that finding the right blog niche is one of the most challenging tasks. Now, we will discuss another challenging task. When it comes to blogging, is to create and publish valuable posts that your readers would love.

With the right content, the right readers will locate your blog. This will gradually work to help improve the search engine ranking of the blog. Once many of your posts have been ranked on search engines, you have already come steps closer to running a successful blog. That said, you need to dedicate a lot of time to research and create valuable content. One that would solve the problems that your readers have.

For a first-time blogger, publishing their first original content often proves to be a difficult task. The reason is not hard to guess. The blogger usually does not know how and where to find the best topic ideas to share with their readers. Some other new bloggers go ahead to copy content on other blogs and publish the same on theirs. That is a very wrong move as Google would see such content as duplicate and not rank your blog for such content. Also, copying content from other blogs can make Google penalize your blog, which will make it hard for it to be ranked on the search engine.

Another mistake that new bloggers make is that they just copy posts from blogs, use article rewriters or spinners to change a few common words or phrases in the article. The bloggers do this because they feel they could fool Google to think the content is original.

However, Google still has a way of detecting content that has been spun using article rewriters or article encoding tools. Google sees such articles as duplicate content, and if you have such duplicate content on your blog, you could be penalized.

Now, how do you find topic ideas for your first blog post? There are several available means of finding the right topic ideas for your blog posts – one of them is through social listening.

## What is social listening?

Social listening involves eavesdropping on social media users' conversations and picking up useful information that you can use to perform various actions. For instance, when you go on Quora, you will find people asking multiple questions – what you are doing is social listening.

When you visit a Facebook group, you will find people discussing various issues – that is, a type of social listening. Now, you can use social listening to your advantage. All you need to do is to be proactive instead of reactive. Rather than just listening to what people are saying on social media, provoke them to tell you what problem they want to be solved.

For instance, if you have a blog that talks about Amazon Kindle Publishing and you are looking for a topic idea to publish on your blog, you could visit Quora and ask a question such as, "What are the major challenges you are facing as a Kindle Publisher?" You could also ask, "What would you advise a new Kindle Publisher?" Or you could try, "What are the best Amazon Kindle keyword research tools?" You will be surprised to find out that many Quora users would be willing to answer your questions. From their answers, you could grab some pieces of information that will help you create your first blog post.

Apart from Quora, you can also do this type of active social listening on Facebook. Search for Facebook groups that are related to your blog niche. Join such groups and proceed to ask the kind of questions you asked on Quora. You will find many useful answers, especially if you come across as someone who is ready to learn.

For instance, if you asked a question on the best Amazon Kindle keyword research tools, you will likely get answers like keyword.io, Publisher Rocket, etc. Now, to utilize such information, you can head to your notepad or word process and produce a topic like, "How to find bestselling Amazon Kindle keywords using keyword.io."

Also, if asked a question like, "What are the challenges you face when you run Facebook ads?" You are likely to get answers like, "My major challenge when I run Facebook ads is how to target the right audience." With that answer, you can proceed to create a topic that says, "How to target the right audience when running Facebook ads."

In the above examples, you can see that your conversations with your target audience already revealed the types of problems that they have. With such information in your hands, you don't have to create topics blindly.

While the method mentioned above is suitable for discovering blog post topic ideas, you need not rely on it alone. Once you have gotten a topic idea, you still need to do keyword research to ensure that the problem you want to address is not a solo one. Proper keyword research will show you how many people are seeking a solution to the same problem. If you confirm after keyword research that many people are indeed searching for the topic, then you can proceed and create a blog post around that topic.

# Keyword research

As mentioned earlier, keyword research is an important step you must take when creating content for your blog. One mistake that many bloggers make is that they create blog posts for themselves instead of considering their audience. For instance, some bloggers only think about a topic that interests them or one they think their audience would love, then they proceed to create a blog post on such issues. What these bloggers often forget is that they are not the ones reading their own blog.

You are writing for an audience, and sometimes, the topics that your audience wants to read may not be the exact topic you want. Since you are not necessarily writing for yourself, you should make sure that enough people are seeking the solution that you want to provide.

Proper keyword research protects you from writing blindly. It shows you the approximate number of people searching for a topic. It also shows you how much advertisers are willing to pay for a specific keyword. All these pieces of information can help you know if it is worth it to spend some time creating a blog post on a given topic.

When we talk of CPC (Cost per Click) or how much advertisers will pay for a keyword, it might sound confusing to the new blogger. However, let's try and explain it.

Google and other advertising networks have a way of determining how much you earn when they place advertisements on your blog or web page. CPC is one of the earning models, and there is also CPM (Cost per Impression). Let's proceed further to explain how all these works.

When it comes to the advertisements that Google or other advertising networks place on a website, there are always three parties involved. The first party is you, the blog or website owner. The second party is Google or any other ad network like Bing, while the third party is a business owner who wants to advertise their business on relevant websites or blogs.

Typically, a business owner runs an advertisement campaign on Google's advertising network called Google Ads. When setting up the campaign, the business owner states how much they are willing to pay each time someone clicks on their ads. Some high-end businesses bid higher than others, while some businesses offer lower.

Now, once the campaign has been set up, Google advertises the business on your blog or web page. Let's assume that the business agrees they would pay $1.5 for every click. Remember, for the ad to be running on your site, Google has found some keywords that are relevant to the business (running the ad) on your blog. So, we can say that the CPC for the keywords that attracted the ads is $1.5. Each time a visitor to your blog clicks on the ad, the business owner running the ad will pay $1.5 to Google, who will take their cut and pay you the rest.

Typically, some keywords that are related to some high-end businesses have higher CPCs than the others. So, when you are doing keyword research, you should be interested in finding out the search volume for the keyword and the CPC. If the search volume is high, it means the keyword will attract a high amount of traffic to your blog every month. Also, if the CPC is high, it means that with just a few ad clicks, you can earn a substantial amount of money.

Another metric you should look out for when doing keyword research is the competitive score of the keyword. For instance, if the competitive score is 1, it means the keyword is highly competitive, and you may find it hard to rank for such keywords. However, if the competitive score is below 1, it means you can easily rank for the keyword.

# Keyword research tools

We have mentioned some of the importance of keyword research - let's proceed to talk about some of the best keyword research tools for bloggers.

**1. Soovle**

Soovle is a versatile keyword research tool – it scrapes the various search engines on the internet and shows you the search volume and CPC of any keyword you enter. It also shows you different variations of a keyword and how users type the keywords when doing searches on various search engines.

What's more? Soovle is completely free. In fact, it works like a search engine. To use the tool, just type soovle.com into your web browser. On the home page, enter the keyword you want to research into the search bar. As you are typing the keyword, Soovle will scrape the web in real-time and show you the keyword's CPC and search volume. If your focus is to rank the keyword on Google, you will need to concentrate on the Google results. If you want to rank the keyword on Bing, you will need to focus on Bing results.

Apart from showing how many people are searching for a particular keyword on conventional search engines like Google, Bing, Yahoo, and YouTube, Soovle also shows you how your keyword is faring on Amazon.com.

While Soovle is a great keyword research tool, it does not show you all the information you need about a keyword, like its competitive score. If you need other pieces of information about a keyword that Soovle cannot show you, you can use any of the other keyword research tools we are going to talk about in this section.

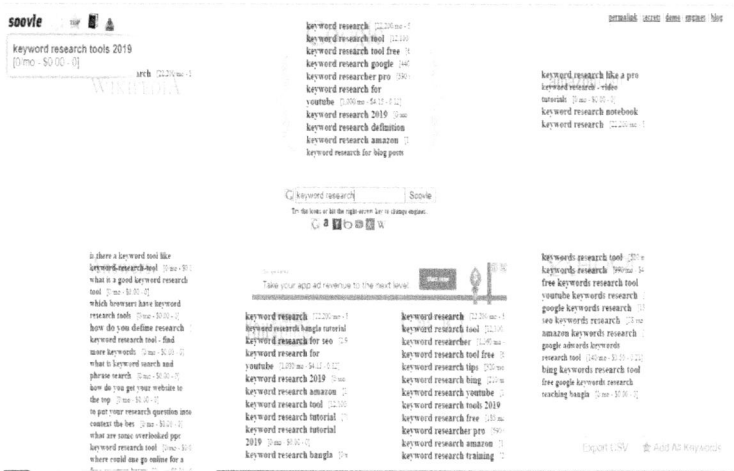

## 2. Jaaxy.com

This is yet another excellent keyword research tool. Unlike Soovle.com, Jaaxy is a freemium tool – meaning you can use the free version with limited features, but if you want all the features, you will need to pay at least $50/month.

Jaaxy, just like the other keyword research tools, shows you how many people are searching for a keyword in a month. One great feature of Jaaxy that distinguishes it from the other keyword research tools is its QSR (Quoted Search Result) feature. This shows you the number of other blogs that are trying to rank for each keyword. Typically, if this number is high, it means that the keyword's competition is high. However, if the number is low, it means you can rank on the first page of Google or other search engines for that keyword.

| Phrase ⌄ | link building | | History ⌄ | 🔍 Find Keywords | |
|---|---|---|---|---|---|

| Keyword ⓘ | Avg ⓘ | Traffic ⓘ | QSR ⓘ | KQI ⓘ | SEO ⓘ |
|---|---|---|---|---|---|
| seo **link building** | 961 | 164 | 365 | Poor | 12 |
| backlink **building** | 334 | 57 | 250 | Normal | 72 |
| one way **link building** | 56 | 10 | 216 | Great | 84 |
| free **link building** tool | 256 | 44 | 91 | Great | 96 |
| affordable **link building** | 213 | 37 | 278 | Normal | 54 |

### 3. Google Keyword Planner

In a previous section of this guide, we talked about Google Keyword Planner. Essentially, the tool owned by Google gives you relevant information about a keyword, so you don't create blog posts blindly.

To use the tool, you must have a Google account, then visit ads.google.com. Use your Google account to log in. On the home page, click on "Tools," then under "planning," click on "keyword planner." Next, click on "discover new keywords," then enter the keyword you want to get information on into the search box.

Your results should look like the screenshot below.

Google Keyword Planner is more robust than the other keyword research tools mentioned earlier. It shows you a lot of information about a keyword that can help you make an informed decision on whether to write on the keyword or not. What's more? The tool is free – you only need to have a Gmail account (which is also free) to use it.

Other notable keyword research tools include:

•        Keywordtool.io

•        Keywords Everywhere – this is a browser extension that we have already discussed in a previous section of this guide.

•        Google Trends – we have talked about this tool in an earlier part of this guide

•        SEMRush.com – a freemium tool that does a great job of helping you find viable keywords

•        KWFinder.com

Apart from these mentioned keyword research tools, there are tons of other ones, both free and paid. Do your research and find out the ones that are best for you.

**Interpreting results from keyword research**

When you research a keyword, you would be shown the average number of people searching for that keyword in a month. You will also see how competitive the keyword is. Typically, you would think that a keyword with a high search volume is the best – while this is true to some extent, such keywords are often very competitive.

The best keywords are those with high search volume, low to moderate competition, and high CPC. However, finding a keyword that ticks those three boxes can be quite hard. A good idea is for you to compromise on one of the requirements.

For instance, you could go for a keyword with moderate or average search volume, low competition, and high CPC. Yes, you can find such keywords. You would want to use your discretion to determine which of the metrics you want to compromise on. For instance, if a keyword has a high search volume, low to moderate competition, and low CPC – you could consider going for the keyword even though the CPC is low because the high search volume will cover up for that.

Additionally, instead of settling for seed keywords, consider their long tails. The long tail of a keyword means the expanded forms that can be derived from the root keyword. Each time you type a root or seed keyword into a keyword research tool, you will see many derivatives from that root keyword – those derivatives are called long tails variants of the keyword.

In most cases, the root keyword may not meet your criteria – it might have a high search volume, and the competitive score would be very high as well, so you don't want to use it. However, when you look closely at the long tails of the root keyword, you will find possible variants with an equally good amount of search volume and low competition. You are to go for those long-tail keywords instead of the seed or root keyword.

For instance, if you search for "celery juice," in the results, you will find "celery juice" as a separate result, and you will also find "benefits of celery juice" as one of the results, which could have high good search volume and low competition. Now, instead of just writing a blog post on "celery juice," a smart blogger would write on "benefits of celery juice."

One good thing about using long-tail variants of a keyword is that you may end up ranking for both the seed keyword and its long tail variant. When you first publish the post, it will rank for the long tail variant of the keyword. Then after some time, it might rank for the main seed keyword – meaning more traffic to your blog.

Now that you have mastered the art of finding and analyzing the right keywords. The next chapter will show you how to write an engaging blog post.

# CHAPTER SIX

# <u>How to Write an Engaging Blog Post</u>

Before we show you how to write a good blog post – let's first analyze the components of such a blog post. Typically, a blog post has three parts – the header or introduction, the body, and the conclusion or calls to action. You need to understand what information should appear in each of these sections if you want to create a high converting and engaging blog post.

**The header or introduction**

Just as the name implies, your blog post's header should introduce the idea or topic of the post. It should let the user know what the issue is all about – you can include definitions here if necessary.

Additionally, the header should let the reader know what they will gain by reading the blog post to the end. You must use emotional triggers to keep the reader hooked and feel they would miss something important if they do not read to the end.

For instance, if you are writing a blog post on the benefits of childproofing your home, you could start by defining what home childproofing means. You could proceed to let the reader know that in addition to learning the benefits of childproofing their home, they are also going to learn the top five ways to childproof their home. This way, you have piqued the reader's interest, and they would want to read your post to the very end.

**The body**

The main body of your blog post comes immediately after the header, and it is where you present your main argument. For ease of readability, you can consider presenting your points in the form of a listicle. You should also use subheadings or subtitles to separate one central point from the other to make it easier for the reader to scan through your points.

As we have always been reiterating, you are not creating a blog post for yourself. Instead, you are doing it for your readers. So, you should present your readers with valuable information in a readable format so that in the end, they could feel you have helped them so that they could continue reading your other posts for more information.

**Conclusion and call to action**

You should use the concluding part of your post to chip in some pieces of information that you did not cover in the main body of the post. Don't start repeating all the points you have already treated in the body of the post – that would be an unnecessary repetition. After concluding the post, include a call-to-action to tell the reader what to do next.

Call-to-action is an integral part of every blog post. Your average reader may know the next action to take after reading your post, but they still expect you to tell them what to do. This is your chance to make them take the desired action. Before writing a post, you should have figured out the goal you want to achieve with the post. You are to use a call-to-action to accomplish this goal.

For instance, if you want the reader to comment, let them know using a call-to-action. If you want them to join your email list, read other related articles, download an eBook, or share your article, let them know. As mentioned earlier, do not assume that the reader knows what to do next – they may know, but they still want you to tell them. The average reader would click away after reading your post if you do not tell them the next thing to do.

## SEO articles and blog posts

Search Engine Optimization involves crafting posts to be easily ranked by search engines such as Google, Bing, etc. When it comes to SEO, some articles are often referred to as SEO articles, while others are not. The significant difference is that SEO articles or blog posts contain relevant keywords in strategic sections of the article, like the header, body, and conclusion.

When you are writing a blog post, optimization must be done for search engine ranking – this way, your ideal reader can discover and read the article. Optimizing your posts for search engine ranking is very important because your posts will be undiscoverable without it. What is the point of writing a blog post if it won't be discovered and read by your target audience?

Before writing a blog post, make sure you have used any of the keyword research tools we discussed in the previous section to analyze the keyword. After your analysis, write out at least three keywords that you would include in different parts of your article. Ideally, you should include keywords in the title, header, body, and conclusion of your blog post.

Ensure you don't stuff keywords unnecessarily in your blog post, as that could attract a penalty. Keyword stuffing will also alter the natural flow of your blog and make it nearly unreadable. For clarity, keyword stuffing is the act of including an excessive number of keywords at different places in your blog post. People who do keyword stuffing think it is a good way of adding as many keywords as possible in their posts to improve ranking.

Most times, instead of improving the search engine ranking of your blog post, keyword stuffing works to reduce its readability and conversion rate. Rather than stuffing unnecessary keywords in your blog post, take your take and learn the proper way of incorporating the right number of keywords in the blog post – this will help improve your article's readability and increase your conversion rate.

# Writing an engaging blog post

The average internet user is not the most patient person out there – they also have a short attention span. This means that if you want them to read your posts, you must make them as highly engaging as possible.

Here are some of the ways to write an engaging blog post:

## 1. Write in a conversational style

When you are creating a blog post, you should focus on the person who will read the post. You can do that by writing in a conversational style. Such a style of writing will increase your post engagement by up to 80%.

Think about this – a lecturer walks into a classroom filled with students, starts talking without even referring to the students; what do you think the students would do? Many of them would fall asleep because the lecture must be boring to endure. However, if the lecturer enters the classroom and creates a conversation where everyone in the class contributes and feels among, what do you think would happen? The course would be lively.

The best way to write in a conversational style is to use "I" and "You" in your posts. Using those two words makes your posts personalized to the reader; the reader would feel you are talking to them directly. It is also an excellent way to create dialogue and encourage your readers to engage with your posts.

You can say things like, "I am happy you are reading this post," "thank you for being here," "in this article, I am going to show you…"

Any reader who comes across any of the above phrases would feel you are talking to them directly and would want to continue reading. Without writing in a conversational style, your post will sound like an academic thesis or a research document, and no one loves reading those kinds of materials except when it is indispensable.

**2. Break down your content into many paragraphs**

When people open your blog post and find it to be one massive chunk of text, they will not hesitate to close the page and go elsewhere. You need to group your points into paragraphs, and each paragraph should contain about four sentences or four lines. Once a paragraph starts getting long, create a new one. It is also a good idea to present your ideas using a list – this improves readability significantly.

**3. Make sure you use subheadings**

If your blog post is a long one – ensure you use subheadings to highlight your major points. Even if your content is not that long, you can still make use of subheadings. Subheadings help to improve the readability of your post because someone could just skim through and grab the main points of your post.

## 4. Throw in images to spice up things

Whenever possible, throw in relevant pictures to lighten your posts and spice things up a little. Many times, when people open a blog post, they scan through for images. They want to draw conclusions from the pictures or use them to understand what the post is all about. Something as simple as a crisp, welcoming image is enough to keep your reader glued to your post. Additionally, well-labeled images help with search engine optimization.

You can follow the above tips and write as many posts as possible for your new blog until you have populated the blog.

In the next chapter, we shall start looking at different ways of monetizing your blog.

# CHAPTER SEVEN

# <u>SEO (Search Engine Optimization)</u>

Search Engine Optimization (SEO) involves designing your blog and modifying its contents so that search engines can easily index and rank the blog. If your blog is ranked on search engines, it means that potential readers who search for keywords related to the ones you have on your blog will find your blog and proceed to visit and read the content you have on there.

It is safe to say that SEO is a way of tricking Google to show your blog or articles to potential readers when they do online searches. In the world of blogging and internet marketing as a whole, SEO is critical, and SEO strategies change from time to time, which is why bloggers are always on the lookout for new SEO strategies.

The average blog reader relies on Google to lead them to the information they seek. If your blog is ranked on Google so that the average blog reader could find it when doing searches, you will have consistent traffic to your blog. If you cannot optimize your blog for search engines, then your traffic will suffer. Unless you run a popular blog that everybody already knows, then SEO is your best hope of getting consistent traffic.

Because SEO strategies take time to yield results, some people think SEO is no longer relevant. However, the truth remains that

SEO is still as effective as it has always been. As a newbie blogger without much financial strength to run social media and other types of online ads, then SEO is your only hope. However, you must do it right; otherwise, it would turn back and hurt your blog. Some careless SEO strategies could make Google penalize your blog. Some other SEO strategies could lead to the suspension of your AdSense account – so, while you are trying hard to make your blog search engine optimized, you need to make sure that you are adopting the right SEO strategies.

Every day, Google and the other search engines change their search algorithms – a change in SEO practices always accompanies these changes. In other words, the world of SEO is an ever-changing one; what is in vogue today may get outdated the next moment, and that's the reason the topic of SEO is always on every blogger's lips.

Many times, new bloggers ask some questions concerning SEO such as, "what is SEO," "what are the best strategies when it comes to SEO for blogs," "where can one outsource SEO services?" amidst other questions. Responding to the subject of the best SEO practices or strategies for blogs can be very tricky because, as we said earlier, SEO strategies are always changing.

Despite the constant changes, the core basics of SEO remain the same. When we say that the core basics have remained the same, we mean that even though some strategies might have changed, there are still things about SEO that have remained relatively the same. In this chapter, we shall not be teaching you specific ways to do SEO. Instead, we shall be concentrating on showing you the current SEO best strategies.

**The best SEO is to stay focused on the visitor**

The mistake that most people make when it comes to SEO is trying out different strategies all the time. Over the years, it has proven not to be the best approach to SEO. Instead of running around and testing out different SEO techniques or tricks, it would be better if you focus on one fundamental concept that states that the best SEO is the human-based one.

Saying that the best SEO is human-based SEO can be surprising to many because they have long thought that the best techniques involve outsourcing SEO services to SEO consultants, or using automation tools, binary code, or shortcuts. While many of these techniques might have worked some years back when they were in vogue, they no longer stand the chance of being regarded as the best SEO practices today.

In today's SEO circle, the best strategies revolve around knowing who your blog readers are, connecting with them, and helping solve their problems. Blog visitors are people looking for solutions to their problems, and if you understand it this way and provide them with a solution to their problem, then you have the best SEO strategy.

The algorithm that search engines use to rank websites might have changed several times over the years, but one single thing remains constant. That continuous thing is that every search engine is out to provide useful content that will serve the needs of website visitors.

Today, we might be talking more about the demand for performance, mobile inquiries, and long voice-based search phrases, yet one thing remains constant – the needs of the visitor must be met. So, as long as humans are the ones visiting blogs, the need for high-quality human-based SEO will always be there. Providing tangible value and placing a strong focus on user experience will always be the best SEO strategy.

Don't be too engrossed thinking about plug-ins, data, and website code as the real SEO. Yes, all these may come into play in ranking a blog, but the essential thing that you must not ignore is to provide the blog visitor with the best user experience so that they don't find it difficult getting the solution they seek on your blog.

You need to understand that following shortcuts or outsourcing SEO services to acclaimed consultants may not really do much for you. The most important thing is the real value and experience you give your visitors. Following shortcuts or outsourcing your SEO services may bring visitors to your blog, but these shortcuts won't connect with these visitors on a personal level. Remember that the people visiting your website are real humans seeking solutions to their pains, and you need to address them as real humans.

**SEO is complex and yet so simple**

The world of SEO is an ever-changing one; everything seems to be getting more and more complex. Long search phrases are now the order of the day. Longer articles are also becoming the standard, and search engines are not left out as they have developed complex algorithms to be able to process all the changes that are taking place. Yet, amidst all these changes, we can say that things haven't changed much.

Search engines are still looking for websites and blogs that provide value to the visitors. So, Google expects that you do the right thing, and the right thing here involves providing value to people every day.

Many times, people want to know if they could game the system and make use of code or automation tools to push their blogs to the top of search engine result pages. The truth is that using these automation tools and codes might have worked in the past, but they no longer work today. If your focus is only on getting your blog way up the search engine result pages, then it means that you have lost focus on the visitor, and once it is not about the visitor, it is not the best SEO.

Human-based SEO is about helping people solve their problems, and you need to know that black hat tricks don't help blog readers to solve their problems. At best, they help you get your blog to the top of the search result, but Google has developed a quick way of removing the websites and blogs that game their system.

The bottom line is that you need to take time to learn about SEO in-depth, especially if you are new to it. Don't opt for shortcuts, don't bother yourself about changing algorithms; learn the basics. Try to understand why people visit and stay on websites, which will help you reach your goals.

Your focus should always be on your visitors, their unique problems, and how you can help them solve these problems. SEO strategies may be changing, but the core SEO principles remain the same: to serve the visitor.

Here are a few things you should do to improve your search engine ranking:

**1. Improve your site speed**

The average blog reader has only a few seconds to wait for your blog to load. If your blog doesn't load within those few seconds, the visitor would be forced to leave. Since Google and other search engines always put the experience of the website visitor first, it means that if your blog loads fast enough, your search engine ranking will be improved.

**2. Reduce bounce rate**

Bounce rate and site speed go hand in hand – the reason is simple – if your blog is slow to load, your bounce rate will be high. With a high bounce rate, Google will believe that your site does not have what the visitor is searching for, and this would negatively impact your ranking.

Even though site speed is not the only thing that affects your blog's bounce rate, it remains one of the major causes. Other things that could cause an increase in your bounce rate include a poorly designed blog. If your visitors find it hard to navigate through your blog efficiently, they would be forced to leave, thus increasing your bounce rate.

Additionally, make sure your blog posts contain value and provide a solution to the reader'sproblem. These days, Google and the other search engines prefer longer articles to shorter ones. This is not implying that you should use filler content to make up your post. Instead, ensure you cover every necessary point so that the reader could say, "Yes, I have value."

Furthermore, if you don't write in a conversational style, you could also chase away visitors, which affects your bounce rate. If you don't know how to make use of calls-to-action creatively, then you could be increasing your blog's bounce rate. With the right call-to-action, you could direct visitors to other relevant and related articles on your blog. This way, they could go on a reading spree instead of bouncing off after reading the first article.

As mentioned earlier, these days, learning all the SEO tricks and strategies in the world will not help you. Yes, you still need to know some fundamental SEO strategies like writing search engine optimized articles, but if your blog eventually gets ranked and you don't retain visitors, you may end up losing your ranking.

So, it is more important to ensure that your blog provides value. Start by improving your site speed and provide useful content. If you do all these, your bounce rate will decrease, and Google would be forced to believe that your blog is valuable; hence, your ranking will improve.

# CHAPTER EIGHT

## Blog **Monetization**

If you have followed this guide religiously, then at this point, you must have found a blog niche, decided on the best blogging platform, designed your blog, written and uploaded posts on your blog.

If you have done all that, the next thing to do is to monetize your blog and earn money from your efforts. In the past, people used to start blogs to document their lives or merely for the joy of it. Today, people consider blogs as a viable online business that can give them money while they are doing the things they love.

In a previous section of this guide, we talked about some of the ways of monetizing a blog. In this section, we are going to spend time talking about the Google AdSense program, which is one of the most popular blog monetization methods out there.

## What is Google AdSense?

Google AdSense is one of Google's integrated services that gives website owners and bloggers the chance to place ads on their website and earn money when visitors click on those ads.

How the program works is: an advertiser approaches Google, creates an ad campaign – then Google looks for a website that is registered in the AdSense program and places those ads on the site. Google goes through every website and ensures that the ads they are putting on are relevant to the visitors of the website.

Google also considers the type of content that a website has when placing ads. For instance, if you run a travel blog, most of the ads that Google would push to your site would be those related to travel. It could be the ads of travel companies, airlines, flight agents, etc.

When visitors come to your website and click on any of the Google ads placed at strategic sections on your website or blog, Google analyses the click action to verify that it is valid. If Google confirms that the click action is legitimate, it pays you according to the amount that the advertiser agreed with Google (CPC). On the other hand, if Google discovers that a click action on an ad placed on your blog is invalid, that could lead to a suspension of your Google AdSense account.

**Who is free to join the Google AdSense program?**

Ideally, anyone who has a blog or website (that doesn't have adult content or promote betting/gambling) can apply and get approved for the Google AdSense program. However, for some reason, some people do not get their application approved. If you visit online forums, you will find people complaining that their AdSense application was declined.

Several reasons could make Google decline one's application to join the AdSense program. Also, there are a few things you need to put in place before applying for Google AdSense. With those things in place, your application would be approved on your first try.

**Why do many people prefer Google AdSense to other online ad networks?**

Before we proceed to talk about some of the things you need to put in place before applying for the Google AdSense program, let's quickly see why many people prefer AdSense. People often ask, "Why do so many people prefer the Google AdSense program to other similar programs?"

The answer to that question is – while there are other online ad networks out there, the fact remains that Google AdSense is the most popular. Because of Google's popularity and its integrated services, many advertisers naturally pitch their tent with Google when they want to advertise on online platforms. Also, Google pays better than many of the other ad networks. Some other ad networks don't have a transparent payment policy, unlike Google, that makes sure you receive what you have earned as long as the click that earned you that income is valid.

Now, let's proceed to talk about how to get AdSense approval on your first try. You must get your AdSense application approved on your first try because if you fail the first time, your chances of failing to secure the approval on your second try are high. Once you have tried the first time and failed, Google kind of places your domain name on a watch list (this is an unwritten rule or code). So, you want to do everything possible to get approved on your first try.

Getting Google AdSense approval is not as hard as many people make it seem. The truth is that if you follow all the steps and do the right things, Google would have no other option than to approve your website for AdSense. If you have followed all the steps outlined in this book so far, then you should not have a problem getting AdSense approval.

That said, here are the things you need to put in order before applying for AdSense approval:

## 1. A decent blog site

Whether you are using the Blogger platform or WordPress, it doesn't matter when it comes to AdSense approval. Google cares more about the functionality of your website. The blog site has to be well designed so that it is attractive to visitors. Google takes the experience of the blog visitor seriously. They want to make sure that your blog visitor gets the best experience when they visit your blog.

Having a good theme can do a lot for your blog in terms of design. You are better off with a premium theme than a free one. Premium themes have better features, and you can customize your blog to look as stunning as possible.

One way to make your blog appealing to both your visitors and Google is to improve its speed. Google hates blogs with low speed – the reason is simple – low speed means high bounce rate, and with high bounce rate, ads would not be clicked, and if the ads are not accessed, both you and Google will not earn.

On the other hand, if your blog loads fast enough, the visitor would be pleased to read as many posts on your blog as possible. While reading posts, they could be prompted to click on ads. Therefore, Google prefers websites that load faster.

In addition to aiding AdSense approval, website speed also impacts SEO. In the past, Google used to rank only blogs that contain the keywords that the reader is searching for. Today, however, Google looks beyond keywords and considers other factors like site speed when ranking blogs and websites.

So, even if you write the best search engine optimized articles, blog posts, and your blog crawls like a snail in terms of speed, you can find it hard to rank on the first page of Google and the other search engines.

In addition to ensuring that your blog loads fast, you need to make sure you include clear navigation on your blog. Google prefers those blogs that have the elements of a proper website. All this still boils down to giving the visitor the best experience.

Typically, Google wants you to include an "About Page," "Contact Page," and a "Privacy Policy Page" on your blog before applying for AdSense approval. Adding all these pages to your blog should not be a huge task – you need to create a new page, name it "About Us," for instance, and include what the reader needs to know about you. Google wants you to treat your blog as a business. That's why it is forcing you to add an "About Us" section.

Your "Contact Us" page should contain basic information on how your blog readers can contact you. You could include your phone number, email, or contact form so that your blog readers can get in touch with you. If you have a physical address for your business, you can include it in this section; otherwise, you are good with just adding your phone number and email.

The "privacy policy page" is the one that Google takes more seriously – in fact, Google may still approve your site if you don't have "About Us" and "Contact Us" pages, but if you don't have a

"Privacy Policy" page, then your chances of approval are almost non-existent.

When creating your privacy policy page, Google wants you to include some specific pieces of information. This article from Google shows you the information you must include. If you find it hard to string together a privacy policy page, consider using this free privacy policy generator.

Additionally, a good logo will contribute to making your blog look as professional as possible. We have already mentioned that severally in the previous sections of this guide. If you have not gotten a logo yet, then endeavor to get one to improve your chances of getting approved for AdSense.

## 2. Quality content

Besides having a decent website, quality content is another thing that Google considers before approving the AdSense application. They want to be sure that the materials you are putting up on your blog are those that can solve the problem of the reader. As mentioned earlier, Google values the experience of the reader more than anything else, and they want to ensure that, at every point, the user gets a pleasant experience. The internet giant, Google, knows that if the user receives a good experience when visiting a blog, then the user will be more likely to click on ads.

So, to increase your chances of getting AdSense approval, you must create useful, articulate, and original content. You cannot just throw up some spammy content you copied from other websites and expect Google to approve your application.

Remember, Google places a premium on user experience, and since spam content irritates the average user, Google would never accept any blog containing such content for AdSense. Posting spam content on your blog will also negatively affect your search engine ranking, so you need to avoid it entirely.

Google wants you to solve the problem that people have – if they find that your blog is solving problems, they will approve it for AdSense. How do you answer people's problems? Through keyword research. After doing keyword research, take the time to write an original, articulate post that addresses the issue you have identified. Make sure you intersperse the post with relevant keywords to improve its search engine ranking.

One mistake that many new and even old bloggers make is that they go on eZinearticles.com, copy articles, and post the same on their blog, then apply for AdSense and expect to get approved. Some even create auto blogs and fill them with copied contents and hope Google approves the site for monetization. If you do that, then you should not be surprised if Google turns down your application. It is good to put yourself in the position of your blog reader. If you were the one reading your own blog, would you be happy to read some of the contents you have put up there? Your answer to that question should guide you.

Ideally, before you apply for AdSense approval, make sure you have posted up to 10 well-written articles. Each article should be up to 1,000 words in length. Make sure you do proper keyword research before writing the articles. Once you have gotten up to the recommended ten (10), don't just jump right in and apply for AdSense. You need to wait for some time and allow the articles to rank on search engines – this will increase the amount of traffic coming to your blog. Note: Google also considers the traffic coming to a blog before approving AdSense for the blog.

Overall, to get AdSense approval, you want to:

• Make sure you have a well-designed blog with all the necessary pages

• Make sure you are posting original search engine optimized articles

Quick tip! If your blog is in one of those popular, saturated niches such as making money online, marketing, SEO, etc., you may find it hard to get AdSense approval. This is one of the reasons why you need to niche down when finding a niche.

Also, you need to wait for at least three months before applying for AdSense. If you create a blog today, populate it with articles the next day, and apply for AdSense the following week, your application will likely not get approved. Also, you need to have a custom domain name to increase your chances of getting approved. Using a subdomain sends a signal that you are not serious.

**Applying for Google AdSense**

Once you have gotten all the requirements, the next step is to apply for Google AdSense and await your approval. If you have followed all the tips mentioned above, then there is a high chance that your application will be approved on your first try.

To apply for Google AdSense, follow this link. You will be asked to provide your blog URL, your name, contact information, email address, phone number, mailing address, and a few other necessary pieces of information. At this initial stage of the application, you will not be required to submit your bank account information or TIN; that will be later when your application has been approved.

Important: make sure that the mailing address and, indeed, all the personal information you are providing is correct. A PIN will be sent to your mailing address for verification purposes, so if you input a wrong address, you will fail the address verification. Also, you will be required to verify your phone number. Although these verifications will not happen until a later time, you need to get everything right from the beginning.

Filling out the application is not hard; you just need to follow the prompts. It is only necessary to provide basic information about you and your blog. You will only spend a few minutes filling out the forms.

**Getting approved to place temporary ads**

After submitting your application, the Google AdSense team will review it to see if your blog should be accepted into the AdSense program. Typically, the approval occurs within 24 to 48 hours after application. If you have followed all the steps and tips in this guide, then getting approval should be the least of your worries.

If you are approved, Google will send you an email that you have passed the first stage of the process. The email will further explain the other processes you need to go through until you are fully verified. At this early stage, what Google does is that they temporarily approve your blog to run ads, and after you earn a certain amount of money from clicks on, you are prompted to do an address verification.

At this point, you will be shown how to place ads on your blog – you will also be able to login to your AdSense account and see how much you have earned from clicks on the ads you have placed on your blog.

From the time you are approved to place ads on your blog temporarily, Google will be monitoring your activities to ensure you are not clicking on your ads, sending traffic from suspicious sources to your blog, or using tricks to increase clicks on your ads. As long as you are not clicking on your ads, sending friends to click on the ads, or using tricks or bots to click on your ads, you should be fine.

If you log into your AdSense dashboard, you will find where Google places AdSense codes, which you can copy and put on your blog. Those codes are what will display as ads when viewers view them on their browsers.

To increase your earnings, place different AdSense codes on strategic sections of your blog where readers can see and click them. However, do remember that the average internet user hates to see ads, so you should know where you are placing ads – you don't want to choke your readers with them.

If you have two or more blogs, you can place your AdSense codes on those blogs and increase your earnings. You don't have to apply individually for each new blog. You simply need to create new ad units and color themes for your different blogs. You are creating a new ad unit and color theme because you want the displayed ad to match the theme of each of your blog or website.

**AdSense verification**

Once your AdSense application has been approved, you can start generating ad units, place the ad codes on your blog, and earn money from clicks. Once you reach a certain threshold, Google will need to verify your physical address, bank account, phone number, and tax information. Without verifying these details, Google will not pay you what you have earned from AdSense.

To start the verification process, log into your AdSense dashboard; you will see a button that will prompt you to begin the verification process. When you click the button, Google will mail a PIN to the physical address you provided. The mail will get to you after seven to ten days. The letter you receive will contain your verification PIN. You will need to log into your dashboard and enter the PIN you received via mail to complete your address verification.

The mail will look like the screenshot below.

Apart from the PIN verification, you may be required to verify your bank account information, but that usually comes later. When confirming your bank account information, you will be required to fill out your tax information. One of the requirements for the bank verification is that the name you applied with must be the same as your bank account name. If you applied with your business entity, the bank account name must be the same as your business entity.

If you want to get paid by ACH (which is the preferred option), you will need to provide your bank account number and routing number. Google will deposit a small amount into the bank account and withdraw it afterward. As part of the verification, you will be asked to input this small amount into your Google AdSense dashboard. If you enter the correct amount that was deposited into your bank account, then your bank account verification has become completed. You can then start getting paid monthly as long as you reach the minimum withdrawal limit.

If you did not verify your phone when you were filling out your application, you would be asked to do so. Google will send a code to your phone number, which you will input into your dashboard or place an automated call with your verification code to you. Once you input the verification code, then you are good to go.

**How to keep your AdSense account safe**

Getting your AdSense account approved and verified does not mean that the account cannot be banned later if you do not follow AdSense's terms and conditions. One common factor that could lead to the banning of your account is invalid clicks.

If you don't click on your ads and you don't recruit people to click on the ads, then you are safe. Also, if you do not use bots or click farms to click on the ads, then you are also safe. If you don't place your ad codes on pornographic sites, then you are also safe.

Publishing copyrighted material on your blog can also lead to the termination of your account. The owner of the copyrighted material could report your blog to Google, and this could lead to an account ban.

One of the reasons why you need to avoid an AdSense account ban, by all means, is that once you have been banned, you cannot place AdSense codes on all the blogs and websites linked with the banned account. So, even if you get a new AdSense account, you will still not be able to generate ad codes and place them on your previous blogs. You will need to start building and growing an entire blog from scratch. This can take a long time.

The best way to avoid the termination of your account is to read AdSense's terms and conditions carefully. Once you follow those terms, then you will have your account all to yourself as long as you want.

**How to earn more with your ads**

Some of the obvious ways to make more money from ads include:

- Research and create posts on keywords with high CPC
- Find keywords with top search volume

Of course, while the two methods above can help you earn more from your blog, there are ways you could play around or be smart with your ads and increase your earnings. For instance, you could do manual tests and ad placements to determine the best sections on your blog to place ads for maximum conversion. If you place advertisements on certain areas of your blog, your readers may not get to see and click on them. So, you need to do an A/B split test to determine the best sections for ads clicks.

To do a proper A/B split test, you need to place ads in one section or location on your blog, then record the number of people that will click on the ad in one or two days. After a day or two, place the ad codes on entirely different sections of your blog and watch its performance over a day or two. Use your AdSense dashboard to monitor how your ads performed across different locations and sections.

Once you have determined the best places where your ads perform better, then stick to placing your ads in those locations. For some people, their ads convert better when placed on the sidebars. For others, their ads perform better when placed horizontally between two posts. For some others, their ads perform better when they place them in between the content of a post. Conducting a proper A/B split test will help you to determine your ad conversion hotspot.

**Can I Use other monetization methods apart from AdSense?**

There are tons of other blog monetization programs like AdSense, which you can use on your blog. If you want to use those other monetization methods alongside AdSense, you need to be careful and ensure you are not about to spam your blog with lots of ads, giving your readers a lousy experience.

Even though Google does not frown at using other monetization methods alongside AdSense, having a competitor monetization program before applying for AdSense could cause Google not to approve your application. There is no official word from Google that affirms this. However, other bloggers' experiences have shown that many times, Google rarely approves AdSense accounts for blogs that already have other similar monetization programs in place.

When your account has been approved, you can place ads from other networks alongside AdSense, but you need to consider the interest of the reader first and ensure you are not bombarding them with ads.

Note: those other AdSense alternatives are not as popular as AdSense. Also, some of them are not as transparent as AdSense when it comes to payment of the amount earned. Furthermore, while AdSense has a stringent approval process, some of the alternatives even have a more rigorous process. So, getting approved into some of the programs is even more challenging than getting into AdSense.

That being said, here are some of the popular AdSense alternatives:

• AdThrive – you will need to have gotten up to 100k pageviews all-time to be accepted by AdThrive.

• Media Vine – this ad network requires that you have up to 50k views all-time to join their program.

• Ezoic

Note: many of these mentioned ad networks still work with Google to serve ads on your blog. So, most of them are still connected to Google in one way or the other. Unlike AdSense, most of them pay you per 1000 visits. They have a specific amount they pay you for every 1,000 visits that your blog records. If you get a lot of traffic to your blog, then you may earn more with these AdSense alternatives than with AdSense itself.

The only downside is that they require that your blog has a lot of traffic before you can apply. Another disadvantage is that some of them don't have a transparent analytics system with which you can track the performance of their ads on your blog.

Apart from placing pay per click ads and other forms of online or display advertisements on your blog, you can also earn money with your blog via affiliate programs. Amazon affiliate program and many others are available to bloggers. We shall talk about the Amazon affiliate program in a subsequent section of this guide.

In this chapter, we have been looking at blog monetization using AdSense. We have seen that placing AdSense ads on your site is one of the best ways of monetizing your blog. We have also seen that getting your AdSense account approved is not rocket science. If you follow the steps in this guide, you will get your account approved on your first try.

In the next chapter of this guide, we shall look at other blog monetization methods.

# CHAPTER NINE

# <u>Blog Monetization – Sponsorships</u>

Apart from placing pay per click (PPC) ads on your blog, you could also consider charging brands to publish their posts on your blog – however, you must let your readers know that such posts are sponsored. This is one of the advantages of running a niche blog – you can publish sponsored posts for companies that sell items related to what you blog about.

For instance, if you blog about mobile devices, phone companies can pay you money to publish phone reviews on your blog. The sponsor will pay depending on how many weeks, days, or months they want the sponsored post to stay up on your blog. The amount you get paid also depends on the traffic that gets to your blog. Typically, if you have more traffic, you can charge accordingly.

**How do you find sponsors?**

There are two possible ways to secure sponsorships for your blog. You could let the sponsors come to you, and you can also get proactive and pitch to them. While the former method is suitable, it means you would be leaving your earning potential to chance. With the latter approach, you are essentially taking the bull by the horns and reaching out to potential sponsors.

The internet has made the world a tiny village indeed. Today, companies understand that inbound marketing methods that involve circulating content about their business on as many platforms as possible are one of the best ways of attracting customers. Hence, you will find companies that scout the internet looking for where to post guest content about their business.

Once your blog starts getting a lot of traffic, you will be surprised to discover the number of businesses that will contact you to post guest articles for them. As mentioned earlier, these businesses search through the internet looking for high traffic blogs where they could advertise their business.

If your blog catches the interest of a potential sponsor, they would get in touch with you and seal a guest posting deal. Sometimes, the business could demand that you post and pin an article they would supply you in specific locations on your blog. Your agreement with the sponsor will detail how many days, weeks, or months their guest posts would stay up on your blog.

While it is great to anticipate businesses to contact you for sponsorship, it is better that you create a sponsored or guest post policy. You can do this by creating a page or section on your blog where you detail your criteria for accepting sponsored or guest posts. Make sure you create a navigation link to this page or section, and the label of the navigation link should read something like, "We accept guest posts."

You could also create a sidebar or banner with the text, "to advertise on this blog, click here." Businesses in your niche that want to advertise on your blog through sponsored or guest posts will contact you, so you negotiate a deal.

If your blog has a lot of traffic and you know how to close deals, you can be rest assured that accepting guest or sponsored posts could give you consistent income. If you are running a niche blog, there will always be a business willing to advertise related products or services on your blog.

One important rule you must follow when posting guest or sponsored content is to let the reader know that what you posted is sponsored content. You could get sued if you pass off the sponsored article as organic content. Also, Google could penalize your blog if you are not upfront with your readers about such articles.

Overall, sponsored posts are a great way to earn money on your blog, but you must be upfront with your readers about such posts. Not being upfront about such means you could be misleading your audience, which could attract severe consequences.

# CHAPTER TEN

# **Blog Monetization – Amazon Affiliate Program**

In the previous chapter, we mentioned selling ad space as one of the ways of making money with your blog. In this chapter, we shall look at another blog monetization method, which is affiliate marketing. There are many affiliate marketing programs; we shall be focusing on the Amazon affiliate marketing program. This is an affiliate marketing program where you promote Amazon products on your blog such that when someone buys the product through your efforts, you earn a commission. Before we go deeply into Amazon affiliate marketing, let's first define what affiliate marketing is.

## **What is affiliate marketing?**

In simple terms, affiliate marketing is a business model that involves promoting other people's products and earn a commission. Essentially, what you do as an affiliate marketer is: you look for companies that have affiliate programs, register with them, promote their products, and if any sales occur through your efforts, you earn a commission.

To promote a product, you will be given an affiliate link – this link is used to track all the purchases that happened as a result of your marketing efforts. You can get an affiliate link from the company or service provider running the affiliate program.

There are different types of affiliate programs – more and more companies today have recognized affiliate marketing as a viable means of promoting and selling their products; hence, most of them have their affiliate programs.

An affiliate program is an organized program developed by companies that allow interested persons to market the products of the company and earn a commission. As mentioned earlier, most of the standard companies you use today and most service providers you will be using as a blogger have their affiliate programs. So, if you could promote these companies' services to your blog readers, then you can earn a commission.

Affiliate marketing is an excellent way of earning money with your blog – the income from affiliate marketing is passive. Also, you do not need to develop a product or create a service. Other people have already done that for you; all you need do is to promote an existing product and earn a commission. The keyword here is "promote," not "sell." You are essentially telling your readers about a product; then, it is then up to them to decide to buy or not.

Affiliate marketing is a win-win for both you, the company running the program, and the customer. It is a win for you because you do not have to stress yourself to develop a product or service. You can promote an existing product.

It is a win for the company running the affiliate program because it is a cheaper way for them to market their products and services and gain new customers. Lastly, it is a win for the customer because the products or services you refer to them can help solve their problems.

If you have grown a massive audience of blog readers, then you need to make money off this audience by promoting affiliate products to them. No matter your blog niche, there will always be an affiliate product or service you can promote to your readers. For instance, if you blog about fishing, you could promote fishing equipment like rods, nets, etc., to your readers. Ideally, someone who is interested in fishing would also love to buy fishing equipment, and if they buy through your affiliate link, you make money.

**Affiliate marketing did not start today**

You may have been doing affiliate marketing for free without knowing it. If you have ever visited a new restaurant down the road, you liked their food, and you talked to your friend and said, "Hey, have you visited that new restaurant? They make some nice delicacies." That's some form of affiliate marketing, even though the eatery did not pay you for it.

Since you have probably done affiliate marketing without pay in the past, why not consider doing the paid one? It is as simple as joining an affiliate program, get affiliate links, write a few things about the product and publish on a section of your blog, and earn a commission when one of your blog readers purchases the product through your affiliate link.

**Amazon affiliate program**

As mentioned earlier, there are tons of affiliate programs that you can join and make money. One of the most popular is the Amazon affiliate program. Amazon affiliate program was developed to help bloggers and website owners like you to earn a commission on sales made on Amazon.

Amazon is still one of the largest e-commerce marketplaces, and millions of people shop on the platform daily. Also, billions of transactions take place on the site daily. Amazon has already developed a reliable brand, so it is not your job to convince your readers on the credibility of Amazon – their strong brand identity already speaks for them. Your only job is to promote their products and earn a commission.

So, how that would work is: on your blog, you have to create a post about a product or a book that is sold on Amazon, you can use a unique affiliate link that Amazon will give you to track everybody that visits Amazon and makes a purchase through you. By that tracking, anything that the person buys on Amazon in 24 hours would be referred back to you so that you can earn a commission. The range of commission you receive varies from 4 to 7% of the price of the product.

**Why beginners should join the Amazon affiliate program**

There are thousands of affiliate programs and affiliate marketing networks out there that you could start with; however, beginners are often advised to start their affiliate marketing journey with Amazon affiliate program for so many reasons, including the ones below:

## 1. It is easier

If you want to start with the other affiliate marketing networks or programs, you need to have strong salesmanship skills. You need to know how to sell and take people through being a cold lead to a warm buyer.

With the Amazon.com affiliate program, you don't need to do that. Amazon is a global brand, and they have perfected their website to the extent that merely visiting the site gets people into a buying mode. This means that most times, when people visit the website, there must be something for them to buy. So, your only job will be to send traffic to the site and make money if they make a purchase.

## 2. There are unlimited products to promote

The products and niches on Amazon keep increasing every day. In fact, thousands of new products are added to the website every single day. If one product or niche becomes saturated, there are thousands of new hot selling products that you can promote and make money. And you can always find something related to your niche which you can promote.

## 3. You can make money from the sales of products you didn't pitch

You can make a lot of money selling products that you have not pitched. For instance, let's say your niche is audio equipment. And you do review all kinds of microphones and recommend them to people. What happens is, if you refer someone to Amazon, and perhaps, the person gets to Amazon.com, changes their mind, and decides to buy a TV set instead, as long as the purchase was made within 24 hours from the time you referred the customer to Amazon, you will still earn a commission, even if they didn't buy the original product that you pitched to them.

## How to join

Joining the Amazon.com affiliate program is free to do. When you visit the website, you will see a button that says, "Join Now For Free," click on the button, fill out the form with your correct information, and you are good to go.

You would want to promote products that are related to your blog niche. For instance, if your blog is about entertainment and music, you would want to promote audio equipment, headsets, and other audio items, along with visual equipment.

The mistake most bloggers make is that they have a blog in one niche while they promote products in another niche. If you do that, your readers will not take you seriously.

Consider this – if someone is already on your blog reading on a particular topic, and they see an opportunity to purchase something related to that item on Amazon, they would grab the chance. This is one of the reasons Amazon.com's affiliate program is great for bloggers.

Most people who read niche blogs are often solution seekers, so if you introduce them to a product that would further provide them with the solution they seek, they would appreciate it. For instance, if you blog about ways of making money online and you promote a book that shows your readers how to set up autoresponders, they would not hesitate to buy the book, thus helping you to earn an affiliate commission.

**How to extract your affiliate link**

To earn money from the sales of a product, you have to extract an affiliate link for that product and use the link when you are making posts on your blog or sending marketing emails. Getting this affiliate link for individual products often seems complicated, especially for beginners. However, it is not that complicated.

• The first step is to log in to your Amazon affiliate program account.

• Then the second step is to search for the product you want to promote

• Extract their affiliate links.

Let's go over these in details:

Once you have logged into your Amazon affiliate program account, look at the top menu, you will see that next to the "Home" button is a "product linking tab." Hover your mouse over this tab, and there will be a drop-down menu. Select the first option that says, "product link." Look further down the new page that opens, and you will see a search bar.

Now, enter the keyword for the product you want to promote. For instance, if you wish to promote training boots for men, type "training boots" into the search bar and click "Go."

Once you hit the "Go" button, some search results related to the keywords you typed will be displayed. Next to each search result, you will see an orange button that will provide the affiliate link for that specific product. Click on the arrow next to where it says, "Get link;" when you click on that, you will receive a pop-up box containing the affiliate link to the product.

On close observation, you will notice that the link doesn't look really nice, and if you use the link as it is on your blog, it could be misconstrued as a spam link.

How do you solve this puzzle? On top of the box that pops up, you will see two buttons. One says, "Copy and paste the link below," while the other states, "shorten link with amazon.to." Now, click on the second button, and the affiliate link will be shortened to something more appealing and shorter. Other link shortening services can serve a similar purpose, like bit.ly, etc. Now, include the link thus gotten in your product reviews, YouTube description boxes, social media posts, or any other place where you intend to be generating traffic for your affiliate products. Repeat this process for all the products you want to promote.

**How to write a promo post for an affiliate product**

When it comes to Amazon affiliate marketing, you must actively promote your affiliate products on your blog for your readers to understand the benefits of the product and hence decide to buy.

For some products, you could consider writing a review post about the product and then include the product's affiliate link in the post. One major problem that people encounter when it comes to writing promo content for affiliate products is that they don't know what to write, primarily if they have not used the product in question.

If you want to get ideas on what to write about an affiliate product, your best bet is to visit the Amazon website, search for the product you want to promote, look at five of the top reviews and see what the customers are saying about the product. Usually, customer reviews are honest and will always highlight the benefits, drawbacks of a product. Now, your job is to take all that information and compile it into a very easy to read article and post on your blog.

That's the value you will be providing to your blog visitors. At the end of the article or blog post, include the affiliate link to the product and earn a commission whenever someone buys the product through your link.

Joining the Amazon affiliate program is a great way to earn money with your blog. There are thousands of products that you can promote. What's more? The earning potential is enormous, and you get to make some money while you sleep.

# CHAPTER ELEVEN

# Blog Monetization – Digital Products (ebooks)

Apart from selling ad space and engaging in affiliate marketing, another way of earning money with your blog is to sell digital products like eBooks and online courses. In fact, eBooks are like hot cakes now – every day, more and more people seek knowledge, and if you package information that people find in the form of an eBook, your readers would be happy to buy.

As a niche blogger, you understand your niche perfectly okay – you know those pain points or problems your readers might have. If you have been paying attention to your audience, then you would have deduced some of their significant issues. You may often find it hard to compile all the issues into a blog post, so you might need to compile everything into an eBook.

**How do you get eBook topic ideas?**

The best way to get eBook topic ideas is to visit Amazon.com, then go to the books/Kindle section. Scroll through the section where you find books related to your niche. Look at the books that are already selling there. Read the reviews left on the books and see what people that have bought the books in the past are saying. Take note of the negative reviews so you can address them in your writing.

A platform like Amazon, for instance, allows you to look through the first few pages of a book published on its platform. You can exploit that feature and look at the table of contents of some of the books that have been published in your niche. Use the information you get to form the table of contents for your eBook.

With the table of contents in your hands, you could proceed to start writing your eBook. Make sure that the eBook contains valuable information such that after reading, your readers could say, "Wow, I have learned a lot from this."

If you do not have the time to sit and write, or if you cannot write lengthy eBooks, you could hire ghostwriters on freelance platforms like Fiverr.com and Upwork.com to help you write an eBook. Usually, you would need to provide the ghostwriter with an outline and discuss other details of the eBook with them.

After writing and publishing your eBook on platforms like Amazon.com and other self-publishing platforms, then it is time to start the aggressive marketing of the eBook. You could create a post on your blog to create awareness for the eBook. You could offer the eBook at a discount price for your readers – then ask them to drop a review after reading the book. The reviews will help improve the book's ranking and make other people want to read it as well.

Remember, when it comes to making money with eBooks, one book is not enough – you must write as many books as possible. To start seeing reasonable income, you need to have at least five (5) books, and you must market them aggressively to your audience. Since each of the books would be in your niche, you need to link them all up so that customers who buy one could buy the rest of the books.

For each sale of your eBook you record, Amazon takes some part of the money and pay you the rest after a specific period. If you want to avoid this commission that Amazon takes, you could consider hosting your eBook on your server and then selling it directly on your blog. For this to work, you need to have a payment processor like PayPal or a merchant account.

Once a customer buys the eBook directly from your blog, and you confirm their payment, send them a download link to their eBook. To make the eBook readable on many platforms, convert it into ePub, PDF, Mobi, or any other popular eBook format. You could never go wrong with selling your eBook directly on your platform as you get to keep all the money.

Asides from selling eBooks, you could create video courses and sell to your readers. The process is the same as that of producing an eBook. You could host the video course directly on your blog and sell it to your readers, or you could host it on platforms like udemy.com, Lynda.com, etc.

If you do not want to create courses or eBooks, you could consider creating a members-only section on your blog. This area will contain gated content or exclusive information that will only be made available to those who pay a subscription fee.

To attract people to join the members-only section, you need to ensure that the general sections on your blog contain valuable information. This way, readers would be longing to see what's in the gated area. It is fundamental human nature – we are always interested or curious to know what's behind the veil. Now, you need to exploit this human nature and make money.

Remember, if people join your members-only section and find out that the information there is something basic they could find elsewhere, they would leave, and that would make your audience displeased. So, you should only create a members-only section if you genuinely have information that you think should not be shared for free.

If you decide to create a members-only section, people could try to guilt-trip you into making everything free. Those are people who think information shouldn't be worth anything. Meanwhile, those same people go to college and pay huge money for the same information. In essence, if you have something of value, don't be shy or guilt-tripped into giving it out for free.

Those who know the value of information will pay anything to have it. If anyone doubts the importance of data and the need for it to be monetized, then that person is not your ideal client anyway, and you should not be worrying yourself with such people. You should be more interested in those who place a premium on valuable information and make sure you provide them with real value.

This chapter has just summarized some passive income methods you could leverage and make money on your blog.

# Email marketing to sell more

No matter what you are selling on your blog, you need to grow an email list – your email subscribers are like your loyal customers – you could market any product or service to them, and they would buy. In the online business scene, it is often said that money is on the list, and that's true. If you know how to leverage your list, then you can make money selling just anything.

**Why is an email list so important?**

For you to understand why a list is essential, let's analyze how the world of business and sales have evolved over the past years. In the past, a company only needed to develop the right product, then send salespeople to market the products. Those days, customers could buy any product as long as the salesman selling the product is convincing enough.

However, a lot has changed today – the average customer now has many options to choose from. They are just a Google search away from finding the right products that would solve their problems. In such a world where thousands of other people sell the same product that you sell or offer the same service that you provide, how do you convince the average customer to patronize you and leave your competitor? The answer is simple – you need to connect with the customer emotionally.

How do you connect emotionally with the customer? First, you need to understand that today's average customer buys based on emotions and justify logically. So, to make them buy from you, you need to excite them and make them feel emotionally connected to both your product and you as a brand. The only way you could do that is by befriending and communicating with them as friends.

When you continuously communicate with your prospects, readers, or potential customers, the propinquity effect will take its course and make them want to patronize anything you are selling. Apart from creating blog posts, you could communicate with your audience through emails.

With the right lead generation strategy, you could collect your readers' emails and make sure that you send them the correct emails. With the right emails, you could turn your followers or readers into loyal customers who would buy your products and continue to read your blogs.

Having a blog makes email marketing so easy – because you already have an audience – you need to nurture them with emails and warm them up about a product, then market the product to them. Usually, the first stage in email marketing is to acquire a considerable audience that could be passed through an autoresponder.

The second stage is to use an autoresponder to warm up the vast audience and narrowly segment your list into those who might need your product immediately and those who might need it later. Continue to use a series of email swipes to warm up the subscribers until they are finally ready to buy and then market a product to them. This whole process usually takes time – from the first time that subscribers join your list to the time they are ready to buy. Research shows that it takes up to 7 contacts for a subscriber to be prepared to buy. This means you need to send messages to your potential customers many times before they are finally ready to buy.

## Let's get practical

Let's assume that you have created an eBook, and you want to use email marketing to promote and sell this eBook. Here are the steps you need to take:

1. First, you need to use something to attract your potential customers to join your email list. Remember, the fact that someone reads your blog posts does not make the person your customer. At most, the person is just a potential customer, and you need to lure them into joining your email list so you could convert them into customers.

To get your readers to join your email list, you need to use something to lure them. For instance, create a free eBook lead magnet or tripwire and offer it to your readers. It could be a short read that would make them salivate and want more.

The lead magnet or tripwire has to be very captivating so that the reader would be asking for more after reading. The free lead magnet is to prepare the reader to buy the paid eBook or to leave their email to receive more information on how to get the paid offer.

2. After creating the lead magnet, make a post on your blog and offer it to your readers. You could use other lead generation methods (discussed in the chapter) to provide the lead magnet to your readers.

3. Create a landing page using ClickFunnels or any of the other autoresponders like MailChimp. Once a potential subscriber submits their email to enable them to download the free eBook or offer, send them a "thank you" message and a link to download their free lead magnet.

4. Now that you have their email, use a series of well-crafted email swipes to inform and educate them about the paid eBook which you want them to buy. Tell them the benefits of the product and why they need to buy it. Your reasons should be strong enough to make the individual decide to buy. Also, you could include social proofs to convince prospective customers further.

5. Once you have warmed up your leads for some time, introduce them to the product you want to sell to them.

The above approach works like a charm because even if the subscribers do not buy the immediate product you are marketing to them, you still have their email, and you could sell other products to them later.

No matter what you are selling on your blog, email marketing will always prove important, and if you learn how to use it well, you will be miles ahead of your competitors.

# CHAPTER TWELVE

## **Platforms to Share Your Blog Posts**

Your brain tasking article deserves more audience than it presently has. Your article is a path to sharing your opinions and mindsets with others. Therefore, each word that deserves to be sent out needs to get out unless you have a secret message that is not meant for this present dispensation. That work you have intelligently crafted out is a real gem.

It is not enough to write your well-designed blog post and publish it on your website. Being relevant in this sphere involves more than just publishing it on your website. There is insanely high competition in the world of blogging. Hence why you should figure out how to be ahead of your competitors and give them a run for their money. Over 70 million articles are being published monthly. No one wants to be caught off guard. The quality of your content is one essential key is to get it in front of many readers. Darren Rowse said, "What you do in the minutes and hours after your post goes live can exponentially increase the effectiveness of the post."

Here is the thing. You have written a detailed and eye-catching new blog waiting to be published, and you are sure it is a piece that will be enjoyed by your readers. You have taken cognizance of the graphic and even optimized it for SEO, and you are looking forward to it being liked, shared, and commented on by your readers. Awesome job! But you have only done half of your job. It would be best to create the required awareness for your blog post to make it go viral and enhance its exposure.

This chapter is geared toward making your content viral and getting it in front of many readers. You will be shown the list of credible platforms to share your blog posts and increase their exposure. The more you share your content on other platforms, the wider you spread your content, and the wider you increase your website traffic. Are you ready to promote your content and increase its awareness? Stay on this ride!

## SHARING

People have been sharing their thoughts and words for many generations. Even before the advent of the pen and paper, messages were scribbled on slates and walls so that a lot of people would see and understand the message. Man has always been evolving in this culture, and several years later, the internet came to be, and there is no limit to the number of people who could be getting a message sent from a person and in just a matter of seconds.

Writing random everyday thoughts or a more tailored and scheduled content to reach people via sites on the internet designed for this purpose is termed blogging. Blogging is one lucrative thing to engage one's self in. As more people get access to the internet, there has been a steaming increase in the number of bloggers. With so many blogs out there, the blogging industry is fast becoming a competitive one. Only SEO-friendly blogs and those who pass Google's qualification for ranking will easily get seen on Google search.

Sharing could either be on the website with a blog page incorporated into it or on a separate site called a blog site. Bloggers use either the free or paid blog sites. The free blog sites operate exactly as their title suggests. Bloggers do not need to pay before access the platform and upload their content; however, the blog site bears the site owner's name. On the free site, there is no payment for a domain; neither is there any payment for any other thing. For example, blogger.com is a free blog site, and owning an account on blogger.com means owning one that goes like this: rokuuu.blogspot.com, instead of rokuu.com.

The sites which are not free have to keep subscribing to a host periodically. But they do not restrict the name a site will bear. There are also other perks like unlimited storage space, SSL protection, depending on the kind of hosting plan accessed. Hostgator, Bluehost, Namecheap, WordPress are some of the numerous platforms available through which these plans can be accessed.

Many bloggers create jobs from blogging, and once they carve out their niche, they go-ahead to develop their skills in this line. Some other bloggers who own huge sites even employ the services of freelancers to get more content on the sites. Others network and get free blogger content on the sites. As long as being true to one's niche is concerned, there are limitless possibilities to being a pro at blogging and gathering the intended growing audience. More on this will be extensively discussed further in this article.

While blogging is emphasized, it is obviously not the only means of sharing one's article with the billions of people on the earth. Publishing one's work either in a journal, book, press, and newsletter is still a few of the other means to get your work out there.

# Making Your Passion a Job

Posting your articles online is more than just projecting your brand or image. Many writers have successfully turned their flair into something that brings them revenues periodically. It can happen in the following ways:

**They could blog and receive revenues from their blogs**

Many bloggers say they didn't start making money immediately they started blogging. It took some months, but they eventually earned from their jobs. If the purpose of starting the blog is to make money, then there must be some real investment in it.

Google's ranking for 2019 showed that google doesn't just care about the SEOs; Google goes further to evaluate the relevance of your content and whether you are the right person to be producing that kind of content based on education, training, or experience.

People who blog about food or give expert advice on burning fat will likely get more audience reach if they come out from that line. They could be health professionals or have some personal encounters in the line of work.

Therefore, the advice here is to be faithful to your calling and be ready to stay there until you achieve the goal. Even if the goal is to make money, ultimately, the contents must add value.

The starting point is always the most important stage in this business, and a well-laid-out-plan is also important.

Starting a blog these days is less like the time when there were very few content management systems like WordPress. With these content management systems, there is little need to be versed in CSS, HTML, or PHP (coding jargon). Platforms like WordPress provides custom designs and help with so many things you would otherwise have paid different experts for.

Blogs are at an advantage when they are SEO friendly. Certain popular keywords that appear in simple searches will increase the visibility of the blog. Buzzsumo.com and google.com/trend are essential tools when searching for trending keywords to add to your article.

A schedule of the times to post content, the types of content to be posted, and how brief or long the content should be is also very important. Some bloggers use schedulers like Iconosquare, Post Planner, Planoly, Content Cal, etc., to schedule their posts, especially on social media.

Blogger.com, wordpress.com, are some of the free blogs. They could serve as platforms for trial blogs before starting the real paid blog, as advised by Neil Patel.

**They could also write for other websites**

Writing for others, either paid or voluntarily, is a way to train in writing. Having to manage ones content could restrict one to a particular writing style. Writing on other website help to improve one's brand and eventually one's audience reach.

There are many editors that will pay good money-from $5 to over $1000 if the article fits their image. A-List Apart, Dame, Longreads, 5Best Things, AppStorm are some of the platforms where you can submit your pitch. Electric Literature is another site that features exciting, relevant, and inclusive articles. They welcome flash fiction, graphic narratives, and short stories. The Balance, HowStuffWorks, Wired UK, Euronews Travel, and Open Democracy are other platforms that pay freelancers to get paid when writing.

Some other freelance bloggers who do stock photography too can include their photographs in their writings and increase the chances of being accepted.

Even if you own a blog, endeavor to offer to guest post on other websites, or offer to participate in other people's podcasts.

So, you see, writing is a gift you can hardly get tired of having because whichever way you decide to channel this gift, it would bring returns both presently and in the future.

The approach could be by writing to the emails of websites you are interested in and offering to help add an interesting twist to their content, which could help their audience; you could also upload a copy of your work.

**Writing for Magazines**

Chicken Soup for the Soul is one of those magazines that offer jobs to freelance writers for relevant content. There are many others who would pay well for good works. There are also online platforms where opportunities like these are usually posted.

It would require basic familiarization with previous contents on the magazines to understand and flow with the magazines. If you intend to promote your writing, a magazine job will get you both money and fame.

**Writing Book Reviews**

Onlinebookclub.org is a platform where e-books are submitted and reviewed. For each successful review, about $5 is paid, which can be received through PayPal. It is a great platform to improve both one's writing and reading skills while earning nothing less than $5.

Writing.com has helped many writers, especially those new, to sharing their work online to grow. The website allows each visitor to create an account and offers free, basic, and other upgraded memberships. Members earn money in the form of gifts for reviewing other posts, posting on the platform, and engaging in forum contests, plus other activities. Since there are different genres of write-ups on the platform, there is always a place for whatever form of writing one is involved with. The website is fun and can also be used to connect with professionals that can help to build one's own community of writers.

Kiyesi.blogspot.com is an example of a free blogger.com account that writes summaries of books for readers who feel too busy to read the whole book.

There could also be offline book reviews where the author shares his new book with a physical (not virtual) group of writers who can help reveal errors and help redefine the book for the intended audience.

### Participating in Contests

Freelancer.com, upwork.com, fiverr.com, among others, are popular sites where writing jobs are offered to freelance writers, and appropriate compensations are made upon completion of tasks. These sites could be one's access to writing on other's websites, magazines, e-books, and participating in contests.

Writing Contest is a fun and engaging way to compete with other professional writers for a sum. It is encouraged to participate in as many contests as possible to improve one's chances of winning. Besides, there is nothing to lose apart from your time and energy. Writing could indeed be time-consuming, but the results are worth it.

There are contests in different categories-according to ages and level of qualification, but they are all always fun.

**Being a Brand Promoter**

We have seen one-too-many content writers that have turned brand promoters. Some others capitalize on niches and engage in affiliate marketing. Social media is not over-burdened by brand promoters, so you can also join this band. Once you have been recognized for excellence, brands that are compatible with your flow will surely have you promote them.

Brands are well-aware of the importance of marketing using individuals who can promote their brands. The brands know that these individual command large audiences as well, so they can easily be swayed into believing in the brand if someone the audiences look up to is promoting it.

Companies know that brand promotion is the hit these days, so you are presenting yourself as a qualified promoter for their brand.

Instagram, Facebook, Tik Tok is the top catches for brand influencing. Promoting your work on these media will help in getting clients' brands.

**Translating their work into books**

The number of books in the world is probably countless, but that doesn't stop new books from being written. Whether they are best-selling books or just any book, there is the right market for them. Many writers have become prolific authors and best-selling too, but that didn't start overnight.

The cool part about writing books these days is that you don't have to author a book before you can write it. There are authors who seem prolific, but they give out book contracts to professional writers and freelancers who anonymously help to translate their thoughts into "best-selling" words.

There are also writers who help edit the work and others who help to review the books, as explained above.

Writing books (whether hard copies or electronic copies) may seem like a lot of work because of the several processes the book has to pass through before it comes out consumable, but in the end, it is worth the work. Many authors still earn revenues for their authorships even many years after producing the book.

As long as producing books is concerned, other platforms like websites, blog sites, and social media can be used to promote them.

**Writing scripts for videos**

While some writers produce their articles for reading, others write for hearing. Writing video scripts is another platform for writers to utilize their talents and promote their work. Whether the scripts are written for short or long videos, every quality video needs a quality script.

Working with a video creator will be of help in fine-tuning the content of your script and how to organize the content.

Even if the purpose is to be a video blogger, it is fine. Video blogging is one of the most effective tools of an influencer.

TikTok, one of the most trending social media apps, is relevant in this niche. Whether they are funny videos or just videos, a good script will highlight the best parts of the videos.

## PLATFORMS FOR SHARING

Here are some of the platforms where articles can be shared. Taking into note the instructions given above, they should work just fine.

## SOCIAL MEDIA

Social media is a great place to share your articles. The media is fast becoming an influence on many people's lifestyle around the world. With several millions of audiences, it is a fast way of propagating your content.

## FACEBOOK

Facebook is great, but with a lot of spam, it is not too advisable to bombard everyone with your content even if it is not relevant to them. It is best to make use of tailored advertising and groups to share your articles. A book club group could be interested in the kind of content you are creating, so why not just go there directly.

## INSTAGRAM

Instagram also has a way of using your preferences or the services you offer to make the content seen by the people who will likely respond. If you happen to run an Instagram ad, it is advisable to follow the regulations and select the right option for which kind of audience views your feed.

## TWITTER

Twitter works best with hashtags. Hashtags can help to increase your reach. But since long articles cannot be shared on Twitter because of the restrictions to the number of characters, there could be a link to the article on other platforms. These days, it is possible to post the same content through Instagram, Facebook, Twitter, and Tumblr. Twitter is also a good avenue to get alerts on writing jobs.

## LINKEDIN

LinkedIn is best for reaching professionals in your sphere and sharing your work with them. Articles can be published on LinkedIn. It is also possible to include a link to the real work. LinkedIn also produces creative briefs. These briefs discuss topics intended for a lot of people to express their opinions on. Just like in other platforms, consistent and creative posts are the most followed.

## REDDIT

Reddit may seem serious against self-promotion. It is a fun platform to reach a lot of people within your niche. The several communities on Reddit are platforms to grow your reach and be aware of issues to write on that appeal to many people. People can also ask questions and get answers on Reddit.

**TUMBLR**

Tumblr used to be for insecure teenagers. Since people could appear anonymous, it gives them the freedom of airing out their views, at least that is what everyone thought, but it is more than that. Young writers grew on the platform. It helps to craft one's audience and create discussions on the writings. Tumblr works like a blog by giving each user a blog account with a blog URL.

## MEDIUM.COM

Medium.com was launched on August 15, 2012, as an American online publishing by A Medium Corporation. The platform can be referred to as an avenue for online journalism that accommodates both amateurs and professionals. Amateurs get to showcase their work and network with others, including professionals. Users can sign up using their emails, Facebook, or Google account.

Evans Williams, who founded it, initially wanted to have a platform that can accommodate more characters than Twitter and blogger.com. The website had struggled with becoming renowned in the past until recently, when writers began to promote it and share. The number of users on the platform was around 60 million as of 2016. And since they started, medium.com had been putting all-hands-on-deck to incorporate features that will make it more used by people around the world.

Writers on this platform can earn money according to the time spent on their articles by readers. This was updated from being paid according to the clap feature.

Medium.com comes with a mobile app, just like other social media applications. Authors on the platform can reach anyone who subscribes to their account or follows them. Authors also get to follow other authors. The only restriction on Medium is in certain countries like China, Egypt, and Albania.

Medium.com also has different writing categories, like space, engineering, health, nutrition, etc. Therefore, it makes it easy to get only articles on preferred topics. Between 2019 and 2020, they launched eight new publications, namely GEN, OneZero, Marker, Elemental, Focus, Zora, Leveland Momentum covering politics, technology health, business, people of color, and anti-racism.

Members on this platform who want to reach a wider audience than they already have, subscribe to medium.com publishing and at a fee. Medium.com articles can also be promoted on social media.

## BLOGGER.COM

You would have heard about this above. Here are some additions. Blogger.com is owned by Google, which is why it is easy to access some tools which are not available on other blogging platforms. Users create accounts using their Google mail on Blogger.com and get to post content on the blog. Their number of reaches and other analytics on their site can be easily assessed using Google Analytics. Blogger.com is the only free blog where google Adsense can run on. This means it is the only free blog that can be used to earn revenue. Google assesses every site under about 35 weeks. Therefore, if you qualify for Adsense, it is possible to start earning money from Ad clicks. As said earlier, it could be used to test the waters of blogging lifestyle and earning for making relevant articles available to your audience.

## NEWSLETTERS

Not everybody enjoys a newsletter, but it comes in handy for busy people. Not everyone can get to read the articles you post but doing a recap of what you do in the newsletter can help inform people about your work. Newsletters can be sent weekly or monthly, depending on the frequency of their needs. However, no matter how important your newsletter seems, it is advisable to send them only to those who will enjoy them by engaging with them.

## QUORA

Quora is a forum where questions can be asked, and answers can be gotten. Experts in various fields will do as much as giving professional answers to questions. Although, this platform is not as strict as Reddit on self-promotion. Answers should be given on the platform and that too, sincerely.

## PRESS

The 'press' may sound too official to share your articles. Still, organizations like the New York Times, Times Square Magazines, Washington Post, The Guardian newspaper, and many others are avenues to reaching a lot of people. Most times, it is only the best of the best articles that will be published, but these influential channels have the potentials to channel your own thoughts and words to influence people. These channels are not only for news reporters; individuals can share ideas too.

## HUBPAGES.COM

This is described as an open community, and just like Quora or Reddit, questions can also be asked and answers gotten. This site uses a lot of informative user-generated content. With over 42 million monthly visitors, Hubpages.com is that platform that, if used effectively, can grow your reach; you can follow other writers and get followed too.

Registration on this platform is free, and Hubpages.com also share revenues it generates. Adsense and Amazon can be used to earn from the traffic one draws as they publish their content on the platform. But unlike having a real blog or website, people do not link to your Hubpages.com account even if there is eye-catching content.

## SLIDESHARE.NET

Slideshare.net has been on longer than Medium. Since 2006 it had been a platform to share articles in word, PDF, open documents, videos, or PowerPoint on slides. Like in presentation, the slides could be very few and very many, depending on the work's bulkiness. It was initially used by businesses to share files between employees. Presently, it has gone beyond that.

Slideshare.net also has a lot of reach. Anyone can register on this platform for free and start sharing with their audience. Slideshare.net has an appreciable amount of traffic, so registering on the platform can draw the right amount of audience. Slideshare.net provides professional content and is mostly visited by students and other professionals for resourceful information. Over 70 million people use this platform today. LinkedIn first acquired it before Scribd took ownership in August 2020.

## LIVE JOURNAL

This is mostly for those who want to project their hobby to others. The writings here are not educational but help portray writing as one's hobby, making writing pretty fun. The site has been on since 1999 and is Russian owned. Each user has a web page, and comments can be made on his post. Guests that do not register can access the platform but cannot post.

## WRITE.AS

This platform helps to wipe out all the distractions that could occur when writing and uploading content. If the intention is just to pour out your heart into your work with minimal distractions, write.as is best.

## SCRIBD

Scribd is a book sharing site, so there are readers and writers on the platform. This happens to be the parent company of Slideshare.net. Apart from ebooks, Scribd.com also offers audiobooks to subscribed users. It has over 60 million documents in different languages. Over 1000 famous publishers work with them. This is also available on Android and other mobile platforms.

## TYPEPAD

This is one of the most popular blogs alongside blogger.com and wordpress.com. It has a free platform called Typepad Micro, but this is very limited as the only thing one can do is just to post articles and nothing else. TypePad professional packages allow more freedom and can be upgraded.

## WRITING ON THE WALL

Writingonthewall.uk is an organization based in Liverpool that offers projects centered on writing development. This non-profit organization holds an annual month-long literature festival that includes a mix of journalism, non-fiction, songwriting, storytelling, and poetry. Writing on the wall also helps to establish new talents in writing.

## STORYBIRD

Storybird.com features millions of writers in more than 100 countries around the world. On this website, one can read, write, and participate in challenges. It is so easy to create picture books on this platform with so many free artworks to choose from. Writers can either register as either students or educators. Storybird is not free but offers a 7-Day free trial for starters.

## WRITING COOPERATIVE

Writing Cooperative is a group on Medium.com consisting of writers. Writing Cooperative was created by Plot Factory. Plot Factory happens to be the online story planning tool for writers to plan and organize their stories.

## PRATILIPI

Pratilipi contains articles written by others. It is a platform both for reading and writing. Just like Wattpad, it has an app. The time it will take to read a piece is indicated in the title of each article. Different writing categories from romance to business and economics, to crime writing, poetry, comedy, etc., can be accessed and in other languages.

## ANY STORIES

Any stories is a story app where writers get to publish their best stories. There are also featured contests on this app. Original stories on the platform can earn money for the writers.

## WATTPAD

Wattpad connects readers and writers all over the world. Their community is growing with millions. The site can be easily accessed on android phones by downloading the Application. Romance stories, teen fiction, and fan fiction are some of the best-viewed stories. The app is mostly used by teens who love writing and books in general.

## WRITER'S DIGEST

Writer's Digest is a platform that does more than just share articles. The website contains a series of resources for writers. Signing up to email mode will subscribe you to a year of writing prompts at no cost. The site contains challenges in different genres-poetry, essays, drama, and so on. Writer's Digest staffs write and post every other day of the week. The site also offers tutorials to writers.

## SCHEDULING YOUR POSTS

Some schedulers have been mentioned above. All of them are great as long as they suit your needs and are comfortable with them. Here are some differences between the different kinds of schedulers available.

## POST PLANNER

Post planner is great if one's goal is to stand out. This scheduler also suggests all other content is relevant and performing well so that one can tailor his/her strength to the right content. It is possible to manage groups, multiple pages, and other accounts using post planner. It also does not waste content as it recycles contents for use.

## CONTENT CAL

This is also great, but unlike post planner, it is good in a business setting where content has to be reviewed by more than one person before going online.

## BUFFER

This is relevant when bulk contents must be uploaded. Buffer manages this well.

## ICONOSQUARE

This is one of the popular schedulers; it is also very useful and provides additional resources like in-depth insight, visual recording, and helps you review how well the content is doing. But it is very expensive, unlike the ones above.

## PLANOLY

This type of scheduler helps to prepare posts, but it does not automatically post content for you. It instead sends you a reminder. Planoly is very effective in quality and a very catchy visual feed on Instagram.

## HOOTSUITE

Hootsuite can be likened to buffer since it also effective for bulk content.

## NOT SHARING YOUR ARTICLES

There are so many advantages to sharing your articles, so why hide them? There are also so many platforms to deliver your thoughts to audiences while remaining anonymous if this is preferred.

Not sharing your articles is like dressing up fully for prom and then going straight to sleep with the dress on; it sounds ridiculous, right?

The stress of posting consistently can be a burden even for writers who like to share their work. Therefore, being resilient is essential.

The internet has made communication easier and has enhanced people's understanding of each other. The #metoo movement started online, #nomakeup, #endsars, #endblackbrutality, and many others took off well on social media. The media is worth more than just sharing articles; people air out their views and get heard a lot. So why not utilize this great opportunity and grow your career in writing?

Paid advertising is another to promote your articles. It is easy to be buried with the competition out there if nothing is done to actively promote the article, especially if it is on a blog. Blogger.com can pay google Ad Words to promote their sites, and if their landing pages are catchy enough, they could gain more subscribers from those clicks.

However, most blog professionals discourage starting with this. It is best to develop the blog to a standard before employing the services of paid advertising or inorganic traffic, as some others call it. Revenue from the blog should be able to take care of the cost of advertising on Google Ad.

Even if the intention is to write for fun and there happens to be a problem somewhere, you can search the internet for help or watch

YouTube videos. The main point here is that you enjoy what you do, whether it brings revenues or not.

It is even possible to employ a group of writers who will manage your blog if it is for revenues. Whether voluntary or paid, it helps to increase your reach network, and each writer can write for different genres. If you are business-minded, it will all come together for your profiting.

One can also have more than one or two blogs. In fact, there is no restriction to the number of blogs one can have if it is their choice. The business gurus have always advised diversifying one's portfolio for multiple streams of income. Freelancers are mostly employed for jobs like this, and most of them work from home and live their lives that way; others have other physical jobs, which they do to double the hustle. Crafting articles is a very interesting task, and it is very important that as you enjoy creating them, there are also readers who are able to access them.

# CONCLUSION

*Blogging is dead!!!*

I am sure you have heard the above assertion many times – it is usually said by those who jumped into blogging without proper research. Some people have ventured into blogging and could not renew their domain name after the first year. Those are the kind of people that make the type of assertion above; as mentioned earlier, they did not do their due diligence before venturing into blogging.

After reading this book, I am sure you have been convinced that blogging is not dead yet and will not die even in the coming years. If there is an online business that will succeed for so long, then it is blogging. Humans are known to be knowledge seekers, and as long as people continue to seek knowledge every day, blogging will continue to be relevant. However, for you to make it as a blogger, you must be ready to work. Don't be like those who see blogging as a side hustle they could fall back on when they are out of a job. Even though many people have touted blogging as a side job, it is not really a side hustle in the real sense of the word.

Blogging is a full-time affair, and unless you treat it like a full-time business, it will not pay you like a business, and you will likely end up joining those who say it is dead. How many hours do you think it would take to research and come up with a good blogging niche? It could take you up to 5 days or even a week. Would you say that something that takes that amount of time to do is a side hustle?

When you have found a blogging niche, you will need to start designing your blog. If you don't have the resources to hire a web designer, you would need to do the blog customization and development yourself. Again, that will take much of your time. Would you call something that demands such an amount of time a side hustle?

After designing and customizing your blog, you will start doing keyword research for blog posts or articles. After rounds of keyword research, you will need to write insightful posts, and they must be search engine optimized. If they are not keyword optimized, Google and the other search engines will not index them, and your efforts will be in vain.

Writing good and high converting blog posts can take you several hours, if not days – is that what you call a side hustle? So, blogging is not a side hustle; it demands that you give it your full attention. With dedication, hard work, perseverance, you will turn your blog into a money-making machine in no time. Then all the efforts you have been putting into it will start making sense to you.

Blogging is the type of online business that ushers in other online businesses. This means that apart from the regular AdSense program that everyone knows about, you can earn money through affiliate marketing, eBook sales, and many other methods. And when you have established your blog to a certain level, you could dive full time into these other online businesses.

So, as a blogger, your earning potentials are just enormous, and most of the methods of earning are entirely passive. This means you can be making money while you are sleeping. For instance, affiliate marketing is an excellent way of earning money with your blog. And affiliate marketing, if done well, will give you passive income.

EBooks sales is also another way of earning money with your blog, and if done well, following the instructions in this book, can make you a lot of passive income. When you combine all the earning opportunities with a major one like AdSense, you discover that blogging is worth it. You just need to give it time and dedication, and it will turn around to take care of you later.

At first, you will have to work your ass off. You will need to dedicate time to the blog. But as time goes on, the blog will be able to stand on its own. When you have created a reasonable number of posts, which are all ranked on search engines, then you could relax and start reaping the results of your efforts.

Also, when you have grown the blog to a certain level, you could start outsourcing some of your operations to freelancers. For instance, you could outsource keyword research and writing of articles to freelancers so that you can have time for other essential aspects of your business or life. You can find good freelancers on fiverr.com and upwork.

To help you get started now, below you can find the best tools recommended by the author (affiliate links).

You can easily scan them with your mobile phone, so no excuses, take action now:

Find freelancers on Fiverr:

SCAN ME

Start doing Email marketing with Get Response:

Affiliate Marketing free webinar:

Thank you for reading, we hope we have been of help! Keep in touch with the author for the upcoming releases:

To Your success!

Robert.

# Affiliate Marketing

## *Earn High Commissions by Selling Products and Services You Don't Have*

*2021 Edition*

By

**Robert Kasey**

# INTRODUCTION

Over the past few years, many people have embraced one online business or the other as their means of earning income. Recently, it is not hard to see someone who has tried their hands on a lot of online business ideas. Look around you, you will find a stay-at-home mom, a student, or just anybody who has looked for a way of earning income online to supplement their current earnings.

Even though many people have tried one online business or the other in the past or presently, the truth remains that most people who go into online businesses do fail. It is likely you have also tried your hands on some online ventures without getting positive results. Perhaps you have asked yourself, "What is it that I am doing wrong? Why am I not making money with this business?"

Most people who go into online businesses will fail— this is the hard truth. And the reason for their failure is not hard to guess. Many of them fail because they listened to people who tell them that they could start an online business today and start making money the next day.

Others fail because they keep pursuing the shiny object, while a vast majority fail because they do not want to put in the effort to see their business grow. For some of these people, they see online business as a money-spinning machine that would make them money even when they do not put in a lot of effort.

An online business, just like your typical offline business, requires commitment, dedication, and perseverance for it to make you the money you desire. Without these mentioned attributes, your online business will not grow. Additionally, an online venture is not something you go into because you lost your job or because you want to make quick cash with which you could use in paying your next house rent. Most people who make it in online businesses are those who take it as a career. When you take an online business as a career, it is easy for you to put in your best to make the business grow.

You could be asking, what is the best online business for someone to go into. If you pose this question to different people, you are obviously going to get different answers, and none of the answers would be more accurate than the other. Typically, there are millions of online business ideas out there, and none of them can be said to be better than the other.

What differentiates one online business idea from the other is the amount of effort, dedication, and commitment that the owner of the business is willing to pour into the business and make it grow. Running a business, whether online or offline is like building a garden. For the plants in the garden to germinate and blossom, you have to tend to the garden every day and make sure that you water it and remove weeds that could choke your plants. Without doing all that, the plants you planted in the garden would wither and die away.

One mistake that many people make when choosing an online business is they tend to chase many things at once. In the online business space, this is called chasing the shiny object. When you keep running to any new online business idea that appeals to you, you are said to be pursuing the shiny object. Shiny object syndrome is one of the most significant impediments to success in online business. So, if you want to be successful, pick one business model, developit until it has become very strong, then you could diversify.

In this book, I will show you how to start and grow an affiliate marketing business. When it comes to making money, you must provide something of value to people so that they can give you their money in return. With affiliate marketing, you are providing something of value to people, and they will pay you money in return. And this is what differentiates real online businesses like affiliate marketing, from online scams that promise you money without doing anything tangible. If anyone says you could make money online by doing nothing, then the person is out to scam you of the little money you have.

If you have been looking for a way of earning income online, then this guide is right for you. You will learn what affiliate marketing really means and why it is one of the best online business models for any serious entrepreneur. You will learn the various ways of doing affiliate marketing so you can see results with your efforts.

So many people do affiliate marketing the wrong way, then they turn around and complain that they are finding it hard to make money with it. Some people do what I call, "hit and run" affiliate marketing – then when they fail to make money, they give up and start complaining that affiliate marketing is dead. Affiliate marketing can never go out of fashion, as long as humans still occupy this earth and as long as humans continue to purchase goods and services both online and offline.

In fact, affiliate marketing is still an untapped market, because at the moment, almost half of the world's population is yet to have access to the internet. Now, imagine what could happen when we have more internet penetration. The earlier you go into an online business, like affiliate marketing and master it, the better it is for you as you get to position yourself early enough for a digital future.

That being said in this guide, you will also learn the different affiliate marketing models and the best one for you. You will learn how to incorporate digital marketing or email marketing into your affiliate marketing business for maximum profitability. Most importantly, you will learn how to run affiliate marketing like a real business and not as a side hustle for quick bucks.

Without further ado, let's dive in and start exploring affiliate marketing and how to make the best of it.

# CHAPTER ONE:
# FIRST THINGS FIRST

If you have heard about affiliate marketing but you do not have explicit knowledge of what it is, then this chapter is for you. However, if you already know about affiliate marketing, you could skip this chapter and go straight to the next and start learning the best affiliate marketing strategies.

That being said affiliate marketing is the type of business model where you help companies promote their products and services and each time a sale occurs through your marketing efforts, you are paid a commission often referred to as an affiliate commission. This is the most straightforward definition of affiliate marketing you will find.

It is as simple as finding a product you think people would like, promote the product, citing its benefits to those you think would love it. Whenever these people buy the product, the company that developed the product will pay you an affiliate commission.

It might interest you to know that affiliate marketing has always been there with us, and there are chances that you have done affiliate marketing in the past, even without knowing it. For instance, if you have ever told your friend about a new restaurant in town that makes delicious delicacies, then you have somehow done affiliate marketing even though, you were not paid.

If you have ever told a sibling about someone you found on Facebook or Instagram who sells nice sneakers or hoodies, then you have somehow done affiliate marketing without knowing it.

So, in one way or the other, you have done affiliate marketing, although you were not paid. Wouldn't it make sense for you to start getting paid for this same thing you have been doing for free?

How does it feel being paid for something as simple as promoting a product or service to people who need them? It feels good – because you did not develop the product – you are not the one who will render the service. Your job is to serve as a middle-man between the buyer and developer of a product. After a sale has been concluded, you get paid.

A lot of companies and service providers have since understood the importance of affiliate marketing and the role it plays in helping them get their products to as many people as possible. This is why it is now rare for you to find a company that does not have one affiliate program or the other.

# Affiliate program, affiliate links, affiliate products or offers

An affiliate program is simply an organized program that a company or service provider develops as a way of providing independent marketers with an avenue to earn affiliate commissions by promoting the products or services of the company.

An affiliate product or offer is the product that an affiliate marketer promotes in order to earn a commission. An affiliate product can be anything ranging from a physical product, digital product, or even a service. If you identify an affiliate offer or product that you think many people could benefit from, you could promote the product and earn a commission.

An affiliate link, on the other hand, is a unique URL that every affiliate product or offer has. The unique URL is used to track all sales that the affiliate offer or product has recorded. For instance, if you find an affiliate product, you are given an affiliate link. When you promote the affiliate product, you give your affiliate link to those you are promoting the product to. When those people want to buy, they will click on the affiliate link which you have provided.

Every traffic that comes to the product through your affiliate link is tracked and recorded. At the end of the day, you are paid for every sale that happens through your efforts. You will be given a unique affiliate link for each of the products you are promoting. For instance, if you are promoting a laptop computer and a hosting service, even if the two products are from the same company, you will be given different affiliate links for each of them.

This is how it works – company A develops a good body lotion. Before developing the lotion, the company already did a lot of research which showed that people are willing to patronize the kind of lotion that they are about to develop. After proper research and development, the company needs to distribute its product to the final consumer. However, to get the product to the final consumer, the company would need to spend a lot of money on marketing campaigns. Add to that; the company would spend a lot of money to acquire distributors who would be willing to take a risk on a new product in the market.

Now, to reduce their marketing costs, company A could develop an affiliate program and pay 20% of the sale price of the lotion to independent marketers who would be willing to market their new product. At the end of the day, the company will get so many affiliates who will promote their products for a chance to earn an affiliate commission.

Working with these affiliates means that company A would no longer spend huge amounts of money on marketing, as the affiliates are the ones who will have to do the active promotion of the products. The company might spend some money to run campaigns targeting affiliates, which would be way less than the amount they would have spent marketing the product.

For company A, it would be better for them to spend a percentage of their marketing budget to acquire affiliates than to spend a huge sum marketing their products itself. When they have acquired the affiliate marketers, they will go into the field and do the marketing on behalf of the company. This is the reason why so many companies now have their own affiliate programs.

If you observe keenly, you will notice that almost all the companies that you use their products or services have one affiliate program or the other. For instance, some online service providers will tell you that you will be offered a 50% discount if you introduce your friend to their business. Now, that's their own affiliate program and all you need to get the promised 50% discount is to introduce your friend to the service provider.

Even financial institutions have affiliate programs – where they tell you that if you introduce someone who takes a specific action, you would be rewarded. It is hard to find a company these days that does not have an affiliate program. From your loan lenders to insurance companies, almost all of them have affiliate programs that you can join.

One good thing about affiliate marketing is that you are not really marketing the product of the company– you are simply recommending or promoting a product or service of the company to other people. When those people you have directed to the product end up buying it, you earn a commission.

You can find people you can promote a product to, in your immediate network. For instance, if you want to promote an insurance policy – you obviously have friends and family members who need insurance cover and you could promote the most suitable ones to them and earn a commission.

Affiliate marketing is vast because there are thousands of affiliate programs out there, which you could join and start earning money. You are not restricted to one particular program. As long as you know how to run affiliate marketing as a business, then you can promote any product to anybody and earn money. The only problem when it comes to affiliate marketing is that some people follow the wrong strategies, then get their hands burnt badly.

# Why should you consider affiliate marketing?

Affiliate marketing is great because it is a win-win for all the parties involved. It is a win for the company that developed the affiliate program because they get to acquire more customers without necessarily stretching their marketing budget. The company only needs to ensure they do proper research and development, then leave the affiliates to do the rest of the marketing job.

Affiliate marketing is a win for the affiliate marketer because they get to earn money by promoting other people's products. Product research and development is one of the hardest parts of starting a business. Now, as an affiliate marketer, you will not involve yourself with product research and development. The company running the affiliate the program must have done that already. The company must have developed an excellent viable product.

Your only job as an affiliate is to identify the selling points of the product, look for people who would be willing to buy the product, and actively promote the product to them. You need to study the product properly because when promoting it, you need to position yourself as someone who has used the product. You do not expect people to buy a product or service you are promoting if they are not convinced that you have used the product yourself.

In addition, in affiliate marketing, there are thousands of products to promote as there are millions of affiliate programs you can join. Apart from the conventional affiliate marketing networks where you could find thousands of affiliate products or offers, if you look around, you will find tons of other affiliate programs you could join.

So, as an affiliate marketer, you do not need to bother yourself about finding the right products to promote. Once you learn to do affiliate marketing the right way, you can easily discover affiliate offers that make sense and promote them. Also, with the strategies you are going to learn in this guide, you will be able to promote just about any product.

Furthermore, affiliate marketing is a win for the customer because the product you are going to promote to them will help them to solve their problems. Without your efforts as an affiliate marketer, many customers may likely not find some of the products they need; hence, their problems won't get solved. So, affiliate marketing is a win-win for everybody involved – the company that has the affiliate program, the affiliate marketer, and the customer that benefits from affiliate offers or products.

If you are now convinced that affiliate marketing is for you, then let's dive deeper and show you how to get started with affiliate marketing. However, before that, you need to know something about shiny objects and how to avoid them.

# **Shiny object syndrome**

One mistake that most people make, which prevents them from earning money online is that they tend to pursue too many things at once. In the internet marketing space, this is called the shiny object syndrome. Often, people see one good online business model; then they jump into it. They see another good model; they abandon the first one and jump into the second. They continue jumping around that way without really going deep into any one product

The same way you cannot go to college to study all the available courses, that's the same way you cannot jump into all the online business models and expect to be successful. If you really want to be successful at affiliate marketing, then you must make up your mind to do affiliate marketing until you have become well-grounded in it before diversifying.

Nobody says you cannot run two or three different online businesses. However, before you jump into any new online business, make sure you have mastered the former one you were into. Do not just jump into a new one because it seems to be more profitable than the one you are doing now.

In online business, it is easy for individuals to get distracted and switch from one model to the other. If you are serious about making money online, you must not be caught switching randomly from one model to the other.

One reason that makes people go from one online business model to another is that they often want the ones that pay quickly. So many people have wrong notions of what an online business is all about. Some people have been made to believe that with an online business, you do not need to put in much effort – you could make money by working for 3 hours a week. All these are unrealistic expectations, and unless you are careful enough, you could find yourself jumping around, looking for that non-existent online business that would give you quick cash.

No real online business will give you quick cash, and no real online or offline business will pay you money for doing nothing. The people who promote such opportunities to you are nothing but opportunists. The moment an individual start telling you that it is possible to make money without doing anything, then know that they have their own hidden agenda. It is either they want to sell you something, or they want to take away the little money you already have.

To make money, either offline or online – you must provide something of value – it is this valuable thing that people are then going to pay for. The amount of money you earn will be proportional to the amount of value you provide. If you provide a service or product that has high value, you will earn higher.

However, if you provide something that is of low value, you will earn lower. And unless you are a scammer or a con artist, no one will pay you money unless you have something of equivalent value that you would exchange with them.

Many acclaimed gurus are notorious for promoting quick money schemes. Before you decide to abandon affiliate marketing, which is a real business to pursue those quick money schemes, know that you might get your hands burnt badly. And if you keep chasing after shiny objects, you will never make reasonable money online.

Now that you know about the shiny objects and how to avoid them – in the next sections of this guide, we shall go deep into affiliate marketing and how to do it right.

# CHAPTER TWO:
# NICHES IN AFFILIATE MARKETING

Anytime online business is mentioned, you are sure to hear of niches. The reason is that in online business, people operate in different niches. Your niche is like your preferred sub-segment of the broader market. This sub-segment of the market is the one you are more knowledgeable in – so you pitch your tent there and become well-grounded in it.

In online business or affiliate marketing, people can operate in one or more niches – but when you are just starting, you need to choose one niche and stick with it. Become well-grounded in the niche before considering going into other ones.

Apart from jumping from one online business model to another, another mistake that people make in online business is jumping from one niche to the other. While there are niches that are considered more profitable than the others, the truth remains that there are potentials in almost all the known niches. Your level of commitment is the only thing that makes a difference. Even if you start operating in a niche that is known to be profitable, if you don't put in the required effort, you will still not make money like the dedicated person who operates in a less profitable niche.

In affiliate marketing, some niches are referred to as evergreen niches – just like the name implies, products that fall under these niches are evergreen. People will always need them to solve one problem or the other. So as long as the earth remains, humans will always buy those products that fall under the evergreen niches.

Apart from the evergreen niches, we have sub-niches that are usually not as popular as the evergreen niches, but you can still make a lot of money promoting products under these sub-niches.

Many times, the sub-niches are directly derived from the evergreen niches through a process known as niching down. When you niche down, you simply take a general niche or evergreen niche and break it down until you have arrived at the smaller more specialized market or sub-niche.

One common mistake that people make when they want to join affiliate marketing is that they rush into evergreen niches. Then after promoting one or two products, they give up due to low income or no income at all. The reason is simple – evergreen niches are popular – people know them to be money-spinners. The same way you want to go into those evergreen niches, there are thousands of other affiliate marketers who are also looking to go into those niches.

So, the competition to go into evergreen niches is very high – and as a new affiliate marketer, for you to break into the competition, you would probably need to spend a lot of money on advertisements and other forms of marketing. The people that often tend to do well in evergreen niches are the established affiliate marketers. Those ones have been in the game for so long – they probably already have an email list or different email lists. They may already know a lot of entrance and exit strategies – and the best types of products to promote.

As a new affiliate marketer, your best bet is to find those sub-niches, which in most cases are often neglected, then start with them. Once you have learned how the business works, then you could work your way up and start promoting products in evergreen niches. Most established affiliate marketers started this way – they started by promoting one sub-niche product, then when they saw positive results, they worked their way up and applied the same strategies they used in promoting sub-niche products to promote evergreen ones.

## List of evergreen niches

Some of the known evergreen niches in affiliate marketing and internet marketing include:

### 1. Wealth and money

Products that fall under this niche are those that teach people how to make money either online or offline. Under this niche also, you will find tools that help people to set up and run their online and offline businesses.

Some of the affiliate products that you will find under this niche include eBooks and online courses that teach people how to start an online business or just how to make money through different ventures. You can also find products like videos under this niche.

Apart from eBooks and courses, you can find tools such as autoresponders as some of the products you can promote under the wealth and money niche.

Additionally, affiliate offers such as web hosting, domain name registration, and lots of other services all fall under the wealth and money niche. Typically, the products that fall under the wealth and money niche help you to make money or create wealth.

Why is the "wealth/money" niche so popular and considered an evergreen one? The reason is simple– money is an essential necessity. Every living soul desires to make money in order to meet their essential needs, which include food, clothing, and shelter.

Because money is quite important, every day, people come online to seek different ways of making money. Even those who already have money seek more ways of increasing their wealth. Apart from those who come online to seek online income opportunities, a lot of others look for offline business ideas. People attend seminars and conferences that promise to teach them how to make money.

This is the reason why the wealth and money niche is and will always remain an evergreen affiliate marketing niche. If you equip yourself with the right strategies and go into this niche, then you are sure to make money promoting products that teach others how to make money.

## 2. Health and wellness

The popular weight loss niche falls under the health and wellness niche. Under the health and wellness niche, you will also find products that help you live a healthier life. Food supplements and other types of drugs that help people improve their life and health all fall under this niche.

In addition, you can find eBooks as some of the products that fall under this niche. Yes, those eBooks that teach you how to maintain a healthy thyroid gland, the eBooks that teach you how to embrace veganism. The eBooks that teach you how to lose excess body fat all fall under the health and wellness niche.

Just like wealth and money, the health and wellness niche is an evergreen one for obvious reasons. It is only the living that can do other things. So, people place a lot of premium on their health. Those who are already suffering from one illness or the other are willing to spend huge sums of money on products that can help them live a healthier life.

Those who are still healthy are also willing to spend a lot of their money on products that can make them remain healthy. Additionally, people who are obese are looking for means of losing excess body fat while those who are fit are actively looking for products and programs that can help them maintain their healthy bodies.

The health and wellness niche is so vast that finding affiliate products to promote and earn money can never be a challenge to you as an affiliate marketer. However, you must know that the same way the niche is popular, it is also very competitive.

For instance, the weight loss industry is a multibillion-dollar one – a lot of affiliates and direct companies are already promoting products in this sub-niche, and if you want to break in, you will need to spend a lot of money on marketing. Also, it takes time to break into such niches as you would have to build your credibility first.

However, once you have found a way of breaking into the niche, you are sure to make a lot of money. Breaking into such niches does require a clear strategy. If you just want to go into the niche and start doing what the others are doing, then you will likely get the results that others are getting as well. For instance, instead of promoting products that show people how to lose weight, you could consider promoting products that show people the types of exercises they could engage in and lose weight. Notice that there is a difference between the two.

### 3. Romance niches

It is often said that man is a social animal – as so-called social animals, we often thrive in the company of others, more so, the company of loved ones. When people go into romantic relationships, they try to make it work. And that's why they spend money on products that can help them sustain such relationships.

Affiliate products you would find under romance niches include those that offer marriage counseling, dating tips, tips for better sex life, etc. You can also promote those eBooks or courses that teach people how to get their ex back, how to get a girlfriend or boyfriend, etc. Yes, they all fall under the romance niche.

Just like the wealth/money and health/wellness niches, the romance niche will continue to be an evergreen one because humans will always go into romantic relationships and when they go into such relationships, they will find means of getting the best out of it.

Apart from evergreen niches, there are also other affiliate marketing niches that you can go into and excel. The products under some of those niches that have to do with hobbies and pastimes. For instance, under the hobbies/games niche, you could find a product that is all about online gambling, gaming equipment, etc.

Gamers and other hobbyists can spend a lot of money just to acquire the tools, equipment, and material they need to practice their hobby – therefore, hobby niches are also as profitable as the evergreen niches.

When you want to choose an affiliate marketing niche, you need to look inwards. Ask yourself, "What do I know about this niche?" Don't just go into any niche because it is popular. You are often advised to go for niches that you are passionate about. The importance of choosing passion over popularity cannot be overemphasized. If you are passionate about a niche, you can spend time and money to learn about it and promote it to others. Remember, in affiliate marketing, you must show that you are knowledgeable about a product before a customer will trust you to buy the product through you.

After discovering niches to promote, you could be asking, "what next?" Well, to answer that question, the next thing you should do is to start looking for affiliate programs to join. There are different available affiliate programs you could join and start making money. Your best bet is to find affiliate programs that are run directly by a company. If you find it hard to find such affiliate programs, then you could join an affiliate network like Clickbank.com and find products to promote.

Even though I don't advise newbies to use Clickbank.com, I will still talk about the network shortly. The primary reason why Clickbank.com is not the best for a new affiliate marketer is that the platform's business model is part of what I call the hit and run affiliate marketing model. You will learn about the hit and run marketing model in chapter four of this guide.

Another reason why you should not consider Clickbank.com is that you will have to promote a ton of products to make a reasonable income. The customers you send to a product on Clickbank.com, do not belong to you.

They belong to the company that placed the affiliate product on Clickbank.com. More on this later.

However, if you join affiliate programs like the ones run directly by a service company, you will make more money while doing less work. In the last chapter of this guide, I have listed some of the best affiliate programs you could join and make money.

That being said, let's talk about affiliate networks.

## Affiliate networks

An affiliate network is a website or platform that aggregates affiliate offers or products from different vendors, businesses or companies which an affiliate marketer can promote.

It is like an affiliate marketing general marketplace – what happens is that vendors register their affiliate products on the platform, then affiliates will promote such products and earn a commission.

There are three parties involved in the business – the vendor who has the product, the owners of the affiliate network and the affiliate marketer. Now, these three parties all must take part in sharing whatever money that is raised from promoting a product – this is the primary reason why commissions on affiliate networks are not often that great.

There are different available affiliate networks – we are going to talk about two.

**Clickbank.com**

This is one of the most popular affiliate networks. The website has a huge list of affiliate products from different vendors or companies that an affiliate can promote.

The network connects a massive number of affiliates to an equally huge number of vendors. When you visit the Clickbank.com website, you are sure to find a product that you can promote and make money. The platform is reputable for prompt payment of affiliate earnings. So, once you earn money on the platform, you are sure to get paid.

**What are the pros of Clickbank.com?**

Joining Clickbank.com is easy – you just need to fill out some information about you and then wait for the approval. The approval process is not tedious like that of other similar platforms. Your account dashboard contains everything you need to manage your account.

Payments are paid promptly, so once you have made money on the platform, you will surely get paid.

Another significant advantage is that the platform contains many affiliate products you could promote, although this could also be counted as a con because you might get confused and start promoting products across different niches indiscriminately.

**Cons**

Since there are thousands of products to be promoted, you could find it hard choosing the right product. You may also find it hard to concentrate on one niche. As an online entrepreneur, the importance of sticking to one niche cannot be overemphasized. Clickbank.com's large pool of affiliate products will make it almost impossible for a beginner to stick to one niche. Even if you decide to stick to one niche, you could find a new product every other day and choose to promote it, making you lose focus.

Another major disadvantage is that the platform subtly encourages you to be a hit and run affiliate marketer. As a hit and run affiliate marketer, you basically don't have a business. You are at the mercy of both the affiliate network and vendors. I talked extensively on hit and run affiliate marketing in chapter four of this guide.

The same way there are many products to promote; there are also many affiliates jostling to grab those offers. So, the competition on the network is high, and to survive, you need to put in an extra effort.

In all, if you feel you have all it takes to join Clickbank.com and excel, then go ahead and register an account. But you are better off starting your affiliate marketing journey with a more specific program like the Amazon affiliate program. The next chapter talks extensively on the Amazon affiliate program.

### JVZoo.com

This is yet another popular affiliate network just like Clickbank.com. However, while Clickbank.com is dedicated to all types of products, JVZoo.com is mainly for digital products like software applications, courses, etc.

Depending on how you perform on the platform, you could earn instant commissions and be paid instantly. This is unlike what happens on other affiliate networks where you must wait for about two weeks or even a month to get paid.

You can run an active promotion using the platform's integrated autoresponders. JVZoo.com is about the only affiliate network that has this feature.

**Cons**

You may not get the chance to be placed on instant commission by all vendors. It is a vendor that chooses who they want to put on instant commission. Usually, some vendors only place people who have achieved certain feats in terms of sales on instant commission. If a vendor does not place you on instant commission, you will have to wait for 30 days to receive your earnings.

Lastly, to promote a product, you will need to seek permission from the vendor of the product. This is unlike what is obtainable on Clickbank.com where you could just browse through a pool of products, find the ones that appeal to you and promote.

So many vendors on JVZoo.com don't like accepting beginners to promote their products. So, as a beginner with no track record, your chances of getting approved by a vendor are slim.

Like I mentioned earlier, I don't often advise beginners to start their journeys on affiliate networks. It is better for them to seek out distinct affiliate programs, join and start making money. In the next chapter, we shall look at the Amazon affiliate program and what makes it great for a newbie affiliate marketer.

# CHAPTER THREE:
# THE AMAZON AFFILIATE PROGRAM

In the previous chapter, I talked about some of the affiliate networks you could join and find affiliate products or offers to promote. In this chapter, we are going to look at the Amazon affiliate program, what it is, and why it is great for any affiliate marketer.

On many occasions, people who are new to affiliate marketing are often advised to start with Amazon affiliate marketing for various reasons. With Amazon affiliate marketing, you could easily learn the rope of affiliate marketing and then move on to join the other affiliate networks and grow your tentacles as an internet marketer.

## What is the Amazon affiliate program?

Just like many other companies, Amazon has since realized that for them to make more money without necessarily increasing their marketing budget; they need to recruit affiliates to do marketing on their behalf. As mentioned earlier, the major idea behind affiliate marketing or the major reason why many companies develop their own affiliate programs is that they understand that it is quite better to earn 50% profit on a product than not to earn anything at all.

For companies like Amazon, they know that if an affiliate marketer helps to sell their products, Amazon will earn from the efforts of the affiliate marketer whereas if the company does not give an affiliate marketer an opportunity, the company might earn less. So, Amazon prefers to give affiliate marketers a chance to make money for both themselves and Amazon.

Anyone can join the Amazon affiliate program, promote any of the numerous products that are for sale on the Amazon marketplace, and earn a commission. Primarily, the Amazon affiliate program was developed by Amazon to allow interested parties to make money from promoting the products on sale on the Amazon marketplace.

Why affiliate marketing beginners should join the Amazon affiliate program:

There are thousands of affiliate programs out there for an affiliate marketer to join – however, as a new affiliate marketer, you are often advised to start with Amazon affiliate marketing program, and the reasons for that are too numerous to mention – in the following paragraphs, we shall look at some of them.

## 1. Amazon is a strong brand, and this will rub off on you

Amazon is one of the largest online marketplaces – the internet giant has done a good job of getting their branding right. One problem that most affiliate marketers do face is that they find it hard to convince prospects that the products they are promoting are genuine or original. This is a huge problem because prospects do not want to spend scarce resources on products that will not meet their standards.

To overcome the above problem, affiliate marketers, many times must spend a lot of time trying to convince their audience or prospective customers that the products the affiliate marketer is pitching are of good quality. Many times, the affiliate marketer must use various marketing methods like sending emails to convince the prospective client. The affiliate marketer may sometimes have to provide testimonials, social proof, etc.

The affiliate marketer does all of that, especially when they are promoting products that are not well known or when they join affiliate programs of companies that are not well recognized. As an Amazon affiliate marketer, you don't have to face such a problem because Amazon, as a company, has gotten their branding right.

Yes, even though there are still chances of people buying fake products on Amazon, there are measures that the company has put in place, help to curtail such occurrences. And if things like that happen, Amazon helps to protect the interest of the buyer by offering them refunds. All these and more are the things that have made Amazon become the trusted online giant that it is today.

Since Amazon is a well-known brand, reputable for its ability to protect the interest of the customer; if you pitch an Amazon product to your prospects, they would likely not have any objection regarding the authenticity of the products you are promoting. Also, your prospect knows that if they do not get the original product, they could simply return it and get a refund.

All this means that promoting Amazon products will be so easy for you. You don't have to say many words; you do not need to provide social proof or testimonials. You also do not need to do aggressive marketing. Simply put, Amazon's shiny brand image would simply rub off on you as an affiliate marketer, thus making things relatively easier for you.

Furthermore, millions, if not billions of transactions are carried out on Amazon every day. This means that the probability of getting someone to buy something through your affiliate link is quite high. All you need to do is to know the right products to promote, and the best ways to promote them and you are already on your way to making a living as an affiliate marketer.

## 2. It is easier

When compared to the other affiliate marketing networks or the other affiliate programs, the Amazon affiliate marketing program could be likened to a walk in the park. To make it into so many other affiliate marketing programs, you would need to meet some requirements, and there are some restrictions too. And as mentioned earlier, when you have been accepted, you will need strong marketing skills to be able to promote the affiliate products of most other companies, and that's not so with Amazon affiliate offers.

As stated earlier, Amazon is a global brand, and they have perfected their branding to the extent that by just visiting the site, you feel like buying something. Many people just get into a buying mode when they visit the platform. So, if you know a good way of sending affiliate traffic to the site, your job is almost done by half. Once the traffic gets to the site, they would likely get into a buying mode, then go on a shopping spree, and you earn a commission.

**3. There are billions of products to promote**

As far as the Amazon affiliate program is concerned, the sky is big enough for everybody as there are billions of products to promote and earn a commission. In addition to the already existing products, more are added daily. Furthermore, newer models of products, especially gadgets are introduced into the market every day, and they would find their way into Amazon.

So, there are always thousands of hot selling products to promote, and if one product starts recording low sales, you could easily research and find new hot selling products to promote. No matter the niche you choose, there will always be something on Amazon to promote.

**4. You can make money from sales of products you didn't pitch**

This is one of the greatest advantages of the Amazon affiliate program. You can make a lot of money selling products that you have not pitched. For instance, let's say your niche is audio equipment, and you do review all kinds of microphones and recommend them to people.

What happens is that if you refer someone to Amazon, and perhaps, the person gets to Amazon, changes their mind and decides to buy a TV set instead, as long as the purchase was made within 24 hours from the time you referred the customer to Amazon, you will still earn a commission even though the customer ended up buying another product instead of the one you recommended to them.

Remember, just like any other affiliate marketing program, Amazon gives you a unique affiliate link for each product you want to promote. It is this affiliate link that is used to track all the traffic that comes to the Amazon website through your efforts. Now, if a sale happens through your link, it is recorded in your name. Amazon uses what is called sticky cookies to make that possible.

The fact that you could earn money for products you did not pitch makes Amazon affiliate, one of the best affiliate marketing programs. The reason is not hard to guess – all you need to make money is to send traffic to the Amazon website. If the customer you send to the site gets there and buys an entirely different item within 24 hours, then you still earn.

The commission you receive from Amazon for promoting their products ranges from 4% to 7% of the price of the product. Sometimes, high ticket items have bigger affiliate commissions while low ticket items have lower affiliate commissions, but this is not a written rule.

# Which niche should I promote on Amazon?

When it comes to Amazon affiliate marketing, no niche can be said to be unprofitable. The reason for this is that you only need to push traffic to Amazon, and even if the customer ends up buying another product, you still make money if the purchase happened within 24 hours.

Nevertheless, there are still some niches that attract the most traffic, and if you promote products in these niches, there are high chances that your audience would buy them. So, you still need to make sure that you are not just promoting any niche that comes to your mind.

The three evergreen niches remain the best that you could promote on Amazon. However, when promoting products in such niches, you need to dig deeper or niche down until you arrive at a specialized sub-niche. The three most evergreen niches include health/wellness, money/wealth, and romance. You may find the games/hobbies niche to be a good one as well.

Let's talk about some of the products you can promote in these mentioned niches. The health niche on Amazon, for instance, has a lot of interesting products that you could promote. Yes, people may not be able to buy drugs on Amazon, but there are thousands of health products they could buy and improve their health.

For instance, Apple iWatch helps people to measure their heart rate and perform a lot of other health checks. Even though the watch falls under gadgets, it could also fall under the health niche as well. So, if you want to promote the iWatch, you could promote it as an electronic gadget and a health product.

There are also thousands of similar health products on Amazon which you could promote and make money. Most of your audience have one health problem or the other, and they might have tried so many solutions to no avail. Now, if you help point them to an Amazon product that could help their situation, they would likely buy the product and put some affiliate commissions in your pocket.

For instance, a lot of people suffer from back pain– and if you show such people that they could get relief from back pain by using an inversion therapy machine which could be bought on Amazon, they would most likely want to try out the product. This would put some affiliate commissions in your pocket.

The Amazon website has lots of products that help people to monitor their health or maintain a healthy lifestyle. These products are not hard to find – and if you promote them to those who really need them, then you can easily make money. Apart from health products, other products you could find in the health niche includes eBooks that teach people how to live healthily and so on.

Just like the health niche, you could find good products in the money/wealth niches, romance niches, and the games/hobbies niches. All these are niches that are evergreen – people spend money on products in these niches. Some people don't even know that many of the products on Amazon exist – so, if you show such people that the products they need exist on Amazon, they would most likely buy and help you earn money in return.

In addition to the evergreen niches, which are unarguably the largest, there are still millions of other niches you could find products to promote. For instance, the gadgets niche is a great one for many reasons. Every other month, new electronic gadgets find their way into the market. However, people do not just go to the market to buy these products, they often wait for others to buy and give reviews.

If you show a prospective buyer of an electronic gadget the features of the gadget, you will help the potential buyer make an informed decision, and they could choose to buy through the link you provided. Mobile devices and other electronic devices are some of the hottest selling products on Amazon.

Remember, by describing some of the niches that sell well on Amazon; I am not by any means urging you to delve into those niches. Take the information you have received here to be for educational purposes only. You still need to do your own research and find out the type of Amazon products you would want to promote. When it comes to affiliate marketing and internet marketing, two people may have the same experience or knowledge and still get different results. So, it is important that you do your own research instead of relying on only the information you have been fed.

The best way to find great niches that do well on Amazon is to visit the website and see what people are willing to spend money on. If you are observant enough, you might find some good products to promote right on Amazon's homepage. On Amazon's homepage, they often list some of their best-selling products.

When you visit the different categories, you will find the bestsellers' list that contains the bestselling products in each category. Explore the products on the list and get an idea of the types of products that are doing well.

If you are new to the Amazon website and you do not know how to find the best-selling products in any category, simply head to google, and type, "Amazon products bestseller's list." When you click on the first result on Google, you will be taken to the Amazon bestsellers' list. If you don't want to go through that lengthy process, simply click on this link (https://www.amazon.com/Best-Sellers/zgbs) and you will be taken to the bestsellers' list directly.

As mentioned earlier, simply exploring the bestselling products list will give you an idea of the types of products you should promote. You will get a lot of ideas and even find some products and niches you never thought existed. So, the key to finding a good niche to promote on Amazon is research – don't depend on anyone to spoon feed you.

# How to join the Amazon affiliate program

Joining the Amazon affiliate program is free – you simply need to visit the Amazon affiliate program website and register. On the site, you will see a button that says, "Join Now for Free," click on it, fill out the registration form with your correct information and you are good to go.

If you already have a blog, then you would want to promote niches that are related to your blog. You could just promote the products to your blog audience and earn. However, if you do not have a blog already, you may need to develop a microblog or a niche blog which you will use for promoting your Amazon affiliate products. We shall look at ways to promote your affiliate offers in a subsequent part of this chapter.

# How to extract your affiliate link

For you to earn money from the sales of an Amazon product as an affiliate, you need to extract an affiliate link for that product and use the link when you are making posts on your blog or sending marketing emails. Getting the affiliate link for a product could seem hard for a newbie; however, it is not all that complicated. Here are some of the steps you need to take to extract the affiliate link of any product on Amazon.

- Log in to your Amazon affiliate program account.
- Use the search bar to locate the product you want to promote. If you have done your research earlier and determined the types of products you wish to promote, then this second step should not be hard for you. Simply type the

names of the product you discovered in the bestsellers' list into the search bar. The products will pop up if they are among those that affiliates can promote.

- Extract the links for the product. Repeat step two above for each of the products you want to promote.

**Let's go over the steps in detail**

Once you log in to your Amazon affiliate marketing program account, look at the top menu, situated next to the "Home" button is a "product linking tab." Hover your mouse over this tab, and there will be a drop-down menu. Select the very first option that says, "Product link." Look further down the new page that opens, and you will see a search bar.

Next, enter the keyword for the product you want to promote. For instance, if you wish to promote training boots for men, simply type, "training boots" into the search bar and click "Go." If you know the exact name of the product, you could consider typing it directly into the search bar.

Once you hit the "Go" button, some search results related to the keywords or search terms you typed will be displayed. Located next to each search result, you will see an orange button that will provide the affiliate link for that specific product. Click on the arrow next to where it says, "Get link." When you click on that, you will receive a pop-up box containing the affiliate link to the product.

On close observation, you will notice that the link doesn't really look nice, and if you use the link as it is on your blog, it could be misconstrued as a spam link. How do you solve this puzzle? On top of the box that pops up, you will see two buttons. One says, "Copy and paste the link below," while the other says, "shorten link with amazon.to."

Now, click on the second button, and the affiliate link will be shortened to something more appealing and shorter. There are also other link shortening services that can serve a similar purpose, like bit.ly, etc. Now, include the link you received in your product reviews, YouTube description boxes, social media posts, or any other place where you intend to be generating traffic for your affiliate products. Repeat this process for all the products you want to promote.

# Traffic sources

Best places to promote Amazon affiliate products

To discover the bestselling products on Amazon that you can promote is not where the problem lies

— the bulk of your problem as an Amazon affiliate marketer is knowing the best places to promote your affiliate offers. Engaging in active promotion of affiliate offers is one area where many affiliate marketers face challenges. It is also what differentiates the serious affiliate marketer and the "off-the-shelfers."

There are many places you could promote your Amazon affiliate links and drive traffic to your affiliate offers. Promoting your affiliate offer involves a simple process – you must create a post, then include a link to your affiliate offer in the post. When people read the post and find it interesting, they would want to purchase the product you talked about in the post. Hence, they (your prospective customers) would click on your affiliate link which would take them directly to Amazon where they could decide to buy the product you talked about or any other one.

Some of the places where you could create promotional content about your affiliate offers include the following:

- Social media
- Blog
- YouTube

**Social media**

Social media is one of the places where you could promote your affiliate offers, but it is not a preferred option for many obvious reasons. One of the reasons is that – people come on social media to catch fun or connect with family and friends. Rarely would you find people who come on social media because they wanted to buy a product or read product reviews. For many people, social media is solely for entertainment, and once a post is not about entertainment, they may find it hard to follow it.

So, when you promote affiliate offers on social media, especially if you are running a free promotion, you may find it hard to record conversions. However, there is a way to overcome that hurdle, and it involves offering social media users a combination of entertainment and a solution to their problems.

You don't just come on social media, paste some affiliate links and go away, then expect people to click the links and buy your affiliate products. It does not work that way. When you want to pitch a product or idea to a friend or someone offline, do you just shove the product in their face without telling them what the product is all about and expect them to buy? The answer is NO.

When you want to pitch a product to someone offline, for instance, you start by telling them the name of the product and the benefits of the product. You tailor your pitch to highlight what the person is going to gain by buying the product you are pitching to them.

If you give the prospective buyer the impression that you want them to buy so you can earn money, the chances are that they would ignore you. However, if you give the prospective buyer strong reasons why you think the product you are pitching is good for them, they would gladly buy.

The same thing applies when you are pitching a product to social media users. You would want to tell them what the product is all about and the best ways they could use the product to harness all its benefits. Additionally, if you present yourself as a friend, your social media followers would be ready to buy anything you are pitching to them.

Even in the real world or offline, true friends often patronize the business of their friends. The same thing applies to the virtual world. The question is – how do you present yourself as a friend to your social media followers and friends? The answer is simple – engage them in a conversation. Be active in their lives and watch them reciprocate the gesture.

It is not a good idea to pitch or promote affiliate offers on your timeline – you should create a dedicated page for that. For instance, if you are on Facebook, create a dedicated Facebook page for your affiliate marketing business. Make sure you use the page to post valuable content that would keep your followers glued to their screen. And don't forget to follow the rule of thirds.

The rule of thirds as it relates to social media posting states that one-third of your social media posts should be informational. Another one third should be purely entertaining while the remaining one third should be promotional. This means you should mix everything up when posting on social media.

If you keep bugging your followers with promotional content every day, they would be tempted to unfollow your page. However, if you throw in entertaining posts, GIFs, memes occasionally, your follows would want to stay. Additionally, posting educational content on your page will be an excellent way to spark up conversations that will help you to retain followers.

One thing that makes the rule of thirds great is that

– it entertains, educates, and informs your followers at the same time. Remember, I mentioned earlier that social media users are entertainment seekers.

So, if you provide them with entertainment and promote offers to them occasionally, the equation becomes balanced, and they would want to stick with you. Also, when you provide people with valuable content, they would want to reciprocate by checking out the different offers you are promoting.

**Blogs**

Apart from social media, a blog is another perfect medium to promote your affiliate offers. If you have a blog already, mainly a niche blog, then you could easily find Amazon affiliate products that are closely related to your niche and promote them to your blog readers.

Promoting affiliate offers on your blog works better because for people to be reading your blog, it means that you already have something of value that they need. Since there is already a kind of rapport between you and your audience, promoting an affiliate product should not be a hard task.

If you do not have a blog already or if you don't have a niche blog, you could consider creating one for the promotion of your affiliate offers. Creating a blog is as simple as ABC – you don't need to be an advanced computer programmer to do it. Blogging platforms such as WordPress and Blogger (owned by Google) allows you to create, update, and maintain a blog.

Both Blogger and WordPress have their distinct advantages and the features that make each one unique. Since you are only developing a blog that you can use to promote affiliate offers, then Blogger should be able to do the job correctly.

With Blogger, you only need to buy a domain name

— and start posting a review or promotional content on your blog. If you are cash strapped and cannot afford to pay for a domain name initially, then you could do with Blogger's default subdomain. Blogger blogs are already hosted for you by Google for free, so you don't need to buy a hosting package.

WordPress remains the best blogging platform — so if you have the funds to pay for both a hosting package and domain name, then go with WordPress. WordPress has hundreds of plug-ins that can ease the job of designing and customizing your blog for you. You also have the chance to choose from thousands of free and premium templates.

Since this is not a book on blogging, I shall not dwell much on how to create and customize a blog. I have an in-depth book that takes you through all the steps you need to create and monetize a blog.

Now, once you have gotten your blog ready — you need to start posting content on it. What are the best types of content for Amazon affiliate products? Let's assume that you want to promote electronic gadgets or mobile phones; then you would want to write reviews about the product and post on your blog.

For instance, if you want to promote the Amazon Echo speaker, you could write a blog on the topic, "10 things you need to know before buying an Amazon Echo speaker." Typically, when people want to buy devices such as the Amazon Echo speaker, they usually come online to read articles about the product. They also search for independent opinions on the product. Now, your job is to post a value-packed content about the product and include your affiliate link in strategic places within the article.

Write at least ten posts and upload on your blog and make sure you include your Amazon affiliate links in all of them. When writing such posts – your interest is to give the reader as much information as possible. You want to provide value and not necessarily promote a product. Even though your end goal is to promote a product, you should not make it obvious.

If you give the reader useful information, they would have no option than to click on the links within the article. And since Amazon affiliate links are sticky, even if the reader does not buy the exact product your promoted or they ended up buying another product within 24 hours from the time they clicked on your link, you will still earn a commission. So, when you are writing your blog posts, don't make them salesy – instead, provide value, and you will reap the results.

## YouTube

Apart from writing and posting review articles on your blog, you could open a YouTube channel for promoting your affiliate offers. Using YouTube is a free way to promote your offers and you get to reach millions of potential customers.

YouTube is currently the second largest search engine, only second to Google. Also, video content has been getting a lot of attention lately, and the reasons for that is not hard to guess – people are more likely to watch exciting videos than reading boring texts. As an affiliate marketer, one thing you need to learn is how to think fast and strategically.

Think about how you can key in and take advantage of videos to market your affiliate offers.

Just like using a blog to promote your affiliate offers, if you are using YouTube videos, you need to observe the rule of thirds. You need to make the videos both informative, educating, and entertaining. When you fuse these three essential elements into a video, then conversion happens naturally without you having to force it.

Depending on the type of product you want to promote, the type of video you create would differ greatly. Generally, review videos do well for a wide range of products. For instance, if you are promoting electronic gadgets, you could use review videos to attract attention to your offers.

If you are promoting a health supplement, you could pick one of the health challenges that the supplement helps to cure. Then proceed to talk about the causes of the health challenge, its symptoms, and treatments. Towards the end of the video, you could then introduce the supplement you are promoting.

Notice that in the above example involving a supplement, I did not advise you to solely base the video on the health benefits of the supplement. The reason for that is – you don't want your viewers to have the impression that you only made the video to promote a supplement. Even though your primary intention is to promote a supplement, you don't want to make it seem so obvious from the very beginning.

Remember, just like the other social media sites; people are on YouTube to catch fun. YouTube is essentially a website that people visit in the evening when they are back from work. When they get to the platform, they watch entertaining videos to cool off. So, if you want YouTube users to watch your videos, you must make them as entertaining as the many "prank" videos that they are already used to watching.

Furthermore, no matter the topic you want to address in a video, there are chances that many other videos have already addressed the same topic. In that case, how do you make the average YouTube user choose your own video instead of the thousands or even millions of other videos on the same topic? The answer is simple – add a distinguishing factor to the videos. This cannot be overemphasized – make your videos as entertaining to watch as possible. Also, you could consider fusing your personality into the videos or just anything to make your videos unique.

Additionally, you don't want to sound salesy in your videos – people do not come on YouTube to watch sales videos, and if you are depicting your video in a way that shows that it is marketing content, you would be chasing away viewers.

Importantly, don't assume that your viewers know what to do next after watching your videos. Even if they know, they still want you to tell them. So, if you want them to click on a link, subscribe to your YouTube channel, or anything else, let them know. Towards the end of your promo videos, you could include a call to action reminding the viewers that if they want to get the products you have talked about in the video, they should click on the provided links.

Apart from using calls-to-action creatively in the main body of the video, you must also include the affiliate links to the product or products you are promoting in the description of your YouTube video. However, when doing that, endeavor to let your viewers know that if they buy any of the products you have talked about through your affiliate link, you will get to earn a small commission at no extra cost to them.

Giving the above disclaimer is very important because a lot of your viewers could get angry or feel that you misled them. Some uninformed viewers could also think that by buying through your affiliate link, they would be charged more for the products.

It is your responsibility to let such uninformed prospective customers know how affiliate links work. You should educate them and let them know that they would not incur extra costs by buying through an affiliate link.

The same way you would not create a single promo blog post and go to bed, that's the same way you should not just create a single promo video and go to bed. You need to keep creating more videos for the number of products you are promoting. Yes, this takes time and effort, but the results can be amazing as well. Remember, affiliate marketing is a serious business, and just like any other business, you need to give it your full attention and resources for it to grow.

Besides YouTube, you could consider posting some of your shorter promo videos on platforms like Instagram. Just like YouTube, visual contents perform well on Instagram too. Lately, Instagram has been recording tremendous growth and only a few businesses are tapping into the vast opportunities that the platform presents. A lot of entrepreneurs are still battling it out on Facebook, leaving Instagram behind. Some only think about Instagram when they want to post vacation pictures.

However, Instagram has grown to become more than just a photo-sharing app. It has become the go-to marketing tool for savvy entrepreneurs. If you join the early stream of marketers who use Instagram to promote their business, you will gain significantly. Even though Instagram does not allow you to include links in the body of posts, you could still attach a link in your bio and ask viewers to check your bio for such links. Alternatively, you could consider using Instagram solely for list building. How that works is – you use Instagram posts to direct your audience on how to join your email list perhaps by downloading free content, lead magnet or tripwire.

**How to get content ideas for your promo materials**

One problem that many Amazon affiliate marketers often encounter especially beginners is that they find it hard to come up with the right content for their promo materials. The truth is that you cannot buy and use all the products you want to promote. You may not even buy half of them – so, how can you confidently describe a product you have not used nor touched? Remember, you are not allowed to copy other people's content, that is plagiarism and could land you in serious copyright-related issues.

Whether you are creating promo blog posts or video, you might find it hard coming up with the right content idea, but you can overcome that problem by doing something simple. Here are a few ideas.

If you want to get content ideas, your best bet is to visit the Amazon website, search for the product you intend to promote, look at five of the top reviews to understand what the previous customers are saying about the product. Usually, customer reviews are often honest and will highlight the benefits and shortfalls of a product. Now, your job is to take all that information and compile it into an easy to read article and post on your blog. You could also use the reviews to derive content for your videos.

No matter the type of content you are creating, make sure you include a lot of valuable information that would make the reader or viewer want to click the "read more" button. You want to make the content convincing enough so that it could drive traffic to your affiliate offers.

In this chapter, we have been talking about some of the ways of earning money as an Amazon affiliate marketer. All the ideas in this long chapter are practical – meaning that if you apply them, you are sure to get results.

Joining the Amazon affiliate marketing program is great for so many reasons – there are thousands of products to promote. What's more? The earning potential is enormous, and you get to make some money while you sleep.

# CHAPTER FOUR:
# AFFILIATE MARKETING MODELS
# THAT BRING RESULTS

Affiliate marketing, just like any other type of business requires that the person involved in it must give it their full attention, dedication, and resources for it to grow and thrive. Unfortunately, many people who want to make money with affiliate marketing have the wrong mindset about affiliate marketing.

In every field of endeavor, mindset is what differentiates those who make it big, and those who just tag along. If you have the mindset that affiliate marketing is a side hustle that you go into when you lose your job, then you may never make a reasonable income from the business. If you have the mindset that affiliate marketing is the type of business you go into in order to raise quick cash to pay your house rent, then the business might not be for you.

The major reason why so many people have developed a wrong mindset about affiliate and other types of online businesses is due to the activities of the so-called gurus. For the most part, most online business gurus do not practice what they claim to teach. They are only interested in selling you something, and how do they get to convince you to buy what they are selling if not by way of tricks.

First, the guru must simplify the business and make it seem as if you would start making money the moment you start the business. The guru also makes it seem as if you don't need any form of commitment, either monetary or otherwise to make it in an online business. All those are false teachings that make many people rush into online businesses without proper planning and get their hands burnt badly.

What is the right mindset that someone who wants to make it big in any online business, including affiliate marketing should have? The answer is simple – you need to have the mindset that this is just like any other business. You need to see affiliate marketing like a real business that it is. The moment you don't see it as a quick cash spinner or something you fall back on when you lose your job, then you are halfway into succeeding as an affiliate marketer.

Apart from having the right mindset about online businesses as a whole, another thing you need to succeed as an affiliate is to adopt the right approach. Many times, people tend to focus on the wrong things when it comes to affiliate marketing – some people believe that finding the right niche is the ultimate key to success in affiliate marketing. A lot of others believe that finding the right product to promote or having a huge audience is the key.

However, it would be shocking for you to find out that while those factors mentioned above could contribute to your success as an affiliate marketer, there is more to affiliate marketing than just those mentioned factors. Unofficial statistics have it that only a small 10% of affiliate marketers make the bulk of the money in affiliate marketing while the other 90% just tag along.

Have you ever paused and pondered why a whopping 90% of affiliate marketers just make enough to pay for their internet connectivity? Have you ever wondered why more than 90% of affiliate marketers do not get to renew their domain name after the first year as affiliate marketers? The obvious answer is – they are doing something wrong. And what's that thing they are doing wrong?

Could it be that they don't know how to find the right products to promote? Could it be that they don't know the right niches to go into? Could it be that they don't employ the right marketing strategies? Yes, all these could contribute to making someone fail as an affiliate marketer, but one of the greatest reasons why people fail in affiliate marketing is that they run what I have chosen to call the "hit n run" affiliate marketing model.

It doesn't matter the type of product you are promoting or the type of affiliate marketing program you have joined; if you run the "hit n run" affiliate marketing model, then you may find it hard to remain in the industry for a long time. Unfortunately, 90% of both new and old affiliate marketers run this model, and that explains why many of them fail.

# Hit n run affiliate marketing

What is the "hit n run" affiliate marketing model?

Let me use a hit and run driver to explain the concept of hit and run affiliate marketing. A hit and run driver, for instance, is one who gets involved in an accident and zooms off without giving appropriate assistance to the victim or reporting to the authorities. Notice that the hit and run driver is always ready to zoom off without looking back – they might go on to hit or even kill other people before they are finally caught.

Now, bringing it to affiliate marketing, a hit and run affiliate marketer is not in any way different from a hit and run driver. The affiliate marketer that runs this model goes about looking for hot selling products to promote. Additionally, they are often very obsessed with the bestselling niches – which is not a bad idea entirely. The problem with the hit and run affiliate marketer is that they are ready to dump one niche and jump into another if there is a slight drop in sales.

At every point in time, the hit and run affiliate marketer is always looking for a "hot-selling" product to market. When they find such a product, they market it, earn some commission from it. And before long, other hit and run affiliate marketers would start promoting the same "hot-selling" product, causing the market to become saturated. At that point, the hit and run affiliate marketer would go looking for another product to promote.

The hit and run affiliate is always in a loop – they are always running around looking for a product to promote. Once a product stops bringing in money, they start looking for the next one – and the cycle continues. The hit and run affiliate marketer does not have a "business." What they have is a "hustle." I would like to say that there is a huge difference between a "business" and a "hustle." A business is something that you have built over time; you have given it your time, attention, and resources so that it can, in turn, help you make some gains later.

However, a "hustle" is something people go into to meet their immediate primordial needs. Many hustlers are driven by hunger – they just want to grab as much as they could to satisfy their immediate hunger. They are not ready or patient enough to build a business. Almost all hit and run affiliate marketers are hustlers. They may get to make a few bucks from promoting a few "hot-selling" products here and there, but they always eventually run out of business sooner than later.

Here is the typical cycle that a hit and run affiliate marketer goes through:

1. The affiliate marketer finds a so-called "bestselling" product
2. They send traffic to the product
3. They earn a commission for sales recorded
4. The company running the affiliate program acquires the client and continues to market their other products to the client.
5. The affiliate marketer goes to scout for more clients. Then the cycle continues.

Notice that at no time does the client belong to the affiliate marketer – because they are running the hit and run model. A better and advanced affiliate marketing model which I shall talk about in a later section of this guide will show you how you can acquire your own clients or grow your own huge customer base as an affiliate marketer.

As a hit and run affiliate marketer, you might be tempted to think that you are making money – but in the real sense, you are just a hustler. If you do not have your own customer base, which is what happens to you as a hit and run marketer, then you obviously have no business.

Here are some of the other reasons why hit and run affiliate marketing is the worst affiliate marketing model;

**1. If the company that has the affiliate program withdraws its affiliate program today, you will stop making money**

As a hit and run affiliate marketer who obviously does not have their own customer base, you are at the mercy of the company running the affiliate program. In fact, as a hit and run marketer, your business is like owning a Facebook account – the owners of Facebook could wake up one morning and decide to delete your Facebook account. And if that happens, what next?

The truth remains that if your business could be deleted by the click of a mouse, then you really do not have a business. While it is true that there is no business that is entirely immune from external influences, you can work hard to make sure that the major control of your business lies in your hands. Hit and run affiliate marketing does not offer you the opportunity to be the owner of your "business" as the company that has the affiliate program could withdraw it any day.

Many companies withdraw their affiliate programs for so many reasons – when this happens, the people that are usually badly affected are the hit and run marketers. For the other group of affiliate marketers who have learned the art of building a business, they just do not bother because they may already have different other programs that they are promoting to their audience.

## 2. The customer does not belong to you

This is one of the greatest disadvantages of a hit and run affiliate marketing – I have highlighted this before; however, it can never be overemphasized. As a hit and run affiliate marketer, your customers do not belong to you – basically, you don't have a business. You are only but a middleman who could be discarded at any given time.

You might be fooled to think that you are making money, but the company that has the affiliate program is the winner in the long run. Each time you direct a customer to an affiliate product, the customer could decide to buy or not. If the customer buys, the company retains the customer's email or other contact information while you are left with a commission.

You go on to look for more customers to patronize the company's products. The company, on the other hand send marketing messages about their products or services to the customers since they got their emails earlier. In all these cases, you see that the company gained more while you, the affiliate marketer earned a one-off commission.

Instead of adopting the hit and run affiliate marketing model, you could kill two birds with one stone – that is – you could acquire your own customers even as an affiliate marketer while earning affiliate commissions at the same time. That is the best type of affiliate marketing model, and we shall talk about it later.

### 3. The advertiser may lower payout

In many cases, advertisers or companies running affiliate programs could decide to lower payouts, and this happens often. When that happens, your earnings drop as a hit and run affiliate marketer. Remember, the advertiser or affiliate marketing network are the ones controlling their business, so they could do as they wish, and you have no opinion whatsoever.

Often, advertisers would advertise a mouthwatering initial payout in a bid to attract desperate affiliates. Once the company or advertiser has attracted affiliates who might have started laboring to acquire customers for the company, the advertiser or company turns around and reduces payouts.

Numerous advertisers do this almost all the time and for reasons that they don't often want to disclose. Just imagine that you have spent money directing traffic to an affiliate offer and then the company turns around and reduces payouts for the product, what happens to you? Obviously, you will lose money because you had a certain payout amount in mind when you were projecting the amount of money you would spend on traffic. This is one of the many disadvantages of being a hit and run affiliate marketer.

## 4. Advertising costs may go up, thus reducing your profits

Affiliate marketers have several ways of advertising their affiliate offers – some use blogs, YouTube, and social media. So many others, especially the hit and run marketers, adopt PPC (pay per click) advertising methods. The other organic means (blogs, YouTube, social media, etc.) of driving traffic to an affiliate offer take time to bring results. And since the hit and run affiliate doesn't want to waste time, they just opt for PPC ads.

One problem with this approach is that the costs of PPC ads are not stable. You could pay $5 today for some clicks and be mandated to pay $7 tomorrow for the same number of clicks. If you continue to pay more money to advertise your affiliate offers, it simply means you will be reducing your profits as well.

Most PPC ads work with keywords – if a keyword starts becoming a bit competitive, the cost of advertising for that keyword will go up. Usually, when many affiliate marketers start chasing one perceived "hot-selling" product, they tend to drive up competition for that product and increase the CPC for the keywords related to the product. It is a simple case of demand and supply – when demand is high and supply is low, the price will go higher.

## 5. You will always be on the lookout for hot selling products

This is yet another problem with the hit and run affiliate marketing model – it is structured in such a way that if you must continue earning money, you will always be on the lookout for hot selling products to promote. Such hot selling products are often like bubbles; they grow in one minute and burst the next minute.

Additionally, any day you stop scouting for products to promote, you will stop earning money. Any business that stops making you money abruptly once you are no longer actively promoting it is not the type of business you want to do. If your business cannot make you money while you sleep, then you should be ready to work until the day you die.

We have analyzed some of the features of the hit and run affiliate marketing model and what makes it undesirable. In the next subsection, we shall be looking at what I have chosen to call the "working" affiliate marketing model. The major difference between the working model and the hit and run model is that in the case of the former, your customers belong to you while in the latter, you don't have any customer base.

## The "working" affiliate marketing model

In business, it is often said that repeat customers or returning customers are the lifeblood of any business. The reason is – if someone has paid for a product you are promoting before, there is a high chance that the person will pay for another of your products or even a similar product later. Also, it is way easier to get an old customer to patronize you than to convince an entirely new person. This is not to mention that the cost of retaining an existing customer is way cheaper than the cost of acquiring a new one.

What the "working" affiliate marketing model does is that unlike the hit and run model, it places the customer in your hands. Yes, you are still doing affiliate marketing, but the customer does not belong to the company running the affiliate program alone. With the working model, you are not just laboring for a vendor or a company that could choose to stop their affiliate program anytime. Since you have your own customer base, if a company decides to stop their program or reduce payouts, you could market as many other products/services as possible to the customer base that you have built.

Running a working affiliate marketing model is not rocket science; you simply need to build an email list. In the internet marketing space, it is often said that money is in the list. The reason is that your email list subscribers are like your loyal audience. For someone to have found it necessary to subscribe to your email list, it means that you have something important that the subscriber needs.

Now, if you promote a product to this your loyal audience, the chances of them patronizing what you promote would be so high. This is not to mention that you would record huge sales at a reduced cost. Email marketing costs far less than other online marketing methods. And with your email list, you can leverage email marketing to get across to a wide range of audiences.

## How the "working" model works.0

Remember, as an affiliate marketer, your principal job is to send traffic to an affiliate product that has been developed already by a company. Typically, what most affiliate marketers do is that they just send huge traffic to a product directly. Then the company that has the product would acquire those clients and turn them into their own. The affiliate marketer would then continue scouting for more clients to send to the company or vendor.

The affiliate marketer only stands to gain once – because they are only paid a commission for each sale that was made through their efforts. However, the company that has the affiliate program gains even more because they would just pay off an affiliate marketer for each client brought in and then continue to market other products and services to the acquired client. The affiliate marketer would not earn any commission for those other products that the company markets directly to the acquired customer, even though it was the affiliate market that brought them.

Now, with the working model, what you do is that you use an email system or autoresponder to collect the email or contact information of the customer before you direct them to the product or service you are promoting.

For instance, if you are promoting a weight loss supplement and you have created a video on YouTube for this purpose. Instead of attaching a direct link to the weight loss supplement in your YouTube video, you will instead attach a link to a landing page. When the prospective customer gets to your landing page, they will have to submit their email. Next, you will send a couple of emails to warm them up or convert them from cold leads to warm buyers.

Once you are convinced that the prospects are ready to buy, you could then proceed to direct them to where they could get the product you marketed or promoted to them earlier. Since you now have the contact or email of the customer, you could simply market other related products to them later.

And even if one company decides to stop their affiliate program, you can find thousands of other affiliates offers within the same niche that you could market to your subscribers. In addition to affiliate products, you could obtain the resale rights of a great product and market it directly to your subscribers and keep all the money to yourself.

The "working" affiliate marketing model is far better than the "hit and run" model for several reasons. With the hit and run model, you don't own "your customers." Once you have sent traffic to a product and gotten paid, your contract ends, and you start scouting for more customers to direct to the product's page.

However, with the working model, the customers belong to you as well as the company running the affiliate program. In addition to affiliate products or offers, you could decide to market other digital or physical products to your subscribers.

The only downside that could be attributed to the working model is that perfecting it takes some time. The patience to perfect a working system is what many affiliate marketers lack; hence, they choose to flow with the hit and run model. The hit and run model does not involve much effort; you just need to find a product, run a PPC campaign for the product, send traffic directly to the product, and earn a commission. Whereas with the working model, you would need to take some time to nurture your prospects with a series of email swipes before sending them to a product – and that takes some time.

The major difference between those who make it big in affiliate marketing and those who don't is the type of model they adopt for their business. All the affiliate marketers who make a lot of money from their business run with the "working" model. It places them in control – it gives them the chance to build a proper business they could be proud of. While 90% of affiliate marketers who do not get to make as much money often run the hit and run model.

## Steps to create a working affiliate marketing system

Here are the different steps you need to follow to create an affiliate marketing system that works:

1. Take your time to find the right niche and choose products in the niche to promote. You must stick with one niche if you are running with the working model because your customers or email subscribers would want to know you for one thing. You don't want to promote guitar pedals, for instance, to your audience today and then promote weight loss supplements to them the following day.

If you do that, they would see you as someone who is not serious. In this online business game, reputation matters a lot, and it is essential for you to be recognized as an authority in a particular niche than a jack of all trades who is a master of none. Just find a particular niche and stick with it – within that one niche, you can find thousands of products to promote.

2. Create a value message and offer to your prospective customers – in our present world where there are thousands of vendors chasing after a few leads or prospects, no lead would hand over their email to you on a first name and handshake basis – you have to give them an ethical bribe.

The ethical bribe, lead magnet, or tripwire could be an eBook or any other value message. With the lead magnet, you get to lure your prospective customers into giving you their email. With their email plugged right into your autoresponder, you send them a series of email messages to warm them up before you direct them to the affiliate product you are promoting.

3. Create a landing page using any of the landing page building tools. Some of the common landing page building tools include autoresponders like ClickFunnels, MailChimp, Aweber, etc. A landing page is a one-page webpage that is used to collect the emails of prospects. It is called a landing page because it contains some instructions and forms which would be filled by a prospect or lead.

4. Send traffic to the landing page and capture emails of prospects. How do you generate traffic? Create a post on your blog, social media page, or YouTube page. Ask your readers to download for free the tripwire or lead magnet you created earlier, then give them a link to your landing page. When they get to the landing page, the instructions on the page will mandate them to enter their email to be allowed access to the lead magnet.

5. Once you have their email in your autoresponder, send the prospects a series of emails explaining the product you are promoting. Remember to use a combination of social proof, countdown timer (which serves to create a sense of urgency) to make the buyer want to buy the paid product or service you are promoting.

After you have nurtured your leads for a considerable amount of time, then direct them to an affiliate product you want them to buy.

Notice that the above model empowers the affiliate marketer to think and run their business like a real business. If you succeed in acquiring a lot of subscribers, then it means you could always promote different products in your niche to them. Even if your subscribers fail to buy one particular product, there are higher chances that they could decide to buy the next ones you would want to promote.

Additionally, the series of email swipes you send to your subscribers will help you to build a relationship with them. If you decide to launch your own products in the future, you could count on them to patronize you since you already have a cordial relationship with them. Your relationship with them could linger on for many years.

In this chapter, we have looked at some of the different affiliate marketing models and the steps to take to create a working model. In subsequent chapters, I shall do an in-depth explanation of each of the above-mentioned steps.

# CHAPTER FIVE:
# HIGH TICKET VS. LOW TICKET OFFERS

In affiliate marketing, you could promote high ticket offers, low ticket offers, or both. The choice of the type of offers or products you want to promote lies solely on you and your goals. A high ticket offer or product is simply one that costs more – consequently, the affiliate commission for selling such offers is often high. Low ticket offers, on the other hand, are those that cost less; hence, the affiliate commission you earn for selling them may be low as well.

For some high ticket offers, you could earn upwards of 80% of the cost of the product. So, depending on the cost of the product, you could earn as high as $1,000 for just promoting and selling one single product. Even if the affiliate commission for a high ticket offer is just 7% or 10%, you will stand a chance of earning high for selling the product.

For instance, if a product costs $1,000 and affiliates are paid up to 10% commission for selling the product, it then means that you stand a chance of earning up to $100 for selling just a single unit of the product. Now, multiply that by as many products as you are able to sell.

Most low ticket offers offer low payouts – typically the commission is usually hovering around 5% to 7%. For such low rates, you will have to sell as many products as possible in order to break even.

Now, one common question that most beginner affiliate marketers normally ask is, "what should I aim for between high ticket offers and low ticket offers?" There is no straightforward answer to that question as each of them has its peculiarities. We can also say that it depends on your goals and your marketing prowess.

For example, if you want to earn $100 in one day, which of the approaches below would you adopt?

Approach 1: Sell ten items to 10 people at $10 each

Approach 2: Sell four items to 4 people at $25 each

Typically, you would want to adopt the second approach because it makes your job easier. If you have the right strategies, it would be quite easier for you to convince four people to pay you $25 each for a product than it would be for you to get ten different people to pay you $10 each for the same product.

The final verdict is – it really depends on you – your goals, strategies, traffic sources, and the type of audience you want to target. With advancements in advertising systems, you can now target the right audiences as long as you know how to create a good ad campaign and a high converting sales funnel.

If you are going to use paid advertising methods to promote your affiliate offers, then high ticket products or offers are just the best bets for you. You don't want to spend a lot of money to promote a lot of products with low payouts instead of promoting a single one that could give you a higher payout.

Additionally, if you are using free traffic sources, then you could consider promoting several low ticket offers. You can also promote high ticket offers even if you use free traffic sources like blogs, YouTube, social media, etc.

# Traffic sources for affiliate products

If you have the best or the most hot-selling affiliate product and you don't have a way of sending traffic to it, then your case is just like that of the person who doesn't have access to or know best selling products. This is to say that traffic is the lifeblood of affiliate marketing. Without traffic, no one is going to see the offers you are promoting.

Typically, there are two traffic sources – free traffic and paid traffic. Free traffic is often referred to as organic traffic while paid traffic is often referred to as inorganic traffic. In this section, we shall examine these two traffic sources and show you how to choose the best one for your business.

Just as the name implies, free traffic sources allow you to generate and send human traffic to a website, landing page or blog for free. It needs your commitment, time, and dedication – although all these could be equated to money, you are not paying cash directly for the traffic.

Popular free traffic sources include traffic gotten from social media pages, guest posting or blogging, YouTube channel, search engine results. Getting consistent traffic from free sources takes a lot of time and commitment. So, if you want to fast track your results, then you could consider paid traffic sources.

Paid traffic sources are those that charge you money to send human traffic to your affiliate offers, website, landing page, etc. Paid traffic can come from display ads, Facebook ads, Google ads, and a host of other forms of online advertising methods. Typically, most paid traffic systems use a PPC (Pay per Click) model to charge you for the traffic they send to your affiliate offer or landing page.

How the PPC model works is – you only pay when people have clicked on your ads. For instance, if you place an ad on Google and state your budget, Google is not going to charge you money unless people have clicked on your ads. This way, you are only paying money for the clicks received.

Now, most affiliate marketers make use of a combination of paid and free sources to drive traffic to their offers. No one traffic source is better than the other – it all depends on your goals, the types of products you want to promote, and your overall strategy.

That being said, before you choose the right traffic source, you need to make sure you have developed what is called a buyer persona.

## **Buyer persona**

A buyer persona is simply a conceptual representation of your ideal customer. In other words, your buyer persona captures a mental image of who you think would be your ideal customer. In identifying your buyer persona, things you have to put into proper consideration include: what is a typical day in the life of this person like? What do they do when they wake up? Where do they hang out? Where do they get their essential needs? Where do they go to seek a solution?

You must identify your ideal customer before you go ahead to start sending traffic to your affiliate offers, especially if you are using paid traffic. Knowing your ideal customer will help you to know where and how to locate them. This way, when you are setting up ad campaigns, you would know how to set realistic metrics. Additionally, with a well-defined buyer persona, you will be able to choose complementary products that will be of help to your customers.

To capture or identify your buyer persona, here are a few essential questions you should ask yourself:

1. What is their demographic – what is the ideal age groupthat would need this product? Are they female or male? Do they have a family? Are they single? What is their average household income? Having answers to these questions will help you to fine-tune your research so that you could develop the right marketing campaigns that will get your audience to buy whatever it is you want to sell to them.

For instance, if you want to promote an affiliate product that teaches people how to make money online – typically, your ideal customer would include younger people from the age of 18 and up to 45 because they are the ones who understand the concept of online income. Your buyer persona would also consist of men and women. With all these pieces of information, you could go on your drawing table and craft out the best marketing strategy and traffic sources for the product you want to promote.

2. What does a typical day in the life of your ideal customer like? Normally, if you have studied the product you want to promote properly, you will be able to understand a few things about your ideal buyer. If you want to promote an inversion therapy table, for instance, then your typical buyer should be older people who have back pain issues. Typically, most of them do not go out much; some are retired and may prefer Facebook to Instagram. With that information, you could choose Facebook advertising over other forms of online advertising.

Furthermore, you would want to find out the kind of jobs that your ideal customers have. Do they have a typical 9-5 job? What activities do they engage in before leaving home for work? What activities do they engage in when they get back from work? What type of TV shows do they watch? How much time do they spend in their car? Answering these questions will help you to determine who your ideal customer is so you can craft your marketing message to suit them.

3. What is the pain point of my ideal customer? This is arguably one of the most important questions you need to ask yourself when creating a buyer persona. Most customers will not buy the product you are marketing unless you prove that you understand their pain points. Normally, if you describe the problems of a person, they often get convinced that you could solve it.

If you don't understand the struggles that someone goes through, you will not be able to describe their problems succinctly to the point of convincing them to trust you. So, when you are developing a buyer persona, part of the questions you should ask yourself is, "what are the pain points of my ideal customer."

4. What are the goals of my ideal customer? Different customers have different goals, and you need to capture all of that so you can develop a perfect buyer persona. What does my ideal customer want to achieve? Do they want to lose weight, for instance? Do they want to maintain their weight? The primary reason why you need to ask this question is that you will need to incorporate your answer in your marketing messages to convince your potential customer.

5. Where do they go for information? Knowing where your ideal customer goes to for information will help you to know your best traffic source. Typically, the first port of call for most information or solution seekers is Google. This means that if you prioritize SEO (Search Engine Optimization) or Google PPC ads as your preferred traffic source, you will be getting a lot of traffic. Again, this depends on the type of product or service you are promoting.

Example: Let's assume that you want to promote weight loss supplements as an affiliate marketer. How do you define the best buyer persona for this product?

To solve the above exercise, we shall attempt to answer the five critical questions that are used to develop a perfect buyer persona.

Question 1: What is the demographic of your ideal customer? Normally, men and women alike tend to be bothered about their weight. However, women are always the ones most concerned about weight-related issues. So, if you are trying to promote weight loss supplements, women should be your ideal gender.

Furthermore, the age of your ideal customer should be between 18 and 60 years because that's the age gap that tends to worry about their weight the most.

Question 2: What does a typical day in the life of someone that needs a weight loss supplement look like? Normally, such a person starts their day by engaging in a few exercises. Some of them skip meals, especially breakfast, and they also go on different types of weight-loss diets. Some of them may have a typical 9-5 job and they mostly live sedentary lifestyles. They usually stay home in the evening, so if you are targeting your ads, you should consider setting it up such that it shows mostly in the evening hours.

Question 3: What is the pain point of the customer? For someone looking to lose weight, their major pain points include the stigma they face daily in a world where being overweight is synonymous with an abominable offense. Another pain point they could have is the issue of dealing with health challenges that are associated with being overweight.

Remember, this is just an example, and the pain points we have mentioned here are only for educational purposes. So, if you are trying to develop a buyer persona, you need to dig deeper and identify real issues that the buyer might be having

Question 4: What are the goals of my customers? Normally, the goal of someone trying to lose weight is to live a healthier life and perhaps get the chance to finally showcase that their perfect "beach body." So, you should include all of that when crafting your marketing message.

Question 5: Where do they go for information? People who might need weight loss supplements are those who are struggling with their weight. Typically, such people often seek information from those who have managed to put their weight in check. It is not uncommon for such an ideal customer to seek information or rather validation from Instagram, YouTube, or any of the other social media platforms. Sometimes, they might also resort to Google.

Now, with the above information, you can come up with a great buyer persona such that when you are crafting or creating your marketing messages, you will not have to do anything blindly, instead, you will be working with facts.

For the type of buyer that we have described in the above example, the best traffic sources for such buyers will include Facebook, YouTube, Google, and Instagram in no particular order.

# CHAPTER SIX:
# SALES FUNNEL

In the previous sections of this guide, we have talked about some of the traffic sources for affiliate products. Recall that we mentioned that traffic is the lifeblood of affiliate marketing. If you have the best affiliate products and no one gets to see them or know about them, then you are not in any way better than the affiliate marketer who does not know or have access to hot selling products.

Some of the most popular traffic sources for affiliate products include YouTube, blogs, Instagram, Facebook pages, etc. Others include paid options such as Google ads, Facebook ads, and other types of online or display ads.

Normally, free traffic sources take time before they start yielding fruits. For instance, if you create a blog for your affiliate products, it will take some time for the blog to be indexed on Google and the other search engines. If the blog is not indexed, you will not get enough traffic or audience. With little or no audience, no one would click on your affiliate links.

Additionally, other types of free traffic options rely basically on blind guessing – for instance, when you post something about an affiliate product on YouTube, you have no guarantee that only the people who need the product would watch your video. You would make the video available to a wide audience who might decide to buy what you sell or not. To convert a viewer to a customer using something like YouTube videos will take a lot of effort and persuasion on your part.

Paid traffic options, on the other hand, are preferred for several obvious reasons. They give you the chance to have a fair control over your business as an affiliate marketer. With traffic options like Facebook ads and Google ads, you have the chance to target only those potential customers who might be highly interested in what you sell. You are not blind-guessing; rather, you are using advanced targeting options to make ensure that only those who need your affiliate products get to see them.

While free traffic sources are good for low ticket offers, paid traffic sources are best suited for high ticket offers. The reason is – you don't want to spend money advertising a product where your commission can be as low as $5 or $10 per sale. When you subtract advertising costs from your profit, you will see that your margins are too low.

Meanwhile, for high ticket offers, when you deduct your advertising costs, you will still have a lot of money in your pocket. Most high ticket offers pay you up to $100 and even as much as $1,000. So, if you used a small amount like $5 to get the customer that purchased the product, at the end of the day, you are still left with a lot of money.

When you are using a paid traffic source, make sure you don't make the mistake of sending traffic to a vendor's offer page directly. If you do that, then you are simply a hit and run affiliate marketer. Many things could go wrong when you send traffic directly to the offer page of a product.

What if the person you sent to the affiliate product decides not to buy at that moment? What if they decide not to buy at all? It simply means that you have wasted the money you used in creating the advertisement that attracted the potential customer. This is why you should build what's called a sales funnel.

## **What is a sales funnel?**

To understand what a sales funnel is, let's use a physical funnel to demonstrate it. A funnel is a plastic or metal object that has two open ends – a wider upper end and a narrower bottom end. Funnels are normally used to channel fluid into containers that have smaller openings. Typically, the funnel's smaller bottom end is inserted into the container that needs to be filled with fluid. The fluid is then poured into the bigger upper end of the funnel.

The major aim of using a funnel to channel fluid into a container that has a small opening is to avoid leakage or wastage. If you attempt to pour a liquid into a container that has a small opening without a funnel, you might end up spilling the entire liquid or half of it on the ground. Another characteristic thing about funnels is that a huge amount of liquid goes in through the upper part and trickles out into a receiving container through the smaller end of the funnel.

Now, when it comes to sales and marketing, funnels are used to perform a similar function. Their main function in marketing is to guide a large audience of potential buyers through what is called a customer journey until they are ready to buy. Just like the physical funnel, a huge audience will go into a sales funnel, but only those who are interested in a product will make it through the narrow lower end.

So a sales funnel is used to channel potential customers through the buying process until they are ready to become actual or paying customers. When buyers are passed through a sales funnel, they are nurtured, and those who are not really interested in the product in question will be placed in a different segment. Those who are interested in the product will be segmented differently and then shown how they could proceed to buy the product.

In affiliate marketing (using the working affiliate marketing model) and online business space as a whole, sales funnels play a huge and important role. It is used to guide the buyer through the entire buying process until they are finally ready to buy.

One of the reasons why a sales funnel is important is that today's average customer does not buy a product the very first time they hear or know about it. Usually, the customer goes through what is known as a customer journey during which they have to consider ways of paying for the product.

Typically, if you want today's average customer to buy from you, you need to keep in touch with them as they go through the customer journey. And the only way through which you might keep in touch with them is through sending emails – email marketing is an integral part of the sales funnel process.

Another reason why a funnel is important is that it helps you to build a good relationship with your audience. If you have a good relationship with your potential customers, they would often want to buy from you. Yes, this happens because the average customer purchases products based on emotions and justifiable logistics and evidence.

Have you ever noticed that friends often tend to patronize each other? The reason is that people attach emotions to the buying process. When you nurture a relationship with your audience to the point that they begin to see you as a friend – if you market or promote a product to them, they would be glad to buy from you.

Additionally, no matter the type of product or service you want to sell or promote, there are already thousands of other people selling the same product or service. The big question then becomes, how do you convince your potential customer to abandon the other options before them and patronize you? To convince them, you would need to build a relationship with them, and having a sales funnel will help to do that.

**Parts of a sales funnel**

A typical sales funnel has three essential parts – these three parts could then be developed into several subsections, depending on the individual, their target audience, and the type of product that is being promoted.

Part 1: Attract
Part 2: Delight
Part 3: Interest
Part 4: Action


**Part 1: Attract**

As mentioned earlier, a typical customer passes through several paths before they finally decide to buy a product, especially if the product is a high ticket offer. Now, if you want to walk your ideal client through the various steps they need to go through before buying your product. The first part or step is to attract them to whatever it is you want to sell.

This first part is where you run ad campaigns or create a blog post to draw the attention of the potential buyer to your affiliate offer or product. For instance, if you are promoting a back pain management product, and you have created a perfect buyer persona, the things you could do in this first step of your sales funnel creation include the following:

- Create an ad campaign on Facebook. The title of the campaign could go like this, "discover how a 55-year-old factory worker is managing his back pain." The aim of the campaign is to draw the attention of your ideal potential buyer to click on the "read more" button. When they click on the read more button, then they are taken to the next part of the funnel.

- If you want to use free traffic, you could create a blog post on your blog that talks about some of the benefits of the product you want to promote. Then ask readers to click a link that would give them more information.

When they click on the link, they are then taken to the next stage of the funnel.

- You could also consider creating a post on social media to draw attention to the product you want to promote.

Basically, this first part of the sales funnel is mostly concerned with piquing the interest of the potential buyer. Things you do in this first part are majorly centered on the creation of ads on social media, creation of posts on blogs, or other traffic methods.

You want to gain the attention of potential customers, so you could give them more information about your product.

Typically, when you have drawn the attention of the potential buyer, you need to convince them to get to the second stage of the process. To do that, you need to provide them with something of value in exchange for their email. Lead magnets or tripwires are normally used at this stage to lure the potential customer to leave their email with you.

Remember, the ad post you created on Facebook, Google, etc. will have a link to your landing page. It is on the landing page that you will collect the email of those who want to download your free lead magnet.

A landing page is simply a one-page webpage that is used to collect email of prospects. The emails collected using a landing page is then added to your email list. You can create a landing page using various autoresponders like MailChimp, Aweber, ClickFunnels, etc.

When the potential customer provides you with their email address, you send them their copy of the lead magnet. In the concluding part of the lead magnet, let your readers do another opt-in. Those who want to know more about what you have talked about in the lead magnet should contact you while those that are not interested should not bother. Some will opt-in a second time while others will not. You should pass those who opted in a second time through the second part of your funnel.

**Part 2: Delight**

At this stage, the potential buyer has provided you with their email; they have downloaded their copy of the lead magnet that you are giving away. They have probably read the lead magnet and are waiting to hear back from you on what they are to do next.

If the lead magnet you gave them for free earlier was really insightful and full of valuable information then this second stage of the sales funnel should not be hard for you. It is at this stage that you begin to send the potential customer a series of emails. The emails are meant to help warm up the buyer and introduce the product you want to promote to them.

For instance, if you are promoting a weight loss product, you could educate your subscribers or prospects on some of the reasons why they have not achieved success with their other weight loss efforts. Ideally, if you know about three reasons why people fail to lose weight, you could divide them into three different emails and send them individually to your prospects.

With these emails, you are gradually nurturing a relationship with your audience. It has been observed by avid internet marketers that you need to send at least seven warm-up messages to your prospects before they are ready to buy whatever you are selling or promoting. It is important that at this second stage, you should not introduce the product you are selling or promoting yet.

The bulk of what you should do at this stage is education – you have to educate your prospects – let them see you as an authority in your niche. If they do not see you as an authority in your niche, then every other thing you say to them will most likely fall on deaf ears. At this stage, you need to send three to four emails to your prospects – all the emails should be educating them generally.

## Part 3: Interest

This part is where you begin to pique the interest of the prospect in whatever it is you are selling or promoting. At this point, you might have sent them a few emails meant to nurture them. You are going to gradually start introducing your prospects to the product you want to promote – all these you have to do with emails.

The first email you should send in this series should introduce the new product you are promoting. Then subsequent emails should talk about the major selling points of the product and why it is better than whatever the prospect is already used to. Remember, the potential customer is not just going to take your words for it; they need you to show them proof that the product works.

To prove the efficacy of the product, you need to show your prospects some testimonials which would serve as social proof. How do you get testimonials since you have probably never used the product yourself? It is simple – head on to the product's page on the vendor's website.

You will find reviews or testimonials left on the product by previous users. Screenshot some of the glowing reviews and include them in your emails. Make sure you throw in as many such testimonials as possible in your emails – it helps to build up your credibility and that of the product you are selling or promoting.

The next thing you want to do at this stage is to create a sense of urgency in the prospect – you can do that by telling them that they have a limited time to get the product at a discounted price. You could come up with other strategies to drive the prospect into believing that the product is scarce and that if they don't get it from you, they would be missing out forever.

**Part 4: Action**

What you do in stage two and three of the sales funnel process is called nurturing prospects or warming up of prospects. You are basically preparing them to be ready for the product you want to introduce to them. If you are good at what you do, before you are even done with stage 3, most of your prospects would already be asking you to introduce them to the product you want to sell.

Additionally, if you do the necessary things you need to do in stage two and three correctly, you will succeed in building a strong relationship with your audience such that they see you as a worthy friend who also is an authority in a particular niche. Remember, when people see you as a friend, it is easier for them to bring out their card and pay for anything you are selling.

The last part of your sales funnel should be where you show your prospects how to get the product you have been pitching to them all along. It is as simple as sending an email to prospects with an affiliate link to the product you have been promoting. As mentioned earlier, if you have done a good job in both part two and part three, then you should have no problem with this last phase of the funnel.

Note: a funnel may have many parts, and some of the parts mentioned above could be compressed into just two parts. It all depends on you, your audience, and the product you are promoting. Using a sales funnel to market a product is actually an art on its own and you need to dedicate time to learn it.

Some of the things you would want to learn as it regards creating a functional sales funnel include the following:

- How to use emotional triggers to get potential customers to subscribe to your email list.
- How to send the right types of emails to subscribers and convert them from cold leads into warm buyers.
- How to create a high converting lead magnet, tripwire and landing page.

- How to segment your email list and make sure that you only send emails to the right audience.
- How to position yourself as an authority in your niche.

This book has only given you some of the fundamentals – so if you desire to be an expert in sales funnel creation, you need to dig deeper. There are some books on that topic which you could find helpful.

# CHAPTER SEVEN:
# AFFILIATE PROGRAMS

In the previous section, you were introduced to some affiliate networks where you could join and find a list of products to promote. In this section, we are going to talk about different affiliate programs you could join and make money.

Earlier, we mentioned that some of the software tools or services you would need as an affiliate marketer or an internet marketer. Many internet marketers have their own affiliate programs. You could join these programs and make money.

Here is a list of a few affiliate programs you could join:

**1. ClickFunnels affiliate program**

ClickFunnels is a powerful autoresponder or a software tool used for the creation and management of landing pages. The tool also allows you to send automated emails and carry out other forms of email marketing functions.

As an affiliate marketer or internet marketer who takes their business seriously, you are likely going to use ClickFunnels or any of the other autoresponders when creating your sales funnel. One thing that makes ClickFunnels stand out is that it is easy to use.

Its "drag and drop" feature allows you to create landing pages within minutes. Even someone who does not know how to click a mouse on the computer can make use of ClickFunnels.

ClickFunnels has an affiliate program that makes it possible for you to also earn money while using the tool.

**How does the ClickFunnels affiliate program work?**

- You earn 40% recurring commission when you introduce people to ClickFunnels subscription-based products such as Funnel U and ClickFunnels. This means that every time someone you introduced to the software renews their subscription, you stand to earn 40% of the subscription amount the person paid.
- You will also earn 40% commission if someone you introduced to the software makes a one-time purchase of ClickFunnels' products like Funnel Scripts and Funnel Hacks.

ClickFunnels affiliate program is among the best affiliate programs out there, and a must join for any serious affiliate marketer who wants to earn consistent and recurring income. One thing that makes ClickFunnels affiliate program great is that their services are subscription-based, and each time someone you introduced to the company renews their subscription; you earn a commission.

This type of commission that you earn recurrently is known as back-end commission. You don't have to continue pitching to the customer over and over again. As long as the customer keeps renewing their ClickFunnels subscription, your earnings are guaranteed.

**How to join**

If you already have a ClickFunnels.com account, then you are already an affiliate, you don't have to go through a special registration process. Additionally, you don't need to purchase any of ClickFunnels products to earn as an affiliate. Once you have registered with the company, you could start promoting the company's products to your audience and earn a commission. When you sign up, you are given a 14-day trial period to check out the company's products. So, this means you are basically signing up for free, and once you do, you can start referring people to the software.

Even though you can become an affiliate without purchasing any of the company's product, the truth is that for you to really convince someone to purchase a product like ClickFunnels, you need to have used the product yourself to understand its ins and outs. Without proper knowledge of how the software tools work, you will lack the proper knowledge to educate others about it and hence convince them to subscribe.

**What is the best way to earn money with the ClickFunnels affiliate program?**

To leverage the ClickFunnels affiliate program and make money, you need to grow an email list of people that are interested in growing their own online business. These could be people who are already running their online business but are not making use of funnels. Your target audience could be "hit and run" affiliate marketers who don't make use of sales funnels. Your audience could also include offline business owners who want to take their business online.

It is better for you to target those offline businesses that are not doing much in terms of online marketing. They are the ones who would appreciate your efforts. One mistake that many affiliate marketers make is that they try to sell water to fish. If you decide to promote a product to an audience that already have it, then you are only wasting your precious time.

For instance, trying to promote ClickFunnels to people who are already versed in one online business or the counter could be counterproductive. The reason is simple – such people may already know about ClickFunnels or other better autoresponders and may be using them already. So, trying to sell them a product that they are already using does not make a lot of business sense.

As mentioned previously, you should try marketing a product like ClickFunnels to those offline businesses that are just on the verge of taking their business online. You could also target those businesses that already have an online presence but have a crappy sales funnel.

If you want to estimate how big the market is for products like ClickFunnels, just do a simple Google search of some businesses within your locality. You will notice that most of them have no or little online presence. Most of the businesses have just a website and no landing page or sales funnel. Basically, they are mostly following the wrong online marketing strategy.

Now, if you target such businesses and make them understand how a product like ClickFunnels works and how they could grow their business with a sales funnel, they would want to purchase the product. That's why affiliate marketing is great – the earning potential is enormous; you just have to be creative and smart at the same time to sniff out opportunities that abound around you.

Do you know that the only online channel that most businesses use in marketing their business is their Facebook page? And perhaps, their boring website? Those are the kinds of businesses that you should target, take them through a funnel, explain how ClickFunnels works, and watch them put some cool affiliate commissions in your pocket. Some of the businesses you could introduce ClickFunnels to cut across several industries – health, real estate, etc.

## 2. Healthywage.com

The weight loss industry has continued to boom for many years and will continue to do so in the coming years. The reason for that should not be hard for anyone to guess – many people do not like their weight and are trying to lose some fat. Those who have a healthy weight want products that could help them maintain their weight.

You could tap into the weight loss industry and be part of those earning billions of dollars that it generates yearly. To do that, simply join the Healthywage.com affiliate program. How the program works is – you earn money for helping people to lose weight.

**How the program works:**

- Each Healthywage sign up you generate earns you $50.
- The company makes it easy for you to market their offers by providing you with text links, banner ads, additional content assets to make a promotional snap.
- You are assigned a dedicated affiliate manager – this manager equips you with tips and instructions on how to excel as the company's affiliate. The dedicated manager also offers you support, assistance, and is always ready to answer your questions.

Ideally, a healthywage.com affiliate program is great for every affiliate marketer because the company provides you with all the assets you need to create a high converting marketing message. The tools provided for you can also help you run an effective sales funnel and convert many potential buyers into willing customers.

**How to join**

- Apply here to become a healthywage.con affiliate program.
- Your application will be reviewed before approval. Once approved, you will be provided with promotional materials. You can then place the materials on your blog, social media page, or your preferred traffic source.
- If visitors click on the marketing materials and sign up to join HealthyWager, one of healthywage.com's products, then you earn a commission.

Ideally, you would want to promote healthywage.com to people who are looking to lose weight. The products that the company offers are not your typical weight loss products – so, you will likely find it easier to get customers.

If you create a high converting sales funnel for healthywage.com, then you can make a lot of passive income with the affiliate program. Remember, a lot of people have weight-related issues, and if you educate these people on how to manage their weight problems, they would want to buy the product you promote to them.

**3. Alidrop-ship**

Alidropship a WordPress plugin used by dropshippers to import products from Aliexpress straight to their WordPress stores. Dropshipping is an e-commerce model where you find cheap products needed by your customers from websites like Aliexpress and many others, then you list the products on your own e-commerce website so that any time a customer orders a product from your website, you send the order to a supplier who then goes on to fulfill the order on your behalf. Usually, your profit is the difference between the amount you listed the product on your e-commerce website and the actual amount the product is selling for on a site like Aliexpress.

To make enough money as a drop-shipper, you need to make sales in huge volumes – so, you have to list as many products as possible on your website. However, importing products individually from a site like Aliexpress to your store is not such an easy job, that's where Alidrop-ship becomes useful.

Alidrop-ship makes it easy for you to import products to your store in just one click. It also has many other useful tools – for instance, an edit option allows you to edit products details before publishing it on your site. You can edit the title, description, change variations, pricing, and image gallery without leaving AliExpress. When you are done, you just click a "publish" button, and the desired product with all your changes instantly appears on your store.

Alidrop-ship is great for any drop-shipper as it reduces the amount of work you have to do. In addition to helping you import products from Aliexpress, you can also use Alidrop-ship to fulfill orders. Basically, the plugin helps you to automate your drop-shipping business and is highly recommended for any dropshipper.

Alidrop-ship pricing starts at $45.5 and goes up to $269.7, and you only have to make this payment once. You can earn a commission for each customer you refer to buy the product. You stand to earn up to 50% commission for every plugin purchase made through your recommendation. You can also earn 30% commission when you refer a customer to order Alidrop-ship's custom store. Also, if a customer you referred to the product pays for extra add-ons or services, you earn 30% commission.

## 4. Hubspot

We live in an age where marketing is no longer about the aggressive pushing of products to potential customers. Instead, what we have now is called pull marketing – with pull marketing, also known as inbound marketing, you pull customers to your brand through the use of various marketing strategies. While with push marketing, you aggressively push marketing contents to your audience and expect them to patronize you.

In inbound marketing, you provide value to prospects and make them come to your business naturally. You can do this by dishing out content materials like eBooks, blog posts, videos, etc. which serve as a lead magnet to attract customers to your business.

Hubspot is a company that develops a wide range of software products and services that can be used for social media management, content management, search engine optimization, and web analytics. Hubspot has an integrated CMS (content management system) – so, if you don't have a website yet, then you can build a new one on the platform. If you have an existing website, you can integrate the software into the site and run your inbound marketing campaigns effectively.

Who should use HubSpot? Hubspot is seen as an "all in one marketing product," so anyone that does anything related to social media marketing, blog marketing, search engine optimization, content management will most definitely find HubSpot's products useful. In other words, bloggers, e-commerce entrepreneurs, online marketing experts will find HubSpot's products useful.

One thing that makes HubSpot special is that it combines all the products and services you need to run perfect marketing campaigns in one place. Hubspot's pricing starts at $250 and goes up to $1,000 – and it is a one-off payment – no recurrent payments. They run an affiliate program which offers you a chance to earn up to $1000 for every purchase that happens through you, depending on the tier of the product.

## 5. Wrike

Wrike is a software product that anyone that works with a team will find useful. It is a project management tool that allows you to track your tasks, work, projects, and everything in between.

If you are working with a team, Wrike makes it possible for everyone on your team to be on the same page as you are and allows them to see the progress of all the tasks or projects being done. This is not to mention that you can sift through hundreds of emails in no time.

With Wrike, you don't have to hold long meetings, as you can simply look through all the work that is being done by each member of your team. Even as a solopreneur, you can still use Wrike to organize your tasks, track ongoing projects, completed tasks, and your emails, all from one platform. Since Wrike is a cloud-based software with both Android and iOS support, you can always work on the go.

Wrike uses a freemium tiered pricing model – they allow unlimited collaboration which includes vendors, contractors, freelancers, and third parties to access approved projects. The service is free for up to 5 users with limited features. If you are looking for expanded features and functionality, you pay $49 per month for five users and $99 per month for 15 users. You stand to earn up to $300 for every sale that happens through you.

## 6. Shopify

Shopify gives you a platform to create your own e-commerce store and use their shopping cart solution to market your products, fulfill orders, and manage your store. Shopify is one of those software products that I recommend that you actively promote to people you know for many reasons. One, Shopify is simple to use, you don't have to deal with anything technical – you can simply focus on marketing or selling your products.

Creating a Shopify account is as simple as making a cup of coffee – with pre-designed themes and a "drag-and-drop" functionality, you can create your own store within minutes. Not to mention, you have access to thousands of plugins and tools that you can use to grow your store.

In addition to selling your own products using Shopify, you can also take advantage of Shopify's drop-shipping option to import products from marketplaces like Aliexpress and sell on your store. Shopify offers you a limited free trial – you can use the fourteen days free trial period to test the waters and see if selling on Shopify is your thing. After the expiration of the free trial period, if you want to continue using the platform, you have to pay a monthly subscription of $29/month.

You can recommend Shopify to anyone who has a physical or digital product to sell and just needs to launch their business online as soon as possible. Even people who don't have physical products can take advantage of Shopify's drop shipping feature and operate a fully functional drop-shipping store.

Shopify promises to pay you $58 for each user that signs up for a paid store with your referral link. You can earn up to $2,000 in commission for each referral.

### 7. Six Figure Mentors

Six Figure Mentors, SFM is an affiliate program that when you join, you will be provided with the necessary training, products, as well as the tools you need to create a highly successful online business. You will be paired with a mentor who will provide you with the training you need.

When you promote the company's products, memberships, and products, you will also earn referral commissions, which is an excellent way to build passive income. The founders of Six Figure Mentors are both successful marketers, and they want to provide you with the tools you need to replicate their type of success.

As mentioned earlier, when you join the program, you will be matched with a mentor who will understand your unique needs and craft a personalized training program for you to make sure you are properly empowered to start your own online business.

Being a member of the Six Figure Mentor program will give you access to pre-crafted and optimized affiliate links, sales pages, and marketing banners in a variety of styles and sizes. So, all you need to do is "copy and paste" the already proven system and get your business running.

Who is this program for? You can refer the Six Figure Mentor program to anybody, both those who are already running their online business and those who want to get into the online business space for the first time. Basically, the program is for anyone who wants to leverage an already working system and create their own online business.

According to SFM's website, they pay $20 on "Introductory" Sales and $200 on "Essential" Sales. You are also paid $20 each month that your referral maintains an active subscription.

SFM has different membership plans – the Essential plan has an enrollment fee of $297 and a monthly subscription fee of $20. The

Elite membership costs $2,500, but you must have bought the Essential plan before upgrading to the Elite membership.

## 8. eToro

eToro is basically a Forex broker but a unique one. In Forex trading, you trade with the currency of other countries and make money by predicting the direction of changes in the different currency rates. You might think that trading requires a lot of skill, experience, and analysis; and you're totally right. However, what makes eToro brilliant is that you absolutely don't need any previous knowledge to make money with it, so you don't need to be afraid that you don't have the necessary skills or that you need a big investment to get started – it's not stock exchange, and you don't have to trade yourself or make any risky decisions.

eToro is more like an online community similar in structure to Facebook and has over 2 million users. You can check profiles of other users, see the trade history, earnings, and the completed transactions done by the person.

To earn money on eToro, you'll need a minimum deposit; however, before you deposit any money, consider opening a demo account. With a demo account, you don't need any investment, and you can test all the functions of eToro until you get familiar with the system. Once you have gotten used to the system, you can deposit money and start earning.

For each user that you refer to eToro, you earn a referral commission. All that is required is for the person that you referred to click on your partner link, register as a user, and fund their trading account. You will be paid according to your chosen commission plan.

## 9. 3DCart

3DCart has functionalities similar to that of Shopify. You can create your own online store and start selling your products online quickly and easily. Creating your own store on 3DCart is as simple as ABC – choose a template, upload your logo and images, and start creating pages – all these can be done within minutes with 3DCart's drag and drop tools.

3DCart offers you a free Facebook app with which you can sell your products directly through Facebook. The platform also allows you to include videos from YouTube in your product pages. You can get a free 15-day trial after which you will have to pay $19/month to continue using the platform. 3DCart runs a robust affiliate program – you can earn up to 300% commission promoting 3DCart's e-commerce solutions, which is why I recommend that people actively promote it and earn.

## 10. Teachable

Teachable is an online platform that provides you with all the tools you need to create and sell courses (slides, videos, eBooks, interviews, etc.) online. With Teachable, you only have to possess the knowledge you want to pass on to others; then Teachable helps you to turn this knowledge into an online course and provide you with the tools to sell it. Teachable hosts the course on their platform and handles payment processing and everything in between.

If you want to brand your courses, Teachable provides you with an easy-to-use page editor which you can use to add your own images, logos, colors, and elements. Teachable charges you a monthly fee for using their platform. The basic plan, which is the cheapest goes for $29/month while the highest package goes for $399/month. You stand to earn a 30% commission when you refer people to Teachable.

Who is Teachable for? Entrepreneurs, bloggers, or basically anyone that has specialized knowledge they would want to share with others.

## 11. Veeqo

Veeqo is an all in one warehouse management tool that allows retailers to synch inventory in real-time across different marketplaces and web stores. You can use Veeqo to list products, fulfill orders, and manage your inventory – you can do all of these without visiting your various web stores. If you sell on Amazon, Etsy, eBay, for instance, you can use Veeqo to sync orders in real-time across these different marketplaces.

Who needs Veeqo? Every entrepreneur, especially e-commerce entrepreneurs who use different online marketplaces to sell their products. These days, more and more retailers are using multiple online marketplaces to sell their products, so, you will always find people who need Veeqo.

Veeqo offers a 14-day free trial ~~to new users after w~~hich you will have to upgrade to one of the paid plans to continue enjoying the services of the platform. The paid plans start at $55/month and go as high as $680/month.

You can leverage Veeqo's referral program and build a solid passive income. The platform pays you 20% commission on monthly subscriptions of your referrals.

## 12. SEM Rush

SEMRush is a powerful SEO tool that is great for finding profitable keywords. We currently live in an age when finding the right keywords is the key to running a successful blog. With SEMRush, bloggers can get to know what keywords internet users are keying in on search engines when they are doing searches.

The tool also allows you to analyze the keywords being used by your competitors. Not to mention, you can use it to run an SEO audit of your blog and find backlinking opportunities that will boost the ranking of your blog on search engines.

SEMRush is such a great tool that both old and new bloggers find extremely useful. No blogger wants to keep writing a blind post anymore; rather, bloggers want to create content that their audience is interested in reading.

It is not only bloggers that find SEMRush useful, even business owners, small and big trust it. So, you can easily promote it to both bloggers and business owners. The tool has different billing plans, with the lowest package going for $83.28 and the highest package goes for $333.28.

The tool also has a robust affiliate program – where you get 40% commission for every new user who buys the tool through you. This commission is paid to you every month.

### 13. SEO PowerSuite

Just like SEMRush, SEO PowerSuite is yet another powerful "all-in-one" SEO tool that lets you be at the top of your SEO game. The package contains the following applications:

1. Rank trackers
2. Website Auditor
3. SEO SpyGlass
4. Link Assistant

All these applications are designed to collectively work with different areas of website management and SEO, including backlinks, on-page SEO, and ranking.

It is an excellent tool for bloggers and business owners who want to take their SEO strategy seriously. The tool has different billing plans, with the lowest package going for $299 and the highest package going for $699.

SEO Powersuite is not just an SEO tool; you can also earn substantial passive income by joining their affiliate program. As an affiliate, you get to enjoy the following benefits:

- Regular 33% commission for all order your referrals make.

- Promo materials — you will be provided with ready-to-use, high converting banners, and links.

- 90 days cookie duration – meaning that if you refer someone to their website, for the next 90 days, you stand to earn commission on orders made by this person.

Don't limit yourself to only these mentioned affiliate programs – you can research and come up with similar programs in different niches. Compare the commission that each program pays and determine the ones you would want to join.

To promote any of the products mentioned above, you will need to create a sales funnel. Besides, you will need to have a blog where you talk about various affiliate offers. The types of customers who need such products do not pay for them on the first contact.

You need to, firstly, educate them on the uses of the product and why they would think to spend money on the product. This education will involve you sending a series of emails. By the time you have sent the right number of emails and the customer has become knowledgeable about the product, then a sale could occur.

One good thing about promoting some of the products above is if a customer buys one of them, you could easily refer to other products on the list that they could need. For instance, a customer that signs up for ClickFunnels.com could benefit from signing up on Wrike, the online project calendar.

Additionally, a customer that needs SEMRush could benefit from having SEO Powersuite. If you have done a good job of winning the trust of the customer, they will be happy to buy any other complementary product you sell to them.

# CHAPTER 8

# NEW PRACTICAL AFFILIATE MARKETING STRATERGIES

So far, in this book, we have been discussing a lot of very theoretical ways and methods of affiliate marketing. But you didn't come here for a bunch of big and smart sounding words, did you? No! You came here to learn how to properly and efficiently market your goods, products, and services to a wide audience in the best way possible.

Although everything that we have talked about and discussed in the previous chapters of this book are very important and vital to the Affiliate Marketing process. The knowledge you have gained from the previous chapters will carry you a long way in your Affiliate Marketing journey but you need to get practical, fast! I have organized two of the most efficient ways to properly promote and sell your products online. Without much talk, let's get into it;

Selling Products with YouTube as a Reviewer:

YouTube is a site where billions of people spend hours on every single day, if you can find a way to get in there and grab their attention and make them see what you have to offer, then my friend, you have struck a gold mine. More than a billion hours of content is watched on YouTube every single day. This mind-blowing statistic makes them the third largest search engine in the world.

The site is constantly growing by the day as new people are signing up every hour, with the increasing use of smart phones around the world, so if you are a person with a large audience on the site, you level of gain will be immeasurable.

Of course, there is the slight problem of how to monetize your channel, but we are not here for that, this is not a step by step book on how to grow your YouTube channel, so go figure all that on your own and come back here when you are ready.

Getting people to be interested in your products all comes down to two basic things; how entertaining and engaging you are willing to be for the sake of selling your products and your ability to redirect the traffic from your channel on YouTube to your online store.

In order to be successful on YouTube, you need to know the algorithm in and out, like the back of your hand, that way you can always stay on op of it and let it work for you, instead of you working for it, or it working against you.

Creating your own videos can be a very tricky thing because you have to walk the fine line between being an entertainer and a successful sales man. Too much of either and you oud have failed your task successfully.

When looking at the most successful YouTube influencers and their content, you might notice a running connection. The more interactive their videos are, the more attention their video seems to generate. This shows how well they walk that fine line we talked about earlier. There's something to be said here about actively engaging your audience. Answering questions about your products in the comments or on live streams, making a Q&A video can be a great way to get your users involved.

Listening to your audience is also not a bad idea. They are often very vocal about the types of content they want to see next, so it can be useful to move forward with the general consensus. Taking into account individual requests and one-off suggestions can also be useful to give you ideas for future content.

Another tip is to always give your audience more of what they seem to like to keep them happy and buying. They are inherently curious and nosey, so a great way to peak their interest is to show the design/manufacturing process of their favorite product of yours through a behind-the-scenes video.

Next, it is time to consider posting reviews of your products. Actions, or in this case reactions of satisfactory happiness, speak louder than confident words of promotion. Reaction videos are one of the most popular types of videos on YouTube. Testimonials are a great way to enhance your brand and its authenticity. Not to mention the added bonus that product reviews make great videos from a content creation perspective, so it is a win, win.

Brutally honest YouTuber merch reviews are honestly the way forward. Next, focus on making topical videos. And always tailor content to your type of viewers. So, if you're releasing a new clothing range, film a video and title it along the lines of 'What outfit suits me best?'

YouTubers are constantly under a lot of pressure every single week to come up with brand new video ideas that will keep their viewers on their toes, guessing what they will talk about next. All this creative thinking should not go to waste by not being applied to your products too. A great example of a person that did this perfectly is an American YouTuber named Jenna Marbles, she managed to sell a whole lot of custom plush toy versions of her own dog to her viewers.

Apparently, you have managed to established your audience and have done all the necessary groundwork to get people watching the videos you make about your products. But the next thing that is coming your way is probably the most important part; which is actually getting them to leave YouTube and go to your website to buy your products.

Applying interactive YouTube cards at multiple points of your videos is a great way to move traffic from your channel directly to your store and increase interaction. Play with the formatting and you can ensure that you are left with a smooth call to action at the end of the video.

Loyal audiences are those that are engaged, and loyal audiences are the best types of audiences because those are the types of audiences that will buy your goods. Creating an open dialogue with your online community can go a long way in the promotion of your brand. Replying to all your messages and comments on social media, sharing your followers' posts and being active in your live streams will go a really long way.

Search Engine Optimization (SEO) simply cannot be ignored. Keywords play a major role in the SEO process of ranking on search engines. And YouTube is certainly no different from the rest. Put a good amount of time aside to invest in YouTube SEO by doing the following:

Always vividly and thoroughly describe the content of your video in the video's description while leaving links to your online store.

Use easily searchable keywords in the title of your video

Use tags containing keywords to your videos

Use SEO approved video descriptions

**Research on the YouTube ranking factors**

Here are four of the most practical ways to move the traffic from YouTube directly to your online store we will be going in depth and detail on each of them, but for now, let us list them out;

- Putting your link in the description of the video
- Making use of custom links that are placed on profile banners
- Making use of YouTube end screens
- Making use of YouTube cards

**1** Putting links to your store in the video descriptions and comment section

This is one of the most cliché ways that YouTubers use to get their viewers to support whatever it is that they are doing outside YouTube. It is also one of the most stereotypical things they say "Link in the description" along with "don't forget to like, comment, and subscribe" its as if they recite these things in the mirror every morning.

It is used so often that the viewers have come to expect to see a link in the description at the end of every video. Some of these YouTubers talk about things that tend to get their videos demonetized so links in the description are how the viewers can show their support for the creators.

Attention spans on sites like YouTube are very hard to come by so you need to be placing your most important links in the first three lines of your description, so as to immediately catch the attention of your view. Also, shortening long links so as t make them easier to read for the viewer won't hurt your chances either. Take a shot for every time I used "so as to" in the past 5 seconds.

A better choice would be to drop your link in the comment section of the video because most people are not rushing to the description to see whatever it is that you might have kept there for them. But I'll tell you something. The number of people that are rushing to the comment section for one reason or the other is enough to make you sell out in a day.

And as the owner of the channel, you can make a pinned comment and drop your ink there, that way any and everybody that comes to drop a comment will definitely see your link.

Here's how it's done:

If you are doing this on your mobile device, open the YouTube app and click on the plus button you see at the lower center of your screen and click "upload video." After uploading your video, type a description foe the video and links to the designated Description box You can shorten your links by using link shortening services such as Goo.gl or Bit.ly. Click on Publish, and you're done.

**2**. Making use of custom link on your profile banner

People see your cover art when they go to your profile as well as the icons you choose to display. This data is vital for people to get a feeling for your channel's brand and how you operate. Furthermore, it is a common page that your viewers visit when they're looking for new content to watch, or when they are considering subscribing.

YouTube allows for up to 5 links to be displayed on top of the profile banner. Those links can be a combination of any external links, such as your different social media platforms, website, or online store. You can make use of this prominent linking opportunity to drive your subscribers to let them know that you have products to offer them, as well as to send them to the right page.

When you add a link to your online store to your YouTube profile, a clickable icon will appear. You can also make use of the ''LINK TITLE'' option to draw more attention to the link you want your viewers to see.

Here is the process of how to add custom links to your YouTube profile:

Go to the top right corner of YouTube, you will see your profile picture, click on it and wait for the menu to drop, select ''my channel''

There will be a ''customize channel'' button in blue, click it

Click on the ''about'' tab of your profile

Click on ''links''

Locate the pencil icon on the right-hand side in order to edit your links

Click on ''add'' and proceed to add the Information about your k and the text you want to be shown

To save what you have done click ''done''

**3**. Making use of YouTube end screens

These are icons that show up at about ten seconds before the end of your YouTube video. They come up in the shape of squares and a circle, they are icons that lead to either a new video on your channel or a playlist that you have created for your channel, these are the squares, the circle acts as a sort of shortcut to the subscribe button to incentivize your viewers to subscribe to your channel. These can be used to promote traffic to your online site too.

Summary of what end screens show:

Different videos or playlists on YouTube

An invitation to subscribe to the channel

Link to external websites that are approved merchandise and crowdfunding sites

The last one is the option we're all most interested in of course.

You can link to one of three options – your own associated site, a merchandise site, or a crowdfunding site, these all have to be approved by YouTube by the way. The merchandise and crowdfunding sites must be on the list of approved retailers, getting on this list is not so difficult.

How to properly add end cards that link to your site:

Make sure you are part of the YouTube Partner Program, you can apply from your account's creator studio

Upload a video, duh

Under your "videos" tab, click the down arrow next to the "edit" button under the video you want to add an end screen to

Select "end screen" from the drop-down menu

Click the blue "add element" button

Click "link" from the drop-down menu

Paste the URL link that you want to send your visitors to and click "Next"

Edit the title you'd like, and choose the most relevant call to action, this could be a custom message that would incentivize your viewers to click your link

Select your image

Click "create element"

**4**. Making use of YouTube cards to drive traffic to your site from YouTube

Cards in YouTube videos appear as a small letter "i" in the top right corner of the video screen, and when clicked they slide out from the right-hand side of the video to reveal their content, which will be what you put there, for them to display.

These cards usually contain an image, a title, and a call to action that gets viewers to click on them, and they link away from your video, so it might be wise to put them in towards the middle or end of the video. There are different kinds of cards you can add:

Cards that display video or playlists - they send viewers to another video or playlist that they might be interested in

Cards that display channel cards – they let you shout out a different channel if you want

Cards that display donation links – these can ask for donations from your viewers

Cards that display Polls – they poll your viewers directly in the video

Cards that display links– these cards send your viewers to external links

With the goal to send viewers to your store and make more sales, the Cards that display Links option is most effective, so we will be putting all our focus on that.

Similar to end screens, Cards that display links have limitations as to what links you can add – they include associated websites, sites from their approved list or retailers and merchandisers, we have discussed all this before.

Step by step process on how to add Cards that display links to your YouTube videos:

Make sure you are part of the YouTube Partner Program – you can apply from your account's creator studio

Upload a video, duh

Under your "videos" tab, click the down arrow next to the "edit" button under the video you want to add a card to

Slide the time marker to the time you want the card to appear, then click "add card"

From the drop-down menu choose "link"

Paste the URL of the link you want to send your viewers to and click "next"

Enter the text, the call to action, as well as the most relevant image, and click "create card"

Repeat the process for any other locations in the video where you would like to insert a card

Helpful tip: Paste the same URL link in your bio on Instagram. Whenever a new customer finds you on Instagram, they're likely to go to your bio page and see your link.

The steps for end screens and cards are very similar but different at the same time. It is very important to make the most of your YouTube audience. Having a loyal following on YouTube is the perfect jumpstart that most retailers need start selling their digital products, and thanks to YouTube's built in tools, it's possible to set up seamless, integrated sales tactics.

For content creators who are just starting their journey, making the most out of tactics like putting links in the description, using pinned comments, and creating custom links in your channel's profile banner will be the best way to send your viewers to your online sites to purchase your digital goods.

Regardless of your experience level or the amount of time you have spent posting videos on YouTube, you'll be able to find creative ways to make money and make the most of that exponentially growing YouTube viewer data base. So, go forth and multiply, use these skills and tools that I have taught you to grow your online stores.

Selling products with Pinterest

Pinterest started out as a site for rare food recipes and do it yourself ideas, but it has now quickly turned into a major global shopping search engine. In fact, 89% of US pinners use Pinterest to research on purchasing decisions. And with the site boasting about 320 million active monthly users, that really is a lot of people going to this one platform just to shop. These are even more reasons why your brand has no business with failing on this platform, one good thing you can do for yourself today is to pay attention and learn how to self on Pinterest.

**Reasons for you to move your business to Pinterest today!**

We have already talked about the mind-blowing fact that a whole 89% of United States citizens are using the platform specifically to plan out and research on purchases for products they need, but that is just the tip of the ice berg.

Almost half of all users on the site are logging in are just there to shop. Forty-seven percent off them to be exact. That's about accumulates to about 150 million potential new customers that could be buying your products. The first thing you need to do is find your target audience, get your products in front of them and wait for those dollar signs to start rolling in, it should be as easy as that right?

Of course, it's not quite that easy, nothing ever is in this life. In fact, the next section of this chapter contains the steps you need to take before you can start successfully selling on Pinterest.

**Preparatory steps needed to get your brand ready to sell on Pinterest**

We know you're excited about the prospect of leveraging all of those potential shoppers on the Pinterest platform. But before you take any serious action, you need to read these quick four steps to help you get your brand ready for selling on the platform.

**1. You need to locate your target audience**

It's always important to have a good understanding of the demographics of a social media platform before starting a new campaign on it. Putting together a customer persona will help you make sure you know exactly who you need to be targeting and selling to on the platform. This will mostly consist of your target audience's optimal income, job criteria, lifestyle and more.

**2. You need to set up an account for business**

A Pinterest business account and a regular personal Pinterest account differ in so many ways. You get access to more features on the business account, such as access your pin analytics, ads and other necessary elements for selling successfully on Pinterest. Do not worry if you created your account as a personal profile.

You can easily switch to a business account by logging into your existing profile and converting it into business account through your account settings. If this proves to be too stressful, you can always create a new Pinterest business account right off the bat. Just head over to Pinterest and sign up!

**3. You need to brand your account**

Each social media that is made for your business profile should be easily recognizable to your customers and followers, and your Pinterest profile should be no different. To brand your profile, make sure your profile photo is a high-resolution logo or it could be a professional headshot of yourself if you are the face of your business, which you should be. And it should match your other profiles, your bio must be optimized and contain details about your business, your cover boards must match your brand, contact information should be current and up to date, and more.

**4. You need to link and verify your website on the platform**

The final step in prepping your Pinterest business profile is to link and verify your business' website. Adding your website through profile settings is simple enough, but then you need to claim that it is your website. To do this, add a meta tag or upload a HTML file to your website. You can learn more about how to do this directly on the Pinterest site.

You can only verify and claim one website for each Pinterest business account, so make sure it's your main site that you make sales from or else you won't be able to create a shop and link products to the account.

**How to successfully sell on Pinterest**

Now that we've gotten the basics out of the way, let's get into the important stuff; how to sell on Pinterest and start making money. There are eight important tips for selling on Pinterest and really turning this visual platform into a new revenue stream for you.

**1. Create stunning visuals for your account**

First things first. Pinterest is a visual platform. Even before we dive into several types of Pins that can help increase sales, you need to make sure that your Pins are actually visually appealing to the eye and make someone want to click. This means that you need:

High-resolution photographs

Beautifully designed graphics

Optimally sized visuals to fit the site's formats

Bold colors and fonts for attraction

Graphics that match your branding

One great way to stand out is by taking professional photography of your product in use, this way your customers can get a sort of personal feel for your goods and not just have them lifelessly on display. You can also create a beautiful, branded graphic Pin that draws users in and entices them to save, click on and purchase what you're promoting.

Or if you are feeling creative, you can do a mix of both, where you create a graphic or text overlay alongside a professional photo, providing information on a product and a product photo.

**2. Focus more on Pinterest SEO**

Pinterest is a visual search engine, which means it has its own search engine optimization rules and algorithms that drives and regulates it.

Focus on industry keywords and use them strategically in your Pin titles and descriptions, as well as your in-board titles and descriptions.

Make sure that you're incorporating your keywords properly and naturally to help ensure that your Pinterest SEO will work. This will expand the reach of your Pinterest content, increasing the likelihood that someone will buy.

### 3. Make use of Rich Pins

Rich Pins extract extra data and information from your website to display alongside the normal pin info, like photo, title, description, etc. It pulls in the price and product descriptions so that users are able to view this information within the Pinterest site itself. On mobile smart phones, users will even be able to click a blue Shop button to head right to your product and check them out.

If the shop offers this info, these Pins will even let you know whether or not the product is in stock or not. These types of Rich Pins work once you claim your website on Pinterest. So, take advantage of the platform's offer to draw in more sales.

### 4. Use promoted Pins

Want to push your Pins to the top instead of relying solely on your Pinterest SEO? Then Invest in promoted Pins! These can be anything ranging from a lead magnet, a blog post or a product. Promoted product Pins can be helpful for generating more sales as they simply take the user directly to your website. When creating promoted Pins, you will be able to target your audience by interest, age and gender. You can create entire campaigns or quick ads for a one-off promotion.

## 5. Organize Pins into Catalogs

Catalogs are an excellent feature on Pinterest business account to use if you have products to promote which is likely true if you're a brand or business!

You should be able to upload your file into Pinterest as long as you have a data source of all your products and their attributes. Once the data source has been approved, any product you add to your website will also automatically create product Pins which you can then use to create shopping ads.

An important thing to note is if it turns out you do not have the right data source to create Catalogs, then you will have to use Rich Pins instead.

## 6. You need to tag your products in Shop the Look Pins

Shop the Look Pins are a great way to link your buyers to several products at once in a single Pin. It does not matter if it is an outfit or a home decor post, each product available for purchase in the photo is shown via a white dot that users can click on in order to see more.

You can share photos of your models wearing an outfit of your latest collection or a room filled with your furniture or similar products to promote more products on the platform. The process for Shop the Look Pins is manual, and once your Pin is linked to your claimed website, you can tag as many products as you would like.

## 7. Share user-generated content (UGC)

Did you find a celebrity or a well-known influencer using your product? You can use that to your advantage. Or better yet, set up influencer marketing campaigns to consistently generate content that you can share on Pinterest and entice your audience to buy.

You can even use User Generated Content as Shop the Look Pins or promote these photos to grab user attention even more. Social proof is everything, and if a user sees a person that they follow wearing your products, they're much more likely to buy because the product isn't really cool until a popular person makes it cool or says it is buy openly displaying their use of it on social media.

## 8. Incorporate content marketing

Blog posts that are geared towards conversions are the perfect things to share on Pinterest. Think in the vain of gift guides, product roundups, or tutorials. These are great pieces of content to save and promote on the site that will most definitely generate clicks, and if you put your content together properly, they will generate conversions too.

Well, that is about it, there really isn't anything else to say, you can go ahead now and take this knowledge and start selling your products on Pinterest.

# CONCLUSION

I hope you have found all the information in this guide useful. The truth remains that the information you have just gotten will not help you in any way unless you put it into action. Many people read books like this purely for entertainment or educational purposes but will never try to put what they have learned into practice.

What is the essence of reading a book if you will not utilize the knowledge you have gained from the book? It is like spending a lot of money to acquire a college degree and then dump the degree for something else at the end of the entire struggle.

Affiliate marketing is by far, one of the best ways of earning money online, and lots of people do it as their primary business. But you will need to get it right from the beginning for it to make sense to you. This guide has provided you with all the pieces of information you need to make that happen.

According to unofficial statistics, 90% of affiliate marketers don't make enough money to renew their domain name after the first year. The problem is that those who are among the 90% don't even understand that they are doing something wrong. If you follow all the instructions in this guide, you will not fall into the 90% category. You will be among the 10% who make things happen. This might take you some time, but you will surely get it right.

You have seen the difference between the "hit n run" affiliate marketing and the "working" affiliate marketing model. Most of the people who have failed at affiliate marketing adopted the "hit n run" model. First, they were sold the lie that they could become overnight millionaires through affiliate marketing. Then they enthusiastically dived in and started with the hit and run model, which failed them woefully.

Hit and run affiliate marketing doesn't work – at most, it will earn you a few bucks but will never sustain you for a long time. Affiliate marketing is serious business, but when you follow the hit and run model, it means that you do not see the business as a long term one. If you want affiliate marketing to pay you like the real business it is, then you must develop a "working" model and run with it.

When you are just starting, you could consider the Amazon affiliate program. It is great for beginners for many reasons – joining the program is simple. After joining, you will need to find products and start promoting. The best medium for promoting Amazon products is a blog – so, you will need to develop a blog and start growing an email list immediately. With proper research, you can learn how to turn your blog into a lead generation machine, and this will help you greatly to grow a huge email list.

After you have used Amazon affiliate program to learn all the ropes, then you would want to start promoting great software programs like ClickFunnels.com that can earn you a lot of money. Do not limit yourself – research and find great affiliate programs to join and earn money. With your email list, you can easily promote any offer, especially if you know how to nurture or warm up your potential customers. With the right marketing messages, you can turn cold leads into warm buyers within a short period.

As a beginner, you would want to stay away from affiliate networks like Clickbank.com and JVZoo.com. Even though some other people will recommend for you to start with such networks, I often advise against that for so many reasons. Joining such affiliate networks is the easiest way to turn yourself into a hit and run affiliate marketer even before you have started.

Additionally, for an affiliate network like JVZoo.com, you will need to request permission from a vendor before you are accepted to promote a product. As a beginner, if a vendor declines your request, the ensuing disappointment could make you lose your enthusiasm and motivation. So, it is better to keep away from such affiliate marketers.

One good thing about affiliate marketing is that it can usher you into many other online businesses – including Amazon FBA and drop-shipping. All these business ideas are also major money-spinners when you do them well. I have a comprehensive guide on both Amazon FBA and drop-shipping – you could consider getting the books.

Also, when you have grown your affiliate marketing business to a certain level, you could start outsourcing some of your operations to freelancers. For instance, you could outsource your article writing and video development to freelancers so that you can have time for other essential aspects of your business or life. You can find good freelancers on fiverr.com and upwork.com.

Thank you for reading! If You appreciate this book, we ask you to leave an honest review on your platform, it is very important for us!

To help you get started now, below you can find the best tools recommended by the author (affiliate links).
You can easily scan them with your mobile phone, so no excuses, take action now:

Start with Shopify:

Find freelancers on Fiverr:

Start doing Email marketing with Get Response:

Thank you for reading, we hope we have been of help! Keep in touch with the author for the upcoming releases:

To Your success!

Robert.

# TIK TOK MARKETING FOR

# ENTERPRENEURS

## The Beginner's Guide to Grow Your Business with Tik Tok and Influencers Marketing

## Robert Kasey

# TIK TOK MARKETING FOR
# ENTERPRENEURS

The Beginner's Guide to Grow
Your Business with Tik Tok and
Influencers Marketing

## Robert Kasey

# Disclaimer

All erudition contained in this book is given for informational and educational purposes only. The author is not in any way accountable for any result or outcome that emanate from using this material. Constructive attempts have been made to provide information that is both accurate and effective, but the author is not bound for the accuracy or use/misuse of this information.

# INTRODUCTION

After the exit of the Vine application, Musical.ly and Tik Tok merged to make the fastest-growing short-form video application. Tik Tok, owned by Bytedance bought musical.ly for $1 billion; today, Tik Tok is the world's number one for short-form video content creation and utilization. Therefore, it is named the world's most valuable startup, $75billion. Tik Tok is the newest trend in social media, with over 2 billion downloads on the App Store and Google Play globally.

It has been downloaded more than 80 million times in the United States and has over 800 million active users monthly. The largest demographic of Tik Tok users is between 16 and 24. The platform consists of 15- and 60-second video recorded by the user that rely on in-application editing functions in combination with the other significant social players. Since its birth in 2018, Tik Tok has developed from a video-creation application exclusively meant for users to communicate their creativity to a marketing and advertising haven.

The beauty of Tik Tok is that anybody can open an account and quickly begin making content and acquire attention from the users. To make it simple, this is how the Tik Tok artificial intelligence or algorithm works. The application has witnessed fast development since the fusion with Musical.ly, and a portion of this development is because of an aggressive promoting procedure or marketing strategy by the organization.

At this moment, Tik Tok's algorithm is genuinely easy to comprehend. It is easy to build upon, which could suggest why numerous creators, entrepreneurs, and individuals are directing their attention toward Tik Tok. The capability of growth for business on Tik Tok is remarkable.

Getting acquainted with Tik Tok and producing your content might prompt a ton of business growth and be an extraordinary advertising strategy for a brand. There are two ways for the Tik Tok advertising technique: working with influencers or creating original and unique content. Each one of these techniques has its advantages and time commitments.

Influencer marketing at its heart looks like storytelling and with enough adaptability to tell their story to their followers to promote and recommend a brand's products and services. Additionally, businesses can use their account to run advertisements and promotions, thereby moving their range to be more global and to younger people in the process.

Lately, Tik Tok launched a native analytics tool for Pro accounts, which are like Instagram creator accounts. Tik Tok's analytics dashboard collects information about your general audience and the performance of published content.

Likewise, they propelled another feature that permits few users to include a link in their bio. This link can help businesses to direct quickly and effectively their customers and other users to their sites from the app, thereby achieving their shopping goals.

# CHAPTER ONE

## <u>What is Tik Tok?</u>

**THE RELEVANCE OF TIK TOK IN THE BUSINESS WORLD**

Tik Tok is the newest trend in social media, with more than 2 billion downloads on the App Store and Google Play and over 800 million active users. The platform comprises 15- to 60-second user recorded videos that allow in-application editing and integration with the other significant social players. The biggest demographic of Tik Tok users are between 16 and 24. Since its inception, Tik Tok has developed from a video-creation application exclusively meant for users to communicate their creativity to a marketing and advertising haven.

Over the last year, brands have created accounts on the platform to explore and connect with customers. On Tik Tok, you can find everybody from influencers and celebrities to legislators and common people. The appeal of Tik Tok for organizations is the sheer number of active users on the platform. It's still unclear how the algorithm works precisely, but it is, by all means, a lot simpler for video content to become a web trend on Tik Tok than on other social platforms.

Tik Tok has different unique effects and features to add to your video, including music. Users usually make lip-sync videos in the style of Musical.ly, where they spell the words of well-known songs. In a way, it resembles making your music video. Tik Tok has pretty much every well-known song on the radio accessible without copyright infringement issues.

Tik Tok is an application for iOS and Android where users can make and share 15-second videos. It works like most social applications with followers who like and comment content. Hashtags let users find content by theme. On paper, Tik Tok doesn't sound different from most applications; however, it is a great deal of fun and has some intriguing content. Lip-synching videos are accessible, yet so are short videos of band promotion, enchanting stunts, and various tricks. Probably the best feature of Tik Tok is its editing options, giving users assets to make fun videos. It gives them intriguing features, for example, the possibility to record their reaction to a video while they're watching it. Users can likewise record their very own video utilizing the sound from another video.

Tik Tok was launched in China in 2016 under the name "Douyin" by a Chinese firm named Bytedance established in 2012 by Zhang Yiming; Tik Tok is a video-driven social media platform or a short-video sharing platform. It was rebranded as Tik Tok for a global market a year later. Today, it's one of the fastest-growing applications available, ranking as the third best free app in the Apple Store of free downloads in the Apple Store. Its parent company, ByteDance, merged Tik Tok with the mainstream Musical.ly application to acquire a more extensive user base. The Tik Tok name was kept. However, the entirety of Musical.ly's content was brought into Tik Tok.

Tik Tok bought the prevalent music-focused application Musical.ly for about $1billion, taking on it's entertaining, casual, heavy-lip-sync content style and snowballing the social platform's popularity. By 2018, Tik Tok surpassed all other social applications, including Instagram, with over 100 million downloads. The application has been downloaded worldwide more than 2 billion times and has been elected the world's most valuable startup at $75billion US. Its reach and scope are tremendous, as the application is hugely prominent in 150 markets and 75 languages globally. Its average user spends about an hour on the app every day, Tik Tok represents the rise of the video-sharing apps.

In the early years of its existence, Tik Tok slid under the vast majority's radar. Still, in 2020, one can no longer overlook the influence it has had around the world or the opportunities it has created for individuals, brands, and businesses. Due to these unprecedented times we are all living through, engagement on social media has increased radically, and more people are exploring the new platforms. Tik Tok is at the forefront of those platforms; Tik Tok has started to compete with Instagram in popularity, and this is something that the digital landscape is continually reminding

Tik Tok shares some aesthetic and functional similarities with Snapchat and Instagram, but it has its core characteristics as well; Tik Tok turned over the midpoint between the familiar self-coordinated and experience-based feed on algorithmic observation and inference. Tik Tok employs artificial intelligence to analyze users' interests and preferences through their interactions with the content. With other results obtained by the algorithms of other services utilized by the user (e.g. YouTube and Netflix) with a list of recommended videos. TikTok interprets the user's individual preferences and provides content that they would enjoy. One can become famous and make money through Tik Tok.

As the platform Tik Tok continues to surge in fame, numerous brands are thinking about how this platform is shaping culture and relevant discussions. They want to get in on the opportunity to increase their brand's impact. Many new updates are on the horizon for Tik Tok in 2020. Tik Tok is one of the fastest-growing platforms; TikTok is ahead of other popular platforms such as LinkedIn, Snapchat,

Pinterest, and Twitter by the number of active users of about 800million. By comparison, it took Instagram six years before it had the number of active users that Tik Tok has. With such a fast growth rate, there are unlimited opportunities for brands to activate influencer marketing campaigns on Tik Tok.

Tik Tok can make someone become an influencer who helps brands and organizations to promote their products and services for a charge. Tik Tok is a go-to application for short-form mobile video with a sole mission: to inspire creativity and network, and to connect users with people around the world while offering satisfaction. It ultimately wants to build a worldwide community where users can make and share their life spontaneously and discover the world around them. It is an inclusive application built upon the foundation of creative expression. Tik Tok urges users to celebrate what makes them extraordinary while finding a community that does likewise. Tik Tok Is aware and take into account that its users originate from a vast expansiveness of nationalities and societies. It considers the social norms and local guidelines of the countries it operates in.

Nowadays, applications have helped numerous businesses reach their target customers and future markets; looking from one point of view, one would prefer promoting on various channels to attract required and relevant customers.

Social media and influencers are becoming a staple of marketing. Ever-increasing numbers of marketers recognize influencer marketing as an effective marketing strategy; however, with the plethora of social platforms to choose from, it's difficult to tell which ones to target.

Alongside this increasing dependence on social media within marketing, comes the rise of social media user fatigue, a perceived propensity of users to feel the need to 'step back' from social media after becoming overwhelmed by the choices of different platforms and the pressure of keeping followers. The truth is, people are getting bored and tired of the negative aspects of increasing established social media platforms. Many are now looking for a new, native-edited space to express themselves, share content, and connect with other like-minded individuals. This is where Tik Tok kicks in. Tik Tok is a platform that seems to value out of the box creativity, with the option to use filters, augmented reality features, music clips and even dialogue from TV shows and movies to edit together a short 15-second video clip quickly. Tik Tok is a social media mobile app with a large community of users centered on video content. Tik Tok users film short videos and edit them with effects, filters, captions, and music, then post them for their Tik Tok followers. Content creators use hashtags and identify which popular category they fit into to be discovered by non-followers more easily.

Much of the app content is humorous. Some of the most popular genres include short skits, lip-synching, cringe videos, and so on. One of the most popular phenomena is the inundation of "challenges" posted across the platform that creates a ripple effect as everybody contributes with their version.

In addition to direct ads, many brands are using Tik Tok's superstar influencers to support their brand campaigns and reaching millions of users in the process. Tik Tok is generally well-known among people between 16 and 24, making up 41% of the total user-base. Asides age, the other stats about Tik Tok is the reasonably even popularity across the board. 56% of Tik Tok users are male, and 44% are female. The app is available in 150 markets in 75 languages, and iPhone or Android usage is a 52%/47% split. As long as you're in the correct age range, you can probably find your customers.

Considering that, it is recommended to possibly use Tik Tok for marketing if you have a young audience. While there's no doubt that older people will begin to use the platform soon, brand marketing resources will probably be better spent elsewhere if that's your targeted audience.

# CHAPTER TWO

## Why is Tik Tok is Valuable Platform for Brands and Influencers?

### Is it Relevant in the Entrepreneurial World?

Tik Tok has around 800 million active users, which is more significant than Twitter and Pinterest taken together. With this muzzle blast of new content to devour, its hooking power has gotten clear. Tik Tok is probably not going to be a fad. This may seem like a marketing goldmine, mainly because there might be less rivalry while different businesses dither to get aboard. However, engaging in with prospective customers in a place where they go to be entertained requires a nuanced, cautious approach.

Tik Tok advertising and marketing is a significant part of the 21st-century social media marketing strategy. The act of selling and promoting products and services has moved beyond the usual selling in stores and malls or advertising on mass media to social media. This has helped brands and influencers target their customers or the types of people they hope will become their customers.

There are two options for Tik Tok marketing strategy: working with influencers or creating unique and original content. Each of these strategies has its benefits and time commitments; Influencer marketing helps in concentrating on the individuals to whom appeal and to impact target costumers' behavior. If a brand sells to young people, they could consider working with influencers on Tik Tok. Like YouTube and other social media applications, Tik Tok's most crucial component is sharing videos. Any Tik Tok influencer marketing campaign will spin around influencers making, sharing, and once in a while live streaming videos that will promote a brand and make it alluring to their followers. The more engaging the videos, the better they reverberate with the audience.

Influencer marketing at its heart resembles storytelling. The most horrible mistake on Tik Tok would be to post anything looking like a traditional advertisement or trying to give an influencer specific guidelines. A brand needs to give their influencers enough flexibility to tell their story to their followers to keep them authentic. The influencers' followers will instantly know whether the videos promote brand products or not. If the videos are made in a different style from the influencer's typical videos, their followers will react badly.

**Why You Should Use Tik Tok for Influencer Marketing**

As with all influencer marketing, the way to have success on Tik Tok is working with influencers whose followers are linked with your target market. For this reason, for influencer promoting and marketing to be productive and successful for brands and businesses on Tik Tok, you have to interest the Tik Tok demographic because Tik Tok's youthful demographic finds traditional ads disdainful.

These influencers have audiences that might want to purchase your products, so for a piece of your marketing budget, you can partner with them and make an influencer marketing campaign. Pay these influencers to utilize your products on-camera or otherwise promote your product in their videos, and you'll get your products before new eyes. But more significantly, you will earn some of your customers' trust as well. One of every three customers trust an influencer's opinion more than a brand, so utilize that for your potential benefit.

Brands simply need to work with their influencers to think to creative strategies that help them arouse the curiosity of their audience and to build enthusiasm for their brand and product. Similar to much influencer marketing, brands can take most notification of measurements (statistics) relating to commitment and awareness. These can be a brilliant guide for brand loyalty.

The benefit of looking for well-known influencers in your specialty on Tik Tok is that they will have a vast user base who will pay attention to any video that they share talking about your brand/product.

Always take note, relevance is a higher priority than reach. Don't just decide on Tik Tok influencers with the most massive followings. Go for those with the most appropriate audience for your goals; the golden rule of Influencer Marketing is that relevance is more important than reach. When you have chosen suitable influencers, you should get in touch with them and structure a partnership. You need to guarantee that any deal is adequate for your influencers. They will not want any involvement except if there is something for them, and they can perceive how it can support their followers.

Don't just move toward the individuals behind accounts with the most massive followings. It will not only be unbelievably expensive to work with them, but they could fail in promoting your brand or products; however, numerous references to your product and brands could fail to be noticed. Search for those who are posting popular videos in your specialty by exploring the discover tab. Look through a bunch of keywords that identify with your industry, products, or services. Take note of the users with most followers or mainstream videos within this topic, watch their post to decide if they suit your product for your product, and consider connecting with them.

Likewise, marketing can be done without using influencers on Tik Tok. It has taken a while for Tik Tok to implement it. However, there is now a formal advertising system. Brands can also promote their business by using a business Tik Tok account. However, just like any other social network, it can be tough to build a sizeable audience on Tik Tok. This is so especially for businesses that don't have a staff of a similar demographic as their audience and struggle to run a business account. It is far easier for most brands to work with Tik Tok's established broadcasters or their influencers than to build a cherished and much-followed business account.

Making your content can be a powerful, marketing strategy. However, it will take a lot of of time, creativity, and resources. Tik Tok is largely dependent to viral content, so your content must be viral as well, otherwise, it will probably be overlooked by Tik Tokers.

The least demanding, best approach to ensure that your original content becomes mainstream and shareable is to dive into the "trend" culture. Use the find page to follow trending hashtags, and afterward create your version of the trend that includes a component of your business. Bonus points if it's funny or entertaining to increase your chance of virality.

Another easy way to create accessible content is to offer how-to's, tips and tricks, or insider secrets from your industry. If you own a bakery, you can show a pared-down, visually appealing version of the steps in a recipe, such as baking a cake to the tune of a pop song where the final version appears when you show yourself snapping your fingers. This method is a doubly effective strategy in the wake of the COVID-19 pandemic, where numerous in-person services have been compelled to figure out how to offer something different online. Create a Tik Tok of your top yoga models for stress relief or how to create extravagant cocktails in your kitchen to keep your content relevant to your audience while they stay home.

When you have created a content using one of these ideas or an original one you came up with for your business, add a couple of consistent, relevant hashtags to your post before you upload it since this is how users who do not follow you will find it.

Brands can also make a marketing campaign on Tik Tok using Paid Ads: Tik Tok has recently introduced this possibility. It is still early to see how successful or cost-effective these will be, especially when targeting the advertising-hating millennial demographic. Tik Tok has proposed that brands combine the use of one of the following ad formats:

1. **Brand Takeover:** These ads appear in the user's feed before they see any other user content. They're linkable to the advertiser's landing page and are exclusive to different categories. Mostly, just one ad can show in that space for a particular category each day.

2. **In-Feed Native Videos:** regardless of whether brands use them as a paid ad or their company Tik Tok channel, they could consider sharing some in-feed native videos. These can last up to 15 seconds, although they can share brief video clips as short as nine seconds.

3. **Hashtag Challenges:** Tik Tok users respond exceptionally well to challenges. There are usually multiple challenges going on at any time for Tik Tok users to participate. The usual type of Tik Tok challenges involves somebody setting a challenge (beginning it with a hashtag), hence the Hashtag Challenge. The challenge typically challenges others on Tik Tok to make and share a particular type of video.

4. **Branded Lenses:** Branded lenses are like the Snapchat 2D and 3D lenses for faces and photos.

Re-posting videos that were created on Tik Tok in other social media platforms like Instagram and Twitter is a hugely popular practice. If businesses have an engaged audience on those other platforms, they can likewise take advantage of the Tik Tok editing tools to create video content for their followers.

**Why Tik Tok is a Valuable Platform for Brands?**

Tik Tok is relatively new and has exploded in popularity. With Tik Tok on the rise, it is natural that companies are eager to examine and utilize the platform to connect with hard-to-reach but incredibly valuable potential customers. Simultaneously, it is imperative to combine experimentation with an excellent content strategy to make a decent digital first impression with platform users.

Tik Tok is experiencing a period of exponential growth at the moment, which implies that there is a broad audience ready to be taken advantage of by creative and fast-thinking brands. Brands who have effectively tuned to Tik Tok early have received tremendous benefits in term of brand impact, often with very little investment.

Brands must position themselves as a creative force to be reckoned with and possibly shift their reach to another, more global, and younger user base. Besides, it is relatively easy to achieve a viral status on Tik Tok. Unlike Instagram or YouTube, even accounts with zero followers can get millions of views on a new video. Content truly is king on Tik Tok.

With the huge potential for brand impact and reach, Tik Tok could soon be making it much easier to redirect the traffic from the platform by introducing a link in bio. This means businesses can now drive traffic to their websites from the app and direct followers to shopping destinations. Only a few users can currently add a link to their Tik Tok bio, but it is well possible that this possibility will be spread in oncoming months.

And for the time being, all users can add links to their Instagram and YouTube profiles from their Tik Tok profile.

# CHAPTER THREE

## **Finding Your Target Tik Tok Audience**

According to the famous entrepreneur Richard Branson, "Business opportunities are like buses; there is always another one coming." You may have missed the grand opening of Instagram, or the chance to be one of the few first influencers. It is never too late. If you wish to still make it on the most recent trending social media platform, Tik Tok is another opportunity.

Tik Tok may seem pretty much new and have not yet gained a worldwide audience. But contrary to what you may be thinking, influence on this platform is a must to reach a wider audience. It is reported that this platform, like Facebook, Twitter, and Instagram, has a very high percentage of mostly teens and young adult users. And just like any other platform, the user base must define your target audience and your influence on them.

This is necessary because the influence on any social media platform involves gathering several followings and likes. And followers and likes come when the product you're offering suits them. Many people target just anybody in a bid to get fans forcefully, but they may not end up going anywhere, because they are dealing with the wrong audience. Imagine being a law student, and then someone comes to advertise spare parts of an airplane. You have nothing to do with that, even if you fly on a plane. Plane maintenance is someone else's job.

The right audience is as crucial. Chris Guillebeau, in his book, "The $100 Start-Up", gives two ways to gather the target audience. These are:

1.  Traditional demographics of the users which involves their ethnicity, Sex/Gender, Income, Location, and Age.

2.  New Demographics which consists of their interests, Passions, Skills, Beliefs, and Values.

**Millionaire Entrepreneurs**

It is great to have fans on social media, but as an entrepreneur, you need to have an engaged following; people who will be loyal not just to you but to the product you offer. Some entrepreneurs connect their website to their Tik Tok accounts, so people get automatically redirected.

Other entrepreneurs have found the secrets to reach a lot of people on Tik Tok, by creating compelling videos of their luxurious lives, and probably at the end of the video they will tell people they will teach them how to make money so that they can be followed. They have huge fan bases even if they never come to eventually telling them how to make money.

Making money may not be as easy as these people figure it to be, but our Generation Z is never a fan of the rigorous process to achieve great wealth. This is why internet frauds are on the rise every day. Therefore, uploading a video teaching 16 – 23 years old (mostly on Tik Tok), the rigorous steps you took to become a millionaire are generally useless, which is why millionaire entrepreneurs do this.

**Taking a Cue from Other Social Media Platforms**

**Attractiveness**

On Tik Tok, your product has to be saleable to people in a precise age range, and you have to be compelling enough through your videos so they can buy it. Ksenia Zaharova, writes in, "How to Sell on Instagram," that 67% of Instagram users consider clear, detailed images to be even more important than the product description. Therefore, if these quality posts have links to to the site where they they can buy the product, they are likely to make impulsive buying decisions for your product.

**Demographics**

As stated above, taking note of the target audience by knowing who they are, what they are like, what they want, and how they want it is crucial in selling your products. From studies, it is estimated that 90% of Americans make purchase by impulse, which amounts to $200 of extra charges each month. Using these facts will move you toward the right product prices for single products.

If your target is young urban female or male, the right marketing approach will get them buying, if you know their behaviors.

A buyer persona is an example of tool entrepreneurs can use to know the audience. It could be written in an Excel document and it consists of information like:

- What age range do you reach?

- What's your average customer's level of income?

- What is their typical value?

- What their common pinpoint?

- What's the solution?

- Which type of content works best?

Surveys like this could also tell an entrepreneur about the kind of products their target audience wants. It could range from this to asking simple questions like;

- What is the audience's most significant problem with buying products like yours?

- What is the foremost question they may have about the product?

- How can you help to solve the problem?

The survey above was suggested in Chris Guillebeau's book.

**Trends**

It is wise for entrepreneurs to make good advantage of trending campaigns, mostly in the form of hashtags. Using the right hashtags at the right moments brings the right customers. There will be details on using hashtags to increase your influence in subsequent chapters. The description on your page tells whether customers will like you for who you are or dislike you for who you are not. Make the best use of the description part when filling in your information on Tik Tok. The description should be specific and detailed, including a few notes about what you sell, shop policies, and possibly about who you are and the hashtag of your accont.

The audience will be motivated to follow you if they know you have them at heart and show it. Your description could be the start of a beautiful, fruitful relationship with them.

**Collaborate with Other Entrepreneurs**

Collaborating with competitors, people who are where you want to be, or people who have products that are doing well could expose you to their audience and bring you to advertise your product well. Customers are usually loyal to brands they trust, and if these brands happen to be endorsing you, then it's a win.

**Staying Active**

"Being pro-active" is the word. Your willingness to actively engage in discussions goes a long way in increasing your influence on Tik Tok. Follow other entrepreneurs, like their posts and comment. People want to see that you are who you say you are. If there is a current trending movement or happening, give your input on it whether it's some children dying of hunger somewhere in the world, or the Black Lives Matter movement. Show that you are part of it and that you care.

**Connect Other Platforms**

Facebook, Instagram, and Twitter, where other Zoomers are active, are platforms On which to be active, too, as an entrepreneur. Many will like to check you up on other social media platforms to see if they find you. You have to present the same image. As a busy entrepreneur, it may seem difficult to handle all these, but applications such as Tik Tok help you schedule posts for many days ahead.

Other platforms like Facebook also helps to connect to specific niches, which is a big win for your business.

## How Business-Minded People Can Take Advantage of Tik Tok

An entrepreneur is business-minded; that is why there is something like an "Entrepreneurial Mindset." Even if there's no physical product, an entrepreneur will always find a way to do business. And if there is no product, affiliate marketing could be the catch. Mustafa Mohammed and Jide Maduako's story is one example of innovation with an entrepreneurial mindset. These two, one a business economist and the other a Computer scientist, developed an application that helps influencers make money through affiliate marketing. And with the increase of Tik Tok influence during the COVID-19 outbreak, their income increased more than ever in some months. As of July 7, 2020, Yoke Network has over 2000 influencers and over 600 million total audience.

Highlighted below are the different ways business-minded people can do business through Tik Tok.

## 1. Personal Products

Do you have a fashion shop, Artwork, or any other product you will sell? Social platforms such as Tik Tok should not be viewed as distractions. An entrepreneur should see opportunities in most places, which is how you must see Tik Tok. Having over 1000 followers on Tik Tok makes you eligible to go live. This will increase your viewership, and fans can gift money.

## 2. Affiliate Sales

In the absence of one's product, it is possible to sell other products and earn a commission. This is called Affiliate Marketing. A lot of influencers are doing this now. Also, more brands are more conscious of this now and probably get more buyers online than offline. These brands sponsor your videos on Tik Tok if you are an affiliate marketer for them. The figure from this could range from $10,000 and above for over 7 million fans. Keep in mind that the more fans one has, the more influence over their spending habit one can exert.

### 3. Other Products Related to the Application

Like the two entrepreneurs mentioned above, Mustafa and Jide, one can develop products that can be linked to Tik Tok. One beautiful thing about this is that, as Tik Tok grows, the product grows too. For Instagram, as the number of users increases, the number of users using tools like Instagram, Iconosquare, and Latergram increases.

### 4. Teach People How to be Successful Entrepreneurs on Tik Tok

This is another way an entrepreneur can make money from the platform. Like this book you are reading; one can make videos about how to utilize every feature on the app or any other thing. Answering people's questions is solving a problem, and filling a need, which is what entrepreneurs are specialized in.

# CHAPTER FOUR

# **Strategy on Building Tik Tok Content**

Tik Tok's extraordinarily creative and user-friendly algorithm makes it a winning social media platform. It enables anyone to open an account, create content, and gain attention.

Tik Tok videos are a great place to showcase your business and what you plan to offer. If your product requires assembling, you can create user-friendly, step by step videos that can be linked to your packaging. If you just want a full display of the business behind the scene shots, you can create that. And if you just want to express yourself yourself, Tik Tok has provided options for that, as well.

It is an excellent platform for fun and work, but what matters is reaching out to other users. It is how content can be created and presented to appeal and pass over the message they carry.

**1. Creativity:** The most significant selling point on any social media is creativity when delivering the content. Be ready to invest your time and other resources available in building up your content to be user-friendly and appealing. Several options enable creativity on the platform. Creativity is endless, and all it requires are some thoughts on unique and likable content.

You can include utilizing Tik Tok effects on your post. Tik Tok offers a wide range of effects to help to help your content to stand out.

**2. Concept:** Normally, Tik Tok videos are regarded as a particular concept. A search will give you options for trending concepts that you can incorporate into your content. This is also useful for brands and businesses as they get across to their target audience through this.

**3. Profile:** Like other social media channels, your profile description indicates what type of content your audience can expect from you. That is why you need to be unique but still clearly communicate who you are and what you deliver.

This also includes your profile picture. Use a profile picture that is clear, unique, and outstanding. And if you are using a video instead, as Tik Tok made it possible, bring your creativity into the mix.

**3. Hashtag Challenges:** Hashtags are used in many other social platforms for searching and sorting content. The same applies to Tik Tok. A specific hashtag is used for a challenge as part of a viral trend, as an encouragement for users to participate in making similar videos.

The idea is to make the content fun, easy, and meaningful. Brands have made use of this hashtag challenges to promote themselves on the platform successfully.

**4. Make Exciting Videos that are Consistent with the Message You Want to Pass Over:** Tik Tok videos can last as long as one minute, giving you sixty seconds to express yourself and the message you want to pass over. Make them count. And as mentioned earlier, be sure to use creativity.

## Tips for Effective Tik Tok Marketing

If the target for your brand or business includes anyone within the age of 13 to 30, Tik Tok marketing will get you the desired audience, target customers, and future markets. Tik Tok has over one billion users and growing. Its developing range of ad options makes it a prospective platform for marketers to promote their products.

Here is some information you should consider to gain success in marketing your brand or on this growing platform.

**1. Consider the type of market you want to reach:** Tik Tok major users are the generation Z and generation X. But we can say that it reaches out to the Millennials as well. If you expect your market audience to be within this range, you should go right ahead.

The good news is that Tik Tok promises to become a social media app that will be everybody's favorite. So this is the time to build your brand and business on this platform.

**2. If you are sure you want to make your Tik Tok account mainly business-related, you need to change it to a pro-account:** This will enable you to track your analytics and overall growth. You will be able to see how your videos are doing and how much response your content is getting back.

It is just like the analytics you have on Instagram, but here you have Tik Tok analytics.

**3. Be sure to follow current Tik Tok trends:** When you see people use a hashtag on the discovery page or see a topic that shows up a lot on your "For You" page, you should know that it is what is trending at that time. Tik Tok trends can be powerful and useful in gaining attention to your brand or business.

Your creativity helps in making those trends work for you and how you can fit those trends around your business. Following prominent content creators to ensure you stay up to trend could work in scoring numerous interest points. A lot of trends are rapidly going viral, and immediately reacting to these trends gives higher chances to your video to go viral, too.

These trends may vary, from contents to hashtag and challenges. And they can be fast-moving. So be ready to keep up with the craze.

**4. Make use of suitable hashtags:** Making use of hashtags that are popular and people are interested in could bring your brand or business into the spotlight. Like every other social media platform, hashtags help categorize and sort out topics and contents to make them easy to find. Using the most relevant hashtags will prompt engagement on your content. Hashtags can be measured with insights such as clicks, number of views, engagement, and trending slots. So when deciding on hashtags to use, look up for the ones you think will fit your content and make use of of hashtags which are slightly less use. This is because your content could get swamped in a sea of content. That might nullify the effect of visibility And make you invisible to those who are most relevant to your campaign.

Using hashtags will get you more followers, help enhance the range of your content, and identify competitors.

**5. Create hashtag challenges:** This is a significant way to promote brands and events. Like Jimmy Fallon, celebrities that started the hashtag "tumbleweed challenge" and business houses like McDonalds, which ran #bigmactiktok challenge, have gathered millions of views.

The hashtag challenge campaigns are usually non-sponsored. All you need are ideas of challenges that are easy to do and fun, that will pass over the message you want. Hashtag challenges by influencers are positive for extensive reach, and you can make use of that to spread your brand message.

6. **Utilizing influencer marketing:** Using Tik Tok influencers is a great use to generate content for your own Tik Tok profile and get a response to your products from influencers' followers. They enable you to present your content to the world by building a reputation for the quality of the content they share on your behalf. Being in a productive work relationship with people who can influence your potential customers increases your chances of visibility on the platform.

7. **Post often, comment regularly and encourage comments on your post:** Just like most social networks, your followers appreciate regular content on your account. You can say that the more content you post, the simpler it will be for people to find your account and decide to follow you.

Also, taking the time to look at other people's content and making meaningful comments will build meaningful conversations with potential customers.

8. **Let your contents have a theme:** Your business offers a particular or specific product, and that should be the basis for your content creation. Specificity gives you a consistent image. And building this consistency over time will help you gain a following of people interested in what you have to offer.

You want your content to pass over a message and be visually appealing, so a theme would give it a personality at the eyes of your audience.

**9. Make use of Tik Tok campaign options:** Tik Tok's formal advertising system can be utilized to make your product well-known. There are three types of such ads available.

**1. In-feed native ads:** This is very similar to Instagram stories in full-screen mode. These are skippable ads and have the option of adding website links and "Order Now" buttons that enable users to land on your page directly.

**2. Hash-tag challenges ads:** In this type of advertising, a user is served a banner ad that is put up on the discover page depending on the user content that takes the user to a page of instructions of the featuring challenge. This tool targets a specific audience and can be measured with banner views, clicks, number of user-generated content, number of views, trending slots, and engagement.

**3. Brand takeover ads:** This form of advertising uses a mix of images, short video clips, and GIF's that link to a landing page or the hostage challenge of any set. This ad makes use of a category, and only a single brand can take up a specific category per day.

Although Tik Tok still has a long way to go, it shows great potential to become a lasting social media platform. But with the surge in the number of users, promoting your brand and business on this platform would get you your desired audience.

# CHAPTER FIVE

# <u>Why Is Tik Tok's Algorithm Key in the Success of Marketing and E-Commerce?</u>

Tik Tok has carved a name for itself in the crowded social space, turning into a global phenomenon. From comedy videos to lip-synch, from cooking tutorials to do-it-yourself home design, dance videos, and the sky is the limit from there. Tik Tok genuinely makes us feel like we can do everything. There is nothing worse than the feeling of posting one's most recent, perfect work only to wake up the next morning and see little or no views and likes. That is colossal disappointment; to avoid this, the Tik Tok algorithm helps videos receive the sort of affection and attention they deserve. Some factors, like user interactions, video information, and device and account settings along with Tik Tok's algorithm, decide how well video performs.

## How Does Tik Tok's Algorithm Work?

Tik Tok algorithm is not as basic as those of some other social platforms out there, yet that does not mean there are no strategies to improve your reach and engagement because some factors influence your video's prosperity. The first, and ostensibly most significant, idea to understand is how Tik Tok feeds your content to its users. An essential way to understand Tik Tok's algorithm is by separating it into two areas:

First, Tik Tok gets a video and releases an initial push to viewers. When this is done, the algorithm gives your video a performance rating. This includes how many shares, comments, and likes your video gets during its initial release. At this point, the algorithm compares the number of view of the video with the like it gets, setting off the platform to show the video to more people.

Your Tik Tok feed is ultimately divided into two parts, your "Following" and the "For You" page. While the "Following" page may let you see what your friends are doing, the "For You" page is a useful tool to build your visibility and possible fluctuation. This is an excellent and ideal time to note that Tik Tok not exclusively drives you to fame, it can likewise be an incredible marketing tool. The constant stream of edited content is not just addicting, but exceptionally boosted to posts from users, creators, and businesses alike, that you interact with.

As indicated by the Tik Tok Algorithm, the "For You" page is the initial phase in winning the Tik Tok lottery. With a better understanding of how Tik Tok algorithm works, it is much easier for users to gain popularity with a potential user reach of more than 1 billion people. Tik Tok fame isn't unreasonably out of reach, and with viral content creation that is pertinent, trending, and engaging, the popularity is around the corner. As a new user, Tik Tok Algorithm shows you the "For You" page as the first thing you see when you open the application, containing unlimited videos that you could like; as the user keeps utilizing Tik Tok, their "For You" page mirrors the user's preferences. The system suggests content by ranking videos based on a combination of factors, beginning from interests the user expresses as a new user and changing things s/he shows they are not intrigued by and this is the reason why Tik Tok is a triumph. It's not social media, it's social entertainment. Likewise, another primary explanation behind its prosperity is that it hits your sweet spot suggesting you suggesting you content posted by your friends/people you follow.

Tik Tok is utilizing AI to assess the quality of each shared video. Everybody understands that content is king, which applies to Tik Tok; great content equals social achievement. At the point when a video is uploaded, Tik Tok shows it to few users in popular trending videos. This way, the user doesn't get bored. The algorithm, at that point, assess the statics of your video, such as the number of likes, comments, and shares it gets. It is the viral videos that eventually act as the carrot on the stick, hooking users to watch to an ever-increasing number of videos.

The rate of likes brands and users should aim to is one for every ten views. This triggers the algorithm to show your video to more individuals. The algorithm is triggered by the speed of the engagements it gets. Content that gets not as much as the like-view rate of 1/10 will stop growing. The uniqueness of Tik Tok is that you do not need to bother with a strong following to become a web sensation. Anybody can record a video, share it on Tik Tok, and begin to get views based on this algorithm. Additionally, what hashtags you use, your location, music choices, and even the absolute first Tik Tok video you like, they would all be able to influence the Tik Tok algorithm.

What makes Tik Tok different from other applications like Instagram and Snapchat is that Tik Tok utilizes artificial intelligence to decide precisely how great your video is. It ranks you on a scale of ten views to tens of millions of views. Adding to this, the higher the level of fulfillment your video gets , the more it gets spread. As your distribution grows, the algorithm takes into account the time that your video needs to continue to grow at the same pace. This means it is a lot easier to go from 10 followers to 100 followers than from 50,000 followers to 100,000 followers.

Complete views have a great weight in the algorithm, it is suggested to keep your videos between 10-15 seconds if you want to become famous online. Tik Tok has many features that can help creativity, like stickers, filters, and music overlays that can catch the attention of the audience.

Tik Tok has legitimately earned its place among the social media application elites. Brands that can be adaptable and adjust their content and channel to deal with the ever-changing social media scene can reap the benefits. This is some genuine Intel for brands and organizations hoping to get higher engagement with their Tik Tok content and how you can begin to use it for your own benefit.

## How to Use Tik Tok's Algorithm to Get Your Content on the "For You" Page

If you are a brand, business, or content creator on Tik Tok, the point is that you want to get more views, likes, and comments on your content. After all, the more eyes on your videos, the higher the opportunity you have to engage your Tik Tok audience and show off your brand. And the key to getting greater engagement on your videos is working with Tik Tok's algorithm to get your content on as many "For You" page as possible. Be that as it may, getting the desired spot on a "For You" page takes something more than adding #fyp to your caption significantly.

To assist you with creating the best content and get more spotlight on the Tik Tok feed there are a few factors that influence Tik Tok's algorithm, from nailing your hashtag strategy to choosing trending songs and sounds, which are parts of the approaches, to hack the Tik Tok algorithm: Factors taken into account by Tik Tok's algorithm include (but are not limited to): Hashtags, Tik Tok captions, use of trending songs and sounds, posting when one's audience is most active, video content and editing and finally location.

While there's no one definitive formula for hacking the algorithm, there are a couple of different factors that could influence video performance and your follower growth as Tik Tok algorithms continually grow, change, and Acquire information from our actions on the application. These factors include consistency, Tik Tok duets, new features, and completion rate.

**Tracking Your Tik Tok Analytics and Statistics**

Tik Tok is a developing platform that represents a unique opportunity for brands which hope to drive higher engagement on a younger audience. Although the platform has an enormous user base, one reason brands have been hesitant to add Tik Tok to their marketing was the absence of analytics. With no in-application analytics tool, it was hard for brands to value platform outcomes from the resources they were dispensing. It additionally implied that brands partnering together with influencers couldn't gauge the effectiveness of their collaboration.

Presently with the introduction of Tik Tok's native analytics, joined with Pentos' third-party tool, brands can value the performance of their content on the platform. With analytics finally available, they can have a reliable screen of the platform's outcomes and assess what is the best move to do next.

Obviously, before hopping into the platform, brands must ensure Tik Tok is ideal for their brand. If their ideal content does not include the platform's average user, it probably won't be worth it assigning the resources to the experiment. Beyond driving engagement, it's essential to decide whether the platform will assist them with obtaining users and reach their goals.

Social media is buzzing with Tik Tok's explosive growth, and that is why it is so significant to understand Tik Tok analytics. Track the correct statistics, so you can be able to differentiate hype from reality. If your brand is new to Tik Tok, analytics can remove some guesswork from content strategy. Available insights on Tik Tok pro accounts can give you valuable information about anything, from when you post to what you post. So, brands must realize which Tik Tok statistics they should track, where to find them, and how they can utilize them for their potential benefit.

The fundamental distinction between a Tik Tok pro account and a standard one comes down to Tik Tok analytics. Pro accounts offer analytics, while regular accounts do not. Much like Instagram creator profiles, Tik Tok pro accounts let content creators have insight about audience and performance. From the Tik Tok analytics dashboard, Pro account holders can learn about their followers, track their views and engagement, and do a lot more. A regular Tik Tok account can be changed to a pro account.

Changing to a pro account is simple; start by going to your profile settings and tap the 'manage my account' option. On the following screen, tap switch to a pro account. Next, you are prompted to choose a featured category for your account. The category includes media, personal blogs, entertainment, public figure, education, and more. The last step is to enter a telephone number for your account and afterward enter the code you get through SMS. When you've set up your pro account, go back to the Settings menu, then you will see 'observe an analytics' option. Tap the option button to open your Tik Tok analytics dashboard.

Tik Tok analytics will now start to record data; the dashboard will not show any past data. You will have to wait up to seven days for your account to produce enough data to start showing insights. During this period, it is suggested that you share as much content as possible so you can get deeper insights. Once the analytics begins to give you feedback, you can plunge into your account insights. Similar to all analytics, this data will become more precise and accurate after some time, as you share more content.

Brands should quantify views, engagement (likes, comments, and shares) and reach to evaluate their campaign's success. Tik Tok has likewise started permitting users to include profile links, which means businesses would now be able to direct people to their sites from the application and direct followers to shopping destinations.

Regarding statistics, now the most significant challenge with brands attempting to use influencer marketing and promoting on the application is the difficulty of executing and evaluating campaigns with a group of influencers simultaneously. Gathering data manually can turn into an overwhelming task; however, it's an absolute necessity if the effect of a campaign has to be determined.

Influencer marketing platforms can be useful in this regard, since they automatically gather, analyze, and present data in a relatable manner that bodes well and helps one focus and guide future efforts. While thinking about whether Tik Tok influencer marketing is a fit for your brand, it makes sense to apply guidelines similar to those you would use on other social media platforms.

This Tik Tok statistics is a good sign of brand interest. It gauges the number of individuals who appreciated your video enough to look at your profile or individuals interested in seeing what your brand is up to on the platform. TikTok analytics makes your marketing campaign easier as it analyzes any TikTok profile, hashtags, videos, and songs to understand the platform and grow your business very fast.

There are three main classes that Tik Tok displays within your account dashboard:

1. **Profile overview:** The profile overview tab is valuable for identifying how well your Tik Tok profile is generally performing. This information includes your total video views, profile views, and follower number.

2. **Content insights:** The followers' tab in Tik Tok analytics shows a top-line perspective on your audience demographics. You can see the gender split and and the locations of your audience organized by percentage rate. Since Tik Tok has scaled over different nations, you can hope to have audience from all over the world.

3. **Follower insights:** The Content tab in Tik Tok analytics offers the most extravagant insights. Just like in an "aerial view", you can see the total views on every video post from the previous seven days, showed all together from newest to the oldest.

# CHAPTER SIX

# <u>Entrepreneurs on Tik Tok</u>

As the utilization of video keeps on ascending in all aspects of life, from entertainment to guidance to news, it turns into a more significant marketing impact. Wyzowl's state of video marketing 2020 reports that the number of businesses using videos as a marketing tool has expanded from 61% in 2016 to 85% projected for 2020. Part of the reason behind the rising speculation is that customers currently watch an average of 16 hours of online video every week, a 52 % expansion since 2018. Despite everything, they still want more.

86% of individuals might want to see more videos from brands, as indicated by Wyzowl, with 36%wanting more educational/instructive videos and 14% interested in more product demos. In an assessment of how, or where, advertisers plan on using videos, the report found that Youtube, Facebook, and LinkedIn were the top performers; however, 15% intend to invest in TikTok promotions. When asked about their prosperity rates with video over all platforms, 79% of respondents to the Wyzowl study revealed having been productive and successful. On Tik Tok specifically, however, 66%report achievements. Many see Tik

Tok as offering unimagined potential, proposing that now, not later is an ideal time to start using it.

A digital trend report revealed that out of 11 minutes spent on a cell phone, 10 minutes are on an application. That implies the opportunity is there to create brand awareness. Tik Tok may appear just like another app for kids, but if its growth is compared to that of other social platforms, it turns out that Instagram needed six years.

It took some time, but Tik Tok finally introduced ads on the platform. A worldwide overview by Global Web Index found that 52% of Tik Tok users internationally would purchase an item just to be a part of the community. Furthermore, 61% will, in general, purchase advertised products. The application offers exact targeting, so you can ensure that your advertisements are reaching the specific users who would be keen on what you have to offer.

Tik Tok offers four unique types of advertisements. There is in-feed native content; this kind of ad is like Snapchat or Instagram story advertisements and supports different features like website clicks or application downloads. You can gauge the campaign's success through tracking clicks, impressions, click-through rate (CTR), video views, and engagement.

Brand takeovers are those that let brands take over Tik Tok for the day. A brand takeover promotion springs up when somebody opens Tik Tok. They can create pictures, GIFs, and videos with embedded links to landing pages or hashtag challenges. Tik Tok just permits one advertiser for this format per day and ensures five million daily impressions.

There are branded lenses, which resemble the Snapchat 2D and 3D lenses for faces and photographs. As indicated by Tik Tok, 64% of its users have attempted face filters and lenses.

Lastly, there are hashtag challenges; rather than trying to make a hashtag challenge famous online, you can use promoted hashtags to get higher engagement.

TikTok is here, and it doesn't appear to be going anywhere. If you want your business to grow and have success, becoming acquainted with Tik Tok is a good first step. It is a video-sharing platform that rose out of relative obscurity to become one of the leading social companies globally, and one of the most business-friendly for entrepreneurs who know how to make it work.

Tik Tok is specially crafted for personal-brand building, and numerous entrepreneurs are utilizing it in just that way. This is an ideal opportunity to get acquainted with Tik Tok; Tik Tok is a social media platform that gives content, entertainment, and engagement for most millennials. The platform supports just a video format of 15 to 60 seconds to catch users' short attention span.

Tik Tok is winning on social media platforms since it is not difficult to use, it is very creative, and has a user-friendly algorithm. These characteristics put together are a 100% reliable formula for

for taking over Instagram and Facebook. Where Tik Tok stands out is in producing brand awareness and engagement. Users that can combine engaging or useful content in a 15-or 60-second video clip can observe practically immediate results. And the use of Tik Tok for creating videos for advertisements and advancement is cost-friendly as most videos cost nothing; all the cutting and editing are in-app features, so it doesn't require any special tool or editing software.

Businesses ready to be funny and engaging, or to make fun of themselves, can witness a fast growth on TikTok. Right now, this seems to be one of the brands' advertising secret.

## Dos and Don'ts for Entrepreneurs on TikTok

Anyone who wants to build a marketing campaign on TikTok should know the following do's and don'ts:

**1. Keep your videos light and fun:** Tik Tok is an opportunity to show a more creative and entertaining side of your brand. While making videos for advertisements or advancement, such videos should be made simple and Relatable for your audience.

**2. Be spontaneous:** Content that is hilarious, real life, and casual plays the best; videos that jump directly to the point and are around 15 seconds long are preferred.

**3. Use music:** Music is a significant part of Tik Tok and can be used deliberately to make videos all the more fascinating and engaging.

**4. Do proper formatting for the platform:** When shooting videos, ensure that they are vertical and not horizontal.

**5. Start a challenge:** Start campaigns that challenge users to make and share Tik Tok videos related to the challenge, use the hashtag #Hashtag Challenge, and tag three of their friends to challenge them and spread your campaign.

**6. Respond to other brand challenges:** In addition, to starting your brand challenge, take an interest in challenges set up by other businesses.

**7. Mimic content that is trending:** As a brand, you must intently monitor what's trending on a daily basis to rapidly reproduce the content that will spread your products and services to potential users.

**8. Collaborate with influencers and partners:** Brands can engage or collaborate with influencers on Tik Tok; Tik Tok influencer has built an army that can enhance engagement and awareness towards your brand rapidly.

**9. Keep good customer relationships:** Customers should be treated like kings, as their complaints are promptly treated.

**10. Do not make a hard-sell advertisement**: If your business has a product, the best kind of content possible is one that showcases your product, but do not feel just like a simple ad.

# CHAPTER SEVEN

# <u>Understanding Hashtags and Hashtag Challenges</u>

Starting a business could be a confusing experience. You might not know which direction you want to give to your business. Several entrepreneur which are now successful had that experience, too.

Creating hashtags is like creating a brand. You get to see this as you Dive in this new chapter of your life. Hashtags also help you see competitors, as well as your visibility to them. In this chapter, we will be going through the history of hashtags and its relevance in increasing one's influence on Tik Tok.

**History of Hashtags**

Chris Messina, is one whose name cannot be forgotten when it comes to how hashtags started. Hashtag was seen as a nerdy thing on twitter. It enables the user to apply dynamic, and user-generated metadata tag. It could be made in the form of letters, digits, and underscores. So, anyone who looks for a particular word or tag sees all posts in which the tags appear.

Chris Messina's first use of the hashtag was in a 2007 tweet. Although Twitter did not adopt it according to Messina's suggestion, it became a common feature for many people. Many other social platforms like Facebook, Instagram, YouTube, Reddit, and even Tik Tok are not left out from its use. Gen Z, millennials, influencers, celebrities, and even entrepreneurs commonly use these tags.

"Hashtag," due to its widespread use, was added to the Oxford English Dictionary as of 2014. Personalities use hashtags to promote their corporate or personal Twitter accounts and receive mentions and replies to posts. To trend hashtags, it is often encouraged to use it not just on twitter but also on other search engines.

Political protests and campaigns like the #blacklivesmatter movement or the #OccupyWallStreet have been organized thanks to hashtags. These went viral since any hashtag, if promoted by enough people, can trend and become famous.

## Why hashtags?

It is a linking medium; it forms a community of thoughts, words, actions, and characters. It connects people and ideas, which is the goal of most social media platforms; An entrepreneur's proper use of hashtags will determine, to a large extent, how successful he/she is on the internet.

## How hashtags should be used?

## Use popular tags

Using trending hashtags on a post can increase the visibility of your post on Tik Tok. One can find trending tags by being active on social media. Popular tags could build campaigns. Popular videos on Tik Tok have tags attached to them. Find out what they are and use them at the right time. The timing is also a factor involved in the success of the tag. When you use a tag that trended in 2014, there will be very little importance unless there is a current campaign similar to that. It is also possible to create one that will be trending. Experts suggest using one alongside a trending tag. So, when a lot of individuals see the posts according to their popularity, they see that tag you have just created too.

As an entrepreneur, another advice is not to be too eager to use popular hashtags that do not go with your niche. Popular hashtags meet a broader audience, but niche hashtags are more specific and will reach people who are more likely to engage with your post. Niche hashtags, therefore, bring you further in the sales funnel.

**Use specific brand tags.**

This depends on what kind of product or service you are offering on Tik Tok. Since personalities "trend" tags, many big brands do this too. If these tags are relevant to your product, then go ahead. The "Discover" page on Tik Tok is an excellent place to search for the right trending tags. Whether they are industry-related, location tags, or modifies #forsale hashtags, it all goes.

**Keep it simple**

Whatever new hashtag you tend to create for your brand, it shouldn't be too long or complicated. The rule here is relevance (as we've been saying) and specificity. It should also not be too generic. Recently, Instagram banned some too generic hashtags like #photography #iphoneography #sexy #popular and many more. "A hashtag is blocked because it returns inappropriate or pornographic results that exceed a certain threshold," says Ksenia Zaharova in her book, "How to Sell on Instagram." It is also wise to apply these rules on Tik Tok.

**Do not overuse them**

Just because hashtags on Tik Tok are fresh, unlike the ones on Instagram or Twitter, this does not mean they should be overused. Tik Tok limits the caption to be just 100 characters, therefore maximize hashtags, but do not overuse them. Avoid creating a post with more than 30 hashtags. It just displays you as a hungry person, hunting for popularity at all costs. It somehow created distrust in the minds of your fans and others who will see that video.

**The Relevance of self-created hashtags to Entrepreneurs**

Website owners know the importance of Search Engine Optimization (SEO) to online marketing. That same importance can quantify the relevance of hashtags on social media platforms like Tik Tok. Every user on Tik Tok can create their hashtags, whether they are new to the platform or have been there for a while. Using other users' hashtags helps increase one's content reach, so do self-created hashtags apply to a specific niche?

When doing a particular marketing campaign, it is wise to create a hashtag for all content created for the campaign. This also helps to keep track and easily find anything related to the campaign.

If a new project is coming, it is great to create a hashtag for that and make people anticipate the campaign by creating content around it and giving people sneak peeks to fuel their curiosity. Many influential people use it to announce the launch of a new start-up or a new idea and create a buzz about the project.

Customers can also use the hashtag created for a specific product when they buy or review the product. This will increase the popularity of hashtags. This is one of the two ways to get free and quality user-generated content.

The last but not the least benefit is that the hashtag challenge could also increase the popularity of the brand on other social platforms just like the #icebucket or the #pepsicanbalance challenge that went all over social media.

**Some popular hashtags**

Some of the popular hashtags on Tik Tok as of June 2020 are;

#blacklivesmatter

#dadsoftiktok

#yogaglow

#juneteenth

#beyourselfchallenge

#fyp

#thanksdad

**The Hashtag Challenge**

This is an indirect method to drag fans and engage other users on Tik Tok. From Guess to Jimmy Fallon, to Chipotle, it has rapidly increased online engagement and brand impact. The idea behind this is that people create content that increases their brand's impact and brings potential benefits in the long run. On Tik Tok, these challenges are spearheading enormous engagement on the platform. Users

like these challenges because they are dynamic, and each user can interpret the challenge in their own way. Brands are also free to create their own challenge rules, custom sounds and effects, and anything else about the challenge.

However, these challenges could be expensive for start-ups. It is advisable to encourage the audience to follow these challenges with ads and brand takeovers to drive awareness on the challenge. These challenges can then be linked to different landing pages to generate leads for the brand.

Chipotle started a #Guacdance challenge, on The National Avocado Day, which required users to make videos of dance moves dedicated to Guacamole. They got 900 million+ views and tremendously increased sales.

Jimmy Fallon, who was new on Tik Tok at the time, started a collaborated challenge, called #tumbleweedchallenge and had around 30 million views.

Another popular hashtag challenge is the #inmydenim challenge by Guess, a company that markets jeans. Users had to show how they wear their products. This resulted in more than 40 million views.

**Tips to Understand when to create your hashtag challenges**

Ask yourself the following questions when creating a branded hashtag.

- What do you want to be the result of your hashtags: popularity, or engagement?

- What is your niche?

This is an example of a demographic to engage for a particular hashtag. Remember, as discussed in previous chapters, they should be broad, yet specific. Other tips are:

- Follow current trends or people that are doing what you would like to do on Tik Tok?

- Think solely about your product, but make people see that it can give balance to their personality and class.

- Use effects and animation to make it fun, engaging, and create something unique for your brand.

- Create rules and make the users follow them.

- Give users the freedom to be dynamic with whatever content they are creating for the challenge.

- Create social currency.

- Use popular memes.

- Select a name that fits the hashtag challenge. People can easily relate to it and remember it.

- The effective use of sounds should also not be neglected.

It is best to study popular hashtags challenges all over social media, know what made them go viral, and try to implement relevant lessons learned to suit your needs. I hope you will use these tools, "Hashtags" and generate mind-blowing leads.

# CHAPTER EIGHT

# <u>Running an Influencer Marketing Campaign</u>

One of the most important criteria for online marketing (and any marketing) is that you reach the kind of people you think will become your customers. Influencer marketing means you have to do one step back and focus on the people who are liked by your target customers and are able to influence their behavior. If you sell to a young audience, you might consider working on Tik Tok with influencers.

When most people think of influencers and marketing, they usually think about traditional social media channels: Facebook, Instagram, and Twitter. Influencer marketing, however, started long before Instagram became the place for ambassadors for celebrity brands.

**Who is an influencer?**

An influencer is an individual or group with personal authority, attitude, expertise, or relationships which affect others' purchasing decisions. An influencer can be a known figure in a particular industry, topic area, or niche that has gained a following. The main characteristic of influencers is that either through expertise or experience, they have built a relationship with their audience. Examples of people we consider influencers are famous figures, gamers, bloggers, industry experts, and social media influencers.

**Tik Tok Influencers**

Social media influencers (such as Tik Tok) have built a reputation for their knowledge and expertise on a particular subject matter. They make they make posts on their preferred social media channel on a regular basis and generate substantial follow-ups from enthusiastic, engaged people who pay close attention to their videos.

You may also describe social media influencer as someone who, thanks to his/her authority or relationship with target customers, may affect the individual's purchases. The definition of social media influencer goes beyond the number of followers that can attract such people to a social media network or website. The ability to build engagement with the core audience on the street is crucial for a brand.

**Marketing campaigns**

Marketing campaigns promote products via various media, such as e-television, radio, print, and online platforms. Campaigns are not exclusively advertising-based and may include demonstrations, video conferencing, and other interactive techniques. Companies operating in highly competitive markets and franchises should conduct regular marketing campaigns and commit considerable resources to these campaigns.

**Tik Tok's Marketing Campaigns**

Tik Tok's marketing ecosystem is new, but brands jump into the advertisement potential of this app. Below are a couple of different ways to incorporate Tik Tok marketing.

1. IN-FEED ADS

2. BRAND TAKEOVER ADS

3. TIK TOK HASHTAG CHALLENGE ADS

4. TIK TOK SHOPPABLE ADS: THE 'HASHTAG CHALLENGE PLUS'

5. BRANDED TIK TOK STICKERS

6. TIK TOK INFLUENCER MARKETING ADS

**Influencer Marketing Campaigns**

Influencer marketing is a form of social media marketing involving endorsements and placement of products from influencers, individuals, and organizations that have a supposed level of knowledge or social influence in their field. Influencer content can be framed as testimonial advertising; influencers play the role of a potential buyer, or third parties may be involved.

As with all influencer marketing, partnering with influencer's whose followers suit your target audience is crucial to success on Tik Tok. Therefore you need to appeal to Tik Tok demographic for influencer marketing to be successful for you on Tik Tok.

**How to go about an influencer marketing campaign**

The most effective form of marketing on Tik Tok is influencer marketing. You don't suffer from ads' negative implications, and you don't have to worry about building the right audience as you do on your company account with native videos. You just need to collaborate with the right influencer to come up with an innovative approach that will help them pique their audience's interest in building interest in your brand and product.

**How to Build a Tik Tok Influencer Marketing Strategy**

Marketers should follow these steps in order to develop an impacting marketing strategy for Tik Tok influencer:

**1. Understand Tik Tok Platform**

If Tik Tok is unchartered territory, do not immerse yourself without research to determine if your brand is ready to launch a campaign. If you are reading this guide, you are learning if Tik Tok is a good platform for your brand or not. Test new ways to reach your target audience or consider working with a reputable marketing agency, such as Mediakix, who knows the platform and has established relationships with Tik Tok creators.

**2. Determine Campaign Goals for Tik Tok.**

Consider what your ultimate aim is for the campaign of your brand — is it pushing UGC or motivating users to use your app? Consider the goals, and know which KPIs you will use to calculate the effectiveness of the campaign. Clearly defined objectives enable you to measure your campaign's ROI and overall strategy.

**3. Research & Vet influencer Tik Tok.**

The Tik Tok creators you want to partner with ought to be carefully researched. Do they have a proven track record of high-quality content? Do they receive real commitment? Is their audience attuned to yours? Do their preferences and values suit your brands authentically? Do not partner with an influencer based solely on vanity metrics (e.g., followers) on Tik Tok but do some effort to understand if they fit your goals.

**4. Let Tik Tok Express Creativity**

With the newness of Tik Tok, brands might be tempted to exert too much creative control over what is being published. Trust the platform creators who have established authenticity in their space. Refrain from taking away their creative spark and let influencers to get input — this will also go a long way in the growth of a long-term relationship with the influencer.

**5. Measure the results of the Tik Tok campaign.**

It goes without saying, but it is pointless to conduct a campaign without knowing how to evaluate its success. Know general performance benchmarks to continuously test and optimize your marketing strategy for Tik Tok influencers. If your goal is brand impact, see how many views the collaboration earns, how much engagement the post generates.

**6. Ensuring sponsorships for Tik Tok influencers and FTC-compliant.**

Brands should check if their Tik Tok influencers have serve for other brands on other social media platforms. Should know that FTC violations can be very expensive for a brand. Ensure that influencer of Tik Tok use # ad and comply with FTC guidelines to avoid getting into a legal mess.

**7. Seek other advertisement types on Tik Tok.**

Building a strong marketing strategy for Tik Tok influencers can be a lucrative endeavor for your brand. Combine it with other Tik Tok advertising tactics, so to get the most out of the platform. This will boost the presence of your brand and it will strengthen your overall marketing efforts at Tik Tok.

## How to find Tik Tok influencers

To launch a marketing campaign that impacts on Tik Tok, you will need to find reputable Tik Tok influencers to partner with. As in every marketing strategy for influencers, marketers must exert their best judgment when choosing influencers to represent their brand. Failing in examining and assessing influencers puts brands at risk of failing the overall marketing campaign on Tik Tok.

Brands should also be familiar with what is essential to influencers in a brand partnership. See the five tips about how to find influencers for Tik Tok to better prepare your brand for a successful Tik Tok marketing influencer campaign:

1. Know your audience.

2. Do Google Organic Search.

3. Check Related, Trending Hashtags on 'Discover Page' by Tik Tok.

4. Identify existing content sponsored by influencers on Tik Tok.

5. Cross-check known influencers on other social networks.

## Benefits of running an influencer marketing campaign

Here are six significant advantages of using influencer marketing to strengthen your social strategy.

### 1. Builds confidence fast

The influencers have established relationships with their followers. Plus, they have confidence with their audience and they can boast a good reputation with them.

People respect their content and recommendations. By sharing the content of an influencer, you will get their attention soon and and they will start sharing yours, putting your message before an active audience.

## 2. Improves awareness towards the brand

As mentioned above, influencer marketing can significantly increase your online reach and positioning. Social users can learn more about your brand, your background, who you are, and the products you offer. The secret to optimizing influencer strategy is to ensure that you also have meaningful content that adds value to both sides of their social media activity.

## 3. Enriches your approach on the web

Sharing influencer content will help you fill the holes on your posting schedule. It works well in case you run out of ideas about the material to post or when you need some quality material to shar on your social media.

## 4 Reaches the target market effectively

This is one of the most important tips. Your content is placed in front of social users who are already interested in your niche through relevant influencers. You don't have to spend extra money on testing and finding your audience. The influencer has filtered and fostered this audience on social media already.

## 5. Provides the audience with tremendous value

The centerpiece of inbound marketing is to deliver content that solves problems, educates, and inspires your intended public. This concept is embraced by influencer marketing, as influencers are already in tune with the needs of the people they serve. In turn, you can easily leverage their content to give your audience value.

## 6. Builds Partnerships

Connecting and becoming engaged with an influencer may be the beginning of a great relationship. You never know where those connections could end when you are in it for the long-haul. There could be future joint-ventures, live activities, and other partnerships at stake.

## Benefits of working with an influencer

Influencers are valuable because they offer credibility to a growing company which need it. Their peers' recommendations influence 70 percent of millennials. Influencers provide a point of connection between companies and the target market. Working with someone who influences:

**1. Increases brand impact:** Gain access to a global audience with your influencer. This market is already engaged and is waiting for appropriate content.

**2. Builds trust:** Consumers already trust the opinions of those influencers they are following. Influencers instantaneously boost your brand's credibility.

**3. Improves customer relationships:** Strengthen customer relationships through intimate customer relationships.

**4. Improves the brand:** The definite link that influencers have with consumers alone creates a "halo impact" that enhances the business at the consumer's eyes.

**5. Improves SEO:** Working with influencer's offers link-building opportunities. More links lead to better search rankings

Now that you are aware of the pros and cons of marketing with Tik Tok influencers, it is time to build your campaign. Whether you are doing influencer marketing for the first time on Tik Tok or you are trying to optimize your strategy, you can partner with an experienced marketing agency to launch an impacting campaign with a Tik Tok influencer.

Influencer marketing can be incredibly beneficial for startup brands or those who have struggled to gain grip in their marketing on social media. With a strong understanding of how influencer marketing can drive your online goals, you can commit to quickly launch your first campaign to see those results in your company.

# CHAPTER NINE

# **Uncertainties and Certainties of Social Media As Regards To Business**

For months now, advertisers have used Tik Tok to promote their companies. For others, social media marketing can be a fantastic way to work. It sounds incredible, right? It is — but those case studies are becoming quite challenging to find. These days, many marketers find their organic growth stagnating from social media. Although 77 percent of marketers Use at least one social media platform for marketing purposes, less than half (48%) say that they see ROI from this strategy.

In this chapter, the certainties and uncertainties of Tik Tok regarding business will be extensively discussed. Also, it is essential not to forget that there are always two sides of the coin, as far as ROI are concerned, half of the chances is to have good results from this strategy

A business is defined as an enterprise or organization engaged in commercial, industrial, or professional activities. Businesses may be for-profit corporations, or they may be non-profit organizations that work to fulfill a charitable mission or a social cause.

The general concept is when an individual or company profits in return for money by supplying products or services. But profit can include other value items, such as credit and exchange items and services instead of money.

## Business in the 21st century regarding Internet presence

The world wide web has revolutionized and changed the way we do business. The Internet has changed and influenced every aspect of our society. It also affected the business. The Internet has changed the rules of the play. It has put everyone in connection and now anyone can be an entrepreneur if he/she has a little bit of creativity.

It has never been easier to start a business. All you need, except of course a profitable idea, is some hosting money, and that is all about it. You can do everything else, from getting content up on the website and creating the logo, promoting it on social media. That is why there have never been more companies, and the potential to make money has never been this high in past centuries.

## Social media platforms and business

Today, tons of social media platforms are available to marketers, and they play a significant role in your success in social media marketing. Factors such as your industry, your audience and your brand can all influence the social network that you are using.

Social media marketing is a powerful tool to reach prospects and customers for businesses of all sizes. Your customers already interact with brands through social media, and if you don't speak to your audience directly through social platforms, you are missing out! Great social media marketing can bring remarkable success to your business, creating dedicated brand advocates and even driving leads and sales.

**Tik Tok and business**

Tik Tok app has been downloaded more than 750 million times in the past 12 months, outpacing last year's Facebook, Instagram, Twitter, and Snapchat rivals.

By using Tik Tok correctly, you can attract a huge audience to your company or product. In fact, according to Influencer Marketing Hub, Tik Tok has 800 million active users worldwide, and it was Apple's most downloaded app.

If your business has a young target audience, Tik Tok users' largest demographic is between 16 and 24 years of age. Tik Tok is the perfect place to grab their attention. Tik Tok has evolved from a video-creation app designed solely for users to express their creativity into a marketing and advertising haven since its birth in 2018. Brands have created accounts on the platform over the last 12 months to explore and engage with consumers.

Tik Tok's allure to enterprises is the sheer number of active users on the platform. How the algorithm works exactly is still unclear, but it seems much easier for your video content to go viral on Tik Tok than on other social media platforms.

**How to maximize Tik Tok as an entrepreneur**

**1. Create fun content**

One of the easiest ways to promote your business on Tik Tok as an entrepreneur is by creating your content. You can show off your products with a fun video demonstration and a nice song. Make it simple. A simple video that shows off your products will be seen as more authentic than if your business tries to create memes with the goal to make them go viral.

**2. Create a hashtag challenge**

Creating a lively hashtag challenge enhances user interaction and engagement and promotes your business. You can encourage Tik Tok users to create or reproduce content and include your brand's hashtag in it.

**3. Work with Tik Tok influencers**

You can partner with Tik Tok influencers to run marketing campaigns. Influencers have varying numbers of followers, therefore, varying degrees of influencers. Be sure that the influencer's audience is similar to your target audience. Identify online tools that will enable you to look for users' bios, look for other brands' mention, and locate commonly used expressions among an influencer's audience.

## 4. Maximize your influences

When you have worked on increasing your followers, make sure you maximize your influence over them. Make sure you are not just posting content for the sake of views alone. Make sure they are buying your product. Let your followers transform into customers.

## Uncertainties of social media (Tik Tok) as it regards to business

With this understanding, it is best to note that Tik Tok has specific uncertainties in its relation to business.

### 1. Poor use of analytical techniques that do not require high precision.

Data Analysis, an understanding of the network, is one of the most important business aspects of a social networking site. Simply put: you cannot monetize what you do not understand.

Simple statistic models are often more reliable than more detailed models for dealing with highly complex situations. This is particularly good advice for marketers, who may be used with two or more decimal places to see awareness and preference data. The problem with dealing with social networks and other dynamic structures is that a simplistic model is more likely to match well with past data but fails to predict the future. A more basic model is less likely to fit past data but more likely to anticipate different future scenarios.

### 2. Lack of Multi-Outcome Preparation.

It is more probable to have success if you bet on more options, rather than on few specific ones. Place lots of huge bets on a range of options.

### 3. Not finding and not relying on predictable situational elements.

**4. Lack of Emphasis on Inputs assessment of initiatives.**
Randomness will scatter even the best efforts to produce results, so the quality of the decision to undertake it may not be considered when assessing the success of an initiative. Don't rely solely on the project's actual outcome (bad or good), but take into account the quality of the process that went into it.

**5. It requires human power to stay agile and strive to react quickly.**
As soon as they happen, there is no substitute for perception, listening, and detecting events. As an organization, you are asked to focus on "sense and respond," and act quickly and decisively. As a rule, have a precise principle, a strong social media policy but generic enough to be flexible, while keeping that the actual results may vary.

In the end, you have to prepare for failure, success, and everything in between. But as long as others find you trustworthy, you will never be alone. Focus on doing the right thing, and your customers, staff, and other stakeholders will all be interested in seeing your business grow.

**Some statistics**
A quick look at these statistics reveals social media's potential for business. It is also important to remember that most of the figures on the outcomes and the estimates are

closer to 50%, which resonates with the complexities of social media as they relate to the company. The statistics are below:

Social Media for Business:

53% of small enterprises use social media.

53% of active users of social media follow a brand.

Sales increased by 43% of marketers due to social campaigns.

Customer relations and social media:

Social media users who experienced poor service will tell their experience to an average of 53 people. Men and women who are not social media user will tell to 17 people.

20% of social media users would buy on a social media site.

50% of small business owners reported receiving new clients via social media activities.

47% of consumers are somewhat likely to buy online from a brand they are following.

**The other side of the coin**

A lot has been understood, but will one allow even a small company to go global without enormous investments? For example, Brand24 is a business that employs less than 50 employees, but acquired clients in more than 35 countries worldwide, by merely optimizing social networking over the years. How do you leverage these platforms within your company? What is constant about social networking?

**1. It allows for more personal relationships (Show Authenticity).**

Social networking is a twofold platform where you can develop a relationship with your present and future customers. Social media helps humanize a brand and create real group relationships.

**2. It encourages entrepreneurship more effectively.**

According to a study, 78 percent of small businesses attract new customers through social media. Thanks to the advanced targeting and remarketing options, you can send your message to the audience that is more likely to be interested in your products and services. Tik Tok's paid ads are relatively cheap, cheap and, if you have a well knitted web on the social platform, one's efforts will pay off.

**3. It offers useful insights into consumers and companies.**

Users inquire, suggest, but post feedback as well. They are the best source of information about possible product developments. Those who use your service or product know best what can be improved to fit their needs.The feedback is gold to get answers about the preferences and behavior of your customers.

**4. It sparks loyalty.**

According to a study by Texas Tech University, brands actively participating in social media interactions continue to experience improved brand loyalty. When the business is active on social networking platforms, you become more open and credible to the eyes of consumers and potential customer.

Other verified reasons which have stood the test of time remains:

**1. It improves brand awareness.**

**2. It remains cost-effective.**

**3. It amplifies brand authority.**

**4. It increases traffic.**

**5. It enhances SEO rankings.**

Social media is the right tool for all this. If you can take advantage of its possibilities, your company can indeed prosper from it. You can achieve marketing goals with fewer resources with a good strategy, some creativity, and additional tools.

Despite all that has been said, Tik Tok remains a vital tool for business in this century and cannot be overruled. According to a McKinley Global Institute report, over the past five years, the Internet largely accounted for 21 percent of GDP growth in mature economies. The future is even brighter, as the same report concludes: "We are still in the early stages of transformation, the internet will unleash and the opportunities it will foster."

When it comes to the economy and business growth, we also have to enjoy the worldwide network's full benefits. Our culture is changing rapidly, and anyone who fails in adapting will have to face the consequences of it. If you are not applying this valuable advice, you will miss an incredible marketing opportunity because it makes it easy and efficient to spread the word about your product and mission.

# CONCLUSION

There is no doubt that Tik Tok is here to stay. Tik Tok has its unique features although it shares some aesthetic and functional similarity with Snapchat and Instagram. Brands who have effectively tuned to Tik Tok early on have received tremendous brand awareness benefits, often with very little investment.

Brands must position themselves as a creative force to be recognized by a new, global and young audience. This book has presented the various benefits of using Tik Tok as an entrepreneur. It has also explained how to maximize influencers on Tik Tok and run marketing ads in order to reach a wider audience.

Use the tips on how to promote your business on Tik Tok that you found in this book and you will be awed by the sudden, positive turnaround that business will have.

If you want to learn more, get the best comprehensive course here:

Stay up to date on the author's upcoming
publications, write to: robertkasey70@gmail.com

# Amazon FBA

## A Real Way to Make Money Online
### *2020 Edition*

*A Step-By-Step Guide for Beginners on How to Start a Profitable Business from Home with Amazon, Creating an Alternative Source of Income –*
*Best Financial Freedom Books & Audiobooks*

## Robert Kasey

# INTRODUCTION

You are going to get rich.

You are about to start making money while you will 'employ' Amazon to work for you.

And guess what?

Amazon is a big brand. They have a large market and a lot of people respect them. If you keep your items with them, your items are in good hands.

Some time ago, they created what is called Fulfillment by Amazon. This allows you to do less work while Amazon handles the other things like shipping, packaging, and delivery.

In the past, sellers handled these things themselves, and you know that's a lot of work. When you receive an order, you will pack, label, and ship it to the location of your buyer. Imagine you are handling a hundred per day. Imagine you are hiring someone to do the work for you.

You will pay a lot of money. You will not do the job as efficiently as a brand that has a lot of staff and the facilities to perform it. Amazon has a large market, an extensive network, where you can reach many more buyers than you will ever be able to if you were handling things by yourself. This book guides you on how to go about it.

Before starting this book, it is likely you have heard about Amazon FBA as a viable business opportunity. Or you might have heard that it is risky to venture into it; or that you should not go into it.

# Good or bad

If you are ready to make money while doing less work, Amazon FBA is a big opportunity that you should tap into. It is a venture that promises great return. In fact, we have heard stories of many entrepreneurs who took it as a side hustle, and it booms, becoming a source of wealth.

Everything in life has a shortcoming. Those who say it is not viable and should not go into it have a point. If you want to make a windfall of money in a week, this venture is not for you. It is not a start-today-get-rich-tomorrow scheme. But...

If you do your calculations right, picking what will sell in the long run and making use of a market where you will find cheap products, you are going to make money – a lot of it.

This book is written to help you make the best use of Amazon FBA. There are disadvantages of using FBA, of course. You will read about them in chapter two. In that same chapter, you will read about the advantages of the opportunity. The pros definitely outweigh the cons.

**Slow and steady wins the race**

This book did not exaggerate what you will make with FBA. That is up to you. But after reading down to chapter seven, you will be able to sit back, as a business analyst and forecast the amount of wealth you can create for yourself.

In the beginning, there are certain things that you should avoid. Beginners do not often know the depths of the water. This is not to scare you; it limits the risk you are getting into, to give you the future of a certain action before you take them. This is covered in chapter two: tips for beginners.

This is a book you should study, making notes as you go. Of course, you will need to come back to the chapters at some point, to digest and remind yourself of the whole insights this book presents.

You can't have this book and not make money with FBA. Let's adjust that a bit, 'you can't follow the tips in this book and not make money with FBA.'

Slow and steady wins the race.


**You are a true student**

'A true teacher would never tell you what to do. But he would give you the knowledge with which you could decide what would be best for you to do' – Christopher Pike.

In chapter four, you will read about all the methods of making money on Amazon and realize, joyfully, that Amazon FBA is just one out of the many ways. You can start with FBA or somewhere else.

This book presents all you need to know.

In chapter three, you are given the situations where using FBA could open you to a lot of risks. Amazon calculates your fees through certain factors, so when the odds are against you, it is better if you choose another system of selling, Fulfillment by Merchant, for instance. What's that? That too, has been covered in chapter four.

There is competition. If you click on Amazon now, you will find pages and pages of items, sellers all selling the same item. If you hop on the train blindly, your item will be lost in the crowd. This is one reason why people stay out of it, avoiding the system because of the competition. But you shouldn't.

There are certain steps that can give you an edge. They are

- Find a product that is highly demanded
- Source it where it is cheap
- Have it branded to your taste
- Build a listing no one can resist
- Market your product

Then sit back, with a cup of wine, a plate of fried chicken on your table and watch your inventory, a feeling of satisfaction radiating from your face. But how will you do the above steps?

This book has done that for you. In chapter six, you are shown the two kinds of products you can sell. You will be given the details about sourcing the product, branding it, and shipping to Amazon warehouse. In the same chapter, you will be given the details to building an irresistible listing; the one a buyer will click on and make a purchase out of the hundreds of listings on the page. Chapter seven is about FBA fees and how you are charged.

Chapter 9 is for people with little capital. It explains what to do if you have just $500, $200 or even $100. You are the one who should really believe that slow and steady can win a race. Some of your fears and questions are analyzed and answered. What should you sell? What steps should you take? The answers are waiting for you in chapter nine. You are a true student!

After these things that are presented to you, what will you do? Head over to Amazon and put the knowledge to good use or put it aside and wait for some more?

A true student would make good use of the knowledge. Truly, wealth will not come to you by just having the knowledge but by making the knowledge work for you.

It is up to you. Turn the page and find the knowledge.

# CHAPTER 1
# WHAT IS AMAZON FBA?

Amazon FBA simply stands for Fulfillment by Amazon. It is an avenue to sell on Amazon with the organizers carrying out most of the tasks.

Amazon is an online platform where buyers and sellers make exchanges. And here are some of the interesting facts about the platform that might interest you, especially if you are a seller.

- Initially, the idea behind Amazon was to sell books, but things changed, and now we have a big online marketplace.
- Another interesting thing is that anyone can buy almost anything on the platforms – just anything you can think of. The little exceptions include cars, homes, cigarettes, and most live animals. For you, as a seller, this is a huge opportunity to show what you have to the world. Just what is your product that you want to sell?
- Amazon has many other brands that you may not even know about. These include Goodreads, Audible, Whole Foods, etc. In total, the other subsidiaries and brands are 41 in number. In other words, buying stuff from any of these brands is the same as buying from or doing business on Amazon.
- There are about 20, 000 employees working for Amazon. The brand has stores across the USA, Japan, Canada, China, and many countries in Europe. This means you are really leveraging a huge market when you are using Amazon as a marketplace.
- The brand is working towards what is called Prime Air. It is aimed at delivering packages to buyers' locations through the use of drones.
- Amazon is helping small businesses and entrepreneur development.

The last point is worth talking about elaborately. So we will dedicate our time, just a few minutes, to see how and what effort Amazon is putting into other businesses to ensure they grow higher and bigger.

# Amazon FBA as an avenue to help an entrepreneur

Do you have a product that you believe if you could sell on Amazon would make a lot of money? You might be getting into a lot of money if you sign up for Amazon FBA.

The aim of the program is to allow anyone anywhere to make some dollars on Amazon. This is a good opportunity for small entrepreneurs. You will produce a product and put it on Amazon; once you have selected FBA as a channel through which you want to sell, Amazon will get to work and all you have to do at the end of the day is receive a commission on what you want to sell. All the jobs about marketing and delivery will be handled by Amazon. In a short while, you will be earning in American dollars.

This is one of the ways through which the brand is helping entrepreneurs. For instance, there is another avenue for Georgia citizens called the Amazon export hub where consumers are allowed to sell a product on the platform.

Now, think...

Think about the market size of Amazon, which is almost everywhere in the United States, the majority of Europe, some parts of Asia such as China and Japan. Are you having an idea of the market size you are dealing with?

Think about the little effort you will be putting in with Amazon handling other activities. There is a lot to gain and very little to lose.

'You sell, we ship it' - Amazon FBA

This is what you will find if you check Amazon services website. The FBA is classified as one of the most advanced of all fulfillment networks. Amazon will do all the jobs which include:

- Shipping
- A little packaging if you have none (however, it is best to package your product yourself. You will learn about it in the coming chapters)

- Marketing (Amazon has a large market and selling on the platform opens your product to a broader audience and enthusiastic buyers)
- Delivery
- Storage
- Provision of customer services.

For a start, you will deliver your product at an Amazon fulfillment center and the brand will come for it with their truck. Very soon, your business will reach more audience and more buyers than you can imagine. There are a lot of things to learn about the process. So stick around and learn from this book.

# What makes it work?

Amazon has a vast customer base. When you join their program, you are leveraging on this fact and the power of Amazon as a company. Remember, a customer base like that of Amazon is not the only thing you need to sell more while doing less work than your competitors. You need distribution. And using Amazon is like leveraging a massive network in terms of market size and distribution.

The only problem you might have is finding a product. This is the hard part for many reasons. It might be hard to find a good product that already has a huge demand so that your product will not be gathering dust in Amazon's stores.

In chapter six, you will learn how to find a good product, as well as package it. It is not that hard, and it is not that easy either. But the right information will set your feet on solid rock so that you will not make a mistake.

If you are selling a product of yours, you need to carry out some exercise. This is recommended for beginners, though. You can go ahead and sell on Amazon FBA if you are confident that people will take a good chance at it.

# People are already making a lot of sales offline

You have likely heard about Amazon FBA for the first time, and you want to give it a shot since you have been selling a lot offline.

Well, there is good news – many of it – and a little bad news. Bad news first, selling on Amazon will take a percentage of your profit. We will get to how this is calculated in a subsequent section of the book. And if you don't make sales on the platform, your product will be accumulating some bills when lying in Amazon fulfillment center (again more of this information is coming).

The good news now is, selling online is pretty easy. Imagine your product is being ordered in another country. If that seems like a little, think about the entire job you have to do, which is finding a product or creating a product and moving your product to an Amazon's warehouse. The rest will be performed by Amazon.

On a clear note, let's make a detailed explanation of how joining Amazon FBA is an awesome decision.

- When Amazon handles your stuff from the warehouse through to the seller's location, you will be able to focus on other things. There will be more time on your hands to find a new market, create a new product, targeted marketing, and focusing on conversion rate optimization.

- You and your customers will have little headaches. You know how frustrating it is to deal with issues like credit card issues, shipping delays, customer service responses, etc. You will leave all those for the Amazon's staff to handle.

- You will lower the cost of doing the job yourself. Let's assume you have your own warehouse and you want to ship products to another distant location, do you think you will spend more or less than if everything was handled by Amazon? You will spend more, definitely.

- Turn your attention to something else. Instead of chasing or looking for where the next order would come from, you can move on to something else like growth opportunities.

The whole concept of Amazon FBA is to free up more space in your hands to do more things with your time. You can make a lot of money with Amazon FBA.

In this chapter, you have understood the basics of Amazon FBA. In the next chapter, you will read about the pros and the cons.

# CHAPTER 2
# THE PROS AND CONS OF
# AMAZON FBA

You have probably heard that there are two sides to a coin. We have the front and the back, the good part, and the bad part.

To avoid repetition, we have discussed most of the benefits in chapter one. We will review them to bring some important points that will be useful in the coming part of this chapter. Then we will quickly skip to the cons.

### 1. Reduction in the level of stress and hassles

Because Amazon is handling distribution, payment method, storing, and shipping, you will have little to nothing to do.

The first benefit is reducing problems associated with shipping. Imagine you have an order for a product in a day. You will start by packing the product in a box. You will put a label on it, print a slip for packing, and attach a shipping label, after all that, you will call the haulers to pick it up. Then expect them to call you often if they run into any kind of trouble on the way. It will be another kind of story if you receive up to 30 or more orders in one day.

Yes, that's a lot of stress.

With FBA, you only take your product to the warehouse, and the rest is done by the brand. You sleep and wake up, expecting money.

Another source of hassle is payment and returns. If you are doing this process yourself, then you have a lot of work to do if things go wrong at the other end. You will communicate with the buyers. When they receive the item, they will confirm and inspect it to ensure the goods are in good condition. If there is a problem, expect your product to be returned and you are paying a refund. You will re-package and resell the item. Again, imagine you are handling hundreds of these orders in one day.

But with Amazon FBA, you don't have to worry about these things. You might not share any contact with your buyers at all, and you will get paid at the end of it.

### 2. It is cheap
It will definitely cost less if you are using Amazon facilities. Also, they have the staff and the customer base.

### 3. You will enjoy 'Amazon Prime'
This is a package which is open to sellers on the platform. Once you have completed the registration for FBA, automatically, your product can be accepted under Amazon prime shipping. Therefore, prime members will get your product within two days of making the order.

This comes at no extra cost on your part. You have submitted the goods; Amazon does the rest of the job.

This will boost sales for you. People will be encouraged to buy the product when they know it will be delivered in less than two days of making an order, and it is arriving at no extra cost.

### 4. FBA members are up on the 'buy box' ladder compared to others
If you are familiar with Amazon, you would have noticed that those who subscribe for FBA are usually ranked higher than the other sellers. The higher a seller is on the buy box, the more sales he will get. This could translate to hundreds or more orders compared to those below you.

### 5. You are selling not just in one marketplace
There is more than the Amazon marketplace if you are selling on Amazon. You are allowed to sell on any marketplace you wish to sell, and yet you can keep your orders on the FBA program. Even if you want it, some solutions will automatically move your orders towards FBA.

### 6. You are borrowing Amazon's brand to sell yours
What does it feel like to attach a big brand's name to your product? Buyers will award you more confidence and think you more trustworthy than selling things to people who have never heard of your brand's name. The buyers know they are dealing with Amazon and that simply means their goods will be certainly shipped and will get there on its due date.

# The cons of Amazon FBA

### 1.   It's difficult to track inventory

As an example, if you have a few goods in the system, you will be able to track what product is selling and what factors favor sales. Because of Amazon's capacity, it is a good thing you want to put hundreds or thousands of products into the system. And some will likely get more sales and some will not. When this happens, Amazon will continue charging you for storing the item with them.

It's easy to track a few hundred products. You can fit all the data and details on one page of a seller central dashboard. But when the number increases to the thousands, this is where the problem comes in. It will be challenging to process all the details about what you should improve on and what you should do to improve sales. The main thing you will be able to track is your best seller rank.

### 2.   It will cost you

Yes, Amazon FBA will require some amount of money. And this is even real when you are not making sales as a seller. Amazon charges you for keeping your inventory or items with them. This is why you need to understand a bit of forecasting what sales volume to keep with the brand so that you are not making more money for them and making zero income. We will get to that in this eBook.

### 3.   Shipping to Amazon requires a bit of work

You will have to move your items to Amazon's warehouse. And the brand has developed a system called the ASIN/UPC which requires that all products must be well-packed and well-labeled before they can be accepted for FBA. This is a job you must do yourself, or you could hire a third-party company to do it for you.

### 4.   You are not branded properly

If you are handling your own distribution, you will want to advertise your brand as much as you can, to tell the world this is your name, your logo and they would know you. Sadly, when you are selling with Amazon, your products will reach the customer in boxes, using labels with the Amazon logo boldly on it. This is not much of a problem if you are making money, but your brand will not be represented as you wish.

### 5. Sabotaging your marketing tools

Part of the marketing tools you won't be able to capitalize on is the email list. You know with an email list you can reach out to people who have bought your products previously and remarket your products to them. But with FBA, your customers do not have a direct relationship, and getting their email is close to impossible.

**There could be delays**

There could be delays during the peak seasons. Just ask your neighbors what they are getting for Christmas and holidays and when are they getting it. You will be amazed at how many people are planning on using Amazon. You could use this to guess or understand why there are delays during the peak season – everyone is making an order at the same time. You might make an order, and the item might be out of stock. And you might be unable to restock that item for quite a while despite sending more merchandise which is not quickly processed.

Now take what you have just read and place it on a weighing balance. Put the cons on the right side and the pros on the left. What do you see? Which of the two weigh more than the other? The pros weigh more than the cons, of course. This means your hope of earning on Amazon FBA is still valid, and you can proceed.

So we head to the next chapter to talk about when you should go for the program and when you should not try it. The next section is essential to your success with selling on Amazon FBA. You might have heard a lot of success stories; it's time to evaluate your product for a success story.

# CHAPTER 3
# WHEN TO AND NOT TO USE AMAZON FBA?

Here is a story someone shared online.

A guy, let's call him Jack, started selling on Amazon in 2017. He heard so many success stories to make his ears ache and he believed he could be part of the success story if he just opts-in without taking a second guess. How wrong he was.

We are all guilty of this – most of us or to be candid, all of us. We show the world what we are able to achieve, where our success can serve as an inspiration to others, where we can receive applause for what we have done, our hard work.

We keep the bad parts; no one wants to read a post titled 'my failure stories.' We write 'success stories.' And if possible, we exaggerate the good parts and hide information about the days where we thought we rather quit and do something else.

Jack had just finished reading such a success story about Amazon FBA. He would make a lot of money, he thought.

He didn't have information about the program or how to go about it. So he started finding information online. He read books and blog posts and all advice he could find on forums. Then he started.

According to the information he read, he sourced for products in China. They arrived. It was a popular niche, and soon his product was among a million others that are just similar yet not serving any other unique purpose than the others. This was the beginning of his fall.

He sold little, made a meager profit. He tried to beat the competition as his mind give him ideas. He thought about the possible ways to make his product rank better. He sat down, hoping his cost of sourcing for the products and the total investment of his time, knowledge and lessons would not go to waste. An idea came, a simple one, and it is what most people have done or are doing: he gave out some of his products for free in exchange for ranking and reviews.

In the end, it was a 'failure story.' He came out of it a better person but with an empty wallet and money that has gone into oblivion. If you catch him around and you ask for advice about Amazon FBA, he will offer the greatest and the most valuable lessons you may not find anywhere else.

# Research is important

Research is important. If you have a person who is already in the game, they have valuable lessons to offer you. And guess what, it might cost nothing other than sitting down and taking the advice seriously.

If there is no one you can run to, calm down, and read this chapter carefully. You might be at risk of losing your money, depending on how much you invest for the first time.

On the brighter side, your first attempt could seem like you have hit the jackpot. You might decide to relax, cross your legs; Amazon is working hard, really hard to make you richer.

# When not to use Amazon FBA

The best piece of advice is that you should try to verify the profitability of selling your product by employing a strategic process. You might try doing market research to know what people are actually buying. For instance, you can use an FBA calculator.

Moving on, here are the factors that indicate you shouldn't use the system. The risks are higher than the outcome.

   1.   **You have a small number of items**

You only have 40 pieces or less than that or the majority is on another platform, and they are selling fine. Then you should stick with that medium. Let others who have a higher number of items – in the hundreds and thousands use FBA. The process of packaging items and moving it to Amazon warehouse coupled with the Amazon charges and rules will not yield good returns with a small number of items. The stress, return, and bureaucracy may not be worth it.

### 2. You have a small profit

It is good advice to do proper calculations if you want to sell on Amazon. Imagine you are selling a product with a small profit margin. If Amazon deducts sellers' fees and the cost of keeping your inventory with them, are you still making a profit?

This could mean you are not making a profit at all. So ensure you do your calculations. And no, you cannot increase your profit easily. There are competitions and price is one factor that can make a buyer scroll down to the next available seller. The topic about seller fees is one we will get to in this book.

### 3. Your product will attract more fees than average

Some products usually attract more fees than others, not because they are more valuable or expensive. It is important to know how Amazon charges an item (and you will read about that in chapter seven).

These are things you should note about your products

- Small
- Large
- Weighs a lot

Amazon will charge you more if your product is heavy or takes a lot of space. You should use the weight of your product to calculate the amount you will be charged in FBA fees then make a connection with your profit margin. Again, you will learn more when you get to chapter seven.

Your products are with another eCommerce website with an older or outdated system of operation.

If you are selling on other newer platforms, it is easy for you to sell on Amazon. There is an easy automation process that allows you to sell using FBA if you are already using

- Shopify
- BigCommerce

Older platforms are not easy to synchronize with FBA. And this could lower your chances of enjoying all the benefits with FBA.

# When to use Amazon FBA

Once you have done an excellent job in determining the times you shouldn't be using Amazon FBA, it is time to do more than that and focus on when you should use the program. Again, you should be reminded that using the FBA calculator is a good decision which we will talk about later.

When to use FBA:

**Your main sales platform is Amazon**

If you have been using Amazon before, it will be good advice to join the FBA program. This will give you the opportunity to enjoy all the benefits of using Amazon's programs. For instance, you will be allowed into Amazon Prime, and there is the advertising, amongst other benefits.

Amazon will handle other tedious activities. These include:

- They will help you source for new products
- They will help improve your listings
- It is their job to widen the customer base

**You have done your calculations**

You can earn more and do less work when you have taken your time to calculate, and you have done adequate research. In this book, we will talk about the process of starting the Amazon FBA for success. With proper planning with the aid of the right information, you will be making a profit on the program.

**You sell on other brands or subsidiaries of Amazon or channels that have a smooth relationship with Amazon**

Selling on other platforms which are affiliated with Amazon is a huge boost for sales. FBA will enhance the multiple channel or network and help you reach a wider shipping network. Amazon has facilitated the program with what is called Multi-Channel Fulfillment (MCF). This allows you to sell and ship on third-party platforms while using a third party seller.

# Tips for selling For New Amazon sellers

When you are new to something, you need guidance. You are in a new city, and there are no road signs, no poster to follow for directions. Now a blind man is standing on the sidewalk with his little poodle. Would you ask him and expect directions to a place he has never seen before just that he has heard the sound of?

That said, you need to be careful so as not to make mistakes. To that, here is some advice for beginners who want to make money selling on Amazon FBA.

### Ignore the resources with outrageous ideas and success stories

You want to know what products people are buying on Amazon. You will find a lot of them, and many of them are already saturated. Many people will offer you the list of bestsellers on the platform for you to make your next billion. Follow it at your own risk. If you can't do something different from what the market is already offering, it is wise to move on to something else.

The truth is that other people are looking for the same list of bestselling products, and you will end up on the same bus, overcrowded and fighting for fresh breath.

Weigh your options. Look at the market; make sure you stand a chance among the competitors before you dive in.


### Follow trends only if you catch the train early

There is a new trend on Amazon; you find it today, check the number of sellers you see on the platform; they are just five or ten or just a little. You are early to the party, so take a sit and ask the waiter for your own dish. Start selling the product.

But if you are new to the game and you follow a trend which already has a hundred or more sellers, then you are there only to watch others killing it. Back out now before it's too late and your money is gone.

Keep an attentive eye on trends before there is a lot of noise on TV or social media. Those who make a lot of money by following trends are two types, those who are lucky or those who have heard it early. You can be both.


### Research like a drunk

Research everything and everything like a drunk. A drunk person who is not afraid to ask many questions, even the ones that seem stupid. But when you are reading and listening to the results of your research, you should put your ears down and dissect every piece of information like a toddler who has found a bewildering toy.

Another thing you must do is understand the category which you want to sell. You might find out too late that there are restrictive barriers if you are selling in some categories. Also, you will want to research the approval processes before you start selling. We will get to it.

**Sell only good stuff**

So you have a product, or you have outsourced a product, but you don't know if it is good quality. You didn't use it yourself to determine if it is worth the money. Once your buyers find out you are selling a piece of worthless product, you are on your way to lose sales and with that a lot of bad reviews. This could be the end of sales on Amazon. People rarely give a review on Amazon so ensure you are getting the good ones to avoid doom.

For starters, you should have firsthand experience with a product to verify its functionality, quality, and durability. Check other sellers and see what people are saying about the products. Now you can address the issues or simply change the product if you think there is no chance to make a difference.

**Source cheaper products**

You need to do some calculations before you jump into the sales of a particular product. This will also help you to ensure you will beat the competition with a lower price than the others. On Amazon, price is an essential factor that can influence sales.

Before you decide to sell at a price, you need to calculate all the charges Amazon is taking to ensure you are making a profit with your sales. You will want to calculate the cost of shipping, sourcing, Amazon fees, and promotions you have made, and you will want to use that in determining the selling price of your product.

With such additional costs, your price might seem higher. And if you are selling an expensive item, people will run for cheaper competitors. So before you sell, check the prices that other sellers have set for their products and aim to beat them.

Don't forget the previous point anyway.

### Sell products you are passionate about wisely

Although selling a product you are passionate about can bring a kind of joy, you should try to analyze the decisions you are making. When it comes to such products, sellers are likely to get emotional. They wonder why the sale is not moving in accordance with the level of passion that they have. Well, buyers do not share the same passion, and you need to give them what they want to buy if you want to make sales. You need to always be logical about sales, not emotional.

### Check if the product is patented

Selling a product that is patented is illegal. So if you are a private label seller, you must check if the product you are getting from a wholesaler is patented or not. This is something you must examine closely because the wholesaler will not tell you. Selling a patented product can qualify you for a lawsuit.

### Do a lot of work on your product listings

Private label sellers are the ones that do their product listings. You are required to set up your listing and make it stand out. Start with finding a good product, you should always be on the lookout for the best products out there. Next, you will put the same effort in creating a listing that is irresistible for your buyers. Of course, it requires a lot of work. But then you have to remember you are not the only seller on the platform, and people will not know your product unless your listing is doing a good job with advertisement and conversions. So what will you do?

Write a good copy on your listing, using keywords creatively. With this done, you will improve the chances of your product being found, and you will persuade buyers to make a purchase with effective copy. If you can't write one, perhaps you should hire a copywriter.

Another important thing is the quality of images you put up there. You don't want to use a photograph taken with your smartphone and expect to stand out from the competition. You need to invest in professional photography. You can find affordable ones around you.

### Stick to the rules

You will find out some sellers on Amazon are breaking some of the policies of the platform. They call it the 'black hat' techniques. They will increase sales by generating more reviews. They will manipulate the process of reviewing a product. Some of them will get away with it, and you might be lucky or unlucky. Amazon will come down on you like a heavy rock if they find out you are playing games with their policies. They have intensified their strategies on finding out sellers who are engaging in review frauds.

**You must improve your listing**

If you are making sales, you might think your listing does not need readjustment. This is the first mistake most beginners make. Things can change over time; the keywords people use in their search might change over time. You have to monitor your listing and how it is driving results, especially if you are not making sales as expected.

Many private label sellers also make the same mistake, but you cannot afford to. You should also check the competitor's listing and see how they are done. Find new keywords your buyers are using and ensure you are up to date in the business. You can also ask a trusted friend to check your listings on your behalf and give you feedback.

**Put your product in the right category**

You might think your product has a better chance if you put it in a different category. Of course, you might earn the bestseller badge you are craving for, but you are missing out on some buyers. Why? Some buyers will go to a subcategory to search for a particular product, and if they can't find yours, they will go for the available option.

# CHAPTER 4
# MAKING MONEY ON AMAZON

If you are reading this, you believe in one simple fact. Although you might not know the details or how to go about, you believe people are making money on Amazon.

Well, that's true, and so is the statistic below.

Amazon receives a lot of search traffic every day. It is a trusted brand in terms of shipping and delivery as well as payment processing. When people search online for stuff to buy, 50% of those who want to buy products end up on Amazon, 70% of such visitors live in the United States.

You would have heard stories and case studies of how people make 1000, 2000, or 5000 dollars on Amazon. It's possible. The reason is simple to guess – people trust Amazon. And with such trust that comes from many years of being in business and a good history with less disappointing tales, more people are willing to bring out their credit card when they are shopping on Amazon.

## <u>Why it works for almost everyone</u>

Once you know how to source for a product, you are in the game. All other things will follow. You don't have to be a manufacturer or a producer. The majority of sellers on Amazon are not producers; in fact, most of them are third-party sellers. The majority of those in eCommerce on Amazon are selling products that are related to electronics.

Here is another list of random facts about selling on Amazon that might interest you.

- Products that are related to media and electronics are the hot cake; they take about 50% of the total sales on Amazon.
- Furniture, other household items, and appliances follow at 18. 5%
- Food and stuff used for personal care come third at 14 %

- Toys, DIY, and hobbies take 12.5%
- Fashion at 3.4%

With the above facts and statistics, you can see that there is an opportunity for what you are selling and if you fall into any of those categories you are very lucky.

Amazon FBA is one of many ways to make money online. The program was developed by Amazon to help sellers earn more and to build more entrepreneurs. Asides from FBA, here are other ways people are making money on Amazon. Bring out your pen and jotter. Ideas are about to start flying in your head.

### 1. Private labeling

You have read about this briefly in this book. You know you can use this tactic under Amazon FBA But guess what? You don't really understand it. So let's take a few minutes to make things clear.

**How it works**

You will source for a product that has a huge market. You will make them available on Amazon, but you will label it as yours. Yes, people do that.

One thing about this option is that you are allowed to make an amendment to the product according to the feedback and reviews your buyers make. For instance, if your buyers complain about the handle of a toy, you can use another design or type of plastic.

You can do this and still use the Amazon FBA. In fact, this is one of the best shots at making money on Amazon.

### 2. Retail arbitrage

Retail arbitrage does not need to change the labels on a product or make an adjustment on it and in that it looks like the opposite of the previous, the private labeling. You can make a lot of money and in millions if you are dedicated to this style of making money on Amazon.

**How it works**

Like in private labeling, you will find cheap products around you. In retail arbitrage, you will want to find the products in your location or somewhere not too far. The idea is to remove the cost of shipping goods to your location. For instance, if your product is in China, it will cost some money to ship it in. But if you are searching the Walmart store in your area, it will save your on some shipping costs.

Literally, you will head to your local store like Walmart. Pick an item and compare its selling price to those on Amazon. If you see a lot of difference, with the ones on Amazon carrying the higher price, you have a business coming.

You will continue searching and finding cheaper products all around you. You will keep finding them, loading them up in your car and keep selling them on Amazon.

To make things easier, some sites have lists of the locations where you can find liquidated sales at a cheap rate. Also, you can use some scanning apps to compare the cost on both platforms before you leave the comfort of your home.

**The downside**

Well, like everything in life, this idea is not for everyone. Not everyone will joyfully be driving from one store to another to see what they can sell, then buying it in bulk. It will consume a lot of time.

### 3. Earn as Amazon fulfillment associates

People who stay in a good location can capitalize on this option.

**How it works**

You will be assisting Amazon with packing, shipping, and sorting as the case may be. Your work is needed at fulfillment centers, delivery stations, sortation centers, Prime Now locations, customer service centers, and Campus Pickup Points.

You have a choice to either do this job as a part-time thing or as full-time.

**The downside**

Location is usually the downside of this option when trying to make money on Amazon.

### 4. Amazon flex

This is like the elder brother to working as a delivery associate. Yes, you need to be in a very good location, and you might be lucky enough to earn as much as $18 and up to $25 for every hour of work.

If you have ever seen a guy coming with a package you ordered on Amazon, and he's not in uniform, that's Amazon flex. Your smartphone and a means of transport: a car, preferably are the essentials.

**How it works**

You will start by contacting Amazon that you want to take up this job as an Amazon flex. Once you have done that, you will follow the app religiously for instructions and guidance. You will acknowledge availability and flexibility for shifts. If you are lucky, you can finish your shift within a few hours before your period elapses and you will earn just the agreed amount.

**The downside**

The only major downside is that it is location dependent.

### 5. Affiliate marketing (for Amazon)

This is a viable means of earning a livelihood. You need to have a blog and a reasonable number of visitors who will click on the link to make a purchase on the website.

**How it works**

You are working as an advertiser. Your blog has a specific niche, say, soundproofing, and homecare. Amazon sells a lot of products relating to that niche. You will head over to the site and copy the special links and promote some of the products on your blog. Blend the links into your blog posts so that people click on them and make a purchase.

For every sale, you will earn a commission. The percentage is between 4% and 8.5%. You can earn a lot of money if you have a large number of visitors.

**The downside**

The commission is not a lot of money. You need a lot of traffic and page views so that some of the many visitors will click and make a purchase. Without traffic or little traffic, you can't make much.

### 6. Amazon services

This option is for those who have a skill; you can fix things with your hands. This option is for you.

**How it works**

Let's say you are into cleaning, landscaping, etc. You will head over to Amazon and sign up for Amazon services. Amazon will connect you with people in your locality who need to have a clean faucet, a clean house, or some repair work to do. 15% - 20% of the payment will go into Amazon's pocket.

**The downside**
You might not have the skills.

### 7. Publish books

Amazon is a large market for authors. Well, it started as a book store anyway, and now there is a large audience of authors and readers. Through Kindle Publishing platforms, readers can have a lot of access to a lot of books and make good use of their time. For authors, it is a medium to sell what they have worked for. Many people are making money from publishing non-fiction e-books, but fiction writers are the best earners on Amazon kindle. You know about a certain thing, and you want to give the knowledge in a book, say, art and painting, you can write something about it, filling it up with samples of your work.

Oh, I don't know how to write.

Well, you don't have to know how to write.

**How it works**

If you are looking for ways to make money on Amazon, publish books in the categories and let people find it using keywords.

You will sign up for kindle publishing. For fiction authors, building an audience earlier is a good choice (blogging, Facebook page, Instagram). For non-fiction authors, you need to find a good idea and verify that there is a market for the idea.

For the writing part, you will need to do a lot of work, writing, and formatting of your book. If you cannot write, do your research, make a bale of content, head over to Fiverr, Upwork or any other freelance writing website, and hire a writer to do the job for you. You will upload your book on Amazon using the appropriate format. And start selling.

**The downside**

The hard part is finding a good idea if you are a non-fiction writer. Writing is a lot of hard work, a lot harder if you are not a skilled writer. You have a better chance if you have built a list of raving fans who are eager to buy or pay for your content whether you are a fiction writer or not.

### 8. Join Amazon handmade

It is for people who make handmade items like jewelry or bags. Amazon handmade lets you sell a lot on the platform with a huge market.

**How it works**

If you have seen other places like Etsy or eBay, you will understand this better. You are expected to make your product by hand – completely. How you go about it is up to you – how you arrange, craft, or assemble the piece is up to you.

You will apply for Amazon handmade and fill some simple questions in about your product. In 30 minutes, you should complete the process and very soon, the order would come in for your handmade product. You will sell a lot with the Amazon market size. You can also sell on Amazon if your product is already selling on Etsy.

**The downside**

Amazon charges a fee for these services compared with another platform of this kind. Amazon charges about 15% in commission, which is too much if you compare it with Etsy's 3.5%. Amazon requires a minimum of $1 as a referral fee while Etsy just asks for 20 cents.

### 9. Amazon CamperForce

This is targeted at RVers, people who travel and live mostly in an RV. These people have sold their homes and their properties and moved into an RV or a bus. They travel around, always on the move.

**How it works**

You can help those who don't have a permanent home address receive their orders when they order things from Amazon. This is necessary during holidays when there are more and more orders every day. The amount paid is dependent on some factors, and it is hard to get the full detail because it is not as common as all the other methods. There is compensation for working overtime and bonuses for those who do the program for the whole holiday season. Amazon usually pays campsite fee if you work the entire holiday (usually, from fall till December 23).

**The downside**

The location could be a hindrance, and it is usually seasonal.

You have understood all the options you have under Amazon. If you have read to this point, you must have gotten one thing: you can make money on Amazon. How to get started is what you need to find out.

In the next chapter, things will begin to get clearer for you. This guide is called 'a definitive guide to Amazon FBA' for a reason. It contains everything you need to know about getting started with Amazon FBA. It is simple, easy, and detailed.

**How legitimate is Amazon FBA?**

You might have heard it, usually from the people who haven't tried the process or those who have jumped in without the right knowledge or those who followed the wrong resources. They said it was a scam.

They have a story to share with you. It is a story filled with mistakes and wrong steps, taken from scratch to the end. On paying closer attention, you will see that such people didn't check for competition or source their products properly. You will see it in their story. But they won't come out boldly with those parts.

Here is the truth in a simple and short sentence: you can make money from Amazon FBA.

The amount you make is up to you. It is also dependent on the type of products you are putting in the system. The profit margin and some other factors which will contribute to your success on the program.

Why do people think otherwise about FBA? What can you do about it? Good God, there are about 200 million products on Amazon at a time, and some people just want to get rich overnight – that's why they think Amazon FBA does not work or is dead.

There is a huge competition and if you don't do things to stand out, you will sink to the bottom of the sea. You are not the only seller, and you won't be the last. If you are not making sales, Amazon will be making a lot of money off of you by storing your goods in their warehouse.

**How to beat the competition**

There is a lot of demand just as there is competition. If you know the millions of searches and sales Amazon receives every day; you will understand this is a vast and lucrative venture you could tap into. Amazon says it receives more than 90 million visitors in a month. Why? What are they looking for?

Obviously, they want to buy stuff on the platform. And that is your product and others' products depending on how you have presented them.

Another question you should ask yourself is 'why is there competition?' People can't be competing when there is no money to be made. Or you mean they are just competing to see who can display the most beautiful toys, bags, and appliances without making money. It doesn't work that way. For there to be a competition, there has to be a lot of money to be made.

What you need to do to beat the competition is to find a product that will actually sell. If you put every other tip in place, then you are going to make money.

In chapter six, you will find out how to make money with a good product in a short time. Read that chapter and if possible, jot down points. Selling successfully on Amazon begins with finding a really good product.

Amazon FBA is like retail arbitrage. You will find a cheaper product somewhere and sell it on Amazon. The unique difference is that Amazon is going to lessen the burden of work, including shipping and more. It is real. It is worth it.

Unlike some other business models, selling using FBA requires you to invest some capital, which can be small for a start. (If you are starting with little capital, which is advisable for most beginners, you will find chapter nine very helpful.)

This capital is a little risk involved, like most venture on earth. For you to call it a business, there should be a level of an unpredictable future. Big investors also make big mistakes that cost them some of their money. This doesn't make them call the venture a scam or illegitimate depending on what it is. So if you lose, eat your cake, learn and correct your mistakes with the information in this book. If you still care, start small. You will learn how to go about it in chapter nine.

**Final thought**

Amazon FBA is legitimate; you can make money. The amount you make is dependent on you, the type of products you are selling and the demand for the product.

# FBA VS FBM

For newcomers, it is better to be grounded in what will come your way later. And to that, FBM against FBA is one of the things that will come up as you begin to learn the ropes of Amazon FBA. But you are rolling your eyes, clueless, uncertain. You have heard about FBA. But...

What is FBM?

FBM stands for 'Fulfillment by Merchant' or 'Merchant Fulfilled Network' (MFN). Of course, there are benefits of using FBM or MFN (beware, we will be using FBM, and hope that won't confuse you with FBA).

One thing you should know about each method is to think for yourself, what you want. Be selfish. Don't compare what you want with what you read online. Think for yourself on this one. On that note, we dive into the details properly.

**The difference between FBM and FBA**

Essentially, the two terms are used in describing the process of shipping goods. Do you want Amazon to handle it or will you prefer to do it yourself?

**FBA, (recap)**

You have known how FBA works. Your products are stored in Amazon's warehouse. When buyers make an order for your product, the staff of Amazon will receive it, pack the item and ship it to the buyer's address. This is easy for the seller because all activities about packaging and shipping have been shifted to Amazon and its staff. Even the customer service is the brand's responsibility.

Well, there is a bad part of the deal. You have to pay some fee for this service. You will pay a certain amount for storing in Amazon's fulfilment center, the longer your product stays with Amazon, the more fees you incur. This fee is determined by the quantity of the item and the weight of the product. It is that simple. But remember you might not need to do a single thing once your product is with Amazon. The next thing you will need to do is withdraw payment from your bank account.

**FBM**

For FBM, shipping is handled by sellers. The product is stored in the seller's warehouse or store or home. Once a buyer makes an order on Amazon, the seller will go into their warehouse, pack the item, and ship it to the buyer's location. This is a lot of work, and it might mean the seller is working fulltime to make sales happen, depending.

The benefits are many. You will not pay extra cost for storing the product in your room. If you have a warehouse, the cost of storing in your warehouse will not be as expensive as storing with Amazon.

**MFN sellers can enjoy SFP**

SFP simply means Seller Fulfilled Prime. This is awarded to sellers under the MFN program. Once you are awarded this benefit, you will be able to use FBA services, and you don't have to send your products to Amazon fulfillment centers.

Those who enjoy this program are given the same benefits as those who signed up for FBA. You will be put on the same buy box algorithm as those on FBA. And yet you will not have to pay for the Amazon FBA fees.

**Which one should you go for?**

This is where you need to make your calculations and do it right. Using MFN will require you to work as along as your product is being ordered. And if you don't have enough capital and capability, there could be a limit to the areas you can reach. Now, you need to be honest with yourself, can you go as wide as Amazon would go about distribution and without spending more than you should?

To tell you the truth, Amazon FBA fees can make you run. Over the years, they have been changing the structure of their fees, and sellers are being scared to join in. There is a competition to beat in terms of price. You don't want your product to cost more than that of your competitors.

### MFN over FBA

- You will not incur fees for keeping your items in Amazon warehouse.
- Your charges over each item will also be minimal. This means your return on each sale will be a bit higher if you are selling at the same price as those using FBA.

- You will package your product and present as you wish, using your brand's name. The advantage of this is that people tend to recognize your brand. If your product is good, they will publicize such a specific name to others. You can even go further to use your receipt and if you wish, give notes of appreciation.
- You can do things differently, maybe put some passion into what you do. This is one of the things people think they can do when they are handling shipping. They will like to interact with their buyers more and more and have firsthand interactions with their customers.

### The disadvantages
- Packaging and distribution are stressful and could be a full-time job, depending on the number of orders you are receiving. If there are a lot of orders, you might need to hire many hands so as not to disappoint buyers.
- Buyers are not very interested in this kind of shipping. There are not many benefits for prime members, for instance.
- On average, you are not as likely to win the Buy Box as those in FBA.

## FBA over MFN
Since we are talking about FBA in this book, you might think some of the points are sentimental.
- Your buyers will be able to enjoy prime shipping.
- Your chance of earning the Buy Box is higher than others.
- Your level of input and contribution is minimal in terms of advertising, shipping, and packaging.
- You will enjoy all the shipping options on Amazon's list. Their network is wide, and you can be assured that your orders will reach your buyers in the given timeframe. Even this shipping cost will come at a discounted rate.
- Many customers are willing to buy from people who are using FBA. This is according to Amazon, and you might want to make use of this important information. People know that they have

a better chance of receiving their orders without much disappointment, and they trust Amazon to give them a better customer care service than a merchant could.

### The disadvantage

We have talked about most of the cons of using Amazon FBA. You can go over them in chapter two. But in comparison with MFN, here are a few highlights. The cost and charges of FBA are not that encouraging. The cost is charged per cubic feet of your product. The weight will also be considered as an influencer of the cost when it comes to shipping. You can use an FBA calculator to calculate this.

This is especially bad for people who sell items considered as long-tail products or items, the type that weighs a lot and get sales only slowly and steadily. In chapter two, you have read about when and when not to use FBA. One of such times is when your product is a long-tail item. If you ask that Amazon ship your item to many centers, you will incur more charges. But it is a good way to boost sales if your product is selling for a low price. This is a good development or a bad development depending on which angle you are looking at it. Are still making a profit? Or is your entire profit going into Amazon's wallet?

### Final thought

For beginners, the decision is up to you. The best advice is to start with FBA after sourcing for a product that has a huge market. You can later experiment with MFN and see how it turns out. Each has its own benefit; your aim and your product are what will determine which will work for you. You can always make FBA work with this book in your hand.

# CHAPTER 5
# GETTING STARTED

The process is long but simple. Some knowledge will come to you as you begin to use the platform. This is like all things in life.

**Stage one: ship to Amazon**

Here, we assume you have sourced, produced, or you have your product with you. You will need to move it to your seller's warehouse where it will be prepared for sale. To do this without any fuss, you will need to follow Amazon's guidelines for shipping your product to their warehouse.

You will

- Label
- Pack
- Prepare a plan for shipping on your Seller Central Dashboard

**Stage two: Storing and Tracking**

After your product has arrived in the warehouse, the staff will sort it according to your inventory. They might send it to another warehouse or center depending on the demand in your location. As an example, if your product is children's toys, and Amazon observes that there is a huge demand for such toys in New York and Las Vegas, they will move some of your toys to the centers in those places, depending.

This is one of the benefits of joining FBA as a means of improving your sales. This will make sales faster. This is happening with or without your knowledge or approval (now, you know, by reading this book) and it costs nothing more on your part.

**Stage three: add to your listing**

Your product is now in the hands of Amazon. It is now in their database that you have a product with them. You can start enhancing sales with promotions and advertisement so that you assist Amazon in its marketing strategy.

Essentially, you are helping your product by making people know about it. Don't ignore this advice on the certainty that Amazon's advertising is enough. Although you might fold your hands and let Amazon do the marketing for you, it is not good advice. There are other sellers like you and if their marketing plans beat yours down, your products will be left to wallow in the dark. As their number of purchases increase, people will notice their products more than the others in the category.

**What should you do?**

Go for the paid advertisement option. You can use any of the methods you can think of

- Social media like a Facebook ad
- Pay per click
- Blog marketing

**Stage four: you are now receiving orders**

If you have done all the steps effectively, your orders will now pour in like the request for water in a desert. When someone orders for your product on Amazon, the staff will get to work, processing the order and shipping to the location. Also, if you have connected with other third-party sellers, your order is either processed manually or automatically through Multi-Channel Fulfillment.

**Stage five: shipping and tracking**

Each order is selected from a fulfillment center which is nearest to your buyer. It will be packed and shipped to the buyer. You can observe what is happening on your status board as provided on the website.

**Stage six: customer services**

You and Amazon have a part to play here. Amazon is a reputable brand; they will follow-up on every shipment to ensure that the customers are satisfied. If your customer needs an explanation on stuff, Amazon staff will be the one to handle it. Now, if they leave feedback on your product, this is where your attention is needed. You will need to make an adjustment so that good reviews will come next time.

**Stage seven: payment**

Your payment comes every fortnight. All sales will be added up, amazon charges deducted, and your profits will then be sent to your bank account.

As you can see, it is all easy and simple. Amazon is handling the bulk of the work. This is serious business, and it should be taken as such; you should follow up and do your part excellently. Have you really grasped what you have to do?

# What is your duty when you have signed up for Amazon FBA?

### 1. Sourcing products

Sourcing for the product is a topic we will come to later. But here is one piece of advice: sell a product whose sales is moving fast. This is necessary if you don't want to pay a lot more for storing your products with Amazon. You will find details on sourcing in chapter six.

### 2. You will keep inventory of products in stock

This is where you will know if your products are still in stock with Amazon. You should check regularly and ensure you have enough items in stock.

### 3. Advertise and market your products

Many people underrate this step for some reasons. You might get away with it, but that's not the case many times. Here are some of the reasons people ignore this important step.

- They are selling a product that has a huge market
- They are reselling a popular brand's product
- They think Amazon is doing the job

For the first two, you can still relax but do not give up completely on advertising, because you don't know what the other sellers are doing. And if you are a beginner, you will need to build your own name as a seller.

For the last point, Amazon is doing some form of marketing for you. You need to go forward and make people know about your product on Amazon. And if your product is fresh and no one knows about it, you will need to do a lot of advertisements to let them know about it.

Custom products also need the same serious advertisement. You can use affiliate marketing just as explained in the previous section – such as Facebook ads, social media pages, and blog marketing.

And that is enough to get you going on Amazon FBA. But then here is a list of things you will need to know when trying to sell on Amazon.

# What you need to start Amazon FBA

Some people have a vague idea of what they need to get started. Some of the things you need are simple. In this section, you will be reminded of the major ones. You should come back to this chapter after you have finished reading the book.

**1. Research skills**

You will need some time on your hands, especially if you want to sell a product that has a huge market. You will need to ask questions, notice what others are doing to make them sell more. In fact, doing research will give you ideas on what products to sell. You will find more information about this step when you are creating a listing for products.

**2. A brand**

What made Amazon become so big and respectable? If you say 'hard work', you are on the way, say 'quality services,' and you are still on the way. But one thing is certain that makes them stand out from all. They are respected because they have put so much work in building up their brand.

Wherever and whenever you see their logo, just like Apple, you recognize them. It's distinct, unique. All those things you said earlier – hard work and quality services – are part of the things necessary for building a business, but you know it's more than that.

Also, when it comes to building a brand, you don't have to worry if what you love doing cannot be sold on Amazon. Here is the trick – if you are an expert in landscaping services, and you are thinking of selling on Amazon, you can choose to sell items that are related to your brand's purpose. If you are a specialist in home cleaning and fumigation, perhaps you should sell pesticides and fumigation items. You can quickly build your brand as well as earn money.

### 3. Quality products

This is an essential part of your success. People will not appreciate your product if it doesn't deliver the quality they seek in it. It has to be made for them, to serve and without any shortcomings. OK, building a product without any shortcomings is not easy, but you should try as much as possible to make it perfect. If you are sourcing for a product, you should use it first to understand it and detect flaws. This will allow you to know how your buyer will feel when buying. Quality products sell, no matter the price. Just ask any iPhone user.

### 4. Competitive price

Products with a large market are a good place to start. Once you learn the ropes, you can start making moves to branch out into other products that are not that popular.

The bad news is that many people are in the same market you are trying to get in. You have to do more to beat them in their game and you have to put a lot of work in doing that.

How?

Good question. Beat their price down. This is even harder to achieve because you are new and being charged by Amazon multiple times over – for storing, shipping, and marketing.

You need to do a lot of research about where to find products at lower prices. When you do that, add the Amazon charges after you must have used the FBA calculator and always try to be as competitive with your price as possible. People really love to buy things at a cheaper rate.

Or if you can't go into producing the product directly because it's hard to beat the competition, you can sell the alternative of such products. For instance, there are a lot of sellers selling a specific kind of wristwatch made by a particular brand, find an alternative wristwatch made by another brand and which costs less.

### 5. A high-profit margin

You need to have a high-profit margin. If you are really going to make good money from this venture, you must have a reasonable profit margin. Because after Amazon must have deducted its fees, you want to have a good amount of money to take home. Depending on your product, the final profit you will be going home with after the whole deal should be between $50 and 100. Aim for this level of profit, and you will be making a good income soon.

**6. An inventory strategy**

Here is where you can make good money and lower the amount you spend on storing products with Amazon FBA. With an excellent inventory strategy, you will forecast the market demands and make an appropriate plan to meet it. It will also help you make a good guess of the quantity of the item to put in stock at a time so that orders will keep on moving promptly. Because if you put few goods in stock, your customer might be disappointed to find out the products are out of stock. They will move to another seller, and that might be the last time they will ever order from you.

You should spend some time to study the market, forecast sales by looking closely at your competitors, their pricing, the quality of their products, and what people are actually buying.

# What you don't need

As a newbie, you will have ideas, some of which are wrong, about how FBA works. Out of them, here is a list of things that you think you need but you don't actually need them. Read and understand.

**1. You don't need to sell on other platforms to make it big**

You might have heard that you need to support sales on Amazon with selling on other platforms. This is true to some extent. Some sellers use what is called MCF (Multi-Channel fulfillment). A kind of process where you sell on other places other than Amazon while your product is still available for sale on Amazon. It is not compulsory; there is not a rigid rule that says you must sell on Etsy or eBay alongside Amazon. MCF only enhances sales. And it has been discussed in chapter four.

**2. Skill in marketing**

Marketing is a skill everyone must-have. Don't you think? Every day of human lives, we have to communicate – market one thing or an idea or a business or product to others in such a way that it must speak to them and they must understand. We all have convinced someone at some points to do something. So having a great marketing skill will be beneficial to you, but you can learn your way up from scratch.

No, you are not learning to become a copywriter or an advertiser. Instead of learning all the skills to become an expert marketer, you can always hire someone to do it or pay for ads such as Facebook ads.

What some sellers do is to give their buyers incentives and gifts during the holidays. For instance, you might reduce the price of your product for the first 25 days of December. Or you can promise the first 10 buyers in the month certain gifts.

In conclusion, marketing skills will help, but it is not compulsory before you start. If you have a few dollars to spare, you can start by paying someone for marketing. In this book, you will find simple and cheap things you can do to boost sales that you don't have to worry about the cost.

### 3. A package

Well, spending a lot of money on a package for your product will cause you no harm, but you should understand that this is not a necessity for beginners. A custom package is good in the sense that it makes your delivery look more appealing and speak about you as a brand. But it all depends on what you are selling and how much you can afford for a start. At the minimum, you are allowed to package your product in a polybag. Using a package will improve your brand's name and create great awareness about you. That doesn't mean if you have little capital for this thing, you should give it all up. No.

### 4. Selling in many marketplaces

So you think you have to sell on eBay, Etsy and the likes before you can succeed as a seller on FBA. You have been mistaken. Let's do a bit of refreshing of what you read in chapter four.

Selling on other platforms is called Multi-channel Fulfillment. It is like putting what people want in all the places they usually check. You know people always check eBay, so you show them on eBay that you have these things.

Although you are storing your products with Amazon, your customers will receive their orders. The item will reach them under a system called the Multi-Channel fulfillment marketing. You can read about it in detail in chapter four.

Now, signing up for this is optional. It is just an avenue to maximize your sales potential by displaying your product to a broader audience, thereby creating a wider demand for such an item. You will read about this as a form of marketing tips you can use to boost sales. Just hang in there.

You don't need to sign up for Multi-channel if you wish; it will only add to your sales, possibly.

## 5. A huge capital

Even if you have a lot of capital, the best thing to do is to wait some time before you invest it all on Amazon FBA. If your goal is to make a lot of money, like a lot of it, your capital should be high. In other words, your goal will determine how much money you should invest. Because you are retailing, you will need more money to buy more products, make a great sales volume and increase your profits later. For beginners, start small. When you understand the process, and you are well-grounded, you should invest more into the system.

## 6. A Shopify account

This is almost the same point as the one above. Integrating your Shopify with Amazon is just an opportunity to reach a larger market and improve sales at the end. The process is quite lengthy, and there is a requirement, especially on Shopify, which you must meet before you can receive approval. After approval, you are free to sell and make money.

Integrating your product to Shopify is not a must. You can, and you might decide not to. This is worth talking about later in the book.

## 7. Licenses

No is the answer. You don't need any form of license to sell online, LLC, or any other business license.

# CHAPTER 6
# THE TWO TYPES OF PRODUCT YOU CAN SELL

Selling products on Amazon FBA is lucrative. You have two options when it comes to getting products to sell. Your aim is to sell as much as possible in the shortest time possible. You will want to put in a lot of effort into this important step. Your product is the only determinant which will make a buyer keep buying from you or move on to another buyer. If you get this step wrong, it could mean the end of a business that is yet to start.

Here are three things you should keep in mind throughout the chapter.

- Quality, the product must meet the buyer's needs
- Price
- Availability

Now that you have those in your hands, you can get the product in two ways

- Create a product/ improve an existing product
- Source for a product

## Create a product or improve an existing one

This is a difficult path to follow if you are a beginner. You need to be creative and have the entrepreneurial spirit. To translate what it means to have an entrepreneurial spirit, you need to take the risk, do your best and expect the best which might not come. You will create something from scratch, something that solves a specific problem people are facing presently. You will have faith in your creation, put it out into the world, and convince people through strategic marketing that they need to buy your product.

This is a difficult path, mountainous, thorny, and risky. You might have done a lot of hard work before you realize that you have been wrong after all; or that people do not care about what you are selling as much as you think.

The benefit is that you might be the next big thing that would be sitting next on the show with Oprah. A lot of sales and a lot of money coming into your account like water from a burst pipe.

For starters, this is a hard terrain.

Ignore it if you don't have what it takes. Try something else.

# Improve an existing product

Head over to Amazon right now and check any category you like, maybe, it is jewelry or toys. Click on an item and scroll down to the reviews.

You are likely going to see good comments and nice feedback. This is not what you are looking for at this moment, so keep reading and scrolling. Anywhere you see 'but,' pay attention and notice what the reviewer is saying.

I love your pencil, but the handle is slippery.

I have read your book, but I think you can do more explanation on how to live life to the fullest through adventure.

The two examples above are not picked from Amazon; they are imaginary. But you can see what the two products are lacking and needs improvement. That is what you need to work on

Make a better handle for the pencil

Include how to live life to the fullest through adventure

You are going to create something similar, of course but with a little improvement than what is already on the market. This will allow you a competitive edge over other sellers.

What you will do is find an item that is selling, make it better by improving it in some way, and sell it on Amazon.

If that seems difficult, do what most people do under private labeling. Find a product that has great market potential, rebrand it (without making any improvement) and sell. That is the second option we are talking about. Just source for an item, rebrand and sell.

# **Sourcing for products**

Wait, wait, wait!

Have you asked where people are getting the products they sell on Amazon? The first thing you might think of is that these sellers are not producers. They are selling rebranded products. Where do they get them from?

**The simple answer is Alibaba.com.**

Have you heard about it? It is like Amazon but with a lot of differences. Items are sold cheaper, and shipping cost, relatively affordable. It is a China ecommerce marketplace, more like an online wholesale market. You buy items in large quantities and resell on other platforms just as you are about to start doing.

Although it is based in China, it is accessible to anyone in the world. You will find distributors and factories from every corner of the world on this site, displaying their items for sale. The good thing is that many of these distributors and factories will assist you in making items unique. They can customize, rebrand, and make an adjustment to products according to your wish.

Many Amazon FBA sellers have learned this trick. This has made a whole lot of pages on Amazon become filled with products that are gotten straight from China or Alibaba.com. These products are classified as white-labeled products. The majority recorded poor sales; some of them do excellently well.

The products, when they arrive, will come with a brand name. This is usually discussed between you and the vendor, with the vendor showing you samples before making a final mass production. You will pay for the items in bulk, have it shipped to you and sell on Amazon.

As an example, an item could cost you about $7 (including branding your name on it, shipping and all that, depending on your negotiation skills) and you can sell as high as $15 on Amazon. If you look at the profit margin, you will be likely to say 'wow!'

But there is a catch. Many items do not sell as expected.

It is a lot of hard work finding quality products on Alibaba.com these days. You will need to search and search before making a choice.

# Private labeling your product

To ensure you are making a lot of money in this business, you will use Alibaba.com for what is called private labeling. In other words, you will select a manufacturer's item and make it look like your own making. Once you do that, you will be able to sell the product with your brand name on it. It is simple and easy. Although there are other options, this is easier and has a higher potential for success.

You can do any of

- Arbitrage – we talked about it earlier.
- Wholesale – buy other brand's products in a large quantity and retail on Amazon at a higher price.
- Sell used books – buy old or used books at any book store, other places, or yard sales. Resell them on Amazon at a higher price.

These options are good. You can research it and make a good move, arm yourself with enough information so that you are not making moves blindly.

Let's talk about private labeling as a viable option.

The benefits of private labeling in comparison to other adventures

- You don't have to source for many different products. You remember in retail arbitrage you are looking everywhere for cheaper products so that you can sell on Amazon. This is not like private labeling, where you will pick an item, order for as many as possible. It could be only that item, bought in large quantity and branded as yours.
- You have control over prices. This listing is for your product and it is under your control, and you don't have to be bothered a lot about underpricing because of your competition. Unlike

in retail arbitrage or wholesale, you need to beat the price down so as to stand as a competitor.

- There is a chance of higher profit. Once the sales start moving and you are recognized as a brand, you will make more sales than average.

# How to create your product using private label

You are going to use Alibaba.com for creation. But first, you have to know what is going to sell. To know what is going to sell will cost you some money, just a token of $49 for a start.

You will download an App called **Junglescout** and make use of the app to find what people are paying so much to buy and how often they are buying. We shall continue to talk about JungleScout and how to use it many sections of this guide. To really understand what the tool does, you need to use it yourself and gain firsthand knowledge.

1. Once you have used JungleScout to determine that a product is selling well, head over to Alibaba.com
2. Source the product through the website and contact a seller who will brand and help you ship the product to you.
3. Come back to Amazon and create a brand-new listing. This will only take a few minutes, and not up to 40 minutes.
4. After your product has been manufactured and branded, it will be shipped directly to your Amazon fulfilment center of choice. You don't need to ship the product to your house or warehouse first before moving it to a fulfillment center. This will be all done by the AliBaba vendor.
5. It is time to launch your product; all you have to do is a bit of advertisement and wait for your product to start selling. The difficult part is finding a product with an awaiting and eager market. Once you have done the first step, using JungleScout

or any niche hunter you know, all other things have become easy.

This seems hard; let's demonstrate it with an example. We are going over each of the steps one after another so you will not make mistakes.

**Step one**

Finding a profitable Private Label Product in a Few Minutes

This is the hardest part of your journey as a seller whether you are using FBA or not. It is important you know what will sell and how it has been performing. In the end, it will seem like magic, because you will keep receiving orders and making a lot of sales.

This is not hard to do if you read the process that will be explained below. It will only take 15 minutes to learn it and less than that to actually find the product.

The first and most significant thing used is called the Best-seller Ranking (BSR). It is found on the offer page of a product on Amazon.

Every product on Amazon has its own bestseller rank. And one thing you should always remember is that lower BSR means the product is making a lot of sales. In fact, you can pick a BSR and use it to understand how many pieces a product sells in a month.

To do this, just pick the BSR of a product and drop it inside JungleScout free sales estimator. You will see how many sales the product is getting. This is a simple trick, and it makes your work a lot easier if you are selling products on Amazon. You will have an idea on how many pieces of a product you are likely to sell. With such assurance, you will be confident you are putting your money into effective use. In fact, you can use the results to determine how many products you should stock in Amazon's warehouse.

What if you want to know how multiple products are performing?

Well, this is going to take the use of JungleScout chrome extension. Once you install the extension on your browser, search through the Amazon website. The extension will automatically return the BSR of all products on a given page.

The information you will get from the extension include the following:

- Average Bestseller Rank – look for lower ranks. This will give a good idea on how well the items are selling.

- Average price – if the average price is between $18 and $60, then you are in the right niche.
- An average number of reviews – products with about 100 are lucrative.

**Step two**

Sourcing for quality products on Alibaba.com

Now that you have broadened your knowledge on how to find products that will sell, you can now head over to Alibaba.com.

There are many other platforms for such buying activities but Alibaba.com is an excellent place to start. They are the best fit for you.

How to source for products on Alibaba.com

This is worth discussing so that you have a smooth experience on Alibaba.com.

There are many sellers on the platform, and you need to be smart and courteous when using such an online marketplace. People are hiding behind a laptop or mobile phone ready to scam you.

Here are a few tips before you start making orders on Alibaba.com

The world of eCommerce is a large place, and if you want to make a lot of money, you have to plan and follow experts. Below are a few tips on how to use Alibaba.com to source for products:

- Know what you want. It is good if you have understood the product so much that you don't need someone to convince you before you can recognize it. For our purpose, it is likely you are not that familiar with what you want to buy on the platform, so take some time to familiarize yourself with it. Use Google and if possible, put some points down so you won't forget.
- If a seller seems shady, stay away from them. Many people are willing to take away your money and never return again.
- The process is longer than you think. So you will need to make your orders earlier or risk incurring a lot of shipping fees to get it early.
- Create a new mail for this process. This is essential because you will be receiving regular updates in your mailbox.

**Reaching to your supplier and searching for your product**

The number of products you will find on Alibaba.com is quite overwhelming. This translates that there are many trading companies and manufacturers.

This is a wide opportunity, and it is an opportunity for sketchy people who want to extort those who aren't careful. But as you are here, you have had a good understanding of what you want. That's a good start.

**Sort your suppliers**

You will first need to familiarize yourself with Alibaba.com. There are certain features that can help you narrow down your search. Some of them include

- Supplier's location
- Certifications
- Free samples offered or the absence of it
- Product prices
- Minimum order quantity (MOQ)

You can find this information on the sidebar and the top filter. As you are searching, focus more on MOQ, price, and free samples. This is not a standard; you are only selecting factors that will favor you as a buyer. There are different types of sellers and programs that make Alibaba.com great for both buyers and suppliers. We will talk about the importance of using the site. You will find the rest later when you start using it.

**Manual outreach**

Now you can contact as many as a hundred suppliers at a time to ensure you have a wide range of options, a pool to pick from. Or you can use a feature known as RFQ (Request for Quotation).

When you use this feature, suppliers will present you their offers. You will provide information like the type of product, the price, and the quantity that you want, the payment terms, etc.

Suppliers will come in with as many quotes as possible, and this can be overwhelming. If you don't mind, you can still go for it. But if you want to speak to just a few, it is best to use manual outreach and contact suppliers manually.

**How to go about it**

You will search for the products on the website. Profiles of prospective suppliers will appear. Click on the product page and see the details of each supplier and their reviews. Message the ones that meet your needs. And do not forget to keep an eye on the MOQ.

By clicking on the contact supplier button, a new interface will appear where you can type a message and ask any questions.

After sending the messages to as many suppliers as you want to contact, you can click on your account and read about the inquiries, orders, contact requests, and messages. Also, there are a lot of features on your account page that you will find helpful.

You may find it difficult finding a quality product on Alibaba.com

When it comes to the price of the product, you are lucky to be on Alibaba.com. As explained earlier, you will find it easy to buy product and ship it at half the price you will find it on Amazon. But what about quality? This is the hard part, finding quality products on the platform is a hard task.

One thing is certain; if you display poor items on Amazon, buyers will leave a review that will make other buyers run away with their money. You don't want that, so you should source for quality items only.

Ask for samples

When an item is so cheap, and you can't believe it, you need to make a great effort to verify its quality, especially because you are not holding the products in your hands. You should ask for samples.

There are two options, according to the supplier's preference. Some will give you free samples (well, it is not that reliable if you ask an experienced buyer). Some will ask for a token for the samples, so choose according to what you can afford.

After you get the sample in your hands, you can verify the quality, head back to your account and start talking with the supplier about making a bulk purchase of branded items.

**Placing an order and payment method**

This is where you have to give out your money for the goods that you have ordered. You really need to make sure you have done your due diligence before paying for a product. So choose a method that favors you out of all the options. Some of the supported payment methods include MasterCard/Maestro, Western Union, T/ T (Bank Transfer), Web Money, QIWI, Yandex, and TEF.

There is what is called a secure payment on Alibaba.com, which allows them to protect buyers and sellers from scams. You can be assured that your orders will arrive in a few weeks or months, depending.

**Step three**
**Writing a good product description**
If you are going to make a lot of sales, enough to beat your competitors, you need to write a good product description. It is like designing your house, the front yard, and an exterior wall. If it is appealing, people will smile and take a second look or bring out their phones and take pictures.

This is one rule you must take with you when writing product descriptions:

Write to the emotional appeal of your product instead of describing your product. Write the benefits instead of writing the features.

In other words, always think of what you are saying and how it will affect the reader or prospective buyer. If you can't state it will make things easier or convenient for your buyer, you should consider revising. Let's see an example of what you have just read.

Let's assume your product is an oil shampoo. You might write the following bullet points in your product description:

- Soft shampoo
- Contains Almond
- Serves as a base

You see, you have done an excellent job of listing what your product has and you did that without including your buyer in the plan. Your buyer didn't know what you mean; their emotion isn't triggered. You don't make them nod, saying 'I want that.'

But look at this.

- The shampoo has a soft texture that develops beautiful milky foam when you rub it between your palms.
- The scent of almond makes the shampoo smell like a rare and angelic flower.
- Should you want to shave, the shampoo could also serve as a base for shaving.

Whenever you can't picture the exact benefit the product you are presenting will give the buyer, you should consider taking another look at it. Compare the second example above with the first, which one do you think will interest you more as a buyer? The second has connected the points with the exact benefits the buyer desires.

Here some tips that will make product descriptions more effective:

- The first thing is to always appeal to emotion. Let you buyer imagine wearing the jeans, using the gas cooker, or eating snacks.
- Make the title grab their attention when writing your description.
- Show it to others and let them give you feedback.
- Check other sellers and see what you could learn from their product descriptions.
- Use keywords in your descriptions. Use them creatively as if you are writing for humans and not for a robot.

Let's talk about the other parts of your listing

**Product title**

Usually, the title is about 250 characters long. Use it all.

Use target keywords in your title. You can use Junglescout to find the terms people are searching and use it creatively.

Make sure you are appealing to the buyers' emotion in your title. Does your land mower have anti-rust properties, blend it in. Or does it have extremely sharp blades, find ways to include that.

**Product images**

- You are allowed to put up to 9 images. Use all the spaces. The lead image, however, should be the most beautiful, showing the entire product.
- Do not underestimate the services of a professional photographer. So invest in one and let the quality of your images speak about your product.
- It is wise if your lead image is bold, clear, and has no watermark that could deceive the buyer, and has a simple or plain background.
- Other images should show your products from another perspective or angle. If it has features or parts that standout, you use that as an image on its own. Zoom in on the parts you think are important.
- Take pictures of the product in action – a beautiful woman wearing that earring or a man using the vacuum cleaner.
- Explore your inner creativity. You have nine images to make a good impression, use it wisely.

**Key features**
- Use the same tips under the product description for this section and do not forget to use keywords.
- What feature is the most important of all? Put that one first so you can stand in competition and beat your competitors.

**Reviews**

There is nothing much you can do about reviews other than wait for your customer to give their honest opinion about your product. But here are some things that can help.
- Reach out to your customers through email campaigns, telling them the estimated time of arrival of their order and encourage them to leave a review when they get them.
- If you have followed the tips under sourcing products religiously, your product must be of good quality.
- Give your customers the best services, and they will no other option than to leave a positive review.

**Product Rating**

Well, you can't do much here either. But here are some things that can also help:

- If a customer makes certain complaints, improve on such complaints.
- When you are reaching your customers through email, inform them to give you feedback through emails. This will prevent bad reviews from getting public.

Now you have known how to make a good impression with your product. This is essential because it is the last point where your buyers will reach for their credit cards. You have to think about that and make the best decision that will not make them change their mind suddenly. Also, you can skip this step until you have your own product with Amazon, but it is wise to always prepare ahead. So that orders will move fast once they start coming and immediately your products have arrived in the warehouse. For the pictures, you can use samples you got from your supplier. If that is not enough, you can upload more photos when you get your goods delivered.

Let's talk about that – how to ship your product in from China.

**Step four**

Shipping your product from Alibaba.com to Amazon's warehouse

This can be complicated, but if you look at it, it shouldn't be. You think you are shipping from one location to another; there should be no fuss about it. But then Amazon comes in with a list of rules.

There are many reasons that shipping directly to the Amazon warehouse will not be as straightforward as you imagine. One of it is Amazon's rule which enforces packaging and labeling. The other thing is that shipping between countries comes with its difficulties and custom processes.

To make things easy for you, use companies that will prevent the hassles and troubles of shipping items from one country to another. Usually, they are called customs brokers and freight forwarders.

There are many options out there, but Flexport is good. They are created by Google and with an extensive online interface. They have a reasonable price in comparison to others.

**The steps for using Flexport are pretty straightforward:**
- Your supplier or factory will deliver the items to Flexport.
- Flexport (or any another freight forwarder you will use) will get the stock and move it to your country and the destination, handling all paperwork and taxes along the way.
- The freight forwarder will deliver your items to the Amazon partnered courier. The courier will take it into the warehouse (Amazon Fulfillment center), just as you want it.

That is all you have to do to get your sourced products down to Amazon warehouse and become an Amazon FBA seller with a product in the store. Now if you have imagined a series of complicated processes, then you have been saved from thinking too hard.

What you are left with now is launching your product and advertisement. Here is a simple truth which can also serve as a reminder: the hardest parts have been covered.

Note: now that you have understood all that is needed, you can switch between the sequences of things. For instance, you might first head over to Alibaba.com to find a product, before you head over to JungleScout to find out if there is a hungry market for it. The only rule is that you must know if there is a market before you make a final order.

Here is a recap of the steps in sequential order
- Find products with a market on JunglesScout
- Source for the product on Alibaba.com
- Build a good product listing or description on Amazon
- Ship your product from Alibaba (China) to Amazon warehouse
- Launch sales

And you are up and making money on Amazon FBA.

In the next section of this chapter, we are going to talk about marketing. You can ignore it if you think you have a sharp edge over your competitors. Read if you don't want to sink below the sea of other products. Staying above and making sales will happen if you fold your hands, but you don't want to take chances while you are new. So, see how to go about marketing.

# Marketing your products on Amazon

The best way to get Amazon customers is by amplifying your listings' visibility. There are such a significant number of items on the commercial center, and purchasers don't have room or the persistence to filter through each and every one. Make it simple for purchasers to discover your items, and you're on track to win more prominent deals. To make your listings visible, we'll feature nine key approaches to drive outer traffic from outside of the website and inner traffic inside the commercial center to your items. Utilizing these procedures drives purchasers appropriately to your postings, so they can choose your business channel and turn into your repeat buyers.

### Visibility and your Amazon Listings

For your products to be seen, you need to engage in aggressive marketing. You spread items mindfully to the world through promotions and other advertising endeavors to drive traffic back to your posting pages.

Amazon algorithms are progressively tricky to understand —they require both outer and inside marketing. With such a significant amount of rivalry on the marketplace, dealers need to create their postings to be exceedingly apparent on Amazon's site, not only outside of it.

### Promoting your product externally

These are advertisements targeted at attracting people from outside to Amazon's website. So consider

- Social media – If you have a considerable number of followers, you can leverage that. If you don't, you can contact other people who have a vast following. Let them create a link on

their page that will bring them back to your Amazon page. That is called influencer marketing
- SEO – use keywords to promote your products so that people will find them easily. Good SEO strategies will help ensure that your listings will show up when people type keywords into their search engines.
- Get backlinks – affiliate marketing or blogging can be a great way to market your products and lead buyers to your Amazon page.

**Promoting your product internally**

Let's assume you're an Amazon vendor, and you need to sell ladies' shades. You won't be the primary shipper selling this item of adornment on the marketplace — there are more than 40,000 different dealers likewise offering ladies' shades. Shades aren't a special item. You will find many of them on Amazon. To beat the challenge, you need to discover approaches to build your item's listings' and their visibility on the marketplace.

Check out ways to promote your items internally

- Win the Buy Box – At the point when merchants share a solitary listing on Amazon since they all sell a similar item, there's consistently a Buy Box which features choice of price.
- Winning the Buy Box enhances prime visibility; therefore, it's a critical method for drawing in purchasers on Amazon. Amazon uses a vast number of components to choose the sellers who will get the Buy Box — principally, cost, yet in addition, others like seller rating and dispatching type.
- Rank high on Amazon item indexed lists – Most purchasers won't move past the first page of listed items, so getting a high positioning is a primary method to land customers. As indicated by Amazon Seller Central, the commercial center search engine uses a content match, accessibility, price, and the history of sales rank listings.

**1. Advance Your Listings with SEO**

SEO pulls in a broad range of purchasers towards your listing. When you incorporate the right keywords in your listings, both customers who are searching on Amazon and those searching on different search engines will discover your products and patronize you.

There are a couple of crucial tools you can use to determine the keywords that your customers are searching for.

- Google Keyword Planner: This free tool demonstrates the month to month search volume of keywords on Google's search engine. Since Amazon listings rank on Google, this tool is particularly useful.

Scope: A tool which explicitly is intended for Amazon. It enables you to follow keywords' month to month volume or positioning after some time, assessed deals, and the sky's the limit from there.

When you've gathered your keywords, place them all throughout your listing, for example, in the title and portrayal. Identifying these popular keywords, web search tools will perceive your listing as an applicable outcome for your purchasers' requests and rank it higher.

### 2. Purchase Sponsored Product Ads

Indeed, even after using SEO, there's no guarantee that your listing will be put higher in Amazon's listed items. The commercial center's search engine thinks about different components for positioning, which include selling history, cost, etc., so SEO alone doesn't really increase rankings.

To enhance their listings' visibility, Amazon merchants can pay for the commercial center to support their items and rank them higher on the page.

Dealers possibly pay when customers click on their advertisements, so the result with Amazon marketing is ensured. Your listings' visibility is expanded, so customers on Amazon discover your item and possibly buy without much stress.

### 3. Post Listings on Social Media

The average individual spends about two hours of his or her day going through social media. Given this prominence, sharing your Amazon listings via social media through your business' records is an incredible method for getting your items before more purchasers.

Many of your followers hope to get an incentive from your posts; it's ideal to abstain from making posts that are fundamentally promotions for your listings. Instead, post your social media contents in a way that they would provide value to your followers.

### 4. Analyze what your competitors are doing

To be ahead of your competitors on Amazon, people who might have been in the game earlier than you – you must know how they are playing the game; learn from their tactics, try to beat them at it. How? It is easier than you think.

Pick one of your competitors and check their listing, one that ranks higher than yours and see what it is they are doing in terms of

- Price: your competitors' price should not be lower than yours if you really want to sell more than him. If your products are the same or look alike, buyers will prefer the one with a lower price. So, you should keep it low. Also, Amazon uses price as one of the criteria for awarding the Buy Box to FBA sellers. Keep your price reasonably lower to make this work for you.

- Images: look at their images. Do they have what you don't? Buyers are very sensitive when it comes to looking for ways to choose an item they will be paying for. They will check your image over and over to see if it is worth it. Now if they find the images on the listings of your competitors more appealing, then you are out of the competition. To avoid this, you want your images to be as good as or even better than your competitors.

- Text: how did they craft their descriptions? If you have a good knowledge of copywriting, you will beat most of your competitors with your choice of text. Also, you should use keywords creatively so that your buyers can find you. Look at your competitors' listing and include the keywords you see in their listing in your own.

## 5. Work with influencers

Have you heard of influencer marketing? It is such a tremendous way to drive traffic to your listing and increase sales. An influencer, someone who is popular in your niche or industry, will make an announcement about your product and provide their followers with links to your page. A lot of Amazon sellers are leveraging influencers to make more sales.

You will find the names of people who are prominent in your industry. Write a list of their names, ensuring they have a huge number of followers on social media. You can think about them, or you can use places like influence.co. Contact them and let them know what you want. Remember, you will have to pay an influencer before they advertise your products.

## 6. Keep up the good rating

Don't forget that Amazon is one big competitive market. To stay ahead, you will have to be consistent with good performance.

- Get products that are of high quality
- Ensure your rating is good. Many buyers are looking at your rating, and they will buy if it is good.
- Whatever feedback is on your page will encourage new buyers or discourage them, so work towards making an excellent first impression.

Some of the things that could make you have a good rating include:

- Be honest about your product: do not say your product is white when it is grey with a touch of black on the edges. It will backfire when buyers come back to your listing to rate you and leave a bad review.
- Give your customers excellent service: If you are using FBA, there is nothing much to do here. But if people contact you directly, perhaps through mails or other form of marketing that you have done, then you should give the best service always.
- Make out time for people who are disappointed: you cannot satisfy everyone, but you should try to satisfy all of them. Contact people who have one complaint or another and try to

help them in any way possible. In exchange, they should leave good feedback or rate your product highly.

## 7. Check your seller overall performance regularly

We have talked about this briefly. Watch your overall rating to ensure you are still in the competition. If you notice any drop in performance, be quick in making adjustments and offering solutions.

Here is how you can go about it:

Check your rating: this is visible on Seller Central, including all factors that influence your ratings. Check what you can do to improve it.

Respond well to customers: there is nothing much to do here if you are using FBA. But you should try as much as possible to reply as fast as possible to people who contact you.

Remove feedback if possible: Amazon has a guideline for reviewers. If your reviewer is not following the guidelines, you can always remove the review.

The major thing is to maintain a high seller rating. Keep your eye on this goal and work – or walk – towards it every day.

8. Try the lightning deal

This works for many reasons.

- It offers your buyers a good discount. And as you already know, people like discounts.
- It is time-based, which means buyers want to make good use of the opportunity before it elapses.

You should know that Amazon must give approval before you can do this

- Lightning deals only run between 4 and 12 hours
- You can offer this deal once in every 7 days.
- You must have the number of products you want to use seven days before the launch date.

These steps should earn you more sales on Amazon and give you an edge over your competitors. Continue to learn and grow and find new ideas on how to stay ahead of the competition. You will find it rewarding in the long run.

# Product research

Amazon is a large marketplace – this means that the same way you are trying to make money on the platform is the same way that thousands of other sellers are also trying to make money on the platform. This breeds a huge competition on the platform with every seller trying to outdo the other. If you must succeed as a seller on Amazon, then you should be ready to learn how to strategize and position your business in a unique way and to do that requires you must do proper product research. You cannot be selling a random product and expect a breakthrough. You must make a conscious effort to beat the competition.

One mistake that sellers often make is that they just want to go with the crowd. If you do what others are doing – you will get the same results that they are getting. If they are getting poor results, you will also get poor results, and in most cases, people who follow the crowd often get poor results.

Before deciding to start selling on Amazon, some people just browse the internet to get ideas on the bestselling products. They then proceed to procure those products and start selling. How do you think you will experience positive results with such effort? Remember, the same way that you are searching the internet for bestselling products, thousands of other FBA sellers are also searching the internet for such products.

At the end of the day, all the people doing such internet searches will end up having the same product ideas. With almost all the sellers selling the same product, the competition will keep growing, and the sellers will be complaining of low or no sales.

The best way to distinguish yourself from the crowd is to do your own independent product research and come up with unique items you can sell. There are thousands of undiscovered niches and products that many sellers are not aware of because almost all of them are preoccupied with finding hot-selling products.

I am not against finding best selling products, but you need to know that it is just a matter of time before other sellers discover such best selling products and make the market for it to be saturated. Instead of finding hot-selling products with a short half-life, your aim should be to find evergreen products that will continue to sell even in the next ten years, and the best way to do that is through product research.

How do you do product research? There are tools for that, and in this section, we will be looking at some of them.

# Top Amazon FBA product research tools:

### 1. Jungle Scout

We have mentioned Jungle Scout before, and here, we are mentioning it again because it is by far one of the best Amazon FBA product research tools available. Jungle Scout has earned a top spot in the hearts of all FBA sellers, and the reasons for that include the following:

- As the name of the app suggests, it scouts through Amazon's website searching for products in hidden niches which you can sell. It also looks at what your competitors are selling – this information will help you to understand what is already working in the market and model your products after those.
- It has a Chrome extension which helps you to get information about a product when you are browsing through the Amazon website.

### 2. Amazon Product Research Tools: AMZ Tracker

This tool helps you to find the proper keywords which you can include in your product descriptions to improve SEO. Search engine optimization is important on Amazon as it helps make your products visible on the platform. If you don't include proper keywords in your listings, users will not discover them when they are searching for related products on Amazon.

In addition to helping you find the right keywords to use in your listing, AMZ Tracker also helps you to track why some of your products are not selling and offer you helpful suggestions. You can try the tool for free for seven days after which you will need to pay a monthly subscription fee that ranges from $50 to $400.

Other notable product research tools include:
- Informed.co
- Scope
- MerchantWord, etc.

Now let's see what Amazon fees are and how items are charged.

# CHAPTER 7
# AMAZON FBA FEES

As much as Amazon saves you a lot of stress, you know it's not free. They charge you some amount of money for their services. This is called FBA fees. And we will be talking about it in this chapter.

If someone wants to scare you off this program, all the person has to do is say 'Amazon charges you for everything, and you will barely make a profit.' That's it. An evil seed is planted, left for you to research or run away. You are wise, anyway.

You have read a story in chapter three. A man took the risk of investing in Amazon FBA, but the man did not make profits. These kinds of stories are shared with a final note of warning: you don't want to lose your capital, so stay away.

But you are wise!

Buying this book means you are not running away from the program. You want the knowledge. So read this: people are milking Amazon FBA, and they are making a lot of money. What people are scared of, most times is the fees. If you know how it is calculated, you will have a better idea of how to:

- Set your pricing
- Imagine your profit
- Plan to face competitors
- Help when you are sourcing for products on Alibaba
- Assist you in making negotiations with suppliers
- Compare competitors and the possibility of success

There are a lot of benefits when you learn about pricing. So let's start. The first thing you need to know is that the rules and policies of Amazon as a brand can be adjusted at any time. This is expected of brands that want to stay relevant as the rate of demand continues to change and development happens generally. There could be changes tomorrow about how items are charged. Anyway, you need to understand the basics, and every other thing will follow.

There are three main factors that will determine how much you will pay on Amazon:

- The weight of your product
- The size
- The channels which you are using to sell

The weight of your product is measured in volume. The size of your product is quite understandable as the bigger item will take more space inside the store compared to the smaller items.

The channels through which you sell is an interesting topic we will discuss in this chapter. It also influences the fees you will be charged. The topic is Multi-Channel Fulfillment fees.

The fees of Amazon FBA are two types:

**Amazon fulfilment fees**

This is the type of payment for making Amazon do your job. You are hiring Amazon to ship products, handle customer services, and provide marketing services. In turn, you will pay an amount for the entire task they are doing on your behalf. This fee is calculated per unit of every item.

**Monthly inventory storage fees**

Just as you are selling, your items are kept in a warehouse, a place where it is safe and protected. You are charged for keeping your item in this store and as long as it stays there. This is where the amount of space your items occupy matters most. This is straightforward, the bigger the item, as in the more space it occupies, the higher the charge. You can pick two things from the above – they are size and weight. Let's talk about the sizes. There are standard sizes and oversized.

**The standard size**

Products in this category are items that weigh no more than 20 pounds after they have been packed. In addition, the dimension should not exceed 18" x 14" x 8".

**Oversize**

Products with size and dimension greater than the above are considered oversize. It weighs more than 20 pounds, and its dimensions are wider than 18 inches across the length, it is oversize according to Amazon FBA.

Here is a table to show the specific weight and dimensions

| PRODUCT SIZE CATEGORY | WEIGHT (IN POUNDS) | LONGEST SIDE (INCHES) | MEDIAN SIDE (INCHES) | SHORTEST SIDE (INCHES) | LENGTH + GIRTH (INCHES) |
|---|---|---|---|---|---|
| Small standard size | Equal to or less than 12 lb. | 15" | 12" | 0.75" | N/A |
| Large standard size | Equal to or less than 20 lb. | 18" | 14" | 8" | N/A |
| Small oversize | Equal to or less than 70 lb. | 60" | 30" | N/A | 130" |
| Medium oversize | Equal to or less than 150 lb. | 108" | N/A | N/A | 165" |
| Special oversize | Over 150 lb. | Over 108" | N/A | N/A | Over 165" |

Don't forget that the prices might change with time. Now that you have understood what influences the fees on each item, you should know that there is another process for charging those who are selling on external sites. This is called Multi-Channel Fulfillment fees.

You should also know that there are FBA calculators which are easy to use and save you a lot of stress.

**Multi-Channel fulfillment and the fees**

You have different options of selling when you are using Amazon FBA.

- You can put the products in your own store. This is known as fulfillment by merchant, and it has been explained in chapter four.

- You can store the product with Amazon, which is known as FBA, fulfillment by Amazon.

- The third option is what we are talking about here in this section. It is called Multi-channel Fulfillment. You will store your products with Amazon, but you can create listings on other channels. You don't have to stock another set of items somewhere else.

This, of course, gives you an edge, showing your products to more buyers, people who are using other channels different than Amazon. Your sales will increase, and that way, you should expect more charges. Clearly, you are the biggest winner when it comes to MCF. If you have a lot of Stock Keeping Units, you are the one who will benefit more from MCF. You have a higher chance of planning demand and recording more sales. You can scale your marketing strategy. However, this plan does present some challenges.

The first notable one is that you might not have the chance to brand yourself properly. In fact, branding is not something you can achieve if you are shipping directly to Amazon's warehouse.

Using MCF for your orders will work if you are selling a few items every day. Those who have a lot of orders daily will have a tougher job to do.

**The fees**

Like the other types of FBA, there are two kinds of fees.

- The storage fees
- And the fulfillment fees

Yes, as discussed earlier, the first deals with payment for keeping your items with Amazon. The second deals with the activities Amazon staff will be performing on your behalf. This is quite understandable.

Now, unlike the previous version, there are specific options for the products under MCF. They are based on duration or period that it will take to ship the products. There are:

- Standard, 3-5 days
- Expedited, two days
- Priority, shipping the following day

Now go back to the table briefly and notice that this has been shown on the table. There are two tables for both standard and oversize items.

| SIZE | 1 UNIT ORDER | 2 UNIT ORDER | 3 UNIT ORDER | 4 UNIT ORDER | 5 UNIT ORDER |
|---|---|---|---|---|---|
| Small (1lb or less) | $5.85 | $3.75 | $3.35 | $3.25 | $2.20 |
| Large Products (1lb or 2lb) | $5.90 | $3.90 | $3.40 | $3.30 | $2.80 |
| Large (1lb to 2lb) | $5.95 | $3.95 | $3.45 | $3.35 | $2.95 |
| Large (more than 2 lb) | $5.95 + $0.39/lb | $3.95 + $0.39/lb | $3.45 + $0.39/lb | $3.35 + $0.39/lb | $2.95 + $0.39/lb |

Table for standard shipping fees used in Oversize products per unit

| Size | 1 unit order | 2 unit order | 3 unit order | 4 unit order | 5+ unit order |
|---|---|---|---|---|---|
| Small: more than first 2 lb | $12.30 + $0.39/lb | $6.80 + $0.39/lb | $5.80 + $0.39/lb | $4.80 + $0.39/lb | $3.80 + $0.39/lb |
| Medium: more than first 2 lb | $15.30 + $0.39/lb | | | | |
| Large: more than first 90 lb | $78.30 + $0.80/lb | | | | |
| Special: more than first 90 lb | $143.30 + $0.92/lb | | | | |

Expedited Shipping Fees For Oversize Products Per Unit

| Size | 1 unit order | 2 unit order | 3 unit order | 4 unit order | 5+ unit order |
|---|---|---|---|---|---|
| Small: more than first 2 lb | $12.30 + $0.39/lb | $7.80 + $0.39/lb | $7.30 + $0.39/lb | $7.15 + $0.39/lb | $6.85 + $0.39/lb |
| Medium: more than first 2 lb | $16.80 + $0.39/lb | | | | |
| Large: more than first 90 lb | $78.30 + $0.80/lb | | | | |
| Special: more than first 90 lb | $143.30 + $0.92/lb | | | | |

Priority Shipping Fees For Oversize Products Per Unit

| Size | 1 unit order | 2 unit order | 3 unit order | 4 unit order | 5+ unit order |
|---|---|---|---|---|---|
| Small: more than first 2 lb | $20.80 + $0.39/lb | $11.30 + $0.39/lb | $8.20 + $0.39/lb | $7.70 + $0.39/lb | $7.30 + $0.39/lb |
| Medium: more than first 2 lb | $31.30 + $0.39/lb | | | | |
| Large: more than first 90 lb | $78.30 + $0.80/lb | | | | |
| Special: more than first 90 lb | $143.30 + $0.92/lb | | | | |

As stated previously, you can see that the more items you have in the program, the lesser the cost. People who have more products on a channel of theirs will acquire a lesser fee. This will even be lower if you sell more on your website than other places.

**Amazon storage fees**

Putting your products in Amazon fulfillment centers will make you fulfill orders quickly. To ensure that you are not accumulating a lot of storage fees, your products should be moving fast out of your store to your customers. In other words, you must sell them quickly.

Here is a table that shows how storage fees work on a monthly basis

| Storage month | Standard size | Oversize |
|---|---|---|
| January – September | $0.69 per cubic foot | $0.48 per cubic foot |
| October – December | $2.40 per cubic foot | $1.20 per cubic foot |

**Monthly storage cost**

| INVENTORY ASSESSMENT DATE | ITEMS IN FULFILLMENT CENTERS 181 TO 365 DAYS | ITEMS IN FULFILLMENT CENTRES 365 DAYS OR MORE |
|---|---|---|
| Semi-annual (February 15 and August 15) | $11.25 per cubic foot | $22.50 per cubic foot |

**Long term storage fees**

| Inventory Assessment Date | Items In Fulfillment Centers 181 to 365 Days | Items In Fulfilment Centers 365 Days or More |
|---|---|---|
| Monthly (15th of every month) | $3.45 per cubic foot | $6.90 per cubic foot |

**Minimum long-term storage fees**

| Inventory Assessment Date | Items In Fulfillment Centers 365 Days or More |
|---|---|
| Monthly (15th of every month) | $0.50 per unit |

**Referral fees**

Remember, Amazon charges for what is called seller fees. You can also call it referral fees, which is levied over all items that are sold on Amazon. You can check the price of this referral fees on the website. For those who are using Multi-Channel Fulfillment, you don't have to pay for this.

**Any other charges?**

Yes, there are other charges which you must understand how they work before you start selling on the website. Some of them might not concern you; some will. You still need to check them out so that you can have a good idea of what your profit will look like at the end of the day.

**Monthly selling fees**

This is like rent, the money you will pay for using Amazon as a selling point.

**Variable closing fees and referral fees**

You will pay a little commission as you sell each item you store with them.

**Returns Processing fees**

Although this is free; most times, you have to keep an eye on it so that your product doesn't get into the category where they are charged unnecessarily. This is dependent on the situation; you might be charged if you want your returned products to be processed.

**Stock removal fees**

This is the amount you will pay if you want to remove your items from Amazon's warehouse or you want it to be shipped back to you.

### Inventory placement service

This fee is charged when you want your inventory to be shipped or distributed to other fulfillment centers. The levy will be charged according to what you want.

### Export fees

You might want your product to be shipped to other countries. This is a service which Amazon offers at a certain fee which you should consider before asking for it.

# Lowering the amount you pay for Amazon Fees

This is the kind of thought that crosses one's mind as an entrepreneur. You know the motto: reduce cost and maximize profit. This is hard most of the time, but then there is fun in trying the hard stuff and joy when something is accomplished. You might have read some of the tips between the lines in previous chapters. Here is a place you come to directly to find answers to the question of how to reduce Amazon FBA fees.

So, let's see what we can do to reduce the cost of Amazon fees.

1. **Ship a specific item to one particular fulfillment center**

The thing is, not all items are fine to be in an Amazon's store. If it weighs a lot and it is not selling fast, you are in a lot of trouble. So then it would be wise to trade items that don't weigh so much and sell faster.

Another thing is to always consider the size of a product. A beautiful earring might cost the same amount and earn you the same profit as a lawn mower. But you know what? The mower will be charged more when you keep it with Amazon because of its size (and weight, of course).

2. **Monitor how your products are performing**

Ask any stockbroker how they have managed to stay long in the business, you will notice that they watch the performances of different stocks, familiarize with it, and make a calculative judgment. *We are not into stock, but you can learn from that.* There are tools on your seller central account that helps you make predictions and maximize your use of Amazon FBA. On the account; you will notice what is called the Inventory Performance Dashboard. There, you can watch your inventory and make predictions and Amazon will give you insights like advice or, if you prefer a less strong term, suggestions, on how to make the best use of the platform.

Usually, this can be broken down into three

- **Stranded Inventory Actions**: this is a simple term which refers to the problem that your listing is facing, and it shows the various ways to tackle them so that buyers will enjoy buying from you. *How great.*

- **Restock recommendations**: with the performances of your products on the system, this option will advise you when to restock so that your buyers will not try to place an order and be faced with 'out of stock'. That's annoying, you know. You can use this tool in determining the number of items you will be shipping to the store the next time so that you won't bring excess and acquire charges that could have been saved.

- **Excess Inventory Suggestions**: This is the opposite of running out of stock. When you are getting a lot of inventory compared to normal, you run the risk of acquiring long term storage fees.

3. **Bundle your items, if possible**

Think about it, if your buyer wants ten pieces of mower blades and you sell each item one at a time, you are making less, and your buyer pays more into Amazon's pocket. The solution is to bundle the products.Amazon will charge you for one package under the fulfillment fees and this may not have much significance on your Amazon seller fees. You can use this idea to sell your items in bundles depending on what you think the buyers would be more interested in buying.

4. **Play games with your competitors**

This doesn't mean you would sit down with competitors with cards displayed on the table before you. Instead, you will try to understand what game your competitors are playing and how to beat them in it. Look at them, what makes them sell, how do you think they are making their profit? You are in the game, learn from them and beat them. This all you need to know about Amazon fees for a start. Once you are familiar with the system, things will get clearer. Remember that companies change policies; Brands change their mode of operation. So, don't be surprised if what is charged last year goes lower or higher than what you expect. Keep up to date. When you seek special services – MCF, export services, shipping back – expect different charges from those who are using just FBA.

Now let's see what advice would work for those who have little capital.

# CHAPTER 8
# AMAZON SELLING PLANS: PROFESSIONAL OR INDIVIDUAL ACCOUNT

In the previous chapter, you have come across this topic briefly. This is a choice you will make as a seller on Amazon. It always comes to this, and many sellers get confused because they really don't know what this is all about.

Let's use this space to explain what this is about. It will save you some arguments, and if you are making an argument, you will be knowledgeable. On a more prominent note, you will be able to perform an estimation of the costs and the possible benefits you are going to earn.

Before we begin, you should know that listing your products on the two accounts is free. You will be charged when you make sales.

The two choices for sellers Amazon sellers are:
- Individual sellers
- Professional sellers

### Individual seller account

This is how it works

Amazon knows you are in doubt, they know you are doubting whether you will make money on the platform or not. So they created this account to allow you to give it a shot. They exclude you from certain fees, but the number of items you can sell is just 40.

On the surface, it looks like a lot of good benefits. You will not pay for the monthly subscription fees. But you will be expected to pay $.99 for every item you sell on the platform. You will also pay for the referral fees and variable closing fees (the two costs also apply to the professional seller accounts).

You will not be able to:

- Use 3rd party services such as Spotify, Inventory Lab or Repricers
- Apply to make sales on some restricted categories on the platform
- Qualify for the Buy Box unless you sign up for FBA (and you know, Buy Box has the Aladdin factor when it comes to getting more sales).

**Professional Seller Account on Amazon**

We are talking about professionals here. If you want to take your business seriously, you should choose this type of account. It gives you a lot of flexibility and a chance to make your business big. For a start, you can sell more than 40 items per month.

The first turn off is that you have to pay $39.99 every month. The first month is charged when you are setting your account as professional. Also, like the individual account, you will be charged $0.99 for every item you sell.

The benefits of using this account is that:

- Using spreadsheets to upload many items at a time is possible through your seller central
- You are allowed to use 3rd party services like Spotify, Inventory Lab, and Repricers.
- You will have more access to seller reports.
- You will qualify for Buy Box (yes, that thing that makes a lot of sales come your way).
- Access to sell in restricted categories will also be granted.
- Creating a new product listing page is possible.

There is no need for comparison. You realize that paying the $39.99 is actually the best option that you could go for. It is the best option if you want to take this venture seriously. If you start with a personal account, you can upgrade to a professional account. For beginners, it looks wise if you start your first month with an individual account. It would be a good decision since you may not have more than 40 products. What if you sell more than that?

The bigger picture of things

If you are truly an entrepreneur, you are always looking at the bigger picture, the big goal. So let's hold a telescope and see what is there – in the bigger picture.

You will be motivated. You paid $39.99 for this account, you don't want it to go to waste. You will do everything in your ability to earn your money back.

You can use the same amount to sell more than expected. Once you pay the monthly subscription fee, you can sell as many items as you wish. It doesn't matter if you stop selling at 41 or at 500. It is up to you. The only thing that it will cost more is the $0.99 on every item you sell. And it applies to both accounts.

On the other hand, most new sellers will not sell more than 40 items for their first month. There are exceptions, of course. Your first month could be the time to tell if you are really one of those exceptions or not.

So there you go, you can see the positive and negative sides of the two options. Although you can start with an individual account, the professional account is what you need if you intend to make this business a serious one.

# CHAPTER 9
# STARTING TO SELL ON AMAZON FBA WITH LITTLE CAPITAL

Our entire discussion from the beginning till now is mostly related to people who already have an Amazon account, want to switch to FBA and have a little capital. Imagine you are a complete newbie to Amazon, with an account, a little or nothing in your bank account and you want to sell on Amazon using FBA.

**What will you do?**
You cannot start without having a little capital with you. It is that simple. You need to have something. Yes, it can be small. With that little amount, it is now a good thing to listen to what this chapter has to offer. So listen up.

- $0 is enough to open an account and nothing more. With zero dollars in your account, you are free to head over to Amazon.
- Scroll down to the bottom of the page and check on the footer. You will see a link called 'Make money with us.' click on it.
- Now click on 'sell on Amazon.'
- Choose 'professional.' Although you can choose 'individual,' this is not your plan because you will want to look like a brand not like a man selling old stuff he used at home. 'Individual' has its own advantage: you will not be charged the regular monthly subscription fee. Choose 'professional,' the first month is free, and the subsequent will cost about $40.

**What to do next**
Read this book again; you can go back and start again from chapter three. You need to brush up on the knowledge about selling on Amazon, read chapter six twice; this is where you need to make the next move. You need to

- find products that have a market

- ship the product from Alibaba
- build a listing that is hard to ignore
- start selling
- And after signing up, you will need some amount of money before moving further.

You need money to buy the products on Alibaba. This is why you need to save some money. $100, $200, $500 – it depends on what you find that has a market and the price on Alibaba.

A good idea is that you should start considering with about $2000. But since you want to start with little capital, you will have to start with, say $100, and build it up from there. Once you are at this stage – from $100 – you are already a professional, and you are smarter in the business than anyone.

**What can I sell with that little money?**

Do your research? Think of an inexpensive item. And if you have nothing at all, your first step is to find the little amount of money you will start with. Find the $100. It could be a big leap to a lot of money in your life – and a lot of money that comes with working at your own terms.

**What to do next**

Always treat yourself as a brand. This means you have a name, a logo you wouldn't be ashamed to show off to others. It also means you have a plan to treat this as a business; you have a plan for five years or even ten years ahead.

Have another skill or something that can give you an edge

This is quite simple, and a no brainer. If you don't have the money, you should have at least one thing that can give you an edge. In fact, everyone does, some sellers are using it to the fullest. Do you have a blog, do you explain skin care or hair treatment to fellow females and beauty queens? Now, start selling skincare items on Amazon. You could use that as an opportunity to maximize your profit. Other things that could help – and that will not cost a lot to learn or acquire – include

- Building a lot of social media followers – Instagram, Twitter, Facebook

- Vlogging
- Learn copywriting (you can start by reading the books of great copywriters like John Sugarman, David Ogilvy). This will help you when you are building your product listing.
- Generally, improve your marketing skills, through experience or reading or studying.

**What to do next**
Once you have these skills, you are going into FBA not just as a novice but as someone who has mastered some things that can make you stand out in a world where many people are struggling to move forward. One of those skills you have acquired could even launch you to greater things, and FBA will be a second source of passive income.

**Understand what you are getting into before you start**
Congratulations, you are reading this book. Imagine you don't have the money to start, and you don't have the knowledge; it is like having two odds standing against you. Seek first to understand, and then you can think of ways to make your dreams come true.

**What to do next**
After you have understood what you are getting into, take the first step in this chapter. Look for the money to start.

**It's fine to have fears about competition**
This topic of competition has been discussed extensively in chapter four. The competition is there because there is an opportunity to make money. There will always be an opportunity to make money as long as people are using things to make life easier, and the dependency on technology increases. Do not give in to your fear? If you have the said skills listed in this chapter, you know you can still make money despite the competition.

**What to do next**

Go to chapter four and read about why Amazon FBA is legitimate. Read about the reasons why people are afraid of starting and what they can do about it. Then jump to six, where you will read about making your product stand out and marketing your products. Here is a watchword that should follow: add value to the product you are selling; present items in a way that people have not seen before.

**The first sale is the starting point**

You will remember your first sale, of course, because it is your first and you want other buyers to keep buying. The crucial first sale is the starting point of something bigger and unique. To make things work for you; you could do a giveaway at the beginning, just to expose people to your brand. But you are starting with little capital; you can put this idea for the last. Or, if you can, consider giving a bonus when someone buys a certain quantity of your product.

What to do next?

Hopefully, other sales will start rolling in. You can invest some of your profits in the paid advertisement as this will give you a wider audience. Let people know you exist.

Diversify. When you first start making a lot of sales and your profit has improved, then it could be time to try new things. This means getting to a wider marketplace than the USA, the UK, Germany, etc. Or it might be trying a new business altogether.

This is how you build Amazon FBA businesses from scratch. There is a warning, though. Investing in Amazon will not make you rich in a month or a short while. Accumulation of wealth, especially through this process is a very gradual process and dependent on what type of product you are selling.

With that being said, let's see why you have an upper edge on selling on Amazon compared to eBay.

# CHAPTER 10
# EBAY VS. AMAZON

Usually, there is no competition between the two platforms. The real thing is dependent on you and what you really want. This might sound somehow strange, so let's take a knife to it and break it down.

### eBay

Over the years, eBay is like one mighty flea market, the sellers are doing most if not all of the jobs, like setting up your 'stand.' You will handle transactions, offer product, ship it, and perform all the things involved to make sales and purchase a complete chain. You have 100% of the responsibility here.

The reason why this chapter begins with 'it's up to you' is that though it seems like a lot of work, there are benefits in it. One of the advantages is that you will earn more when you are doing more of the work. A larger percentage of the profit will be completely yours, or you will be having more of it than in a situation where someone else or a team is handling it for you.

### Amazon FBA

We aren't looking at Amazon as a whole but Amazon FBA specifically. So what does that look like in the setting we are talking about?

This is like one big mall where you own a shop. There are storekeepers who work for everyone and help them sell their items. Once you sign up for the program, you will get a space in the warehouse. You will pay for it of course, but it also means that when you are at home sleeping or watching your favorite show, someone is handling shipping, packing and delivering your items to your buyer's location.

Of course, the benefit is more than that, and we have explained most of it. The most important one we should talk about here are the charges you will pay for using the services.

Well, you can sell on both channels using Amazon.

You haven't forgotten Multi-Channel Fulfillment, have you? You will keep your item with Amazon, and they will do the job of shipping and delivering the item when people make an order on Amazon or on other platforms.

Go to your seller account. Choose to create Multi-Channel Shipment to a channel like eBay. Let Amazon fulfill the submitted orders. They will also manage the orders you have submitted. Things will be even easier if you are using a professional account. Amazon can automatically fulfill the FBA inventory with MCF.

# CHAPTER 11
# WHAT THEY DON'T TELL YOU
# ABOUT AMAZON FBA

If you have read another book before doing this, you would have seen some things – depending on the course or books you read, you might have been fed some lies. Here is a chapter that lays everything bare.

The truths are emphasized and the lies are debunked.

### 1. You will spend some money

There is nothing like starting FBA with no capital. The only possible thing is starting with little capital. One: you will be charged for using the services. You are renting the space inside the brand's store, and you are hiring the staff of Amazon to help you with shipping, packing, and delivering. These things come at a cost.

If you have been sold on the idea that you can start without capital, you need to take your money back from the book's author or the organizer's course. It is not possible. You are going to need money to ship from Alibaba.

In the long run, the profit is there in the open for you to estimate. You can really make money if you invest some of it in the program.

### 2. Amazon serves everyone

Well, not everyone, but those who use their services. The thing is they don't care about the size of your business or the number of your products that you sell. It is up to you to make the right calculation and bring a good number of products into stock depending on demand. If there is a demand, the products will sell. If there is no demand, your product will remain in stock. Amazon serves everyone truly.

### 3. You can sell on Amazon without FBA

What did you just read in the previous chapter? You can sell books – without FBA. In chapter four, you read that you can choose FBM (Fulfillment by Merchant). You will do the job and keep your money; it is as simple as that. But do you know what you are doing, what you are missing? You might want to read chapter two and see the pros of using Amazon FBA.

4. **Shipping to Amazon and shipping to your customers are two different things**

You will handle one, and Amazon will handle the other. Although it is said that you will pay Amazon fees and it covers shipping; please, do not misunderstand it. Amazon fees only cover the cost of shipping products to your buyers. You are responsible for shipping the products to the fulfillment center. Amazon will take things up from there.

The good news is that Amazon has noticed this little difficulty and has joined hands with the courier service providers. This will make shipping your products to the center easier and cheaper.

If you are using this courier service, the company will give you a label you that can attach on your items. You will receive your bills inside your account in the form of 'Inbound Transportation Charges.' Depending on the size of your merchandize, you might go for full truckload or partial truckload as Amazon provides.

5. **Shipping is up to you, and the number of items on the truck is not Amazon's business.**

There is no rule that says you can't keep a certain amount of items on the truck that is heading towards the warehouse. What matters is the charges you will pay for keeping the items in the center and the fees for other services Amazon will perform. If you choose to ship it twice, on different trucks or you choose to ship it all at once, you are free.

6. **The brand utilizes what is called the FIFO method for calculating storage fees**

This means First In, First Out method. This is how it works: the first item that arrives in the store will be the first to get out of the store when customers make orders. When the items are shipped to customers, you are no longer charged for storage fees for those items.

If you restock your products into the store, you are going to pay storage fees for those new set of items.

### 7. Do your homework

To avoid being charged a long term storage fee, you should really do proper research to find products that will sell fast. This will prevent your products from sitting in the warehouse and lower the amount you will pay for storage fees.

You should also know that there might be slight changes to storage fees during certain seasons.

### 8. Spend less time on packaging; you are not saving cost.

Do not think that by spending a lot of time packing your item; Amazon will compensate you. Of course, you are expected to package your items, and you want your buyers to receive your product in a good state. That's very thoughtful of you.

Add to that; you should not expect that you are not going to pay the 'pick and pack' fee. That fee is compulsory, no matter the hours you spend on packaging.

### 9. Start small

This book has broken down all you need into bits and bytes of chewable information. You can digest it and make a lot of money on your first attempt. The best advice, however, is to start small, at least for your first attempt. After that, you can go all in and invest big. You are going there the second time with firsthand experience.

### 10. Your money stays in Escrow for a while

It will be there for a very short while. Why? One advantage that Amazon offers buyers is that they can return items that do not meet their expectations. So they put your money in Escrow after deducting their cut. It will be there for some weeks before you can get it.

### 11. FBA fees are added to Amazon's commission

Maybe you have decided to sell on your own, using the Fulfillment by Merchant. Amazon will take a commission for every sale you make. This is as true as the color of your tongue.

Now opting for FBA, you will be charged FBA fees which will be added to the commission. In other words, you will be charged both commission and FBA fees. The commission is still there, and it is added up. So set the price of your listing correctly. You may want to refer to chapter seven to read about FBA fees.

### 12. Create a shipping plan of your own

When your products get to the Amazon fulfillment center, the brand will decide some things on your product. They might ship to another center if there is a greater demand for the product in that area. The cost of shipping will fall on you.

But take the initiatives. Do some market research and create a plan of where you want your items to be shipped to. Request for a shipping plan and Amazon will oblige, shipping to where you have planned your items to go. The hard part is making market research of where you want your items to go.

### 13. Play by the rules

What do you think has kept Amazon all these years? They set rules and try to keep to them. They have rules for their FBA sellers too. If you play by the rules, you will be in business. If you break the rule, your account will be suspended. Here are some of the rules.

- Do not create more than one seller account – you can ask for permission before creating another seller account.
- Do not manipulate reviews – many sellers know that reviews can enhance sales, so they have developed strategies of creating fake reviews. Amazon has upped its game and is coming down on the guilty ones with a hammer and a blow. Your account could be suspended.
- Sell quality products – once people buy your products, and it is fake, they will complain about it to Amazon. When the number of complaints pile up, and they think 'this is enough,' your account will be kicked from where it is causing trouble.
- Do not tamper with property laws – you cannot take someone's creative work and call it yours. If Amazon finds out, your account will be suspended.

Now you should be able to make a lot of money with FBA. The tips in this section are the uncommon ones that people do not talk about. So go ahead and continue to make a lot of money.

# CONCLUSION

You have come to the end of the book.

When people talk about selling, they clench their teeth and frown. They hate the idea of coming to someone, a stranger, a friend to try and sell them.

This should not be, though.

Every human has to learn how to sell some things, an idea or a message or point of view. If you want to create a product, you have to learn how to sell it.

Then the internet came. The use of eCommerce emerges.

People began to sell without having to see who they are selling to until the transaction reaches a certain level.

'You sell it. We ship it.'

Ecommerce businesses begin to create a program that will make it easier for their users. Some programs are set up to make users have a better experience with the program. Some are forwarded to make small entrepreneurs scale up their businesses.

Amazon created FBA.

People are making money with FBA, the guided ones. Some tried it and lost their money. Now listening to these two sets of people can create confusion. One side will tell you what you need to make money. The other might discourage you from making a move. But one thing is true. You can make money with Amazon FBA.

If you are guided on what steps to take and what steps to avoid, you should be able to make good money in the next couple of months.

And this is where this book comes in. Everything has been explained. In chapter one, FBA is introduced. In chapter two, the pros and cons are analyzed. In chapter three, you are warned about certain situations where you shouldn't use FBA. Chapter four and six should be read twice. This is where you can make the best out of FBA, in terms of creating a listing, sourcing for products and finding products that will sell.

'Action is a great restorer and a builder of confidence. Inaction is not only the result but the cause of fear.' – NormanVincent Peale.

The book is in your hands. Make use of it.

# Dropshipping & Shopify

## 2021 Edition

*A Step-by-Step Guide for Beginners on How to Start
Your E-Commerce Business and Make Money Online*

## Robert Kasey

# INTRODUCTION

To make a living in the past, you would have to get a job and work all the days of your life. If you don't want to go the job route, you would need to start your own business. Most people who lived in the past, just got jobs because it was the most natural option for them. Most of the jobs were very tedious and required a lot of physical strength. No wonder people still detest going to work even up till this day, even though most of the jobs we do today don't require a lot of physical strength.

For those who wanted to start a business in those days, they needed a lot of money. There were just a lot of things to be paid for. You would need money to acquire a business space, do the necessary registrations, obtain all the licenses, pay staff remuneration, and bear huge risks. All these made starting a business in those days very hard and an option that was only available to a few.

I am not trying to imply that starting a business today is easy, but it is relatively easier compared to what was obtainable in the past. In those days, there were not a lot of tools that would make your business grow fast and flourish. However, we now have so many tools at our disposal that we could deploy and grow our business. We have a lot of business options or models available that a smart entrepreneur can exploit; unlike in those days where the possibilities were limited.

Today, thanks to the internet, starting and running a business is not seen as something reserved for a few. The internet has introduced a paradigm shift in the way we do most things. From the way we eat to the way we interact with each other, the internet has changed it all. An aspect of our existence in which the internet has played a critical, decisive role is in the way we do business.

There has never been a time in the history of humankind that starting and running a profitable business has been as easy as it is today. This ease of doing business that the internet has brought, made it possible for different types of online and offline businesses to spring up. Today, we have blogging as a form of business which is putting a lot of money in the pockets of smart entrepreneurs. We also have affiliate marketing, e-commerce, and a host of other types of online businesses.

The interesting fact is that starting any of these mentioned types of online businesses does not cost so much money. In most cases, you need a computer, internet connectivity, and a little money to pay for subscriptions. Once you have sorted out these things, then you are already in business. This is why I mentioned earlier that there has never been a time in history that doing business was easier than now. No wonder we now have so many young people who make millions just from the comfort of their bedroom.

One type of online business model that has gained grounds in the past few years and will continue to grow in popularity is e-commerce. People used to walk down to the store down the road to get supplies, but we have become so lazy. Technology has continued to make us desire the easy way out. So, more and more people are now resorting to buying the things they need online.

Large scale internet penetration has made eCommerce become a vast industry. And in the coming years, as more and more people continue to adopt easier ways of shopping, e-commerce will continue to grow. This is why e-commerce is one of the best online businesses that a smart entrepreneur should start today.

The word e-commerce is derived from two words, electronic and commerce. It simply means commerce that is performed on electronic devices or over the internet. Ecommerce is a wide field – there are different types; we have retail arbitrage, white labeling, online wholesaling and retailing, etc.

In this definitive guide, we shall be focusing our attention on one type of e-commerce, known as dropshipping. The word dropshipping seem to be on the lips of everyone recently, but only a few people truly understand what it really means. Dropshipping is not a new concept or idea – you might have dropshipped in the past without knowing it. Dropshipping is the easiest way to get into the e-commerce space. It requires a minimal investment of capital and effort. In fact, as a dropshipper, you are basically a middleman who sells other people's products without even seeing or touching the products.

So, what is dropshipping, how does one go into it, what are the best tips for success as a dropshipper? What are the best dropshipping platforms for anyone? How can someone create their own dropshipping platform? All these and more are what we shall be discussing in this guide. Without further ado, let's get started.

# CHAPTER 1
# WHAT IS DROPSHIPPING?

Dropshipping is an online business that involves connecting a potential buyer of a product with a seller or supplier. What happens is that you as the dropshipper is only but a middleman between a supplier and buyer of a product.

It is a type of retail system where you don't have to keep inventory – your job is to find someone who wants to buy a product and then connect them with a supplier. If a buyer indicates interest that they want to buy a product, you will go scouting for a supplier that has the product. Next, you take money from the buyer, pay some of the money to the supplier, and give the supplier the address of the buyer. The supplier then packages the product and ships to the buyer, and the transaction becomes complete.

In order to reach a wider audience of buyers, you will need to create an online store. Once created, you will need to populate your online store with products that the buyer needs. You will write clear product descriptions for each product so that the buyer knows exactly what they are about to buy.

Ideally, what you are creating is a typical online store. However, unlike conventional online stores where the owners need to have an offline inventory; as a dropshipper, you are not keeping any inventory. The reason is simple - you are not selling your own products; you are instead selling the products of other people.

After you have created your online store, you market it or send traffic to it so that buyers who want the products you have listed could contact you and place an order. Once an order has been placed, you take the money paid by the buyer and then head over to the supplier. You pay part of the money to the supplier so that they ship the good or product to the buyer.

It is just like your typical buying and selling or what is called retail arbitrage. However, in everyday buying and selling, a seller would buy from a cheaper source, keep the product in their store or inventory house, and look for buyers. When a buyer comes around, the seller hands over the desired product to the buyer. Dropshipping is a bit similar; however, you are not keeping an inventory of any kind.

You don't even get to see the good or products you are selling. You only list them on your online platform, and when you are contacted or when an order is placed, the supplier sends the product directly to the buyer.

How do you make a profit as a dropshipper? Your profit is the difference between the price for which you listed the product and the actual price that the supplier has set for the product. For instance, if a headset sells for $100, you could set the price at $150. Now, when a buyer contacts you for the headset, they will pay you $150 – you will take $100 and send to the supplier of the product who will then ship the headset directly to the buyer. Your own gain or profit in the entire transaction will be $50.

Dropshipping is a risk-free business model, and that's one of the reasons why anybody that wants to go into e-commerce is advised to start with dropshipping. Dropshipping is risk-free in that you don't get to handle the products you are selling – you are only a middleman or intermediary between the buyer of a product and a supplier of the same product.

Additionally, since you don't keep the inventory of the products you are selling, the risk that is associated with stock keeping has already been lifted off your shoulder. With minimal risks, you stand to gain more while doing minimal work. Furthermore, you don't have to be the one that develops the product you sell. One of the hardest parts of being an e-commerce entrepreneur is product research and development.

Many businesses fail because they did not do proper product research and development. However, as a dropshipper, you don't have to bother yourself with such burdens. The supplier of the product has already done a good job of researching and developing a hot-selling product. Your only job is to connect this supplier to a buyer of their product.

If one supplier stops making good products or if you find out about cheaper alternatives, you could switch suppliers, and your business will not be affected in any way. Many suppliers are happy to work with dropshippers because they (dropshippers) help them to grow their business and increase their customer reach. Some suppliers are even happy to stamp your name or company name on the product to make it seem as if you own the product.

That being said, dropshipping a win-win for all the parties involved. It is a win for you the dropshipper because you get to sell products that you don't manufacture and make money while at it. It is an easy way to make money online, and if done well, it can make you rich. Remember, e-commerce will continue to grow in the coming years. And as more and more people embrace e-commerce, your dropshipping business will continue to grow. Dropshipping is a win for the customer or buyer because the products they buy through this means help them to solve their problems. When many people have issues or when they need products, they often do not know where or how to get the products. If a dropshipper helps such a buyer to find the products they need, then the buyer has benefited from dropshipping as a business model.

Besides, dropshipping is a win for the supplier of a product because dropshippers help them to sell more products. Think of this – if you are a supplier of a product, which would you prefer – to work with dropshippers and sell more or to shun dropshippers and sell less? Every smart business owner/supplier understands that it is better for them to partner with others and earn 50% than not to partner up and earn 0%. So, it is safe to say that dropshipping also helps suppliers to sell more products.

# Why can't the buyer source products directly?

One of the most common question that people ask when they hear of dropshipping is, "why can't the buyer just source their products directly from the supplier?" While that is a logical question that anyone should ask, there are real reasons why buyers do not source for a product directly from a supplier. One of the reasons is that most buyers prefer to sit in the comfort of their bedroom and order the products they need.

Think of it this way – how many times do you go directly to a farm to source for your groceries? Even though going to the farm to source for supplies will cost less, and you are guaranteed of getting only fresh farm produce, many people still prefer to get their supplies from the grocery store. This is despite the fact that grocery stores sell at a far costlier price than what would be attainable in a farm. Also, before the products get to the grocery stores, they may already be losing their freshness; yet most people prefer to buy from the grocery stores. Why is that so?

The simple answer is convenience. We live in a fast-paced world where people want things instantly. That's why we have instant noodles - instant this and that. Everything is instant – no buyer wants to go through the rigorous stress of finding a direct supplier for a product that they want to buy. Rather, they choose to pay a little more for someone to do the job for them.

So, instead of sacrificing their comfort to look for a supplier, many online shoppers prefer to spare a few dollars to have someone else do it for them; and that's one of the reasons why dropshipping is booming and will continue to remain relevant in the coming years.

Even if a buyer decides to go scout for a product directly, they might just give up after a few tries. The reason is – even though the internet has made the world a global village, the truth still remains that it takes a special skill for someone to search and find desired products even on the internet. Going through many sources searching for a product can be time-consuming and tiring, and many online shoppers do not have that energy and time.

Another reason why online shoppers don't approach the suppliers directly is that they do not even know that an e-commerce store is a dropshipping store. A typical dropshipping store is just designed to look like your standard e-commerce store. There is no difference – when you get to the store, you see different products listed there with their individual prices. Then you also see an "order" button or instructions on how to order for the desired product.

On the surface, everything looks like a typical online store – then after the online shopper has ordered a product, the dropshipper does the rest of the job at the background or behind the scenes. The dropshipper will take the money paid by the online shopper and place an order on the website of the supplier. Then the supplier will fulfill the order and send the ordered product to the address of the online shopper. So, the online shopper does not even know that the online store they are ordering their product from is only but a dropshipping store.

We could summarize the reasons why online shoppers don't buy from a supplier directly as follows:

\endash        Dropshipping makes the buying process easier for an online shopper.

\endash        Many online shoppers don't know that they are buying from a dropshipper. They just want to have their ordered product delivered to their doorstep, and it does not matter if they pay a little more.

\endash        In many cases, the online shopper has gotten to trust the dropshipping store, and won't want to trade with another brand that is yet to be tested and trusted. It is often said that the devil you know is better than the angel you don't know.

\endash        That being said, it is interesting to note that most of the independent online stores you come across on the internet are actually dropshipping stores. At the surface level, you would never know that such stores have dropshippers behind them. When you place an order for a product, dropshipping is then done behind the scene. Even on popular e-commerce marketplaces like Amazon and eBay, there are dropshipping stores there.

These popular marketplaces allow independent vendors to open stores on the platform – so, dropshippers also open their stores on there. If you have ever bought a product from Amazon or any of the other popular e-commerce marketplaces, then there is a high chance that the product was drop shipped. All this goes to show that dropshipping is more pervasive than you think – so starting a dropshipping store could never be a wrong business decision.

If you plan to run a successful dropshipping store, you don't need to spend a lot of money. However, you need to be a good researcher – this will help you to research and find hot-selling products which you can list on your store and make more money. Dropshipping business thrives on large volume sales – since the profit margins can be small sometimes, you need to sell in large volumes if you intend to make more money. This is one of the reasons why you need to research and come up with hot-selling products. You also need to design your store to be catchy enough and put SEO (Search Engine Optimization) into consideration when designing the store. We shall get to talk more on these tips in a later section of this guide.

# Three ways to run a functional dropshipping store

There are two main popular ways to run a dropshipping store and one unpopular approach – let's talk about the three of them briefly. The first method or approach is to create a storefront on any of the popular e-commerce platforms. Once you have created the store, you need to research and find hot selling products and then list them on the store. When people order the product, you send their information across to a supplier to fulfill the order for you.

One advantage of having your dropshipping store on already established marketplaces, is that you get to leverage the brand image of the e-commerce platform to sell more. Online shoppers already have a good perception of the major online eCommerce marketplaces. So, once you have a store on such marketplaces, the brand image rubs off on you. This means that a buyer would be more than likely to purchase from you.

For instance, Amazon is a well-recognized e-commerce marketplace – the platform is also well known for its customer satisfaction policy. Now, if you create a dropshipping storefront on Amazon, an online shopper will trust your store just for the mere fact that it is on Amazon or that it has Amazon's branding on it.

The role that branding or brand image plays in the success of a business can never be underestimated. So, if your store has a positive brand image as a result of its association with Amazon (associative branding), then you are sure to gain the trust of your potential buyers and record more sales. Another advantage of having your dropshipping storefront on established e-commerce marketplaces is that you get to enjoy the enormous traffic that gets to such platforms daily. There is no doubt that platforms like Amazon welcome a barrage of human traffic every day. And all those visitors are on the platform for one thing – which is to buy something. If you position your store before such a vast audience, then you are sure to record sales.

With the type of traffic that gets to the platforms, you may not need to spend huge amounts of money on advertising your products or store. Yes, you may still need to pay some money to the different platforms for improved visibility, but that would be significantly lower than the amount you would have spent on PPC (Pay per Click) advertising, for instance, if you were trying to pull your own traffic to the store.

The only disadvantage or rather drawback that comes with selling on popular e-commerce marketplace is that the competition can be stifling. Since it is pretty easy to create a storefront on those platforms, the competition is quite high as there are many vendors jostling for the traffic that comes to the sites.

However, it is essential to note that competition is a normal part of running a business. There is no type of business that does not face competition, but your ability to position yours uniquely is what will differentiate your store from the millions of others that are available.

Another way through which you could run a dropshipping store is to create your own independent online store and then connect it to an order fulfillment platform like Shopify. To go with this approach, you will have to buy a domain name, hosting package, and then design your store from scratch. After designing the store, you will then populate it with products. Some plug-ins allow you to automatically import products from various order fulfillment sites into your own online store. Using such plug-ins or software applications will make the job of populating your store with as many products as possible easy for you.

Note: as a dropshipper, it is essential for you to add as many products as possible to your store. The more products you add, the more your sales. Remember, we said earlier that dropshipping thrives on volume sales. Since you are not even the person fulfilling the orders, you don't have to bother about the stress of fulfilling many orders at once.

The major advantage of creating your own independent dropshipping store is that you are entirely in charge of your business. If you create a store on a popular marketplace like Amazon or eBay, you could wake up one morning to find that your store has been deleted or restricted. If another company can delete or restrict your business, then it is safe to say that you don't have a business. Running your own independent store puts you in control. You decide the types of products you want to list on your store and those you don't want.

A significant disadvantage of running an independent store is that you would have to do your own branding yourself. Getting prospects to trust your store and leave their money with you can be a hard task. You will work extra hard before you could gain the trust of your audience. This is unlike what happens when you are selling on a popular marketplace – the brand image of the marketplace serves as an umbrella that covers you.

Another disadvantage of running your own independent dropshipping store is that you will have to spend a lot of money on marketing. You will be responsible for driving traffic to your store, and this can often be expensive. Running PPC campaigns all the time can take a huge toll on your income and reduce your profit significantly. And unless your store has become very popular, you will always need to run ads for people to keep coming to your store.

The third, albeit unconventional method to run a dropshipping store, is the social media approach. This involves showcasing high in demand products on social media – when your followers or other social media users like any of the products you have displayed, they would order them. You will then need to source for a supplier who will deliver the product to the online shopper.

This type of dropshipping could best be described as manual dropshipping, although some people would choose to call it retail arbitrage. Many dropshippers usually start their journey on social media and then proceed to build their own platforms or create stores on e-commerce marketplaces.

One major advantage of this dropshipping approach is that it is the least expensive option. You don't pay any money to create a post on social media. It is also easy – you are not required to set up anything. Any regular social media user can create posts and ask people interested in a product to get in touch.

A major disadvantage is that you will have to gain the trust of your followers first before they are willing to do business with you – and this can take time. Also, you will need to grow a large social media following – again; this can take time. If you want to work with social media influencers (people with large social media following), you will have to spend a lot of money.
Another disadvantage is that your business will be at the mercy of the social media platform in question. The social media platform that you are using could decide to restrict the number of your followers who get to see your ad posts. If that happens, you will have to run PPC campaigns, which can be quite expensive.

Often, people who are new to dropshipping do ask, "Which is of the three approaches is best for a newbie?" There is no straightforward answer to that question – some dropshippers start with social media while others start with e-commerce marketplaces. It depends on you and the level of technical knowledge you have. You could even start with your own independent store if you are sure of what you are doing.

Since we have looked at the different ways of running a dropshipping store, let's proceed to talk about how to actually create and run one. But before then, let's summarize some of the reasons why dropshipping is excellent for every e-commerce entrepreneur.

# Why bother about dropshipping?

Here are a few reasons why you should consider starting your own dropshipping business today:

### 1. It is easy to start

As mentioned earlier, starting a new business used to be hard – however, business models like dropshipping have made owning a business a simple process. As a dropshipper, you don't need to worry about getting office space; you don't have to worry about hiring and paying staff, at least when you are just starting. You may need to hire virtual assistants to assist in running the business later, but that's when you have grown to a reasonable extent.

Furthermore, you don't have to bother about securing huge startup capital – essentially, you are not using your money to run the business. You are only but a middleman, you take money from an online shopper, pay some of the money to a supplier of a product, and you keep the remaining as your profit. So, you don't need huge funds – if you already have a computer or even a mobile phone and an internet connection, then you could start and grow a dropshipping store.

Since you don't fulfill your own orders yourself, you don't have to worry about product research and development. The product's supplier has already done an excellent job of researching and developing the right product so that the burden is no longer on you. If a product stops selling well, you will only need to research and find other hot-selling products and list them on your store. As you may already know, product research and development is one of the most challenging aspects of running a business. But as a dropshipper, that aspect is already taken care of. So, you are hugely in luck.

Once you have found a good product that you want to sell, you only need a platform to display them or make them visible to buyers. You could leverage existing and already trusted e-commerce marketplaces to display your products, or you could create your own independent online store. Social media is also a great place for displaying the products you are selling.

## 2. Easy access to millions of products

As a dropshipper, you could list thousands of products on your store and make more money. The more products you list, the more your chances of recording sales, which translates to more money for you. Listing as much as a thousand products on your store is extremely practical, since you are not the one developing the products or fulfilling the orders.

You are not restricted to one type of product – you could source for products from different suppliers and list them on your store. Whenever a product is ordered, you simply send the order details to the affected supplier to fulfill the order. To list different products, you just need to create different sections on your store, especially if it is an independent store. For instance, you could list headphones, totem bags, phone cases, belts, shoes, etc. on the same dropshipping store.

## 3. You can set the price of products

A supplier will often give you products at wholesale or reduced prices – you could then add your own profit to the cost and sell to the buyer. If you desire to make more money, you could raise your prices slightly while ensuring it is still reasonable.

## 4. Easily scalable

As a dropshipper, you can easily scale up your business by hiring virtual assistants to assist in the running of the business. You could also create more stores on other marketplaces where you don't have one already. You could research and list more products to increase your profitability.

# Downsides

Dropshipping has its own downsides – so, it is essential that we also mention some of them. Without romanticizing everything, here are some of the disadvantages of dropshipping:

**1. High competition**

If you have a store on any of the popular e-commerce marketplaces, which is what most dropshippers do, then you will have to deal with stiff competition. Dropshipping has a very low barrier of entry – it is a business which anybody can join – and as expected, the competition is very high. However, you could always overcome competition by developing unique strategies. And you have to understand that there is competition in every business. Even those businesses that have a very high barrier of entry, still face competition.

So, you have to see competition as a regular thing in business and work out strategies on how to stand out from the crowd. The best way to beat the competition in dropshipping is to find and sell unique products that many people are not already selling. Most dropshippers have a herd mentality – once they hear that one item is selling like hotcakes, they will all rush in to sell the same product. Do not be like most dropshippers; you should be different if you ever want to stand way above the competition.

**2. Supplier error**

Sometimes, you order a different thing, and the supplier sends an entirely different item to your buyer. This happens more often – and in such situations, the buyer might escalate the situation and hurt your business. Supplier error can make you lose money as you will need to use your money to pay for the actual product that the buyer wanted.

### 3. Shipping times are usually longer

Most suppliers are based in distant countries like China – as a result, ordered products will often take a longer time to get to the buyer. While many buyers do not care about long shipping times, some others will not take it. Some potential buyers will not purchase from your store if they discover that the shipping time will be longer than necessary – making you lose out on money you would have made.

The above are just some of the downsides of running a dropshipping business. Despite these assume downsides, dropshipping is still a great business model for anyone who wants to become financially independent while keying into new global trends. If you are now convinced that dropshipping is for you, then read on as the next sections of this guide will take you by the hand and show you how to create and grow your own e-commerce empire.

# CHAPTER 2
# DROPSHIPPING ON SHOPIFY

In the previous section, I mentioned that you could create your own independent dropshipping store, add products, and then sell to your customers. You could also create a store on any of the popular e-commerce marketplaces and sell your products. Additionally, you could grow a massive following on social media and dropship products to them. We also saw some of the advantages and disadvantages of each of the options.

In this chapter, we are going to talk about how to create an independent dropshipping store using Shopify. This is going to be a step by step guide, covering everything you need to know about creating a store using Shopify. When you are done reading this chapter, you should know how to create your own Shopify store, customize it to your taste, and import products from aliexpress.com, one of the most popular Chinese e-commerce marketplaces, into your Shopify store.

You will also learn how to fulfill your orders, customize your product listings to make them unique and general tips on how to succeed as a Shopify e-commerce entrepreneur. Without further ado, let's dive in and start exploring the various options that Shopify present.

# First things first – what is Shopify?

Shopify is a software tool which allows you to create an e-commerce website – it does not end at that, the tool has a shopping cart solution which you can use to create product listing, manage your listings and fulfill your orders. Shopify does not just allow you to create a website; it helps you turn the site into an online store.

What makes a website an online store? A website becomes an online store when the administrator of the site can create product listings and manage them on the site. Also, when users visit the store, they could be able to add desired products to a shopping cart, manage the items in their shopping cart and check out when they are done shopping. Shopify's shopping cart solution gives you all the tools to turn the website you will create using available themes into an online store.

# Why do people prefer Shopify?

Shopify is an e-commerce management tool of choice for several reasons – one of the reasons is that it is easy to use. To create a store, you simply need to create an account, choose the desired theme, customize the theme, download all the necessary plug-ins, then add products, and start selling. It is as simple as that.

Creating an independent e-commerce website without using Shopify may be difficult for you. There are several things you will need to do to make that happen. However, with Shopify, most of the tools you need are already available. You only need to download the necessary plug-in that offers the functionality you need.

A plug-in is a piece of software that is designed to complement the functions of a bigger software tool. Most plug-ins are usually developed by third parties to perform added functions, ones not available in an already existing software solution. Shopify has a shopping cart solution; however, there are still some functionalities that the tool lacks.

Those missing functionalities can be replaced by plug-ins. For instance, Shopify originally doesn't have the functionality that allows you to import products directly from another e-commerce platform into your Shopify store. But a plug-in like Oberlo enables you to import products directly from aliexpress.com into your Shopify store. You can also use the plug-in to organize your products, manage your listings, modify or update product details, and perform a host of other exciting functions.

Another thing that makes Shopify great is that anyone from anywhere can use it. And most interestingly, the products you want to sell doesn't necessarily need to belong to you. You can fulfill orders both manually and automatically. Manual fulfillment of orders becomes an option when you have just a few listings, but if you work with third-party e-commerce platforms like aliexpress.com and you have a ton of products and a lot of orders as well, then automatic order fulfillment becomes a preferred option.

Some plug-ins help you to fulfill orders automatically – for instance, if you import your dropshipping products directly from aliexpress, the plug-in known as Oberlo can help you place orders on Aliexpress and fulfill the orders automatically. With such a plug-in, you only do little work and still earn money.

For Shopify, there are plug-ins for most functions you could think of, and these plug-ins all help to make your life as a dropshipper easier. We shall talk about these plug-ins in a subsequent section of this guide. With the right use of plug-ins, you could turn your Shopify store into a passive income spinner. This means you would just need to do little work, then go to bed and sleep while you keep making money. We shall talk about that later.

For all these features that Shopify has and the fantastic opportunities it offers, the tool is almost free. In fact, the price is just negligible, and when you start making money, you will not remember that you are paying a subscription fee for the tool. Furthermore, Shopify runs an affiliate program, which means that if you talk to people about Shopify and they get to register an account, you will earn an affiliate commission. The more people you talk to about the tool, the more the affiliate commission you will make.

So, if you have a massive audience of e-commerce enthusiasts, you could show them the fantastic functionalities of Shopify, then convince them to sign up, and when they do, you get to earn affiliate commissions. Now, if you add your earnings as an affiliate and your actual earnings from the sales of your dropshipping products, it means more money in your pocket. This is not a book on affiliate marketing; so I won't delve too deeply into the subject. I have a comprehensive book on affiliate marketing – if you would want to learn more about the topic, then consider getting the book.

Let's now talk about Shopify and how to create an e-commerce website using the tool. To create your own e-commerce website using Shopify and start selling dropshipping products in a few hours, here are the steps you need to take:

**Step one: Start with a free Shopify store**

Shopify, just like many other internet service providers allows you to start with a free account and then start paying for the tool when you are really convinced that dropshipping or e-commerce as a whole is for you. The truth is that if you follow the advice in this guide religiously, you will have no reason to abandon dropshipping. Dropshipping can be the channel you need to go through to become an e-commerce giant, and it starts with creating a free Shopify account.

Shopify understands that not everybody who creates an account will get to continue after the trial period. So, they give you a 14-day trial period to test the waters – if after the 14 days, and you are convinced that this is what you want to do, then you can start paying for the tool.

To create a Shopify account, you simply need to type www.shopify.com into your browser. On the homepage, click on "start free trial." you will be shown a registration form that will mandate you to enter your email address, password and store name. Enter your correct email address – this is important because a confirmation email will be sent to the email you provided. You will need to click on the link in the confirmation email to continue to create your store.

Additionally, you need to choose a password – and when doing that, do not forget to follow password creation guidelines. You would want to make your password a combination of upper- and lower-case letters. You also want to include numbers and special characters in the password. Don't worry about forgetting the password; you can always use the password recovery feature to reset the password.

Just like your other online accounts, it is important that you keep your password safe because if the password gets compromised, someone could gain access to your Shopify account and modify some things. For instance, an intruder could hijack your store and even change some vital details like your bank account information.

After choosing a secure password, enter your store name. It is important that you choose a unique store name – do not just enter the first word or phrase that comes to your head. Remember, you are trying to build a long-term e-commerce business, and it all starts with the name you choose for your store.

Giving your store a random name means you only see it as a "hustle" or something you do because you want to raise quick money to pay your house rent or settle some urgent bills. If you really see e-commerce as a business of the future, then you would want to sit and think of a better name for your store.

Even if it would take you a few days to come up with a good name, then pause the registration until you have figured out a perfect name. The reason why it seems as if I am emphasizing on choosing a great name is that the name of your store forms part of your branding. What do you think differentiates Apple phones from any other random phone out there?

The answer is branding! Your store name alone could make a customer decide not to buy from you. Remember, we still live in a world where people buy things based on emotions. Something as simple as a name could sway a potential buyer's emotions and make them not to buy from you.

Choose a name that depicts the types of products you want to sell. Also, make sure that the name is not too long. Ideally, shorter names that just consist of a single word are preferred. Names with two words are also great – you just need to ensure it is unique. In fact, if another store is already using your chosen name, Shopify will let you know and ask you to choose a different one.

Once you have entered a valid email, created a secure password, and entered your desired store name, then you are ready to create your first Shopify store. Next, click on "Create your store," and your store will be created by Shopify. This may take some time to be completed – you have to be patient and wait for Shopify to complete the process.

After your store has been created, a new page will come up requiring you to fill out some additional information about yourself. Filling out the information on this second page is not mandatory; if you don't feel comfortable doing it, you could simply skip it and go to the next page. Even though filling out this page is optional, you might want to do it anyway. For Shopify to include the page, they must have a tangible reason for doing that. However, if you don't want to fill out the information there, just click on "Next" and move on to the next page.

On the next page that comes up, you will be required to enter some personal information about yourself. For instance, you will be required to enter your personal information like your first name, last name, address, zip code, phone number, website (optional), etc. When you are done filling out the required information, click on "Enter my store," and Shopify will take you to your brand-new Shopify store. Your account is fresh, with no products listed and no customizations. You need to get to work and customize the store and start listing products.

Important tip: when you make your first sale, Shopify will send your earnings to the email you used in opening your Shopify account. What this means is that if you used an email that is not already linked to or associated with any PayPal account, your money would remain in the email until you link it to a PayPal account before you receive your payout into your PayPal account.

Shopify uses PayPal as the default payment method – so when you are creating your Shopify account, at the point where you are asked to enter your email, it is important that you use an email address that is already linked to your personal PayPal account. As mentioned earlier, Shopify automatically assumes that the email you have used to create your Shopify account is linked to a PayPal merchant account – hence when you earn money, Shopify will send the money to the email you used in creating your account.

Now, if the email you used in creating your account is not linked to any PayPal account, you will need to create a PayPal account using the email so that Shopify can always process your payments into the email. Otherwise, your payouts will keep hanging in the email until you link it to a PayPal account.

After creating your store, the next thing you want to do is to choose a theme, customize it, and start adding products to the store. That takes us to step two, which is theme customization.

**Step Two: Choose a Shopify theme**

A theme is simply the overall style, feel, and look of your Shopify store. It shows how your products will be displayed in your store. It also shows how the various layouts and components of the store will be positioned. Without a theme, you would have to do a manual design of the layout, style, and outlook of your website. With a theme to the rescue, you only need to do a small job of customizing what is already there.

You have two options when it comes to choosing a theme for your Shopify store – you could decide to buy a theme from a third-party vendor or buy directly from Shopify. One disadvantage of buying from a third-party vendor is that Shopify may not approve the theme. Shopify prefers that themes used on the platform should be mobile responsive and user-friendly as well. If Shopify feels that the theme you got from a third party doesn't meet those requirements, the theme could be rejected.

Normally, you don't need to even go to a third party to buy a theme for your Shopify store. Shopify's theme store has a wide variety of themes you can choose from. If you choose a theme from Shopify itself, you won't worry about having it approved or not.

To get to Shopify's theme store, simply click on "Themes" on your Shopify dashboard. If you don't want to use that option, you can visit the theme store directly by clicking on https://themes.shopify. com. As the name suggests, it is a theme store where you can find thousands of themes you can use to customize your Shopify store.

You will find two types of themes on Shopify's theme store – you will find free themes and paid ones. The cheapskate in you would want you to just pick a random free theme and run along. However, you need to understand that e-commerce is serious business, and if you want it to pay you like a business, you must treat it as a business. If, on the other hand, you treat it like a hobby, it will pay you like a hobby. That being said, one of the primary ways to know that you are treating your e-commerce or dropshipping business as a hobby is when you decide to go for free themes.

Dropshipping using Shopify is a business that will make you money, and for something that has such potential, you need to invest money into it. One reason why many people don't often want to invest in their dropshipping business is that they were sold a lie. They were told that you could start a dropshipping business without capital. While it is true that you can do dropshipping business with little money since you are not purchasing any products directly; you still need a little money to set up the business and run marketing campaigns to attract customers.

That being said, you are better off with a paid theme. Even the layout of the free themes should send a signal to you that says, "This is not what I want for my business." Paid themes look more professional, inviting, and user-friendly. With such a user-friendly theme, converting your store visitors to actual customers will not be a hard task for you.

Imagine that you have spent a lot of money running PPC campaigns and then the potential customer gets to your store, heaves a sigh, and clicks away, how would that make you feel? Do not forget – people buy things based on emotions. Someone could just decide to buy from you because they love the color or layout of your store. Some people could decide to buy based on the sleekness of the store while others could decide to buy from you based on how fast your site loads. So, it is not ideal for you to lose customers because of something that is within your control.

Different themes come at different prices – some sell for $180 while others sell for $160. The price of a theme depends on so many factors – for instance, its layout, color schemes, and most importantly, the industry it is designed for.

You also need to consider your industry when choosing a theme – some themes are best suited for some industries than others. For instance, if you want to sell clothing items, then you must select a theme that is for the beauty or fashion industry.

Apart from the above considerations, here are some other things you need to factor in when choosing a Shopify theme:

## 1. Aesthetics

Before choosing a theme, consider its aesthetics, its feel, and how it blends with your industry and brand. A common mistake that most dropshippers, especially beginners, make when they want to choose a theme is that they go for the ones that suit their taste. Yes, it is good to look for a theme that you think is nice; however, an important fact you should always keep in mind is that you are not designing your e-commerce store for yourself. Yes, you heard that right – the store belongs to you, but you are not serving yourself. Your store serves your customers – so it is safe to say that the store belongs to your customers.

Since the store is not for you but for your customers, you should design it to appeal to them. One way to know what would appeal to your customers is to consider your industry and ask yourself relevant questions. Ask yourself a question like, "What color scheme would someone in the fashion industry like?" "What theme would appeal to someone in the healthcare industry?" Once you ask the relevant questions and get your answers, then you are sure to understand what your customer would like.

Themes come with predesigned elements which you can replace with your own materials. Before you choose a theme, check out the layouts, design, and be sure that what you have will fit into the theme's layout and elements.

## 2. Think about your logo

Remember, your e-commerce store is like your typical offline business – if you are running an offline business, you would want to ensure that you get your branding right. Before even creating a store, make sure you have gotten the branding of your e-commerce business right. For instance, make sure you have chosen a name – this should be the same name you will use as your store name. Additionally, make sure you have designed a logo. This logo will appear on your branding materials and marketing materials. The logo will appear on your website, social media pages, and every other place where you market your e-commerce business.

Since your logo will appear on your store, you need to be sure that the theme you want to choose will accommodate the logo well. Every theme has a logo placeholder, where your logo will fit in. Check and ensure that your logo will fit into the provided placeholder. If the available placeholder makes the logo look odd, then consider choosing another theme.

Also, you need to be sure that the color scheme of the logo matches that of the theme – you don't want the colors on your e-commerce store to riot with each other. Remember, it is the simplest of things that often turn off customers. You might think that it is not necessary, but a logo that looks out of place could spell unprofessionalism, and customers don't want to deal with such vendors or merchants.

## 3. Think content

Every theme comes predesigned with layouts and content. You will only need to replace the available content, design, graphics, and images with your own. Now, look at the layout, content, and images available on the theme and ask yourself, "Will my content, images, graphics, etc. fit into the available placeholders without the content spilling over?" If the content you have wouldn't fit into the available layouts perfectly, then consider another theme.

For instance, if a theme has heavy images and lengthy texts, but your store is meant to contain only a few images and very few texts, then you don't want to consider such a theme. You have to look further until you find a theme that fits the type of store or design you have in mind.

## 4. Will the theme accommodate the types of products you have?

If the products you sell fall under many categories and subcategories, will the theme accommodate those categories? This is one important question you should ask yourself. If the theme cannot contain all the categories of items you want to sell, then you might have problems fitting all your products into the theme.

A theme will have some expanding menu that helps you put your products under different categories. If the theme you want only allows for 50 categories, whereas your products will be classified into 30 categories, then you should not choose that theme. In the same vein, if your store has 50 categories and the theme's expanding menu or dropdown menu only allows for 30 categories, you should also look elsewhere.

You want a theme that will accommodate all the different categories of products that you would want to sell. This is important for many reasons – one; it helps you maintain a clean looking store where items are not spilling over each other. Secondly, it helps your customer locate the items they want in the right categories.

Many customers don't have the time nor patience to start looking for the products they want. Once they look for the product in the category where it is supposed to appear, and it is not there, they automatically assume that you don't have the product and look elsewhere. You should never allow avoidable mistakes to make you lose customers.

## 5. Can you get support?

All the themes available on the Shopify theme store were developed by third party software developers and placed on the platform for sale. While the themes are being made available to you by Shopify, it is not the responsibility of Shopify to ensure that you get support from the developers of the theme when the need arises.

Something could go wrong when you are trying to install your Shopify theme, and you might need to get in touch with the support team of the developers for help. Before settling for a theme, make sure you will be able to get support when necessary.

The best way to know that the developers of a theme offer support is to look at what other dropshippers or e-commerce entrepreneurs have said about the theme and its developers. The themes available on the theme store are showcased like your typical products on a typical e-commerce store. You will see a sample of the theme and how it looks, you will see its price, and you will also see reviews that other people have left about the theme and its support team.

Go through the reviews and see the common complaints that people have made about the theme. As always, you are advised to leave out the shiny five-star reviews – but you could still look at them, especially if they don't appear to be too good to be true. You might also want to leave out the "one-word reviews." One-word reviews include those that just say, "Nice theme." Such reviews are not explicit enough to tell you what the problems are that are common with the theme or what makes the theme great. Look for the three stars and two stars reviews. Often, those are the most honest reviews.

When going through the reviews, watch out to see if a reviewer would comment about the availability of the development theme to offer support when needed. If a lot of people complained that they were not able to get support when they needed it, then you might want to consider looking for another good theme.

Often, developers of a theme leave their contact information in the description box of the theme. Don't be shy to contact them to ask relevant questions before finally committing your money. Remember, you are paying for the theme, so it is your right to get all the information you need before making the final commitment.

Now that you have gotten yourself a suitable theme, it is time to customize it and start uploading products to your store.

# Customizing your Shopify store's theme

Remember, a theme is just a designed layout that contains several placeholders which you will need to customize to make it yours. Theme designers normally create placeholders with generic texts and images which you need to replace with your own texts and the images of your products. Customizing a theme is as easy as ABC – with an available drag and drop feature, all you need to do is drag your own texts and images into the available placeholders, and you are good to go.

The image below shows the skeleton of a theme. The theme has been stripped of the images and texts.

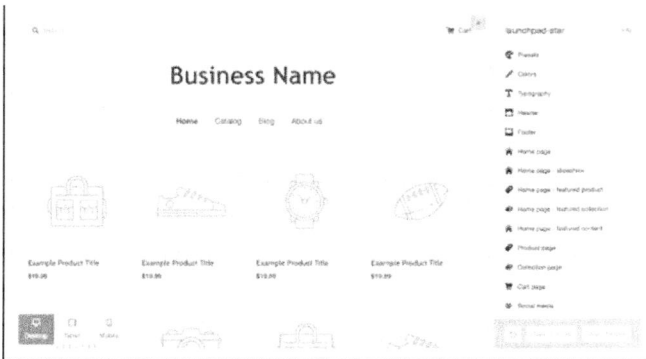

As you can see from the above image, there is a placeholder for your business name, which in this case is your store name. There is also a placeholder for your logo – you need to fill out those placeholders with your correct data.

**Here are some of the things you need to change in your new Shopify theme:**

A      Change the random generic logo on the theme and replace it with yours

B      Change the generic business name on the theme and replace it with your store name

C      If you don't like the background color of the theme, you can simply replace it. You are often advised to go for a theme that already has the color scheme you desire so that you don't have to start changing color all over again.

D      You can change the font if you don't like the default fonts – you can increase or reduce the font size, font style, and font name if you desire.

E      The navigation menus will obviously contain generic text; you are to replace that with your own custom texts. If the texts of the navigation menus and boxes are the same with what you already have in mind, then there is no need to change them again.

F      If there are areas, layouts, or elements on the theme you don't need, you can remove them.

G      If you intend to grow an email list, you can add your link or subscribe form to the theme. If you don't want to start building an email list just yet, simply hide the newsletter layout until you are ready to start using it.

H      Other things you can adjust on the theme include the following:

I      The labels of the categories and subcategories

J      The large featured images on the homepage of the theme

K      Links to social media pages

L       The texts that appear on information pages. Information pages include "about us," "policy pages," "contact us," and all those other similar pages.

M       As you already know, you can add or remove product listings

N       Information that appears on the header and footer of the theme.

Since this is not a book on theme customization, we shall not go deep into how to perform the above functions. You can find books or even videos on how to do any of the things listed above. If you a perfect DIYer, you can modify the theme without consulting any source – it is simple, and the "drag and drop" feature available to you makes everything even simpler.

Once you are done customizing your theme, adding everything that needs to be added – next, you want to start uploading products to your store. Normally, if you are the owner of the products you want to sell, you would do the manual addition of products. Even as a dropshipper, you can still do manual product listing – however, seeing as you will be uploading hundreds of products, you will need to install a plug-in that helps you automate product listing.

To list a product is just a simple process – but for you to understand what it involves, let's look at what you will find when you visit a typical e-commerce store. When you get to an e-commerce store, you will find hundreds, if not thousands of products on display. If you click on one of the products, you will be taken directly to the offer page of that particular listing or product. On the offer image, you will see a clearer picture of the product, its description (which is basically a description of its features), the price of the product and a button that says, "Add to cart."

Now, if you want to list a product, you simply need to upload photos of the product, write something to describe the product, state the price of the product, and you are done. For the checkout button, it is added automatically by the e-commerce platform you are using – in this case, Shopify. If the product goes out of stock, the order now or "add to cart" button changes to "out of stock." Shopify does all of that for you – that's why it is called a shopping cart solution or tool.

As an e-commerce entrepreneur who just wants to add ten original products they own – the product listing process will be so easy for you. You only need to take photos of the product and write the product descriptions; and you are good to go!

Just imagine that you are a dropshipper who wants to add close to hundred products from other e-commerce marketplaces into your Shopify store, how are you going to get that tedious job done? Will you have to keep uploading the details of the products one after the day until you get to the hundredth product? Of course, that will be a cumbersome process – you will need a tool to make the job easier. You will need a plug-in that can automatically import your desired products into your Shopify store.

**Step Three: Install Oberlo**

Oberlo is a powerful plug-in that makes the job of importing products into your Shopify store easy and straightforward. Oberlo is specifically designed to work with aliexpress.com and Shopify – if you install the plugin, you will be able to import products directly from the Aliexpress website into your Shopify store. Most dropshippers who get their products from aliexpress.com suppliers make use of Oberlo to import products and fulfill orders automatically.

Here are some of the reasons why Oberlo is such a great plug-in:

**1.** It helps you to easily add products to your store – with Oberlo; you don't need to add or list products manually. The tool helps you to import products directly from Aliexpress into your Shopify store. All you need is to indicate some of the products you want and click a button; then the tool uploads the same products into your store with the same product images, description, etc. You might consider changing some of the product's details before finally importing them.

**2.** You can change suppliers easily as you desire – if a particular supplier stops performing well, you can change suppliers using Oberlo – and the process is such an easy one.

**3.** Oberlo automatically manages your inventory – what is inventory management? This involves the supervision of the products you have listed in your store to know when they are in stock and when they are out of stock. Since you are using suppliers on aliexpress.com to fulfill your orders – what Oberlo does is that it monitors aliexpress.com so that if any product you have in your store goes out of stock on aliexpress.com, Oberlo automatically changes the status of the product to "out of stock" on your website as well.

It is necessary that Oberlo does this automatic stock inventory because you don't want the status of a product to state "in stock" on your e-commerce website whereas it is out of stock on aliexpress.com. If a customer orders a product from your store because it is showing "in stock" and the product turns out to be out of stock on aliexpress, you may have a hard time fulfilling the order.

Oberlo also updates the price of the products you have listed on your site automatically. The plug-in is always crawling aliexpress.com to see that the prices of the products you listed on your Shopify store have not changed on aliexpress.com.

Let's assume that you are selling phone cases and you initially listed the price as $50 on your Shopify store. If the price of the product changes to $60, for instance, on aliexpress.com, Oberlo will automatically update the price of the product on your store. That is, Oberlo will change the price of the product in your store from $50 to $60. This automatic price update is important as it saves you from making a loss.

Imagine that the price of a product has increased on aliexpress.com and you listed the product at a lower price in your store, it means that when customers order the product, you will use your own money to make up for the difference. You don't want to start telling a customer that you listed the wrong price. That would spell unprofessionalism and show that you are not serious with your business. Such a customer might choose to cancel their orders with you, and that would mark the end of their business relationship with you. The customer could proceed to write scathing reviews about you and your business on your social media pages, and that would likely drive away potential customers.

Oberlo helps take the stress of monitoring your listings and updating them manually away from you. As said earlier, if a product goes out of stock on aliexpress.com, the tool marks the product as out of stock on your site. If the price of the product you have listed changes on aliexpress.com, Oberlo updates the price of the product on your site automatically.

**4.** You can use it to customize your product before listing – normally, you can import products with all of its attributes (product image, product description, etc.) directly from aliexpress.com into your Shopify store. But sometimes, the product might have a photo which you don't want, or you would want to change. Also, the product's description might look too unappealing to you, and you might want to change it. With Oberlo, you can do all the customizations you want to do before importing the products into your Shopify store.

5. Automated pricing – this is part of the automatic inventory management that Shopify helps you to do. As explained earlier, one of the beauties of Oberlo is that if the price of a product changes on aliexpress.com, the plug-in automatically updates the cost of the product in your store to match that on aliexpress.com.

6. Automatic order fulfillment – when you use aliexpress.com suppliers, and you get an order, what you do is to order the product from aliexpress.com supplier and then ship to your customer. This might be an easy thing to do when you get about 3 to 5 orders in a day. What happens if you have close to 50 or even 100 orders in a day, how do you handle all of that manually?

Oberlo takes the burden of order fulfillment off your shoulders. Once you get an order on your site, Oberlo takes over, places an order for the product on aliexpress.com and provide the shipping address of the customer. Oberlo also tracks the orders and provides tracking details to your customer. You can also follow the tracking details that Oberlo provides you until the product arrives at its destination.

7. Track your sales – Oberlo helps you to track and record your sales so that you know how your store is performing. Without properly tracking your sales, you will not know if you are making profits or losses. You can look at your sales history over a given period to see if you have been making progress or if you have been doing poorly. With the sales report, you can modify your strategies if need be or stick to your current strategies.

In addition to the above benefits of Oberlo, you can also run multiple user accounts. This means that if you have more than one Shopify store, you can create another user dedicated to your second store on the same Shopify account.

Oberlo is the plug-in of choice for most Shopify users because of the many benefits it has. The only assumed problem that Oberlo has is that it is specifically built for Shopify. If your dropshipping store is built using WordPress, for instance, then you cannot use Oberlo. But there are also alternatives to Oberlo which you can use on WordPress – a good example is Alidropship. Alidropship is a plug-in that works just like Oberlo – what it does is that it converts your WordPress website into a functional dropshipping store.

Now that we have looked at some of the benefits of Oberlo; let's proceed to talk about how to install it on your Shopify store.

# Installing Oberlo

As mentioned earlier, Oberlo is a Shopify plug-in which also has a Google Chrome extension – you have to install the extension on your Google Chrome browser. To install Oberlo, visit app.oberlo.com, then click on the signup. After you have signed up, you will be taken to your dashboard – on your dashboard; you will see instructions on how to link your Shopify store to your Oberlo account. The instructions are pretty straightforward – just follow it and link your store to the Oberlo app. You will be needed to grant Oberlo some permissions to manage your Shopify store. Once you have done that, you will be able to install the Oberlo app on your Shopify account. After linking your store, the next thing you want to do is to install the Oberlo extension on your browser.

The job of the Oberlo Chrome browser extension is to make the job of importing products into your store easy. When you have installed the extension, you just need to click a button to be able to import products directly from aliexpress.com into your Shopify store. If you don't have the Google Chrome browser, then you will need to download and install it at this point. Chrome browser is free – so you don't have to pay money to use.

After installing Google Chrome, simply type "Oberlo Chrome extension" into your search bar. The first result that Google will pop out will lead you directly to the download page of the Oberlo Chrome extension. Download and install the extension on your Google Chrome browser, and you are good to go.

Once you have installed the extension, look at the top right-hand corner of your browser, you will see the Oberlo icon there. If you see the icon, then it means that the extension was installed successfully. If you don't see the icon, then you might want to reinstall the extension or activate it.

With your Oberlo account created and linked to your Shopify store and with your Oberlo Chrome extension properly installed, everything is now set for you to start importing products from aliexpress.com into your Shopify store using the Oberlo app.

**Step four: Importing products into your store**

To import products from aliexpress.com into your Shopify store, you will need to use your Chrome browser. Your Chrome browser is where your Oberlo browser extension installed. So, you need to use it to make the process of product importation easy.

Open your browser and type www.aliexpress.com into the address box. You will be taken directly to the Aliexpress website. You will find some products on the homepage, but they may not be the exact products you want to import into your store. Remember, before getting to this stage; you must have carried out in-depth product research to know the exact types of products that do well and those you would want to avoid.

You have two options when it comes to finding the products you want on aliexpress.com. One, you could simply browse through the different categories, locate the category for the product you want to import and proceed to look for the exact product.

Another approach is to just type the keywords for the product or the name of the product if you know it into the search bar. You will see a lot of results. When you have found the product you want to import, how do you continue the process?
Simply hover your mouse over the product of interest or place your mouse over the listing and the Oberlo icon will appear on the listing. This is why you need to use a browser that has the Oberlo extension installed. If the Oberlo extension is not installed on your browser, the Oberlo icon, which you will click to import products into your Shopify store will not appear.

If you have found the particular product you want to import, and you have placed your mouse over the product listing, you will see the Oberlo icon. Click on the icon, and you will get a confirmation message that shows that you have successfully imported the product into your Shopify store.

See the image below for clarification.

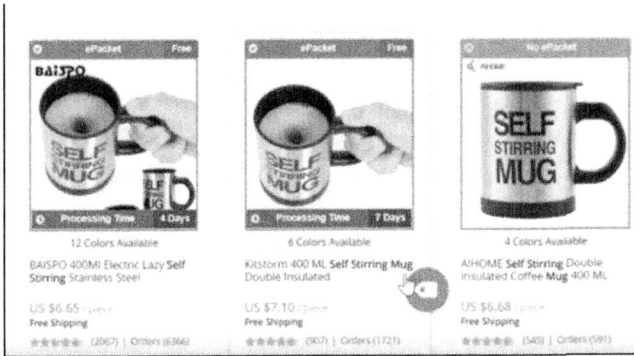

In the above image, I tried to import the second product into my Shopify store, so, I placed my mouse over it. You can see that the Oberlo icon only appeared by the side of the listing because it is the only product of interest to me. Remember, I am only using this as an example.

Now, if I click on the icon, I will get a notification message that shows that I have successfully imported the product.

The image below shows the notification message you will get when a product has been successfully imported.

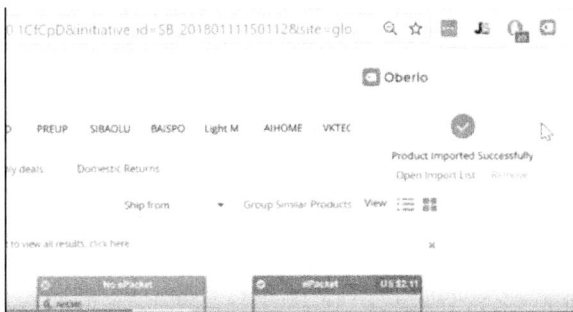

As you can see from the image, you can open your "import list" and see all the products you have imported. You can also remove some products and add others as much as you want.

If you want to add more products to your import list, you simply need to repeat the above process. First, search for the product or go through the different browse categories to find the product. When you have seen the product, hover your mouse over it, and the Oberlo icon will appear. Click on the icon and add the product to your import list.

Earlier, we mentioned that one of the advantages of using Oberlo is that it lets you modify or edit the products you have imported before you finally add them to your Shopify store. Once you have added all the products you want to import to Oberlo import list, click on "open import list" button. See the image above for clarification.

When you open the import list, you will see all the products you have imported. You can change the product description of any of them. You can also change the product photo by uploading your own custom photo. Sometimes, the product images of some products on aliexpress.com may not be clear enough – so you might want to change some of them.

An important detail you will definitely want to change is the price of the product. You want to make a profit – which means that the price you list a product on your Shopify store must be higher than the price of the product on aliexpress.com.

For example, if a product is selling for $40 on aliexpress.com, you might want to list the product for $50 on your store. Anytime the product is bought, you will make a profit of $10, which is fair enough since you are not the one fulfilling the order yourself.

You have to be sure that you are giving your products reasonable prices – remember that the dropshipping space is super competitive. High prices could chase your potential customers away, and low prices can lower your profit margins. You need to find a balance – if possible, search for other stores and see how much they are selling similar products.

Once you are done editing all the details you want to change – description, image, price, etc., then click on "save" and all the products you have added to Oberlo import list will automatically be imported into your Shopify store. Visit your Shopify store, and you will find the products being displayed there.

Notice how the Oberlo app makes the process of adding listings to your Shopify store as simple as ABC. You just have to click a button, and your preferred product will be moved from aliexpress.com into your Shopify store. With the Oberlo app, you can import as much as 50 products at once. If you want to do that manually, you may end up spending a whole day to upload just 10 products.

After importing products to your store, then it is time for you to go on aggressive marketing and watch orders start rolling in. In a subsequent section of this guide, we shall talk about some of the marketing methods you can use to drive traffic and potential buyers to your Shopify store.

## Step five: Enable payment gateways

When you make money from your store, you will be paid through PayPal. We mentioned this earlier when we said you need to make sure that the email you use in opening your Shopify account is linked to a PayPal account.

If the email used in opening your Shopify account is linked to a PayPal, Shopify will be exiting your payments to your PayPal via the email. However, if the email is not linked to any PayPal account, you need to create a PayPal account using the email; otherwise, your payments will be stuck until do so.

If you don't want to receive your payments through PayPal, you could consider setting up Shopify payments which you will use to receive the money you made selling on Shopify store. When you set up Shopify Payments, Shopify will send your earnings directly into your bank account.

To set up Shopify payments, go to your Shopify dashboard and click on "Settings" at the bottom left side of the page. Click on "Payment Providers" and proceed to click on "Complete account setup" under Shopify payments. Next, add your bank account details so that you can start receiving your earnings into your bank account.

Note: when you click on "Complete account setup," you will be shown a form that is already partially filled with the information you provided earlier. You need to make sure that all the information is correct. Then fill out the new required fields and submit the form. For instance, make sure you have provided the correct zip code, phone number, home address, etc.

We have been talking about setting up a Shopify store – before we end this chapter, let's talk briefly on other ways of creating a dropshipping store without using Shopify.

# Shopify alternatives

After the 14 days trial period, Shopify charges you $29/month (for the basic plan) if you want to continue using the platform. Some people consider this expensive, especially new dropshippers. If you think Shopify is expensive, there are cheaper options you can explore.

# WordPress and AliDropship

You can create a fully functional e-commerce website, just like the one you could create using Shopify. The process is similar to what you would do when creating a Shopify store. You need to create a WordPress site, install an e-commerce WordPress theme, and install the AliDropship plugin on your WordPress site.

The WordPress site with e-commerce theme installed will give you all the functionalities of an e-commerce website. The AliDropship plugin you will install will be used to import products from aliexpress.com directly into your store. We can say that AliDropship plug-in is to WordPress what Oberlo is to Shopify.

WordPress is a popular content management system that can be used to create, update, or manage a website. Just like Shopify, you can create an e-commerce store using WordPress by simply installing an e-commerce theme. Once you are done customizing the site, you will then install the AliDropship plug-in which will help you to import products directly to your store.

Using WordPress to create your e-commerce store will require that you will buy a domain name and a hosting package. Your domain could be the name of your store while your hosting package is for storing the contents of your website on the internet. An example of a domain name is www.janestores.com.

While many people prefer Shopify because it is a platform that is solely dedicated to the creation and management of e-commerce websites, and it actively supports dropshipping; the truth remains that Shopify is a bit expensive.

Apart from the monthly fees that Shopify charges you – you are also charged a certain transaction fee for every credit card transaction. Shopify's cheapest plan, which goes for $29 per month, still doesn't offer you all the options. The biggest package that Shopify offers goes for as high as $2,000/month. That's a lot of money for a new dropshipper to pay.

Creating your dropshipping website using WordPress and AliDropship might be a better option. You only need to pay for a domain name, a hosting package, and then AliDropship. Unlike Shopify's fees, you only pay for AliDropship once – no monthly fees. You could get a domain name for as low as $10 per annum and a hosting package for $12/month. So, when observed carefully, you see that going the WordPress/AliDropship option is cheaper.

Here are the steps you need to take to create a dropshipping store using WordPress (this is a quick summary):

\endash Buy a hosting package

\endash Buy a domain name

\endash Download and install WordPress

\endash Download and install an e-commerce WordPress theme

\endash Customize your e-commerce website

\endash Install AliDropship

\endash Import products from aliexpress.com into your store and start selling.

The above is a quick summary of how you can create and manage a dropshipping store using WordPress and AliDropship. I did not want to do over the steps in detail because this is not a book on WordPress development. If you want to learn how to customize a WordPress website, then you might consider sourcing materials on that. Alternatively, you could outsource the customization of the site to a professional website developer.

In a subsequent chapter, we shall look at ways of marketing your products and driving traffic to your store.

# CHAPTER 3
# MARKETING YOUR PRODUCTS

As a Shopify dropshipper, no one will see the products you have in your store unless you market them aggressively. If you must make sales, then get ready to go out there and let people know about the products you have in your store.

Now, there are several ways through which you can advertise your store and drive or generate traffic. In this section, we shall be looking at some of those ways. Typically, we have two main ways of driving traffic to a store – organic and paid traffic.

When you make posts on your social media timeline about the products you have in your store and leave a link to the store or product page, that's a good example of organic traffic. You are not paying for it. You can also get free or organic traffic when you create guests posts on blogs and include a link to your store in the call-to-action section.
One problem with free or organic traffic generation methods is that they take time to yield results and the result just trickle in like water. Unless you are a big social media .influencer, relying on organic traffic sources should not be your best option. Rather, you should facilitate your results by paying for traffic.

One of the best traffic sources as far as dropshipping is concerned is Facebook PPC (pay per click advertising). What makes it great is that if you do it well, you will receive huge traffic in your store.

Facebook ads as it is often called allows you to target people who are actively interested in the types of products you are selling.

It doesn't give you room to guess randomly – you can target people within a certain demographic; you can target people who live in a particular area. You can also target those who have purchased something online in the last few months or weeks.

Facebook collects the data of users on almost every other online platform – that's the data they use to improve their ads service. Another great feature of Facebook ads is that you are only charged when someone sees or clicks on the ad. It is not like some other ad methods where you are charged whether people see the ads or not.

If people don't get to see your ads, Facebook will not charge you – so, it is a win-win for you. Interestingly, running Facebook ads is cheap – with as little as $5, you can run high converting ads and send a lot of traffic to your store. When you compare the amount, you will spend on the ads and the massive traffic you will get; then Facebook ads is worth it.

To run Facebook ads, here are the steps you should follow:

**Note:** creating high converting Facebook ads is a course on its own – and it is not something we can cover in this guide. If you desire to learn more about how to run effective ads, then consider getting some materials on the topic. What we shall present to you here are just the necessary steps.

**Step 1: Create a Facebook page** – you need a Facebook page to run Facebook ads. You cannot run ads using your personal Facebook account. When creating a page, make sure the name of the page represents the type of products you sell.

**Step 2: Go to your page, and click on "Ad center," then "create ad."** You will be required to give your campaign a name and state what you want to achieve with your ad. The options are there for you to choose from – do you want to increase exposure for your page? Do you want to send traffic to an external source like a website or e-commerce store? You will see many options you can choose from.

**Step3: Select your target audience** – you can set up your ad so that only people within a certain location will see them. You can also set up the ads so that only people who earn a certain income range will see the ads.

**Step 4: Ad creative and ad copy** – ad creative is the image or video that accompanies an ad. People prefer using videos as their ad creative – the logic is that videos convert better than images. You can also use images. Whatever you are using as your ad creative, make sure it relates with your product. In fact, if you are using an image, it should be a photo of the product you are advertising. It should be catchy enough to make the impatient Facebook user scrolling through their timeline to stop and look.

Your ad copy is the text that accompanies your ad image – you use it to explain what's in it for the viewer. If your ad text is not convincing enough or doesn't have a lot of incentives for the Facebook user, they would not bother to click on your ads.

A good way to learn how to write ad copies is to start observing some of the different Facebook ads that pop up occasionally on your Facebook timeline. Whenever you are scrolling through Facebook, watch out for ads and see how the advertisers crafted their copy and the type of creative they have used. This will help you to learn to craft your own ad copies and develop the best ad creative.

**Step 5: Set your budget** – Facebook allows you to set or determine how much you would like to spend running an ad every day. If you want to spend only $5, you can set it. Facebook will not charge you more than your daily budget.

Once you are done setting up and customizing the ad, publish the ad and wait for approval from the Facebook team. Normally, your ad will be reviewed to ensure that it meets all the standards. If you have followed the guidelines, then your ad should be approved without delay.

Once the ad has been approved, you can then sit back and watch the traffic that comes to your store. Create more ad campaigns using different ad sets and learn the one that performs better. This is called A/B split testing. When you have determined the ad sets that give you the best results, stick to it.

Remember, the steps above are just an overview – like mentioned earlier, learning how to run effective Facebook ads is a course on its own. You could consider getting some materials on the topic to broaden your knowledge. Also, as you continue to run ads, you will learn more about how to customize and optimize your ads for better results.

**Other means of driving traffic to your store**

# Instagram influencers

Instagram has gradually moved from being a photo-sharing platform to a powerful marketing tool. Businesses have since learned that they could attract a lot of customers by simply posting about their business on Instagram.

What makes Instagram great is that it receives a lot of monthly visitors. At the moment, more than 800 million people visit the platform monthly. Do you know what that means? You will be exposing your business to many people.

Another thing that makes Instagram great is that many business owners are yet to see the hidden potentials of Instagram as a marketing tool. Many of these marketers still look at Instagram as a photo-sharing app that is only good for sharing vacation pictures. Other marketers are still digging it out on Facebook to care about Instagram marketing. However, if you should take your business to Instagram, you will be among the early birds who will leverage the platform to record huge sales.

There are three ways you could promote your store on Instagram:

5. Build a huge audience
6. Run Instagram ads – similar to Facebook ads
7. Pay Instagram influencers to promote your products

To build a massive audience on Instagram takes time – you might need to spend months to achieve it. Also, you will need to be consistently posting useful content to retain your following. For the average dropshipper who just wants to send traffic to their store and make money, this might seem like a long process. The other options available to such a dropshipper is to run Instagram ads.

Even though growing an audience on Instagram takes time, and won't give you instant results, you still need to do it. This is how to go about it – while running Instagram ads or working with influencers, make sure you are also growing your own following at the same. By the time your audience has grown to a reasonable number, you could stop working with influencers and start posting marketing content directly on your page.

While you are waiting for your audience to grow, start with Instagram ads – the way to run it is just similar to the way you run Facebook ads. You decide your target audience, set up ad creative and copy, set your budget, and you are good to go. Instagram ads convert just like Facebook ads, if not better. When it is set up correctly, it can be a huge source of traffic to your store.

Apart from the two options above, you could work with an Instagram influencer to help you drive traffic to your store. Who is an Instagram influencer?

An Instagram influencer is just an Instagram user that has grown a large following through the relevant content they share on the platform. Influencers also record huge engagements on their posts – so, it is clear that if you pay them to market your product, you will get good results. Typically, anyone that has up to 50k followers could be considered an influencer. Although it depends on the industry – for some industries, people with 10k followers are considered influencers too.

Influencer marketing, which involves paying influencers to market a product started becoming popular the moment social media started taking center stage in the lives of many people. Today, influencer marketing is considered a viable way of marketing a product or service. It will also continue to be relevant in the coming years.

One thing that makes influencer marketing work well is that people who follow influencers see them as a hero and would be glad to do something that the influencer has asked them to do. Influencers are seen as people who are more knowledgeable on a subject, and when they recommend a product or service, their followers follow their recommendations.

To find an influencer in your niche, use the Instagram search feature. Search for users in your niche with a huge following. Observe their posting patterns and how many people engage with their posts. Go through their posts and observe if they have helped people to post sponsored content in the past. Send the influencer a direct message and let them know you would want to work with them.

When searching for an influencer, you have to be careful, so you don't pay money to someone with fake followers. How do you know someone with followers? It is simple – observe the number of their followers that engage with their posts and juxtapose it with the number of followers they have. If someone has 100k followers, for instance, and less than 100 people engage with their posts, it goes to show you that the majority of the followers are bot generated.

You don't want to pay money to someone whose posts don't record a lot of engagement. Some dishonest people pay money to get bot-generated followers on Instagram – make sure you don't work with such people as that will amount to a waste of your resources.
If you have done your due diligence and chosen an influencer to work with, send them a direct message. Let them know you want them to give you a shoutout. Shoutout means a promotional post. Negotiate a price with the influencer and send them the image of the product you want to promote. The influencer will include a link to your store in their bio and ask their followers to click on the link to get the advertised product.

When working with an influencer, make sure the influencer does not make the promotional post sound so salesy. Rather, you would want them to craft the post in a way that would seem that they are only trying to recommend a product they have used before. Even without being told, good influencers know that they are supposed to make promotional posts seem like recommendations.

Depending on your agreement with the influencer, the shoutout post might remain on the page of the influencer for a day, week, month, or several months. The amount you will pay for the post to remain on an influencer's page for one day will differ from the amount you will pay for the post to be there for one month.

How much does an influencer charge? There is no fixed amount for influencer marketing. The amount you will pay will depend on so many factors such as your negotiating ability, the influencer involved, how many days you want the post to remain up, and even the type of product you are promoting. On average, the cost of influencer marketing will not dig a hole in your pocket, and the results can be quite encouraging. Many Shopify dropshippers use influencer marketing to drive traffic to their store.

Remember, when using influencer marketing, you need to be building your own audience at the same time. You might one day become an influencer and start marketing your products yourself and that of other people. In this chapter, we have just talked about some of the popular ways of marketing your dropshipping business to attract huge sales. In the next chapter, you will learn about how to do product research.

# CHAPTER 4
# PRODUCT RESEARCH

Deciding to sell a product without, first of all, researching about the product to determine its viability can be likened to placing the cart before the horse. One of the things that differentiates a good dropshipper from the average one is that the former does a lot of research before selling a product while the latter just sells every product that comes to their mind.

Product research in dropshipping is like keyword research in blogging – it should be the first thing you do before deciding to sell a product. That being said, here are some of the top product research tools for a Shopify dropshipper:

## 1. salesource.io

This is a product research tool par excellence – it does so many things, some of which include:

- It helps you to know how many other stores are selling a particular product. Why is this information important? So, you will know the number of stores you are competing with. If the competition is too stiff, you could consider leaving the product.

- The tool, even though it is mainly for product research, helps you to find good themes for your store. It also helps you to customize your listing by giving you product description suggestions.
- The tool compiles a list of products you could list in your store and start making sales immediately. The products span across more than 20 categories, so you are sure to find something that fits your niche.
- It has a Google Chrome browser extension which you can install to make it easier for you to use the tool.
- As you can see, the product has many pros – the only perceived downside is that the tool provides you with a lot of information which could leave you confused and wondering the exact one to use.

## 2. nichescrapper.com

This great product research tool has both a free version and a paid version. The paid version costs about $13 per month – if you can afford the cost, the tool is totally worth having. As a beginner dropshipper, this tool is a must-have – it does provide you with a list of hot selling products which you can start selling immediately. The tool also has a Facebook ad generator, which you can use to create effective Facebook ads that convert.

The only downside is that since the tool provides you with a list of already researched products to sell, there will be many marketers selling the same product. Other than that, it is such a great tool.

## 3. ecomhunt.com

This product research tool is similar to the one mentioned above, with a slightly different user interface. The price of the tool is quite okay for all the useful information it provides you. The only downside is that it just shows you products that every other dropshipper is already selling.

## 4. productlistgenie.com

This product research tool is great for finding hot selling products that you can list on your store – some people have complained that it is a bit overpriced. It has a lot of cool features which include review generator, and it also integrates with Oberlo to help you find the best products. It provides you with a list of about 10k products which you can sell, especially if you don't want to start doing your own research from scratch.

## 5. Saturation inspector chrome extension

This is a Google Chrome extension – if you install it – anytime you are browsing the aliexpress.com website searching for a product, the tool lets you know if a product is saturated or not. This way, you don't have to import saturated products that everyone is selling into your store.

Here are you have it, some of the top product research tools for Shopify. Make sure you do product research before listing any product. Note: you can do your own research and come up with your own preferred product research tool.

# CHAPTER 5
# DROPSHIPPING SUPPLIERS

To work as a dropshipper, you need to find a fast-moving product and look for a supplier who will supply this product to your customers. The earliest form of dropshipping was done as a form of retail arbitrage. Sellers would typically look for cheaper products manually and sell the products at a higher cost.

In those days, the prevalent avenue for selling such products was social media – that was in the early days of social media. Although so many people still do retail arbitrage today, the number of those doing it has reduced significantly. It is safe to say that retail arbitrage gave way for dropshipping to take center stage.

Dropshipping became popular when people realized they could source for a cheaper product directly from manufacturers in China and ship same to Europe and America. Since labor is cheap in China, the cost of producing goods is also significantly cheaper than what you would get in the United States or Europe.

So, dropshippers took advantage of that to make a profit – even after adding shipping cost and production cost, the dropshippers found that they still made a profit. And that was how dropshipping grew to become a viable business model that we know it to be today.

Just like any other business, dropshippers soon discovered that there was a problem with their business model. It takes close to two weeks and sometimes three weeks for goods ordered from China to arrive in the United States or Europe successfully. This started to raise concerns because customers were beginning to get angry and raise eyebrows.

To solve the problem, dropshippers have resorted to sourcing products in the United States to deliver to a US audience. This is an advanced form of retail arbitrage or digitalized retail arbitrage because unlike the conventional person that does retail arbitrage, the dropshipper has developed means of using automation tools to source for cheaper products and sell the same on platforms where they are costlier.

The most popular platform where dropshippers source their products is Alibaba.com. This is a well-known Chinese e-commerce marketplace where customers could buy anything ranging from electronic gadgets to clothing items. One good thing about Alibaba.com is that the site displays in the English language, unlike other similar platforms where you would need to translate the language for you to understand it.

In addition to Alibaba.com, aliexpress.com is another good Chinese marketplace for sourcing products. In fact, aliexexpress is way more popular than Alibaba.com. The platform also has a lot of plug-ins or software tools that have been developed to help dropshippers source products from the platform and ship to different countries of the world. In the previous sections of this guide, we have looked at ways of dropshipping products from aliexpress.com to different locations.

As mentioned earlier, shipping products or goods from aliexpress.com to any part of the United States or Europe takes nothing less than two weeks. As a result, so many customers complained that shipments arrived late. Another problem was that some customers do get angry and cancel their order before the goods arrived, making the dropshipper to lose money.

To contain the problem, dropshippers started to source products directly from their location. This is referred to as local dropshipping in some quarters. So instead of heading to aliexpress.com or any of the other Chinese marketplaces to scout for products, dropshippers used automation tools to find products that are cheaper in one place and sell the same in another place.

The only problem with the above model is that the profit margins are way lower than what you would get had you shipped from China. Also, some of the local merchants from whom dropshippers get their products also frown at dropshipping as a business model, although the number of merchants that are cool with dropshipping far exceeds the number of those that don't vibe with the model.

We have talked about dropshipping from aliexpress.com extensively in a previous section of this book. For now, we want to talk about some of the suppliers within the United States who can help dropshippers deliver their products.

# Dropshipping suppliers within the United States

As mentioned earlier, one of the benefits of using a dropshipping supplier that is based in the United States is that your customers will get to have their orders delivered in record time. Typically, it takes about three days or even a day for a supplier within the United States to deliver orders within the country.

Remember, we live in a world where people want everything to be instant. Imagine having your customer wait for close to two weeks before they get their orders delivered. Some customers will get angry and cancel their order with you. Some might even forget that they placed an order with a dropshipper. It happens all the time; you would get in touch with a customer to remind them that their order has arrived, and you would hear things like, "I cannot remember placing such an order." In that case, you just have to count your losses or start using the product.

In the e-commerce business space, customer satisfaction is more important than any other thing. Customer satisfaction has to do with many things – it has to do with how the products you are selling is helping to meet the needs of the customer. It also has to do with the overall experience of the customer ordering a product from you. If you keep a customer waiting for more than two weeks, they might have negative things to say about your business and would never order from you again. So, you want to give the customer a positive experience.

That being said, here are some of the reasons why using a US-based supplier is preferred:

**1. It offers fast shipping** – the importance of fast shipping cannot be overemphasized. When customers order a product from you, they expect it to be delivered as soon as possible. Imagine delivering a product to a customer the day after they made the order; it means you just got yourself a satisfied client. Remember, a satisfied client will turn to a repeat client, and in business, repeat customers are the lifeblood of the business.

It costs way less to keep an existing customer than to acquire a new one. For an existing customer, you have to say a few words to convince them to buy another product from you. However, for a potential customer, you will need to deploy so many marketing strategies becoming convincing them to buy from you. This is why it is often emphasized that you should prioritize the experience of your customers. Give them a positive experience and ones to remember. Once you do that, then expect them to keep buying from you.

Most United States based suppliers will deliver an order within a day or two, I have mentioned this severally. This is unlike what is obtainable when you are ordering from China where it could take up to 2 weeks or even a month in most cases for ordered products to get shipped to the destination.

**2. Reliable tracking** – most foreign-based suppliers make use of courier service companies that don't offer reliable tracking for shipped goods. When you use such suppliers, it is hard to track the progress of an order. You will not be able to pinpoint the exact location where your order has gotten to until it arrives at its destination. Sometimes, an order could get lost in transit – this is something that happens more often.

If you have ever ordered anything online, you will understand that online shoppers often want to know where their ordered product is at every point in time. They want to know the exact time they will get the product. They don't want to be kept in the dark as regards the location of the product they paid for. Many times, if the customer is unable to locate their product, they could get anxious, and some even decide to cancel their order.

Aliexpress.com, for instance, is just a marketplace, and like every other marketplace, different vendors create a storefront on the platform and market their goods. Now, when you order a product from an aiexpress.com supplier, they are going to try to reduce shipping costs. Most often, they go for the cheapest shipping options – some of those courier service providers used by the suppliers in China do not offer you a tracking code or anything of such with which you could track your order. Even some of them that give you a tracking code, you may find out that the data you get through the code could be incorrect.

On the contrary, when you use a local supplier, you are sure they are going to use a reliable tracking system to point you to the location of your order or product at every point in time. Most of the US suppliers use trusted courier service providers like DHL, FedEx, UPS, etc. to ship products. These courier service providers will offer you a tracking code which you can then forward to your clients. Your clients will use the tracking code to track their orders until it arrives at their destination successfully.

In addition to fast shipping, reliable tracking adds to the positive experience of the customer and would make them want to buy from you over and over again. Note: most customers don't want to be left in the dark – if you turn out to be the vendor who gives them the least anxiety, then you have gotten yourself some repeat clients. Remember what we said earlier about repeat customers – they are the best types of customers you would want to do business with.

**3. You have a wider range of shipping options** – US-based suppliers use better courier service providers, as mentioned earlier; as a result, they offer you a wide range of improved shipping options. For instance, you could choose that you want your customer's item to be delivered the same, the next day or within two days. Of course, if you choose same-day delivery, you are going to pay a higher fee, but then, you will be giving your customers a better experience, and you could also transfer the cost to your customer.

This is not possible when you are sourcing suppliers from China or other overseas locations. For the most part, the product ordered will not arrive until after several days. So, if your customer needs their order urgently, you become handicapped. If many customers discover that you don't offer a shorter delivery time, they may be pushed to look elsewhere to get their needs.

The above are some of the shipping benefits of using a US-based supplier. The idea is that since the supplier is within the same location as the customer, the delivery time is greatly reduced and contributes to the overall experience of the customer. Do not forget that a happy customer will become a repeat customer.

Now, apart from the shipping benefits attached to using a US-based supplier, there are several other benefits that come with such practice. We shall get to talk about all of them one after the other.

# Product benefits

There is no denying the fact that the product you get from US-based dropshipping suppliers will trump the ones you get from Chinese dropshipping suppliers in terms of quality. This is why such products are generally more expensive than the ones you get from China and other places.

For the most part, labor is way cheaper in China than the United States – this contributes to making the products gotten from there to be cheap. Also, there are not a lot of regulatory standards or guidelines – that's why many of the manufacturers in China tend to compromise on quality.

Now, to get United States-based dropshipping suppliers, you will be paying a higher amount of money for each product. But it is worth it – you will have the assurance that your customers are getting the best quality. Also, you will transfer the cost of the products to your customer – this is one of the joys of doing business, you will always transfer costs to the customer. Initially, your customer might protest about the price of your products, especially when there are several other dropshippers offering cheaper options. However, after attesting to the quality of the product you sell, they will have no other option than to stick with you.

To get your customers to patronize you, what you need to do is to convince them that your products are of higher quality than those that come in from Vietnam, Taiwan, China, or any of the other Asian countries where labor is relatively cheaper. As mentioned earlier, it just takes your customers knowing that they are paying for quality for them to patronize you.

Furthermore, if you source your products from the United States, they will have that "American-made" stamp of approval. There is no doubt that most patriotic people will prefer to buy a product made in the good old America than the ones that come from other sources. This is not saying that Americans wouldn't buy from other sources, but they will place a premium on their very own before considering other options.

If you are getting your products from United States-based dropshipping suppliers, most of the goods will be made in America and will carry that stamp of approval. This will help to distinguish you from the average dropshipper on eBay or Shopify who just orders supplies from outside sources.

Additionally, when your customers are assured that they are paying for a quality product that has met all the regulatory standards or guidelines, they will be more likely to buy at higher retail prices. You just need to know how to state it that your products are from the US and your customers will be more than happy to pay a higher price for it.

Yes, there will be those who will prefer the cheaper alternatives from China and other Asian countries, but the vast majority of customers who understand what it means to pay for quality products will happily pull out their wallet and pay you the right monetary worth of the product you are selling.

Apart from the above benefits of using US-based dropshipping suppliers, there are several others. For instance, it helps you to give your customers better satisfaction and experience. Imagine delivering the orders of your customers to them within a day, something that takes other vendors days or weeks to do, what do think would be the experience of that customer? Of course, they are going to speak good things about you and your business.

Imagine making sure that the customer gets a comprehensive tracking system that lets them know the exact location of their ordered product at every point in point. Again, what do you think will be the experience of the customer? Their experience will be positive, and you will reap the benefits in that you will acquire a repeat customer for yourself.

The benefits of using a US-based dropshipping supplier are just too enormous. We have not mentioned that it is a perfect way to distinguish yourself among the crowd. The majority of dropshippers are still using Chinese based dropshipping suppliers to fulfill an order. This makes it really hard for such dropshippers to give their customers a better experience all the time. If you join only a few dropshippers who use local dropshipping suppliers, it means you will make more sales, since there are not a lot of people doing that. How will you make more sales?

Simple – once you explain to your customers who are mostly based in the United States, Canada, Europe, etc. that they will get expedited shipping, then you have already won yourself a customer. Some customers might protest the higher cost of the products you are selling as opposed to what is available in other places. You could calm their mind or neutralize their fears by letting them know that they are getting better quality.

This is not to mention that the "Made in USA" stamp that your products will carry will further improve your credibility and make more customers want to order from you. While some customers may not really care about where their ordered supplies are coming from, many others do care, and once they are sure that the products are made locally, they will pay you the money you have quoted for the products.

In order not to romanticize things a lot, it is good that I mention that many US dropshipping suppliers charge considerably higher than their foreign-based counterparts – there are some customers who still prefer the cheaper options. For some of them, they often don't tend to understand why they should pay a higher amount for a product that they could get cheaper elsewhere.

If you are a focused business owner, you should be able to know how to make your business distinct and know who your customers are. If you have determined that your audience are those who can willingly pay a higher price for quality, then stick with them and forget about the customers that prefer cheaper options. In business, it is called knowing your audience or market segment and sticking with them.

# What to consider before choosing a US dropshipping supplier

Remember, as a dropshipper, you are a business owner, and as a business owner, you need to think critically and strategically. No matter the type of dropshipping supplier you want to use, it is still necessary that you do your due diligence before pitching your tent with anyone. You do not want to work with a supplier solely based on the fact they are based in the United States. That will be a really infantile reason to work with someone. On the other hand, you don't want to work with a supplier solely based on the fact that they are based in China, Vietnam, or other overseas locations.

Also, you don't want to work with a supplier on a first name and handshake basis. Remember, as a dropshipper, your supplier is one of your most critical business partners. If they mess up or if you choose the wrong one, then your business suffers. In fact, it is safe to say that you are at the mercy of your supplier. If they decide to mess you up and continually send wrong packages to your customers, then your business will be as good as gone. If the supplier sends damaged products to your customer, you will get nothing but negative reviews, ratings, and feedback – which will impact you negatively.

There are just so many ways through which your supplier could ruin your business – and that's why you must properly vet any supplier before settling for them. One thing I normally tell people who want to go into dropshipping for the first time – find and join forums or communities of other dropshippers. In those forums, you can ask questions about suppliers and get the most honest answers from people who have had firsthand experience with the suppliers in question.

There are several active dropshipping groups both on Facebook, Reddict.com, and other online mediums. You just need to search, find, and join as many forums as possible. When you join, make sure you contribute to discussions – that way, when you ask questions, other members of the community will be more willing to answer you.

That being said, here are some of the things you should consider when choosing a US-based dropshipping supplier:

**1. Trust and reliability**

The best way to know the reliability of a supplier you want to pitch your tent with is to ask for recommendations If you are a member of a community of dropshippers, there is a chance that other dropshippers have used the supplier you are asking about. You can ask the supplier for references – let them refer you to some of the dropshippers they have worked with – this is a good way of sieving out the unreliable ones.

Additionally, you could check websites like TrustPilot.com to read what other people are saying about the supplier. Do note that some suppliers or companies do pay individuals to leave positive reviews about their business on TrustPilot. So, if you want to depend on what you see on the platform, make sure you ignore the shiny positive 5-star reviews.

If you really want to get an honest opinion about the supplier and any other company at all on TrustPilot, look out for the 2 and 3-star reviews. Those are the real unbiased opinions of people who have used the services of the company. You could also check the 1-star reviews, but in most cases, it has been discovered that some of the people who leave such reviews are disgruntled elements who just want to pull down other people's business.

You can also go through this webpage that provides you a list of more than 8,000 vetted dropshipping suppliers you could work with. This is not expressly saying you should just pick one or more suppliers from the list and work with them without doing your own due diligence. Of course, you will still need to ask other dropshippers about the suppliers you want to work with – this is to help get the opinions of others.

If you want to take things, you could arrange to meet the supplier face to face and talk over things with them over a cup of coffee. Although this is a stressful option, the result will be worth it. At least, you get to know who you are working with as well as know who to hold accountable if anything goes wrong.

## 2. Friendliness and communication

What is the ease of doing business with the supplier you want to choose? Are they friendly? Can they work with you to resolve issues should there be any? Will they cooperate with you and ensure that your customers get a good experience or do they suddenly go cold once you have paid them? Yes, there are some suppliers that will display a totally different before you have made payment and then turn around to cold uncooperative, difficult fellows once they have gotten your money. Working with such suppliers will dent your business because they may refuse to provide tracking codes or when they might provide the codes late, making your customer be anxious.

Remember, when working with a supplier, you would want to partner with them for a long time. The reason is that you want to be going through the hassle and vetting and choosing a new supplier every other week. This means you should do your best to choose someone you can easily get on with. Again, it is important to ask other dropshippers their experience with a supplier you want to work with. When asking, don't just focus on the reliability of the supplier, ask about how friendly they are and how they treat dropshippers that work with.

Even without asking others, if you are discerning enough, you could tell a lot about the character or personality of a person through their emails or voice. If they exude some irrational nastiness when you are still talking or negotiating with them, then there is a high chance they will exhibit their full unruly attitude when you have committed you and/or your client's money into their care. Once you have ascertained that the supplier you want to work with is friendly and approachable, then go on to check how much they charge for shipping products.

## 3. Shipping costs and information

You opted for a US--based dropshipping supplier because you wanted your customers to receive their orders as soon as possible. Now, would it make sense to choose a supplier that delays delivery? If a US-based supplier cannot facilitate fast shipping, then there is no difference between them and the one based in China, for instance.

Before choosing a US-based supplier, ensure you know about all the shipping options they offer. Do they offer same-day shipping? Next day shipping, etc.? You would want to know. In addition, you will need to know about their shipping costs. By knowing the shipping costs for each item beforehand, you will know how to charge your customers for products ordered properly.

## 4. Production capacity

Some dropshipping suppliers are also the manufacturers of the products they supply. If you want to partner with such a supplier, you need to ask them about their production capacity. This will give you an idea of how many products they can make at a time. Why is this important? You don't want to run into a situation in the future where you will have to start sourcing for another supplier when your main supplier has run out of stock.

During the holiday seasons, a lot of people are often shopping for supplies, if you partner with a supplier that doesn't have enough production capacity, the frustration that comes with not finding what one wants could drive your customers away. If a supplier is able to meet up with your demands, it means you will never have to put up that "out of stock" label that many customers hate to see.

## 5. Additional fees

So many suppliers charge what they call a dropshipping fee – this is normal, and you should expect it. However, the supplier has to be upfront with you about these fees – you don't want to be greeted with surprises when you have already ordered for some supplies. Additionally, you need to know what the price you are being charged covers.

Some suppliers will remove every branding symbol that has to do with them. Some others will package the product in your preferred packing style or box. Some of them will also issue an invoice in your business name to the customer. These are some of the things that the dropshipping fees cover, but you should not just assume, ask first.

If a supplier cannot state what they plan to do with the fees they want to charge you, then you are better off looking elsewhere. Also, if they charge inordinate fees that cannot be justified, you should look elsewhere too. You are in business to make profits – if you have to lose all your profits through random fees, then how are you going to make a profit?

## 6. Warranty and returns

As a dropshipper, your customers are humans, and as humans, they could change their mind after ordering a product and then decide to return it. If such happens, what will your supplier do? Will take part of the responsibility or will they shift all the responsibility over to you? Remember, when you pay dropshipping fees to a supplier, these are some of the things they are supposed to protect you against.

So, before you choose a supplier, make sure you read their returns policy. They should also provide you with information about product guarantee and warranty. What happens in the event that a customer receives a damaged product? Who bears the cost? This is a sensitive area in dropshipping because most suppliers like to absolve themselves of any form of blame or responsibility when an issue arises.

If a supplier sends the wrong product to your customer, will they bear the risk of reshipping the right product to the same supplier? Or will they require you to pay more money? If a customer decides that they are not happy with their order, will the dropshipping supplier gladly receive the product back without a fuse?

Sometimes, you have to go beyond what the supplier says concerning their return policy. Most of the time, some suppliers say things they do not put into practice. To get the best opinion about the return policies of a supplier of interest, you are better off getting the views of other dropshippers who might have used the supplier. Nothing beats the firsthand opinions of real dropshipper in issues like this, so don't take it for granted.

Note: depending on the different types of products you are selling, you will need more than one supplier. Even if you are selling only one item, you may still need more than one supplier depending on the location of your customer. Some suppliers are better suited for customers based in a particular area than the others. So, no matter the number of suppliers you need, make sure you put the points mentioned above into consideration before settling for anyone.

Now that we have covered the top six things you should consider when choosing a dropshipping supplier in the United States, here are the top ten dropshipping suppliers in the United States.

# 1. iFuncity (mostly supplies electronics like cameras and photography equipment)

Since its inception in 2007, iFuncity has been a dropshipping supplier of choice in the United States. The company has served more dropshippers in more than 60 countries and partnering with them for the supply of electronic gadgets will not be a wrong choice.

One thing that makes the company stand out is that they offer what is called blind dropshipping service. What is blind dropshipping? If a company offers blind dropshipping, it means that they customize the products and brand it with a dropshipper's branding material or after the taste of the dropshipper.

For instance, if your brand name is, "Grupo," and you want to order digital cameras from iFuncity, the company can brand the cameras to bear your business name and carry your logo. Also, the invoice will carry your brand name and every other information you want. This way, your customer will not know that the product was drop shipped. Blind dropshipping is also great because it helps to build your own brand and name.

In addition to offering in-demand electronics, the company also offers fashion accessories. The company gives you an option to choose between branded items and non-branded ones. So, if you want to brand your products before shipping, you indicate. On the other hand, if you want them to ship without branding, you can also state it.

If you want the company to be your dropshipping supplier, you can browse through their product inventory – you can also request for a product data feed, and the company will provide.

# 2. Teledynamics (mainly supplies computers and electronics)

Teledynamics is based in Austin USA, and they are mostly into the wholesale supply of electronics. They are one of the major distributors of electronics from manufacturers such as Polycom, Siemens, Motorola, Sony, SBC, AT&T, NEC, Panasonic, Plantronics and a host of others.

One good thing about the company is that they do require that you must order a certain quantity or what is called minimum order quantity (MOQ). And that's why they are a great option for dropshippers. Another exciting thing about the company is that, just like iFuncity, they also offer bling dropshipping and this they do at no extra cost.

To get started with Teledynamics, you will need to obtain reseller identification. To find products from the company to resell or dropship, simply request for the company product catalog. The companies generally prefer working with individuals with good credit rating.

### 3. FootwearUS

If you want to be dropshipping footwears, then this particular company is your best bet. One unique thing about the family-owned company is that they manufacture their footwear. Just the two other companies mentioned above, FootwearsUS offers blind dropshipping – if you want them to brand the wears with your name, just let them know and they will do it.

### 4. FragranceNet

This company has been in existence since 2007, and the name suggests, they are majorly into the supply of perfumes and colognes.

To drop ship the company's products, you will need to sign up on their website as a dropshipper. Once you have signed up for the dropshipping program, then you will have access to all of the company's products.

If your customers are within the US, the company will charge you approximately $6 to ship each item. You will need to factor this shipping cost when giving your customers the retail prices of the products you sell. The amount the company will charge for shipping a product overseas will depend on the weight of the item and other factors.

### 5. I&I Sports Supply Company

This is a major supplier of airsoft products, martial arts merchandise, arcades, paintball products, etc. in the US. Like most of the other companies we have mentioned, this one also offers blind dropshipping.

### 6. Whitney Brothers

This is another great dropshipping supplier – the company is mainly into the supply of baby gear including children's furniture – great for daycare centers, nurseries, playrooms, etc. they offer a lifetime warranty for all their products.

### 7. New Concepts Distributors International

This dropshipping supplier is majorly into the distribution of underwear, shapewear, and other related clothing items. The company adds a nominal fee of $3.00 to all drop shipped products. So, if you want the company to drop ship products to your customers, they will add $3.00 to the price of the product – which is fair enough. The company doesn't have a minimum order quantity so they can happily ship a single item to your customer.

## 8. Innovative beauty

Just as the name of the company implies, they are mainly into the supply of beauty products – quality ones at reasonable prices. They have a special price for drop shipped items which will be made available to you upon request.

## 9. Fashion stories

This company offers drop shipping services for pieces of jewelry and other fashion accessories. The good thing about them is that they don't have a minimum order quantity – so they can happily ship even a single item to your customer.

## 10. Parkflyers RC

They are into the distribution of remote-control toys. They offer blind dropshipping – if you want to join their dropshipping program, you will pay a one-time fee of $99 after which you will not pay any other extra fee per order.

Now, we have talked about some of the dropshipping suppliers in the US – you could be asking, "What can I do with such information?" Since most people who use Shopify to create their dropshipping store normally source their products directly from aliexpress.com suppliers, what can one do with US-based suppliers?

Let's face it, while drop shipping products from China is still largely popular, if you want to build a brand, one that will be attached to your name for a longer time, you need to start thinking strategically.

How do you think strategically? Ask yourself, "Will dropshipping products from aliexpress.com make me known?"

The answer is no – you will make money, but you still do not have a brand. The ultimate winner in this whole game is still the aliexpress.com supplier and perhaps, Shopify. You might ask, "Why are the suppliers the winners?" Shopify is well known all over the world – whenever you mention Shopify, people already know that it is a platform for building dropshipping stores. In the same vein, if you mention aliexpress.com, people see the platform as a popular e-commerce marketplace. But when your brand or business name is mentioned, would anyone know you? The answer is no.

When you are just getting started as a dropshipper, it is good for you to use Shopify to make quick money, then start thinking of how to build your own brand. By building your brand, it doesn't mean you should start producing your own product. Rather, you should start branding the products you sell. You can still be a dropshipper, but you will no longer be the type that just dropships products from China to a customer.

The type of dropshipping that anyone should aspire to become is the type where you source products directly from the types of suppliers mentioned above, then list the products on your e-commerce website. When an order is placed, you send the details over to your supplier for them to fulfill the order. You could ask, "How is this different from the typical dropshipping?"

The difference between the model I have described above and the popular one is that you are using suppliers who offer blind dropshipping. The supplier will brand the product with your business name before shipping to your customers. The supplier will also make sure that the invoice sent to the customer carries your name or business name instead of that of the supplier.

By making sure that the products you dropship are branded with your name, it will really be easy for you to grow your assumed small dropshipping business into a global brand in no distant time. When your brand has grown quite huge, you could go into direct production of your own products and start charging as much as you want.

Like I have been reiterating all along, the problem with most dropshippers is that they don't see dropshipping as a long-term business. For some people, dropshipping is just an avenue to raise quick cash or something they fall back on when they have lost their job or when they want to make some money for rent.

For such people who see dropshipping as a "hustle" rather than a business, they will often be trying to grab as much quick money as possible. Don't be like the others who see drop shipping as an interim hustle – instead, you should see dropshipping as a business that can launch you into global prominence.

If you want to work directly with a local supplier, you could do so with your Shopify store or a WordPress store. The process is basically the same – instead of importing products from aliexpress and the other popular platforms, you simply do manual product listing. When an order is placed, you take the order details and send over to your supplier.

By the time you have developed a good working relationship with some supplier, you could arrange or negotiate better deals with them. For instance, you could tell them that for you to keep working with them, they should offer you reduced prices. A considerate dropshipping supplier will be happy to keep you and honor your reasonable demands.

Another significant advantage of this approach of dropshipping is that you are mostly in charge of your business. If Shopify, aliexpress.com or any of the others decide to restrict your operations or do something in that line, you could simply design your own e-commerce platform and work with your trusted suppliers to fulfill your orders.

Before we end this chapter, let's have a recap of all we have seen in the section so far.

We started the chapter by stating that dropshipping as a business model has come to stay and will continue to remain relevant as long as individuals are willing to stay in the comfort of their bedroom and have their products delivered to them.

The first set of dropshippers were basically doing retail arbitrage, then graduated into sourcing cheaper products from China and selling the same in the US and Europe. We identified that one of the problems associated with such a dropshipping model is that customers have to wait for up to two weeks to have their orders delivered. Another problem is that customers have to deal with inferior or low-quality products.

We were able to establish that the best way to contain the problem is to work with US-based or local dropshipping suppliers. These types of dropshipping suppliers mostly offer blind dropshipping service – they can brand your products with your business name or brand name before shipping them to your customers.

The choice of using local dropshipping suppliers is a better one as you are sure of the products you are getting, and your customers get to have their orders delivered in record time. Working with a local supplier who offers blind dropshipping service also helps you to develop and build your own brand so that you don't spend all your years working to help other people's business or brand grow at the detriment of yours.

In the next chapter, we shall look at the possibility of dropshipping on Amazon.

# CHAPTER 6
# AMAZON DROPSHIPPING

When most people hear of dropshipping, the first thought that comes to their mind is Shopify. The reason for that is not hard to guess – Shopify has become a household name in the dropshipping industry and is the first name that comes to mind when dropshipping is mentioned.

Little do people know that they can also build their own dropshipping store or a general e-commerce store using WordPress and some plug-ins. Many others do not also know that they could dropship on eBay – yes, eBay actively supports dropshipping, but you have to play by their rules. Another platform which supports dropshipping, albeit surprisingly is Amazon.

Amazon allows dropshipping, but you must read and abide by their dropshipping policy. Some of the information contained in their dropshipping policy, which can also be found on their website include the following:

\endash     You must identify yourself as the record seller of the products you dropship. What this means is that Amazon doesn't want a situation where a customer buys something from a supposed seller, and another supplier with a totally different name supplies the product.

\endash     You must remove every label, invoice, marketing material, etc. that indicate that the products you are selling are coming from a third party. For instance, if you are using iFuncity as your supplier, the invoice of the product must not bear iFuncity. The packaging of the product should not have anything that links it with iFuncity. Basically, Amazon wants your supplier to offer you blind dropshipping services. Some of the suppliers we mentioned in the previous section do offer blind dropshipping; you can work with them and drop ship their products on Amazon.

\endash    If a customer seeks to return a product, the seller, which in this case, is you must be the one to process the return and offer every needed assistance to the customer. Amazon does not want you to refer a customer to the supplier that drop shipped the product. To amazon, the customer does not know the dropshipping supplier; you and Amazon are the only parties known to the customer, so you must be available to process all returns.

\endash    You cannot order products from another online retailer and have the retailer drop ship the product directly to a customer. By that, you are already prohibited from sourcing products from aliexppress.com or any of the other popular online retailers. You are then left with the option of ordering from local suppliers.

\endash    You must be able to comply with all other Amazon policies regarding selling on the platform.

Apart from complying with the above rules, Amazon also expects you to drop ship using their FBA program. FBA simply means Fulfilment by Amazon – it is a program developed by Amazon where the company fulfills your orders on your behalf. When fulfilling the order, Amazon indicates that this product is sold by XYZ seller and fulfilled by amazon. The product also arrives at the customer's destination in Amazon packaging.

Amazon has what they call fulfillment centers that are scattered all over the country. When you join the FBA program, you will ship your products to any of the fulfillment centers, then when you get an order, Amazon ships the product on your behalf, Amazon also does customer support and everything in between for you. Then they will take a certain percentage of the price of the product and pay the remaining to you.

Amazon expects that you should dropship using their FBA program – this basically means you will get products from your suppliers and keep them in Amazon's fulfillment centers. When you get an order, Amazon helps you to ship the product to your customer. One problem with that arrangement is that your supplier might not agree to release their products to you without an initial or down payment. Also, you may have your reservations about making down payments for a product that no one has indicated interest in buying.

Normally, if you own your product, either through white labeling, or you manufacture the products yourself, then dropshipping using the Amazon FBA program can be a great option. However, when you are using a third-party supplier, joining the FBA program might not be the best option for you.

Amazon will start charging you what they call long term storage fees if your products stay in their fulfillment centers for more than six months without getting sold. As a dropshipper, you cannot afford to pay money to keep a product that people may not be interested in buying. The FBA program also has many other fees that may eat deep into your profit. Amazon has what they call FBA calculator, which you can use to calculate all the fees you will have to pay for dropshipping a particular product using the FBA program.

Since the FBA program is a total NO for a dropshipper, are there still ways of leveraging Amazon to make sales as a dropshipper? The answer is YES. However, you will have to be the one fulfilling your orders – Amazon calls it fulfillment by merchant.

Typically, you will create a seller account on Amazon, list some products, when you get an order, you send the order details to your supplier who drop ships the product in your branded package. Once your supplier has shipped the product, they will provide you with a tracking number which you can then supply to your customer for them to monitor the movement or status of their orders.

# Advantages of dropshipping on Amazon

Dropshipping on Amazon has a lot of benefits that are too numerous to mention, but we are still going to talk about some of them.

One of the significant benefits is that you will be selling products on a platform that records millions of human traffic every day. Amazon currently has close to 30 million active users – this means you will be selling to this vast number of an active audience.

With such a huge user base, if you know how to position yourself before them, then you are sure to make money. Also, though the competition is high, you can still grab your own cut from the huge pie. Even if you are just able to convince only 0.001% of that audience to patronize you, that means you will still be smiling home at the end of every day.

Another major advantage of selling on Amazon is that the marketplace is already well known – you will enjoy what is called associative branding. By virtue of being on the platform, many customers will trust you enough to patronize your profits. Amazon has worked well over the years to perfect its branding – it is perceived as a company that places a premium on the interest of the customer. It is also seen as a company that wants to give every customer a positive experience. This is something that many customers are aware of, no wonder they like to patronize the huge marketplace. As said earlier, selling on Amazon will make you enjoy associative branding.

Unlike dropshipping on other platforms where you have to work really hard to convince the customer to trust you, Amazon's solid image will serve as an umbrella that covers you. Now, you can leverage this positive brand image and the massive traffic that comes to Amazon to make money. All you need is to position your products in a way that they are discovering on the platform. You can do that by ensuring you follow SEO best practices when listing your products.

The majority of buyers who come to Amazon do not bother to visit the different sections of the website when searching for a product. What they simply do is that they type the product they want into the search bar and follow the search results. Most of them don't even type the full name of the product; they just enter a few keywords that are associated with the product, then follow the search results to find the products they want.

Now, if you want such a customer to discover your product and buy them, then you have to think like them. See yourself as a potential buyer who has come on Amazon to buy your own product. What are the keywords you would type into the search box to be able to find your products? Think about those keywords and use them intuitively when listing your product. Include the keywords in the title and description of your product – that's the way that customers will find the product and buy it when they are doing searches.

What I have just described is called search engine optimization (SEO) – you are optimizing your listing and loading it with relevant keywords so that when potential buyers search for the type of products you sell, yours will pop up in the search results. One thing about Amazon is that if you master SEO and how to do it well, you will be making consistent sales on Amazon.

If you know how to do SEO on Amazon, then you may not need to pay money to advertise the products you sell. This is yet another huge advantage that is attached to selling on the Amazon platform. As mentioned earlier, Amazon has up to 30 million active users – with such a vast user base, you don't need to pull external traffic to your listing. All you need is to position your listing before the already present traffic and watch the magic that will happen.

Yes, you may wish to advertise your products using the Amazon PPC (pay per click) ad method, but it is not entirely necessary. In fact, if you have many products that are selling on the platform, and you know how to craft the best product descriptions, then you may not pay Amazon to run ads for your products. By saving the money you would have spent on running ads, you will actually have more money in your pocket.

# Cons

Yes, dropshipping on Amazon does have its own drawbacks – it is like displaying your products in an open market where there are thousands, if not millions of other vendors like you who are also selling the same products. As expected, there will be stiff competition in such a marketplace.

Amazon is a vast marketplace, and many vendors have storefronts on the platform – no matter the type of products you would want to sell, there will be many other vendors who will be selling the same product. So, you will need to position yourself to make potential customers choose you instead of your competitors.

Many sellers set the prices of their products to be ridiculously low – it is their own strategy or way of beating the stiff competition. Most of them are usually dropshippers who order from an online retailer, who then ships directly to the customer – something that Amazon clearly frowns on but people do it anyway.

For such people, they don't really care about following set down rules; they are only happy when they make a profit no matter how little, even if it is just $1 on a profit. When vendors resort to making their products dirt cheap in order to beat the competition, how do you survive or compete with such people? That's one of the disadvantages of dropshipping on Amazon. Even though the competition is stifling, if you use a combination of good SEO practices combined with other factors such as good rating/feedback, then you can survive the competition.

Another major disadvantage is that you cannot order from another online retailer, who will then ship the product directly to the customer. This means you cannot order from an aliexpress.com supplier and have them ship the product to your customer, something you can do when using Shopify. It is one of the don'ts that Amazon included in their dropshipping policy.

Even though some people see that as a con, you can actually look at the bright side of things and see the policy as an advantage. At least, you will get to work with local suppliers, who will brand products using your name or brand name and then ship to your customers. Something that will help you grow a huge brand in the long run.

Another disadvantage, although some people may not really see it as a disadvantage, is that many Amazon customers have very high expectations. Once there is a little mistake, they would leave scathing feedback on your product, which would scare away other potential buyers. And if more people continue to leave such feedback, Amazon could close your account or withdraw your seller privileges.

Lastly, Amazon could wake up one morning and decide to restrict your account – as I always say, if another company can delete your business, then you don't really have a business. Yes, no business is immune from external influences, but the greater control of your business should be in your hands.

That being said, when you consider the cons and pros, you will see that dropshipping on Amazon is still worth it. Now, if you want to get started, here are a few steps you should take.

# **Getting started**

### **Step 1: Decide on the type of products you want to sell**

Amazon has more than 20 product categories and ten more are available to sellers with a professional account. Before proceeding to create an account, you need to decide on the type of product you would want to sell on the platform. Your choice has to be as unique as possible – you don't want to start selling the same product that millions of other sellers are also selling.

One common mistake that most dropshippers often make is that they go on the internet and search for "best products to sell on Amazon," then they just dive in and start selling the products they found in their search. One problem with selling the same products that one website described as hot selling is that you are not the only person searching for such products.

The same way you are searching the internet for hot selling products, thousands of other dropshippers are also searching for such a product. All the people searching for such products will end up flooding the Amazon marketplace with the same product and then start complaining of low sales.

Think outside the box – don't go to the internet searching for a hot selling product. Instead, use your intuition and think about the products that you feel people really need. While brainstorming, you might just get product ideas that will change your story. Now, once you have determined the types of products you want to sell – the next thing you want to do is to negotiate with a supplier who will drop ship the products to your customers. Consider some of the dropshipping suppliers we mentioned in the previous section.

Remember, Amazon does not allow you to use online retailers to fulfill your orders – so, don't expect to use a marketplace like aliexpress.com to fulfill your orders. Even though many sellers do it, you don't want to be among them. If found to be using online retailers to fulfill orders, Amazon could suspend your account and make sure you don't receive the money you have earned.

**Step 2: Register and choose a selling account**

After deciding on the type of products you want to sell, the next step is to register an account on Amazon as a seller and choose your preferred selling plan. To register an account, click here, then click on "Start selling" to start the registration process. You will need to enter your email and name, as shown in the image below. Choose your password and proceed to the second stage of the registration.

**amazon** seller central

## Create account

Your name

Email

**Password**

At least 6 characters

*i* Passwords must be at least 6 characters

Re-enter password

Next

Already have an account? Next ›

Once you have created your account, you will need to choose your selling plan. Amazon offers two selling plans – individual seller and professional seller. If you intend to list 40 products or less, then you have to go for an individual seller account. With an individual seller account, Amazon will charge you $0.99 for every sale you record.

The professional seller account offers you more flexibility in terms of the number of products you can sell. Unlike the individual seller account that allows you to list only 40 products, with a professional seller account, you can list an unlimited number of products. You can list as much as 10,000 products – that's if you will be able to fulfill all the orders that you will be getting.

Additionally, a professional seller account has a monthly fee of $39.99 every month. Once you have paid the fee, you will not have to pay $0.99 for every product sold, unlike what is obtainable with an individual seller account.

**Step 3: List products**

After creating a seller account and getting it approved, the next step is to list products and start selling. If you are using an individual seller account, you will only be able to list products individually. However, with a professional seller account, you can list or upload products in batches with the help of third-party services or tools.

**Step 4: Start selling**

If the products you have listed are truly ones that people desire, you will start receiving orders in no time. Remember, Amazon is a huge platform with lots of available users – so if the products you have listed are truly relevant and needed, then you should expect to get your first order on the same day you listed your products. This is one of the reasons why you need to do proper research and ensure that you are not just selling the same product as thousands of other dropshippers.

**Step 5: Fulfil your orders**

Earlier, we mentioned that the FBA program is not the best for a dropshipper – you should go for FBM (Fulfillment by Merchant). Once you receive an order, send the order details to your supplier – remind them that you prefer blind dropshipping. The supplier should not include their marketing material in the packaging of the product, and they should remove everything or material that will link them to the product. You want the product to have your brand name as the shipper.

If your customer confirms that they have received their order, the money for the product will be added to your Amazon balance, which will be paid to you at regular intervals. When you receive a payment, Amazon will send you a payment notification. Payments are usually sent directly to your bank account, which you must have provided during registration.

The above are the steps you need to follow to dropship on Amazon. Next, let's talk about another form of dropshipping – which involves dropshipping from Amazon to eBay.

# Dropshipping from Amazon to eBay

This type of dropshipping is one that many dropshippers engage in – they find cheaper products on Amazon and sell them on eBay. Amazon is known for selling items at low prices – so dropshippers leverage that to make money on eBay. When the product is ordered on eBay, the dropshipper orders the same product on Amazon and ships to the customer. The profit the dropshipper makes is the difference between the price of the product on Amazon and the price the dropshipper listed it on eBay.

The above model cannot be said to be strictly dropshipping – retail arbitrage will be a more suitable term for it. The retailer scouts through the Amazon website looking for cheap deals, when they have found it, they list same on eBay and make a profit.

Now, there are a lot of problems with this model of dropshipping – one; the product usually gets to the buyer in Amazon packaging. If the customer discovers that their product arrived from Amazon instead of eBay, they could get angry. Also, the customer could find out that they could have gotten the product cheaper on Amazon rather than buying it from eBay. All this will contribute to a negative customer experience, which could make the customer leave negative feedback or even escalate the issue with eBay. In cases like that, eBay could suspend the account of the dropshipper.

Furthermore, if the Amazon seller that has the product discovers they have been used to drop ship their own product, they could get angry and take drastic actions. This was exactly what happened sometime in the past when an Amazon seller discovered that someone on eBay was selling his exclusive product at a far higher price. The Amazon seller went on eBay and purchased the product, then went on his product page on Amazon and increased the price of the product.

If the eBay seller fulfills the order, he will incur a huge loss – so, he canceled the order. The Amazon seller proceeded to leave a scathing review on the eBay seller's page, which affected him greatly. While eBay is not against dropshipping, the platform does not allow sellers to drop ship products from Amazon to eBay.

Apart from the argument that it is ethically wrong, eBay thinks that since customers will receive their orders in Amazon packaging, dropshipping from Amazon to eBay would mean helping Amazon grow their brand. Do not forget, Amazon and eBay are operating in the same market, so they are competitors, and no business would want to promote their competitors at their own detriment.

# Other dropshipping options

Apart from dropshipping using your own e-commerce store, Shopify, Amazon or dropshipping from Amazon to eBay, you can dropship products from aliexpress.com suppliers or other suppliers to eBay. Yes, eBay fully supports dropshipping from other suppliers. What they don't support is dropshipping from Amazon to eBay. Recently, they have been restricting the privileges of accounts they suspect are dropshipping from Amazon to eBay.

To drop ship on eBay, you must be ready to abide by the rules – one of the rules states you must guarantee that customers will get their orders in less than 30 days. And as stated earlier, you should not drop ship from Amazon to eBay, although you can get your products from other suppliers. In fact, eBay states it clearly that you are not under any obligation to state that your products are coming from other suppliers – this means they support dropshipping fully.

In all of these, creating your own independent dropshipping store is still the best option although you will have to drive traffic to the store by yourself. You won't enjoy the huge traffic that comes to the big marketplaces. You won't also leverage associative branding to sell more. But it gives you control and flexibility.

# CHAPTER 7
# THE OBERLO ALTERNATIVE IN 2021

E-commerce, otherwise known as the Internet commerce is described as a business pattern that promotes swift buying and selling of products and services on the internet, and the circulation of data and currency needed to carry out these activities.

As the name implies, E-commerce represent any transaction performed on the internet. It's no surprise that the e-commerce platform is popular among business owners, hence the need for e-commerce store. Industry experts describe e-commerce as a powerful initiative poised to transform the means by which we market our products and represents our brand.

**E-commerce has 6 categories:**

**1. Consumer to Administration (C2A)**

Consumer to Administration is quite similar to Business to Administration (B2A). In customer to administration, a consumer offers a solution to the government which could be applying for a new government ID or making payment for parking ticket.

## 2. Business to Administration(B2A)

Business to administration connects the data of businesses as well as their goods and services to government. For example, government taxes. Third parties are put in place to transfer these taxes to the government and they include social security, goods and services that explains legal documents, and several others.

## 3. Consumer to Business (C2B)

In consumer to business, consumers are able to sell their goods and services to businesses. For this e-commerce business model to work, there are some websites that allow customers display their goods. When the goods and services are displayed, businesses can now bid for the opportunity to transact with the customer. This e-commerce model avail customers the opportunity to set their price offerings and have businesses compete to meet their demands. Affiliate marketing is also considered C2B.

## 4. Business-to-consumer (B2C)

Business to consumer model is described as the most effective e-commerce solution as it allows consumers to connect to your business. For example - when you purchase goods from an online store, you have done business to consumer transaction.

## 5. Business to Business (B2B)

This model of e-commerce improves business transactions between two businesses. An example of business to business transaction is transactions between businesses who designs a feature on their websites to offer products to small and large businesses.

## 6. Consumer to Consumer (C2C)

This model of e-commerce goes way back and it is described as one of the reliable models considering that it protects business transactions between consumers. For example - consumers operating on amazon eBay.

In other to fully grasp the subject of e-commerce, there is a need for us to divert briefly into the evolution and it's impression in the business world.

A brief history - E-commerce was launched about 40 years ago, and it has since driven business expansion thanks to its existing and new technologies.

Back in the year 1980, Compuserve brought the attention of the market to one of the earliest forms of email and internet connectivity, which dominated the e-commerce space throughout the mid-1990s. Fast forward to 1995, Jeff Bezoz launched Amazon designed as an e-commerce platform to keep books. And in 1998, PayPal was introduced to provide secure payment solution on the e-commerce platform.

This brings us to the big question - what are the ways to promote e-commerce?

Since it's launch, the e-commerce industry has been thriving and expanding. Thanks to its expansion, you only need Internet and website access for your business to thrive. Having an e-commerce website improve your transactions as it makes shopping at your virtual store easy for customers regardless of which part of the world they are shopping from.

There are some basic things you must do before you consider promoting your e-commerce website. For one, you need to list your products with catchy descriptions and high quality images. Secondly, you need to set up a reliable payment gateway, enter your shipping information and more importantly ensure that your website is mobile friendly.

Today, major sales are transacted on a mobile device, and experts predict that mobile commerce will grow 2.58 times more than total e-commerce sales. So you have to ensure that your e-commerce store is mobile friendly for consumers to browse through your products and make payments on their tablets and smartphones.

Perhaps you are looking for strategies to adopt in other to enhance your e-commerce site and stay on top of the competition. Consider personalization, as it could be the solution and should be on top of your list.

Having put the right things in place, you can now proceed to promote your e-commerce website to get some sales for your business. Although an online store allows you reach more customers and give you full control over their transactions, there is a need for you to promote your e-commerce business. If you don't promote your online store, customers will not find it (it's as simple as that). Create your store, put the necessary things in place and start promoting your website.

**Promoting Your E-commerce Store**

## 1. Optimize your site for SEO (Search Engine Optimization)

SEO covers several things. Search engine optimisation will make it easy for search engines such as Bing and Google to find your website. But for it to work, you need to use keywords that are relevant to your niche all over your website to draw search engines to the site. Use relevant keywords in on-page content; in images, and product descriptions. The idea here is to use natural keywords that customers at likely to use when searching for your products. Say for instance you are selling second-hand phones. You should use phrases and keywords such as "UK/US used phones" or "buy used phones." Do not overuse Java script or Flash as too much can make it difficult for search engines to see your content.

Also, consider meta tags and title tags. Make sure to give each page of your website unique title tag. Title tags are like headlines which search engines use to deduce what each page is about. Meta tags on the other hand are short synopsis of each page. This is how it works - when a customer searches for a keyword and your site comes up, the customer will see you title tag and meta tag before any other thing.

## 2. Check out Ads on Google

Check out Google ads; one advantage of using ads for search engine is it avails you the opportunity to obtain keywords that will make you show up on the first page of search engine results pages. Since showing at the first page is what search engine optimisation delivers, Google ads will give you a heads up - you will always show on consumer's screen.

Search engine marketing is one of the leading ways to advertise your e-commerce website. For one, it doesn't demand any special design and it helps to drive traffic real quick. You can use your results to modify your campaign strategies if need be.

### 3. Create and Maintain a Blog to Support your E-commerce Website

Say for instance, you want to sell women's clothing on your website, create a blog to publish articles about women's clothing. Write useful and engaging interest that will pique the interest of customers in your brand. Include a link to your e-commerce website on your blog for readers who loves your content to visit your website.

### 4. Search For Forums that Relates to Your E-commerce website and Participate in Online Events

If you are given permission, activate your site's URL as a forum. Participate in forum meetings. Search for other participants and share your website with them.

### 5. Take Advantage of Social Media Platforms Such As Facebook, Instagram and Twitter

Connect with customers online and share your e-commerce website. Who are your target customers? On which platform do your customers spend the most of their time online? Is it Twitter, Facebook or Instagram? And what time of the day are most of your customers online? When you have answered these questions, you can then focus your attention on the platform where your customers spend their time. Perhaps it's Facebook, create a Facebook page for your e-commerce site and encourage users to become your fans. If majority of your fans are on twitter, open a twitter account and tweet about your products and special offers.

## 6. Look for other websites related to your e-commerce site

Search for other websites that are related to your website. Then ask the site owners about the possibility of including a link to your website on their websites. Should they agree, return the favor by also doing the same. In other words, creating partnerships with other website owners or brands will help to promote your e-commerce store.

## 7. Buy Pay-Per-Click (PPC) ads

Pay per click ads show in search results. Though effective, these targeted ads are quite expensive. When a customer clicks your ad, they are directed to your website and you pay a certain amount.

## 8. Design fliers and business cards with your e-commerce URL printed on them

Hand out as many as you can whenever appropriate.

## 9. Encourage returning customers to share your website with their friends

Encourage your existing customers to share your website with their friends by offering them a discount on the next purchase.

## 10. Boost your organic social presence

If you are running an online business, you want to use every chance you get to improve your digital engagement. And one of the effective ways to do that is to engage your customers through your social media channels. Stock your Facebook, Instagram and twitter account with engaging videos and cool images.

Perhaps you already have a solid following on your social media channels. Don't relent, continue building on that. Post more engaging videos, short rich visual content and images. In other words, up your posting frequency. As you boost engagement with your audience, you are also increasing your brand awareness with their followers. Maybe you don't have much followers or your social media channels are dry. Now is the time to have a solid presence on your social media platforms. While you don't have to be everywhere, make sure to have a solid presence on the social media platform where the bulk of your target customer spends their time.

## 11. Consider using influencer marketing.

Who are influencers? Influencers are online users who have a large following and are able to influence the purchasing habit of their followers. Using the right influencer to promote your e-commerce website can increase your brand awareness thus putting your products and services in front of potential customers. To get the best of influencer marketing, ensure that the value of the influencer you want to employ aligns with your brand. More importantly, make sure their followers are your target audience.

Some of the tactics that influencers use to increase brand awareness includes writing an article or a blog post about products, recommending products at an event, demonstrating products or reviewing products.

## 12. Build your email list

When it comes to e-commerce website promotion, it's important to develop an effective email marketing strategy. Save as many email addresses as possible, from your prospective customers, customers and even people who have picked interest in your events. Even if you haven't launched your event, you can send an email to your list before the launching date.

You should also consider offering the customers on your email list promotion or a discount to encourage them to refer their friends and loved ones. In the e-commerce industry, Email is considered one of the most surest marketing tools. So collect as much email addresses as you can. Another way to build your email list is to use a pop-up box on your website to prompt customers to fill their email addresses in exchange for a discount or promotion, say free shipping, a free gift or 20% off their first purchase.

More importantly, keep the communication steady with your contacts. Don't just build email list, write to them. Have a regular email consistency to send new content, promotions, newsletters, product launches, and other news that can push them to checkout your website.

Though selling online as a newbie can seen somewhat confusing, it is doable provided you take it a step at a time. Be patient, show up everyday but don't do too much at once. Follow some of the marketing and promotion tactics discussed above and your business will reap great rewards. Feel free to tweak and modify your tactics as you begin to see results.

## Is There a Relationship Between E-commerce and Drop Shipping?

Again, e-commerce which is otherwise known as Internet commerce or Electronic commerce is a business structure that promotes swift buying and selling of products and services on the internet, and the circulation of data and currency needed to carry out these activities. Dropshipping on the other hand is an online business that works by connecting a seller or supplier of a profit to a potential buyer.

## The Useful Tools to Perform a Good Market Research in 2021

If you are considering dropshipping business, you need to know whether the goods you want to sell are good for the business. There are specific tools that you can use to uncover details about the products before your launching date. In addition to helping you uncover details about products, market research software or tools provide support for your business, from the beginning of product discovery to the final stage. Using market research tools for your dropshipping business will open you to the current trend in the market and also help you understand how your customers think. What's more? Market research tools help to collect data for you to know the products the consumers find satisfying.

Today, every business including the dropshipping business is using the software to carry out market research. Shortly, you will find the list of top market research tools for your dropshipping business.

### List of Best Market Research Software/Tools

### 1. Dropship Spy

Dropship Spy is a useful and reliable software that tracks the performance of various products across multiple online stores and social media platforms. With Dropship Spy, e-commerce store owners do need to do much work researching products and getting their analytics. This tool is great for store owners who are new to dropshipping. Dropship Spy will show you winning products, promising products, product information and analytics, and engagement rating.

## 2. Intelligynce

Intelligynce is not just one but a bundle of software and tools that helps dropshippers perform an in-depth research and analysis, and then identify the most profitable products. Intelligynce has spying access to millions of products across over 500,000 stores. Also, it allows you search for profitable products on eBay and Amazon market places.

## 3. AdSpy

AdSpy is a tracking tool that business owners can use to gather information on competitor's keyword strategies. This tool offers valuable insights on who's dominating your keywords. It helps you compare how your ad ranks against your competitors.

## 4. Niche Scraper

Niche Scraper is a useful market research software that helps dropshippers research the thriving products to sell on their website. Imagine you have access to a tool that allows you find out the best selling and trending products in both AliExpress and Shopify stores. How great would it be if you are able to check the essential information on the products? Like the sales trends and sales difficulty level? That's what Niche Scraper offers.

## 5. AliShark

AliShark is a spy tool for dropshippers; it gathers information on AliExpress and informs the products that you should trade. AliShark is a useful and advanced tool as it provides you with data needed to find the right products for dropshipping. The features of AliShark includes live chat, product information, product trend, and advanced filters.

## 6. SurveyGizmo

SurveyGizmo is an enterprise survey tool for reliable and effective market research. SurveyGizmo provides data insights that business owners can use to make smart business decisions. With the filtering benefit of the software and segmentation, business owners can make selected products successful in the market. Thanks to the exclusive prediction of market trends provided by SurveyGizmo, business owners can stay ahead of the competition. With the SurveyGizmo tool, business owners can analyse data about products, including the positive and negative feedback of products. The features of SurveyGizmo market research tools include Statistical Analysis, Benchmarking, Survey Management, Compensation Management, Paper-Based, Data Management, Phone-Based, Sample Management, Face to Face, Panel Management, and Email/Online.

## 7. SurveyMonkey

SurveyMonkey is an effective market research tool that business owners can use to perform market research tools. With the software, business owners can reach a specific audience easily. SurveyMonkey allow users to measure brand awareness, research and analyse a target market, and get insights intb future market trends. SurveyMonkey is also a useful market research tool that business owners can use for market segmentation and to measure how their strategies stand against their competitors. The features of SurveyMonkey market research tool includes Survey Management, Statistical Analysis, Paper-Based, Email/Online and Data Management.

## 8. Qualaroo

With this market research tool, it is easier for business owners to analyse the market, target the right audience and collect feedback. The tool has unique templates that serves everyone, from educational technology companies to e-commerce. The surveys can be used to perform market research, check CX and UX metrics, check NPS, prototyping and many more on apps and websites with the feature of advanced targeting.

The features of Qualaroo includes A/B Testing, Exit Intent Surveys, Nudge for Prototypes, Confirmation Page Surveys, Mobile iOS & Android, Survey Templates, AI Sentiment Analysis, and Question Branching.

## 9. SurveyLegend

SurveyLegend is an effective mobile friendly free online market research tool that users can use to perform reliable market research for future products. Users can create surveys on their computer or tablet without hitch. SurveyLand offer different themes for brands to use according to their requirements. SurveyLegend makes it easy to do a survey - the tool offers emojis and pictures that makes the survey beautiful and encourage the audience to participate. It also works well! It is easy to use and should you encounter any problem, there is a support system available to help.

This tool allows you to share your survey to other channels such as blogs, twitter, Facebook, and emails to help you reach your audience. Also, this marker research tool provides real-time data analytics for users to have access to real-time insights.

The market research features of SurveyLegend includes Survey Management, Phone-Based, Email/Online, Data Management, Face to face, Sample Management, Panel Management, and Statistical Analysis.

## 10. Typeform

Typeform is a data collection tool that allows user to transform data collection into an amazing experience. The market research tool offers unique ways for business owners to ask questions and get answers. Using the conversational feature of the market research tool, business owners can gather data. With the user-friendly interface, business owners have access to templates that can aid their market research.

The market research features of Typeform includes Survey Management, Email/Online, and Data Management.

## 11. QuestionPro

QuestionPro is a web-based online market research tool for business owners to perform easy market research. The tool is free to use and fully automated thus giving users access to real-time insights. Business owners can use QuestionPro as a market research tool to create online surveys, create questionnaires to perform market trend research and gather responses of the audience. The tool also allow users to analyse research results easily.

The market research features of QuestionPro includes Survey Management, Sample Management, Panel Management, Data Management, and Benchmarking.

## 12. ProProfs Survey Maker

ProProfs Survey Maker is a leading online survey creator which allow users to gather employee/customer feedback to improve their product offerings for better future experiences. ProProfs survey maker creates NPS, scored surveys, on-app surveys, sidebar and other forms that simplifies the feedback collection process. The market research tool has more than 1,000,000 survey questions and 100+ beautiful survey templates to help business owners create a beautiful survey for their brand. What's more? ProProfs survey maker is the best for conducting market research. Thanks to it's instant reporting and analytics, business owners have access to detailed insights on their target audience.

The market research features of ProProfs survey maker includes Survey Management, Statistical Analysis, Sample Management, Email/Online, Data Management and Benchmarking.

## 13. Latana

Latana is an advanced brand tracking tool for fast growing business owners who are looking to make informed marketing decisions. Unfortunately, even though they spend millions of dollars on marketing and advertising, some companies today still base their sales campaigns on gut feeling rather than real facts. The reason is they do not understand that their marketing and advertising campaigns have a massive impact on their target audience.

The market research features of Latana includes Survey Management, Statistical Analysis, Sample Management, Panel Management, Email/Online, Data Management and Benchmarking.

## 14. SurveySparrow

SurveySparrow is a free online market research software that convert surveys into real conversations. SurveySparrow helps business a owners to create engaging and useful surveys for their brands. With this tool, business owners can get access to all the answers that they need to grow their business. The tool offers different templates for users to design the survey according to their brand requirements. SurveySparrow also offers rich analytics, customization, live preview and audience management.

The market research features of SurveySparrow includes Survey Management, Statistical Analysis, Sample Management, Panel Management, Email/Online and Data Management.

## 15. SurveyLab

SurveyLab is an effective and reliable survey tool. The software is easy to use and offers data analysis and reach reporting benefits. SurveyLab can be integrated with several tools such as LiveChat, Slack, Zendesk, Sales force and many more. SurveyLab can be accessed from anywhere regardless of your location and it supports different devices. SurveyLand boasts of a dedicated customer support and has different themes which businesses can customise according to their needs. Also, the software detect browser language settings and supports multi-language surveys.

The market research features of SurveyLab includes Survey Management, Statistical Analysis, Panel Management, Compensation Management, Data Management, Paper-Based and Email/Online.

## 16. Survicate

Survicate is a market research survey tool for researching customer experience and collecting actionable feedback from all digital channels. With this tool, business owners can collect valuable insights to improve their business, grow their business and more importantly increase customer satisfaction. The software offers user-friendly interface and a diverse survey library with different survey examples that business owners can use to perform research, and gather website visitors and leads faster. The software integrates with some marketing automation platforms such as Marketo, Intercom, HubSpot, Pardot, Salesforce and many more.

The market research features of Survicate includes Survey Management, Email/Online and Data Management.

## 17. QuickTapSurvey

QuickTapSurvey is an offline survey tool that allow users to gather data from anywhere using mobile forms and surveys. With this tool, business owners can easily create mobile forms to perform market research. Through customer feedback surveys, business owners can collect customer feedback to better improve their business. Also, business owners can use this tool to gather leads for their business.

The market research features of Quick TapSurvey includes Panel Management, Survey Management, Statistical Analysis, Paper-Based, Face to Face, Email/Online, Data Management, Benchmarking, Phone-Based and Sample Management.

## 18. Dub InterViewer

Dub InterViewer is a data collection software that uses a platform to provide business owners with Internet, telephone and face to face market research. Dub InterViewer is an online Cati/Capi/Wapi system that merges distribution of surveys and centralized management. Also, the tool allows users deliver surveys to their devices through a browser or the Nabu native apps for Android and iOs. Dub InterViewer offers users the most flexible and reliable robust data collection in the market. When you choose to use Nebu Dub InterViewer, it means you are choosing to benefit from Nebu's 25 years of experience in developing and implementing reliable solutions for market research companies.

The market research features of Dub InterViewer includes Survey Management, Statistical Analysis, Sample Management, Phone-Based, Panel Management, Face to face, Email/Online, Data Management, Compensation Management and Benchmarking.

## 19. Voxco Survey Software

Voxco Survey Software is not only reliable but also flexible. It is a multichannel survey software for data collection which can be used at any time and from any location. With this software, users can easily perform market research and gather public and social opinion research. Also with this software, users can manage phone based interview, emails, face to face interviews, Panel Management and many more with the Voxco Survey Software. Likewise, Voxco survey tool also allows statistical analysis.

The market research features of Voxco survey software includes Survey Management, Statistical Analysis, Sample Management, Phone-Based, Panel Management, Face to face, Email/Online, Data Management, Compensation Management and Benchmarking.

## 20. MediaRadar

MediaRadar is a sales enablement tool with customized solution for ad tech, agencies and media to close more deals. Considering that it is a Saas software, MediaRadar provides users with real-time advertising insights. More importantly, this software helps users to know who makes the buying decision and close more sales. With this software, users can access relevant data, insight, and advice to grow their business. The crucial features of MediaRadar are Statistical Analysis, Data Management and Benchmarking.

The market research features of MediaRadar includes Statistical Analysis, Face to Face, Benchmarking, Email/Online and Data Management.

# Oberlo alternatives in 2021

Oberlo dropshipping has a 30-day free trial. You won't be billed until after that free trial period has ended and the cheapest plan in oberlo is $5.00 per month. Oberlo is one of the most well-known dropshipping apps on the e-commerce platform, but can only be applied with Shopify.

So, what happens when this free trial has ended? Would you want to continue using oberlo? Or better still what happens when you want to branch out to other ecommerce platforms like WooCommerce, wix, aliscraper etc. well that's entirely up to you.

Regardless, whenever you're faced with either of these scenarios, you do not need to fret especially when you intend to start looking for alternative ways from Shopify because, there are other alternatives for you to choose from apart from oberlo.

A world where you have different varieties can be both freeing and at the same time confusing especially when you're unsure of the one to settle with. Well if you're confused that's fine seeing that this is your first time entering into dropshipping and you're trying to uncover the best app for your business.

A good app will help you schedule your business activities and allows you to concentrate on the marketing and selling of your product.

Keep in mind that its your business and you have to decide on the best choice for you, cost wise and efficiency wise, requires minor effort to create and invest, and promotes the growth of your business. Now let's dive straight into the exciting oberlo alternatives for shopify that will be revealed to you:

1. Spocket
2. Dropified
3. Modalyst
4. Product Pro
5. Importify
6. UniteXpress
7. Spreadr App - Amazon Importer
8. Dsers
9. ShopMaster
10. Nimble Dropshipping App

**1. Spocket**:
Spocket syncs effortlessly with your online store and all orders automatically appear in your app.
80% of Spocket's dropshipping suppliers are based in the US or Europe. Spocket is integrated with Shopify, BigCommerce, Wix, and WooCommerce.

Spocket's huge range of US and EU-based products guarantees fast shipping.

It has a 24/7 customer support, with in-app chat facilities, so that no matter what problem you confront, you receive assistance. The sites navigation is great with a call to action that is tempting.
Spocket allows you to choose the best products with great quality to sell from thousands of dropshipping suppliers and also allows you to order product samples right from the dashboard in a few clicks. You can easily test out the products and suppliers to build a reliable dropshipping business.

Suppliers go through a strict procedure, they're vetted individually and interviewed

With Spocket, along with unbiased and generic packaging,

3. suppliers go an extra mile to attach your store's invoice to the box- with your store's name, contact details, your logo and a personal note from you to the customer.
4. Spocket allows order tracking to all users, which is important for customer satisfaction.
5. Spocket Automates product pricing, inventory updates, and automatically syncs the tracking number to Shopify, while with Oberlo, you have to manually enter them through Oberlo to the Shopify interface.

when using Spocket, you can import products to your store by following the steps below:

\endash        Login to your Spocket account.

\endash        Search the product that you want to sell.

\endash        Go to the product listing and click Add to Import List.

\endash        Next, move over to Import List and view the product.

\endash        Click on Push to Store to import the products to your store.

\endash        Finally, visit the Product List page and click on View Listing. This will let you see the item on your Shopify or Wix store.

products on Spocket have a 30-60% discount off of retail price, in order for you to make a good profit for your efforts.

Spocket Pricing offers you four paid subscriptions starting from $12 per month. All four plans come with a 14-day trial period.

Your suppliers' inventory levels are updated in real-time, which avails you the opportunity to stay up-to-date with the stock of your products, and never accidentally sell products that are out of stock.

**2. Dropified:**
Dropified allows you to seamlessly import and manage dropshipped products into any e commerce platform of your choice
Dropified is integrated with aliexpress, eBay, Groovekart, woo commerce etc.

Dropified has a 14-day free trial with any plan you choose and upon its termination, you begin to get billed with 17 dollars per month which is its lowest plan.

1.      All you need with Dropified is, find the products you want to sell, market your store, and Dropified automates the rest with its one-click order fulfillment feature that provides sellers the opportunity to increase the efficiency and accuracy of orders.

2.      It makes it easy for dropshippers to sell better products,

3.      save more time,

4.      manages dropshippers Product inventory,

5.      customizes products and has a 24/7 customer service support.

6.      Dropified automatically syncs any changes the suppliers make to product pricing.

Dropified automatically updates product availability in your dashboard to ensure you don't sell something that's out of stock by accident. So, if the supplier removes a product, you will know and have the chance to remove it from your store.
Dropified helps you promote your business by providing a **60 DAY ECOMMERCE TRAINING which** is designed to teach you what you need to start a profitable dropshipping business within 60 days and this is dependent on where you are in your

e commerce journey and provides tools to import and sell profitable products,

**3. Modalyst:**
Modalyst not only knows how to sell its services, it also has a vivid and spontaneous user interface.

They make it simple for an online store to source, list and sell niche products.

If you're in the category of launching a new ecommerce store, you have the option to add millions of low-cost products to your store instantly at no charge with a 25-product limit.
Until you're ready to offer more varieties to your customers, you have the option to choose the $35 plan per month with a 5% transaction fee and a 250-product limit.

Modalyst suppliers range from private manufacturers to handmade Indian businesses to aliexpress suppliers. They also feature hundreds of US dropshipping suppliers as well as international suppliers from all over the world.
Vendors are vetted and offer fast shipping, affordable products and discounted rates.

With Modalyst automation:
- you have the option to add products with one click,
- import all products information, images and variants,
- easily edit all product information, oh and
- Real time inventory update notifications,
- price discount notifications,
- variant mapping, and you can add products in bulk to your ecommerce store.

When it comes to Modalyst return policy, the retailer may provide their customers with a 14- day return policy during which a customer may return an item that is undamaged, unworn and with tags still attached.

The brand also provides a return policy for damaged items as long as any claims are placed within the agreed upon 14 days of the item being received.

Ranges of goods can be acquired with Modalyst, including men's and women's apparel, shoes, children's clothes, bags, bridal wear, beauty products, plus-size clothing, homewares, and accessories, etc.

## 4. Product Pro:

Product Pro offers instant access to quality products to sell from vetted US suppliers and offers a 100% automated fulfillment for orders once sales are made, giving you enough time to grow your business.

Upon installing the app, which by the way has a warm user interface you're enrolled on the free plan which allows you save product edits and add draft products to your account. A paid subscription plan is required to import products and process orders.

Users with steady sales and a desire to scale up are recommended to use the premium plan which is $45 monthly and includes:

- an expanded inventory,
- unlimited orders,
- custom product recommendations,
- 15-minute product consultation,
- $10 towards first order.

In the scenario whereby you're just beginning your dropshipping business, you're recommended to use the pro plan which is $89dollars monthly which includes:

6.  a full product catalog,
7.  100 orders per month,
8.  automated fulfillment,
9.  Real-time inventory sync,
10. chat + email support.

98% of orders made in product pro are shipped in 1-2 days this is good news because customers no longer have to wait weeks to enjoy your products all you need to do is focus on sales.

With over 60,000 US products available, you'll find plenty of quality products to add to your catalog for new promotions and sales.

Product pro gives a step by step guide on how to:

2.  import products,
3.  edit products,
4.  searching for products and how to bulk update pricing.

In product pro, packaging of orders varies and vendors are required to remove any promotional material and pricing information from dropship order.

Refunds on damaged, missing, or incorrect products are offered but to receive refunds, you have to be prepared to provide images of the products/packaging.


**5. Importify:**

Importify is compatible with the biggest wholesalers, and fully integrated with Shopify, WooCommerce & jump seller.

Each plan on Importify starts with a day trial and your billing cycle starts after the free trial has ended and you can change your plan at any time directly from the Importify dashboard.

With importify's research tool, you're able to find proven hot selling products to your online store. You are provided with a step-by-step dropshipping guide that educates you on the best way to promote and start driving traffic to your shop.

Your business is automated with importify's semi-automatic order fulfillment to quickly fulfill your orders.
You are availed the opportunity to:

2. import products from hundreds of suppliers,
3. to spy on other shopify stores and find proven products in your niche,
4. 1-click to import products from the most popular ecommerce platforms,
5. Built-in editor for product descriptions, edit title price images, tags category variants, etc.

You get to easily change suppliers when product is out of stock, or you have a better source. The override function is available for you to migrate from apps like oberlo, dropified Ali orders, or other dropshipping apps and keep your current product link.

Towards the end of each page Importify says Importify "was created with love for dropshippers to easily import products into your shopify store and fulfil orders with only a few clicks". Now that sure is lovely!

Importify shows you immediately how user-friendly it is as soon as you start using it,
This is thanks to its vibrant user interface.

6. Unitexpress

Here is another great app for dropshipping with its headquarters based in Cairo Egypt

Unitexpress automates your entire order process from shopify to AliExpress. Unitexpress is active in shopify app development and ecommerce solutions. With unitexpress, your dropshipping is accelerated and you can modify and edit your products in many ways, from changing titles and descriptions to adjusting prices with little effort to suite your style. The pricing automation feature helps you save time by creating a pricing rule and setting the pricing for a chosen set of products.

## 7. Spreadr App -

Spreadr is an amazon affiliate and dropshipping app that provides its users with both options of either dropshipping or earning from affiliating by linking them directly to Amazon. There is a:

4. Spreadr plugin for WooCommerce,
5. Spreadr app for shopify and Bigcommerce

Spreadr offers an advanced import tool which can be used to search what's popular on Amazon which can in turn be added to your store with a one click upload. It also provides features of auto-sync, customize product descriptions, Bulk import, making it quick and easy to dropship, and many more.

Spreadr offers a 7-day free trial to new users who register with the site and the account is charged according to your chosen subscription at the end of the free trial.

All purchases are non-refundable.

You can cancel your subscription at any time and will take effect at the end of the current paid term.

## 8. Dsers:

DSers delivers products within a 10-day period, and it is integrated with Aliexpress, shopify, WooCommerce etc.
Dsers pricing is quite impressive as it has a:

2. basic plan which is forever free,
3. standard plan which is $1.99 per month,
4. advanced which is$19.9 per month and
5. pro plan which is 49.9 per month.

With dsers you can manage suppliers easily by simply connecting to the supplier you want to work with,

2. save 96.7% ordering time in a few clicks, track orders automatically,
3. map your store product to any aliexpress supplier without changing anything on your store,
4. auto-syncing of tracking numbers to your store and pay-pal,
5. auto update order status, preselect your favourite shipping method according to the order destination,
6. pre-set pricing rule to mark-up your product price automatically when you publish them,
7. link and manage multiple stores in one dsers account,
8. integrate with Admitad to get commission when you place orders to Aliexpress.

Dsers mass supply program works with high qualified suppliers. It enables you to do what other order management tools like Oberlo can't.
Dsers is an amazing Oberlo alternative for Shopify.

## 9. ShopMaster:

Shop master supports dropshipping suppliers from aliexpress, bang good, Gogo mall, Taobao.com, 1688, Alibaba, dropshipping.com etc. All these are great options because you can make use of Shopify to dropship across multiple platforms. Shopmaster is also integrated with wish, ebay, 3dcart, WooCommerce.

With Shopmaster, dropshippers can eliminate the busy work and use automation features to engage more prospects, it is fast and reliable, centralized and low cost,

Another amazing thing about Shopmaster is, just like Dsers, it has a forever free plan.

## 10. Nimble Dropshipping App

Nimble has a 14-day free trial period after which there's an:

5. $18 basic plan which carries the capacity of 250 Orders
6. $60 regular plan which carries the capacity of 1000 orders
7. $129 advanced plan which carries the capacity of 3000 orders and much more

In the case whereby you need more than 3000 order per month, a customised plan will be made available depending on your order volume.

Nimble provides all the tools needed to create and scale a 100% automatic Aliexpress dropshipping store.

Nimble will help you fulfil your orders automatically the moment your customers place them.

The app has developed many automation features to help you run with the least amount of your involvement possible. It literally works while you sleep. Here are the amazing features that you will get from using Nimble Dropshipping.

\endash        Push products from Aliexpress to your store with one click

\endash        Chooses the best shipping option when placing an order.

\endash        Keep your customers updated with order status emails.

\endash        Corrects shipping address mistakes made during shopify check out.

\endash        Detailed spending breakdown of aliexpress payments.

\endash        Tries again if a payment doesn't go through on Aliexpress

\endash        Fulfils your orders without needing help with captchas.

\endash        Automate order fulfilment for your existing products, and so many more.

## Ultimate Facebook advertising guide for Shopify in 2021

Facebook is an excellent marketing channel that will provide you with more traffic and sales. To obtain these Shopify business results, you need to combine different Facebook marketing strategies to create a bulletproof Facebook marketing system. To make the Shopify Facebook marketing system impeccable, you need to:

O Promote your content on Facebook
P Create a Facebook business page
Q Run contests

R Create a Facebook group (optional)
S Grow your email list from Facebook
T Sell products
U Create Ads
V And others

Advertising on Facebook and Instagram in 2021 is essential for every commercial project. This guide will help you learn how to create Facebook Dashboard ad campaigns and do it profitably.

## Embedding Facebook Pixel in Your Project

The first thing you need to do is install the Facebook Pixel. Pixel is simply an HTML tag that you place on your store's website. In a nutshell, Pixel will capture Facebook profiles of people who visit your store.

## How do I install the Facebook Pixel?

Simply. If you are using Shopify you can integrate Pixel, then you can create and install a pixel in just a few seconds.

## Installing Facebook Pixel with HTML Integration

1. Create an account in the Facebook ad cabinet.

2. Insert a pixel into the Head of the site

## Installing custom Pixel events

You've probably noticed this situation: you buy clothes or something with Ali Express, add a lot of things to the basket, and then suddenly change your mind or decide to check competitors' offers. After a while, ads with specific products that you added to the cart begin to catch up with you in social networks and browsers. Not really. These are the very same custom events. They are the ones that allow you to do such retargeting campaigns.

## The best audiences for your ad campaigns

The "golden audiences" that will work for any niche and budgets do not exist. Otherwise, there would be no point in the services of agencies and targeting experts.

### Traffic levels concept

Every marketer targeting specialist and business owner should understand that your target audience can be divided into segments. The audience is usually divided into "Cold", "Warm" and "Hot". We believe that the normal human body temperature is 36.6, so we divide the audience not by the conditional temperature, but by the funnel's position.

### Top of the funnel (ToF)

People who have just entered the funnel. They don't know your brand and don't explicitly express a need for your product. This audience is relatively easy to find. We are looking for it by various combinations and bundles of interests.

### This magic block

We recommend using split tests and trying different combinations. The bigger, the better. Even if you've already found an audience that works for you, chances are there are better audiences. Facebook ads tests shouldn't stop. A kind of continuous development, if you know what I mean.

### Mid of the funnel (MoF)

This is targetted at those who are familiar with your product but haven't bought it before or have bought it for a long time.

**Look-a-like and simple retargeting**

Once the Pixel has collected enough data (roughly 30 days, depending on how much traffic you get), you can build an audience using the pixel data. This audience is called the "custom site audience".To put it simply: these are people who visited your site, poked something and left. Launch retargeting for these people without hesitation. With a high degree of probability, it will give positive results. It is also a good idea to collect look-a-like for this audience.

**Bottom of the funnel (BoF)**

People who are already ready to buy a product like yours, or may have recently bought a product from you. The most successful campaigns are done with this audience. One of the most valuable types of user audiences is called "Custom audiences from the customer list"... You can upload a spreadsheet (.csv file) to your Facebook ad account with your customer names, email address, and phone number. Facebook will try to match your customer data with social media profiles to create an audience for you. You can load different databases. The most successful bases are the bases of previous buyers and the bases of customers of your competitors (did not even think about where people get them from).

**Best ads for ad campaigns**

Advertisements are just as important as audiences—a single answer to the question: "Which creatives will convert?" not. Constantly test new ideas and keep a close eye on competitors. Below are examples of ads that work in our campaigns and those of leading foreign agencies.

**Bottom of the funnel (BoF) creatives**

Previous customers who abandoned a purchase (who added an item to their cart but did not dare to pay for it) and even users viewing the product page are the most likely audiences to buy a product directly through Facebook ads. This means that this audience will have the best ROAS. Here are the best ad types to serve these audiences: Your loyal customers, people who abandoned a purchase at the last moment and people who just viewed the product page -the most likely audience to buy a product directly through Facebook ads.

**Dynamic ads**

The first type of ad we recommend setting up is dynamic product ads (DPA).

DPA - Ads generated automatically from your product catalogue you integrate your online store's product catalogue with your Facebook ad cabinet, you can automatically create ads using the image, title, description and price of your products. The easiest way to set up DPA is to let the platform your store is on do it for you. If it is of course supported. If you use Shopify, for example, you can use one of their apps to integrate your product without any problem. To add a product catalogue manually, you can go to catalogues in your Facebook account settings.

After you have integrated your product catalogue with Facebook, you can create a new catalogue sales campaign that will allow you to use your catalogue as an advertisement. Here's an example of an ad generated from a store's product catalogue: DPA continues to be one of the easiest and most effective ways to advertise a product on Facebook in 2021.

**Video ads**

Video advertising has been and remains one of the most effective types of advertising. But not every video will give an impetus to the buyer, and the video must be convincing. What is a compelling video? A compelling video is a video that tells the story of solving a buyer's need. There is one type of video ad that has really become popular with advertisers: User Generated Content (UGC). UGC ads are (usually) ads containing video testimonials from customers. UGC ads work well because they give potential customers the confidence that they will love their purchase. UGC ads are especially powerful when an influencer is talking about a product.

### Carousel ads

Another type of ad that remains effective in 2021 is carousel ads. When creating a carousel, you have complete control over each image (or video). This allows you to get creative to grab people's attention when viewing their news feeds. Here's an example of a commonly used visual cue that prompts Facebook users to scroll through one carousel image after another. Not only are they effective in engaging Facebook users, but they also have high engagement rates. High engagement leads to lower advertising costs because it tells Facebook that users are getting high on your ads.

### Creatives for MoF (people in the middle of the funnel)

An audience that is only slightly familiar with your brand and product requires a slightly different approach. If you want to test DPA for MoF audiences, they may not give you a high ROMI, as DPAs are just a reminder to buy. Since MoF audiences are not always ready to buy, you need to nudge them a little. The best format for this ad is video and carousel ads. The goal of advertising is to tell a compelling story about why people shouldn't care about your product. Here are a couple more ideas:

### Short repetitive videos

Another option is short videos (fifteen seconds or less) that will automatically loop. Make a Loop. Even if you only have one image, you can turn it into an attractive looping video by adding several effects. This ad from Magic Spoon Cereal has animated text that reveals the benefits. "Zero Sugar Porridge" and "High Protein Porridge". The great ad that will push your audience to buy.

## Show the range of uses for your product.

Perhaps your customers don't understand how to apply your product. Take advantage of the power of your ads to demonstrate different use cases. In this ad, Honey demonstrates how the service can be used not only to shop online but also to order food online.

## Ads for people at the top of the ToF ad funnel

The purpose of serving ads targeting ToF audiences is not to sell directly. It would be a terribly ineffective campaign.

ROAS will not be as high as BoF campaigns, so you should get the most out of your BoF and MoF audiences before setting aside any budget for ToF audiences. Your strategy should be to get the maximum number of people to your site. This solves two problems:

1. Introduce them to your brand.

2. Collect their data for cheaper retargeting.

In other words, the goal is to get people to join the MoF. Below is an idea for advertising.

Tell the story of one of your customers.

In this ad from Moleskine, they showcase their client's lifestyle - a creative, a thinker, a modern classic. In just 13 seconds, this ad shows how Moleskine products are integrated into that person's daily life. The company wants so you can imagine how their products can integrate into your life. If you see yourself as a creative and thinker, then Moleskine is for you. This approach can also be effective for MoF audiences. The ad style and format you use at each stage of the funnel is less important than the message conveyed through them. The above are just examples to help you get on the right track.

To facilitate the creative process, you need to always be on the lookout for interesting solutions that other companies use. Here are two ways to do it:

**Look at your competitors' ads**.

Did you know that you can see all the ads shown by any company at any given time? Now you know. Now let's tell you how. To see ads for any company, go to the Facebook page and click "More" in the "Page Transparency" field in the right sidebar. The pop-up window at the bottom has a section called "Ads from this page". Click on the link "Go to the ad library, and there you will see all the advertisements that the company places. In Facebook's ad library, you can search for any brand and see the ads it shows.

### Join Facebook advertising groups

Look where no one is looking. We look, and this is one of our advantages. We recommend joining the Facebook Ad Creatives Only group.

### Strategies for scaling Facebook ad campaigns for online stores

You need to scale. If you hit a break-even point in your campaigns, it's time to think about how you can increase your budget by improving ROAS or at least maintaining it.

### Use Facebook Automation

You can use Facebook Automation to automate most of your day-to-day ad work. Automation can help you focus your attention on activities where your expertise is really needed, such as creating new ads and finding new audiences, with Facebook doing most of the work.

Facebook automation is essentially a simple algorithm "If this" then "this "... For example, you can create an automatic rule to pause an ad if your ad's average ROAS has dropped below 1.0 over the past few days. In fact, Revealbot helps us create the exact rules needed to run fully automated campaigns - you just add new ads to the system, and automation does the rest. We recommend that you try it 100%.

### Let's sum up

Facebook advertising is an incredible tool for online shopping. Once you set the Pixel, understand which target audience is best, and make the right ads for that audience, you can take your company to the next level. If there is no time for this and there are more important tasks, then use the services of agencies. Trust the experts.

# Google ads

To successfully sell products from a Shopify store, you need to be in front of as many people as possible. With the power of Google Ads, you can introduce yourself to people who are looking for the products you sell.

### Google Ads term

There are many terms you need to know when using Google Ads, so let's take a look first.

Google Ads-an online advertising platform where you can pay for advertising Shopify stores, content and products. We have five forms of ads; the most important for you is research and shopping.

Display-how often the ad is displayed.

Bid-the highest amount you are willing to pay for an ad click.

Search ads-text ads displayed at the top of Google search results.

Shopping ad-a product-based ad that appears at the top of Google search results along with pictures and prices.

Keywords-words or phrases that determine when and where the ad is displayed.

Negative keywords-words or phrases that determine when and where your ad will not appear.

Budget-the average daily amount you will spend in a month.

Cost per click: (Cost per click) The average cost charged to users who click on your ad.

Click-through rate: How often users who see your ad click on it.

This is a lot of information to know, so let us use it to help.

First, you need an account. Use your email address and website to log in to your Google Ads account and fill in the required information.

Prepare for your first campaign.

Now it's time to create your first Google Ads campaign. Google Ads will guide you through four main steps, namely:

1. Name your campaign

Give your campaign a self-explanatory name so you can easily identify it.

2. Set a budget.

Determine how much you want to spend on this campaign each day by dividing your monthly advertising budget by 30.4 (the average number of days in a month). Start small when you start learning to master Google Ads.

3. Choose your audience

Determine who will see your ad by determining the following.

location

Adjust your campaign to make it focus on a specific location of your target audience. For example, you might want your ad to show only in the country where the ad is served, or you can run a very specific campaign for a specific city.

the Internet

In this guide, we focus on the Google search network, where your ads will appear on the Google search results page. However, please note that you can also choose to display ads on the Google Display Network, which includes other websites, programs, and videos.

Keywords

What search terms or phrases do you want your ad to show in search results? Enter a list of keywords related to your ads and Shopify store, and then use the following tips to help you.

• Consider related keywords and phrases that potential customers can also search for.

• Use terms and phrases that customers use in real life.

• Target long-distance keywords as specific as possible.

4. Bidding

Set the highest price to be paid for customers who click on your ad in the Shopify store. To calculate a quote, you need to balance the return on investment (how much might these customers cost?), which comes at the cost of the competition.

5. Write your ad

Now is your time to shine. Write an ad that grabs your audience's attention and encourages them to click through to your Shopify store home page.

\endash  Incorporate your keywords and phrases
\endash  Incorporate a convincing call to action
\endash  Make for ads link to your landing page.
\endash  Includes a single point of sale such as two-day delivery.
\endash  Lastly, confirm your billing information (not forgetting to add your coupon), review your settings, create your campaign and see how the clicks arrive. But it is not over yet.

6. Add the fast shipping badge

Do you want to stand out from the competition and grab customers right at the beginning of their shopping journey? Take advantage of the fast shipping promise with Google Free and Fast.

7. Analysis

Regularly review your campaign metrics to see results, adjust your budget, change your wording, and compare overall results.

**Different types of campaign**

So that's what you've established with your first campaign. But to really dominate Google Ads for Shopify, you want multiple campaigns to run at once. To inspire us, we have put together five types of campaigns to drive new traffic to your eCommerce website.

1. Brand search

Brand search campaigns engage those who actively search for your brand by name. It will protect you from competitors bidding your name. Cost per click is generally low.

3. Generic search

This type of search targets generic keywords and phrases related to your products. For example, lipstick, skincare travel kit, or eyeliner. Depending on how generic your keywords are, the CPC can be high, and the CTR can be competitive.

3. Search for competitors

Competitor search campaigns accomplish the opposite: capture those who are actively searching for their competitors by name. The CPC is again generally low, but so is the CTR.

4. Search for related products

A related products campaign targets keywords related to your products, with the goal of cross-selling and targeting buyers with similar interests. For example, if you sell female wears, you could target the long-tail keyword phrase: "fashion at its peak." The more specific the keyword phrase being searched for, the lower the CPC, however the CTR can below.

5. Purchases on Google

The campaign target specific product searches, matching them to the product for sale in your Shopify store. By displaying the product image, price, and star rating, these campaigns are very effective, but depending on the search term, they can be expensive. They convert well. You must be prepared to handle and fulfil an increase in orders in your Shopify store.

**Pinterest**

When it comes to direct sales, Pinterest has a lot of advantages. This is partly due to the longevity of a pin's life, which tends to present itself. As a result, to search engines for years, and due to the purchasing power of Pinterest users. A survey by Shopify, in partnership with Pinterest, found that a typical user tends to spend $ 50 per purchase. But of course, for users to become traffic or sales, strategic planning is required.

Generate traffic and sales using Pinterest :

Create buying personas: One of the maxims of marketing says that if you try to sell to everyone, you will end up not selling to anyone. This weakens the message and further demonstrates that you have no idea who your potential customers are. One way to do this is to identify exactly who your products are for and develop purchasing personas. Such a persona outlines the key facets of his buyer and includes information such as age group, gender, education level, income, hobbies, challenges, curiosities, among much other information. It is essential to know who you are trying to reach in order to know the type of pin you will create and what content to use. In other to create your buyer persona, think about the profile of the people who usually shop with you (or your customer) and write down the main characteristics of these buyers. At the end of the process, you should have a brief descriptive text that will show you exactly who your ideal buyer is.

Always optimize: the optimization of your pins must be done in two parts. First, you need to adapt your content according to your purchase persona. Now that you know exactly who your audience is optimize everything to attract these unique individuals.

Second, you have Pinterest's optimization mechanics. The more information Pinterest has about your pins, and the more likely users are to become involved with it. In addition, pin optimization can increase the likelihood that the platform will show the material to individuals similar to the one described in your purchase persona. This can help your company generate traffic and sales using Pinterest.

To boost your efforts, do a few quick checks. First, check your site and authenticate it with Pinterest. This makes the platform recognize its content as a more reliable material. Then, add Pinterest buttons to your site. This gives users the ability to pin their products directly from your website.

Once your site becomes more friendly to Pinterest, start using titles and links with keywords that are important to your business. Using what you have learned from your purchasing persona, you can identify keywords that align with your ideal customer's interests. Pinterest can also help through the search feature guided. When you type a search term on Pinterest, it automatically pulls related categories. In addition, while you're typing your search, Pinterest offers self-populating suggestions, which provide relevant insights into what people are searching for. After gathering keywords from Pinterest, you can use the AdWords keyword planner to expand your selection and observe search volumes. It is worth mentioning that, by optimizing your pins, you lay the foundation for a strong global SEO strategy for your business.

Use Rich Pins: When the rich pins were launched, a lot of people thought they would make a lot of money from it. Ultimately, however, they solved the challenge of creating targetable pins rather than making money from Pinterest. However, rich pins can generate profit or at least traffic to your site. Transforming your products into rich pins can be advantageous to reach the buying personas and generate sales more quickly, as well as to direct those same people to your website and start to contact them there too.

Create "Gifts Ideas" and "Theme Boards": These are good ways to attract people. Creating a curatorship of gift suggestions and thematic pictures can lead many people to become interested in the images, click on them and then on the link to the website to see more. It is always worth curating interesting topics for your personas, as there is a tendency in the person who has seen interesting material on your page to return to it to consume more material and still share the content with other people who have the same interests. Creating relevant content is a good way to keep your audience attracted and generate sales.

Implement Pinterest best practices: Sending a bunch of ready-to-buy customers to your store means increasing access and sales. And you can achieve this by implementing best practices on the platform, improving the company's overall performance on Pinterest. When it comes to selling products, one of the best practices is still to create attractive pins. Take advantage of the possibility of using a more vertical layout to generate beautiful and different pins, which will attract users, allowing them to see the product as a whole without having to click on the image to open it.

Part of the appeal of buying an item is to adopt the lifestyle it creates, and you can use your pins to capture that essence. Also, notice how companies often use high-quality images on their pins. Therefore, always try to work along the same lines. Blurry or pixelated photos can give the impression that you don't know what you're doing.

Keep track of what's working: even with the creation of a consistent buy leg that helps your business grow on Pinterest, it is likely that some previous strategies may continue to be used. First, check what types of pins will generate traffic and sales using Pinterest, so you can continue basing part of your work on what is already a success. Also, compare your efforts on Pinterest with website traffic and sales to see what efforts are generating the most sales.

Another important tactic is to assess what people are saying about your pins. This can help to understand how people see your material, what they like best and what is expendable, leading to the refinement of different materials, from the type of content to the images used as pins.

## Instagram influencer

The good and fast results brought by Instagram's influential marketing indicate that the platform is certainly a marketing channel worth exploring - Instagram statistics don't lie! With 1 billion active users, Instagram surpassed Facebook in the number of interactions 20 times. Instagram digital influencers, also known as digital influencers, cultivate large audiences that convert when they see the right product (that's where you come in). You can use the partnership with a digital influencer to promote new products, get more customers or even communicate directly with existing customers. That is why working with a digital influencer is so effective for your Shopify website! And it is clear that, just as content marketing takes a specific approach, the strategy to be adopted with a digital influencer must be one that creates attractive content and is not very artificial. That's why Instagram influencer marketing can be so good for your brand in 2021. With the right digital influencer, messages will reach your customers without appearing to be "forced": every salesperson's dream.

## Create an account

Instagram Marketing: How to Create Your Own Target Audience? There are two different ways to use marketing on Instagram: the first option is to build your own list of followers, and the second is to use the work of promoting a digital influencer from Instagram.

## Creating a follower list: tools to build your Instagram audience

You can build a list of followers in a variety of ways: tools such as Webstagram and IconoSquare, for example, can be extremely useful in finding the most popular hashtags in your niche. Conducting a search on Webstagram is an excellent way to find the best Instagram hashtags for your e-commerce - not to mention that everything is done in a few seconds, leaving you with more free time to focus on other marketing efforts.

To personalize your search, just type the keywords relevant to your e-commerce in the search bar at the top of the page, marked in the image below with the red arrows. The platform is free and easy to use, so it's worth doing a quick search on Webstagram to try to identify key information relevant to your Instagram marketing strategy. Another marketing tactic for Instagram is always to be aware of the best times to post on social networks. Using IconoSquare, you can find out the exact times during which you will be most engaged and the ideal times for publication. It is a great tool to start your work of dissemination through a digital influencer.

## Creating your own follower list: marketing with Instagram targeting

Do you know what segmentation marketing is? There are numerous ways to segment your audience, and one of the best strategies is to build your own list of followers from the followers of your competitors - after all, people who follow a competitor's account have already shown an interest in the type of product you are trying to sell. This means that by attracting this audience, you practically guarantee the construction of a personalized list. Go to a competitor's account, click on "followers" to see the list of people who follow you and then approach them 1) following them, 2) enjoying your photos or 3) commenting on your photos.

An informal Shopify test, conducted to analyze how to gain followers on Instagram, collected some interesting data on the number of followers you could achieve with this type of approach:

\endash  Follow: 14% followed back;
\endash  Follow + Like: 22% followed back;
\endash  Follow + Like + Comment: 34% followed back.

You can use numerous tactic to build your follower list from scratch, but it can be quite difficult at first.

## Instagram influence marketing: what is a digital influencer?

A digital influencer is a user who has an established audience and who is able to persuade others because of their high level of credibility and reach on Instagram. Instagram digital influencers can help build a large audience from scratch in a relatively short period of time, with the potential to generate a lot of sales: just ask them to advertise and advertise your products. That is, if you want to know how to make money on Instagram, this is the way to go.

When you post images to your account without an existing base of followers, you may be unsure if someone is looking at your posts or if everything wasn't a huge waste of time - after all, it's hard to say what works and what doesn't and it takes time to see results. With a digital influencer, the thing is different: the idea is to establish partnerships with these virtual celebrities, who have a large list of followers and ask them to share their publication. This way, you can get tens of thousands of people to find your brand overnight.

That's why influencer marketing on Instagram is so relevant. Hundreds or even thousands of potential customers will get in touch with your products and probably convert to your brand because they trust digital enough to influence you to follow it.

## Example of marketing on Instagram

For products with good visual appeal, marketing through a digital influencer from Instagram can be a great way to build a large list of followers in a short period of time. That way, when you publish promotions, or new product offers to sell, and you will have a greater number of users who will see your publications, which can generate more sales. Now that you have an overview of marketing on Instagram, let's take a step-by-step approach to build your own list of followers.

## How to advertise on Instagram with a digital influencer

For beginning entrepreneurs, using a digital Instagram influencer to build a following can seem daunting. How do you know who the best influencers are? How to contact in order to make a good impression? Will this really generate sales? The whole process can seem confusing, especially when we don't know much about the work done by digital influencer. In fact, all you need is the right approach - and you will soon master the process.

## Instagram influence marketing - Step 1: find the right digital influencer.

You need to begin with getting the right influencers, that is those who are popular in the specific niche of your e-commerce. Using Instagram influencers that are already popular will increase the likelihood of sales as followers are already engaged. One way to increase your chances of achieving a good ROI using a digital Instagram influencer is to know as many details as possible about your target audience. If you have a store that sells formal shoes, you can go after influencers who specialize in "professional men's shoes" instead of "men's fashion" influencers. A quick way to find the best Instagram influencers in your niche is to use a tool like Ninja Outreach or Snapfluence.

If you prefer to move away from the tools, you can just search for relevant keywords within Instagram as part of your marketing strategy. Also, remember to choose specific hashtags and keywords that interest your audience in finding publications with a lot of likes and comments. It is important to note that this stage of marketing on Instagram can take a long time, since you may have to see many publications and hashtags to find the digital influencer that is a good choice to tell the story of your brand. But it's worth taking it easy and doing it carefully. If you find a suitable influencer for your target audience, you can achieve a very good ROI on your marketing investment. And if you choose inappropriate influencers, you may have to pay a high price.

## Marketing with the digital influencer on Instagram - Step 2: form a partnership

Once you find the right digital influencer for your Instagram campaign, you need to make contact and form a partnership. This is an important part of your Instagram marketing strategy: if followers of a digital influencer realize that the person is promoting the same product over and over again, they are more likely to trust the product. Typically, Instagram influencers will have a contact email in their bio. As there is usually monetary compensation in such cases, they are generally willing to work with entrepreneurs whose products align with the type of content they publish. It is a symbiotic relationship.

However, you must keep a few things in mind before entering into a partnership with a digital influencer. The first is to send the person a "summary" of the type of content you would like them to publish. Since influencers like to have creative freedom when creating content for their publications, you can at most give a general idea of the type of images you want to see associated with your brand. The good idea is to prepare a mood board in advance.

The boards' mood is collections of images that give a general sense of the kind of aesthetic that you like to have on your images. Below is an example of a mood board that Neil Waller uses to promote his store, Shore Projects.

**Marketing on Instagram - mood board**

The best part of mood boards is that they put digital influencer in touch with your branding and help you get a good idea of how to get the message out to the public, which contributes to the success of your marketing strategy. You will pay your digital influencer for various services, such as creating content, promoting content to the public and rights to use the created content. The amount paid for an influencer post can vary between R $ 271 and 763, depending on the size of the audience.

**Influencer Marketing on Instagram - Step 3: Evaluate Marketing Results on Instagram**

Before launching any campaign, it is important to have a good structure for measuring and evaluating results. That way, you will know exactly what works and what doesn't. When it comes to marketing on Instagram, it can be a good idea to create trackable links for influencers. Tools such as Bit.ly, for example, can create several trackable links for each influencer who works with your brand.

**Instagram marketing and drop shipping - how to put it all together**

Marketing on Instagram, more specifically working with a digital influencer, proved to be beneficial for entrepreneurs who own their own online store; in addition, if your product has visual appeal, you will have the potential to earn big with dropshipping on Instagram. Building a list of followers should be part of the marketing strategy on Instagram to establish your brand as a reference - but, as this requires a time-consuming approach, doing a search on Webstagram, planning publications with IconoSquare and targeting followers of competitors can help accelerate this process. A quick way to build a large list of followers on the platform, as we have shown, is to take advantage of the audience from a digital influencer. We hope that you now have a good answer to the question "What is a digital influencer on Instagram?".

Remember that influential marketing on Instagram is one of the most useful things for dropshipping entre How to start a Dropshipping business in 7 easy steps:

Step 1: Find a niche.

You need to delve into the right information to choose the best dropshipping business idea. You need to do proper research to avoid getting stuck in the product testing phase for so long. At best, the dropshipping business model works perfectly with niche products, compared to commoditized items. Tools exist to help you identify an untapped market with remarkable growth potential. Let's see them:

Amazon's keyword tool: This search tool consists of four well-connected metrics; the search volume, trend, CPC and competition. Each KPI aims to boost Amazon's SEO, and you get to sketch cool product descriptions that help customers discover your products very quickly. Its autocomplete feature feeds you with keyword suggestions from Amazon's keyword listing database.

Google Trends should also help you to discuss seasonal and popular products in various regions. It's a one-stop-shop for the 'Johnny who's been around lately' who wants to learn how to start a dropshipping business and has no idea what to sell. For simplicity, Google Trends allows you to analyze all the necessary and difficult to unmask competition factors. While it is usually not the only tool needed to measure the volume of search for a product on the market, it is still a useful analysis tool that will help you establish yourself in a constantly growing niche.

Along with the tools mentioned above, Ubersuggest offers the same benefits to help you have an advantage over your competitors. You can classify your dropshipping business ideas based on what people are looking for in the search engine. To ensure that your dropshipping products have great potential to generate sales, you must strongly validate your search volume through keyword research. And that's what Ubersuggest was designed for - helping you find a profitable niche.

As a dropshipper, your main goal is to make a profit on every sale transaction. This is quite to the point. But not every niche is profitable. An ideal solution here is to learn from the thriving dropshipping stores.

Professional tip: it is worth solving the defective points of customers and solving a consumer problem in the market. That way, you will escape saturated niche products and win the daring competition. There are prominent factors that go into successful dropshipping. And the battle to beat the competition cannot be won overnight.

Subscribe to your competitors' newsletters and social media accounts to learn how they engage with your customers. If your dropshipping competitor runs a blog, check out their call-to-action and conversion optimization strategies. Choose an item from your competitor's product page, but don't check it out. Notice how they handle cart abandonment. Monitor the effectiveness of your ad recovery and redirect emails.

Monitor all order fulfilment options. This will give you a fair understanding of how to manage the shipping process in your dropshipping business.

Analyze all comments/analyzes generated by users by your competitors' customers on factors such as product quality, delivery and customer engagement. In the end, this should provide information on how to improve the relationship with potential buyers. See your competitors' pricing structure. Your business model must take into account how much the target market is willing to pay.

To beat your competition with a landslide, you can issue incentives, such as loyalty programs, gift cards, and gifts to repeat customers. Again, make perfect use of SEO tools to spy on relevant keywords ranked by your competitors.

# CONCLUSION

Dropshipping has become popular within the last couple of years and will remain relevant in the coming years. The reason is simple – as more and more people gain access to the internet and mobile devices, they would want to order products online – which means more business for dropshippers.

There is no better time than now to join into the dropshipping bus – it is still largely profitable. You only need to do proper product research and be sure that you are not just doing what everyone is doing.

Also, if you want dropshipping to pay you well, you must take it as a business and have long term plans for it. If you see it as a side "hustle" that you run to when you are out of a job, then it will pay you like a side hustle.

Lastly, while drop shipping using Shopify, think about building your own independent e-commerce store. Then work with local suppliers to supply your own branded products. This should be your long-term plan – you don't want to be a Shopify dropshipper forever – rather, you should be thinking of building your own brand.

Thank you for reading! If You appreciate this book, we ask you to leave an honest review on your platform, it is very important for us!

To help you get started now, below you can find the best tools recommended by the author (affiliate links).

You can easily scan them with your mobile phone, so no excuses, take action now:

Start with Shopify:

Find freelancers on Fiverr:

Start doing Email marketing with Get Response:

Thank you for reading, we hope we have been of help! Keep in touch with the author for the upcoming releases:

To Your success!

Robert.